Twelfth Edition

THE SCHOOL AND COMMUNITY RELATIONS

Edward H. Moore
Rowan University

Don Bagin
Rowan University

Donald R. Gallagher
Rowan University

 Pearson

Director and Publisher: Kevin Davis
Executive Portfolio Manager: Aileen Pogran
Managing Content Producer: Megan Moffo
Content Producer (Team Lead): Faraz Sharique Ali
Content Producer: Deepali Malhotra
Portfolio Management Assistant: Andrea Hall
Executive Product Marketing Manager: Christopher Barry
Executive Field Marketing Manager: Krista Clark
Manufacturing Buyer: Deidra Skahill
Cover Design: Pearson CSC
Cover Art: Pgiam/E+/Getty Images
Editorial Production and Composition Services: Pearson CSC
Full-Service Project Management: Pearson CSC, Jean Acabal and Billu Suresh
Printer/Binder: Courier/Westford
Cover Printer: Courier/Westford
Text Font: 10/12 Times LT Std

Credits and acknowledgments for material borrowed from other sources and reproduced, with permission, in this textbook appear on the appropriate page within the text.

Every effort has been made to provide accurate and current Internet information in this book. However, the Internet and information posted on it are constantly changing, so it is inevitable that some of the Internet addresses listed in this textbook will change.

Library of Congress Cataloging-in-Publication Data
Names: Moore, Edward H. (Edward Hampton), 1953- author.
Title: The school and community relations / Edward H. Moore, Rowan
    University, Don Bagin, Rowan University, Donald R. Gallagher, Rowan
    University.
Description: Twelfth Edition. | New York : Pearson Education, [2018]
Identifiers: LCCN 2018052191| ISBN 9780135210659 (alk. paper) | ISBN
    0135210658 (alk. paper)
Subjects: LCSH: Community and school--United States. | Schools—Public
    relations—United States. | Communication in education—United States.
Classification: LCC LC221 .G35 2018 | DDC 371.190973--dc23 LC record available at
https://lccn.loc.gov/2018052191

5 2022

ISBN 10:   0-13-521065-8
ISBN 13: 978-0-13-521065-9

ABOUT THE AUTHORS

EDWARD H. MOORE

Edward H. Moore is a Professor Emeritus in the College of Communication and Creative Arts at Rowan University in Glassboro, New Jersey. Moore started his career as a school public relations practitioner and went on to serve more than 25 years as a public relations counselor, journalist, and educator working with a variety of corporate and educational organizations throughout North America, Europe, and Asia. Moore was managing editor of *Communication Briefings*, an international communications newsletter, and he previously served as Associate Director of the National School Public Relations Association. Moore taught public relations for more than 20 years. At Rowan University he was a Professor and Coordinator of the M.A. program in public relations. He holds an M.A. in school information services from Glassboro, New Jersey, State College, and is accredited in public relations by the Universal Accreditation Board.

DON BAGIN

Dr. Don Bagin founded the graduate program in public relations at Rowan University, where he was a professor of communications, and went on to direct that program for more than 30 years. He served as president of the National School Public Relations Association and received the association's award given to the educator who has contributed the most to improving the relationship between schools and communities. Dr. Bagin was the founding publisher of *Communication Briefings*, a newsletter read by 250,000 people. During his long career, he wrote eight books and hundreds of articles on public relations. He earned his first two degrees from Villanova University and his doctorate from Temple University.

DONALD R. GALLAGHER

Dr. Don Gallagher's career included more than 40 years of experience in public relations and communications with the U.S. Navy, two school districts, a community college, and as a professor. He served as a professor at Rowan University, where he coordinated graduate programs in public relations. He was one of the owners of *Communication Briefings*, an international communications newsletter. Dr. Gallagher conducted many public opinion polls, published numerous articles, recorded national videotapes and audiotapes, and gave numerous workshops throughout the United States. A graduate of St. Francis University in Pennsylvania, he earned a master's from Villanova University and a doctorate from Temple University.

PREFACE

Rapidly evolving communication technology, tremendous shifts in the way educational services are funded and delivered, and increasing demands in what the public expects from schools continue to challenge school communication professionals and school leaders.

Importantly, most of these evolving issues are adding to and not subtracting from the complexity of school communication programs. New technologies are supplementing communication tactics in the school communicator's arsenal while not supplanting conventional tactics. Traditional school systems now face a constant struggle for students and resources in a tough, new competitive environment. And increasingly segmented publics are making more nuanced and specific demands on school leaders.

But there is a precedent for such shifts in communication demands. Rapid changes in traditional media, public demands, and government involvement in education gave birth to the formal practice of modern school public relations in the 1930s. Education leaders today must seek ways to successfully confront similar struggles in different environments.

School leaders must effectively deal with the ways in which traditional news media now cover and comment on schools in the converged world of print, broadcast, and online reporting; the realities of non-stop, two-way communication and engagement that digital and social media have spawned; the vastly expanded expectations of parents in particular and taxpayers in general for transparency and instant, on-demand access to information and data; and the new realities of ties between effective communication and community involvement and the resulting impact on student and school success.

This revised edition has been updated to reflect the new ways in which school communicators can organize and operate to meet the new demands this changing environment presents. It seeks to offer practical insights and guidance on how schools can build trusting working relationships with their communities to create sound foundations supporting student success.

NEW TO THIS EDITION

- Interviews with school communication experts and professionals offer practical insights for current issues in all chapters.
- Key issues identified for all school employees—central administrators, building and program administrators, and teachers, counselors, and staff—in all chapters.
- Links to videos offering examples of how schools are addressing many key communication challenges.
- Updated chapters in the "Essential Considerations" section reflecting the expanding roles for school communication programming in a time of rising demands for accountability and unprecedented competition for resources and students; the rising importance of community engagement in an era of constant change; and the evolving skill sets demanded of communication practitioners.
- The "Relations with Special Publics" section has been updated to address emerging communication challenges, such as the complexities of identifying internal and external audiences in a new-media environment, the growing need for objective-driven planning to inform and influence key audiences, and the growing importance of effective interpersonal communication among school employees to support student success.
- A revised section on "Communication Tools" addressing the new need to fully address the integrated nature of communication through online and traditional media tactics and emerging trends in planning for special communication campaigns and school-finance communication.
- An expanded look at accountability metrics for the evaluation of institutional and personal assessment of communication performance.

ACKNOWLEDGMENTS

For this edition, special thanks and recognition are extended to the National School Public Relations Association Executive Director Rich Bagin and NSPRA's members devoted to school-communication excellence and student and school success. NSPRA's commitment to documenting best practices in school–community relations serves school leaders throughout North America in their work to engage communities, build understanding and support, and promote student achievement and school success. Special thanks also are extended to Kathryn Moore for her tireless efforts at analysis and commentary, which contributed greatly to this work.

Our thanks also are extended to Ethan Aronoff, President, Millville (NJ) Public Library Board of Trustees; Devra Ashby, Public Information Officer, Colorado Springs (CO) School District 11; Kelly Avants, Chief Communications Officer, Clovis (CA) Unified School District; William J. Banach, Ed.D., Chairman, Banach, Banach and Cassidy, Ray, MI; Dr. Joseph Basso, Professor, College of Communication and Creative Arts, Rowan University, Glassboro, NJ; Melissa Braham, Public Information Specialist, Capitol Region BOCES/Queensbury Union Free School District, Queensbury, NY; Timothy Carroll, Director of Public Information, Allen (Texas) School District; Fairfax County (VA) Public Schools; Sandy Cokeley, CEO, SCOPE School Surveys; Dr. Suzanne FitzGerald, Professor and Chair, Public Relations and Advertising Department, College of Communication and Creative Arts, Rowan University, Glassboro, NJ; Anthony J. Fulginiti, Professor Emeritus, College of Communication and Creative Arts, Rowan University, Glassboro, NJ; David Hackney, College of Communication and Creative Arts, Rowan University, Glassboro, NJ; Susan Hardy-Brooks, Chief Communication Officer, Cooperative Council for Oklahoma School Administration, Oklahoma City, OK; Dr. Randy Hines, Professor, Susquehanna University, Selinsgrove, PA; Keith Imon, Associate Superintendent, Prince William County (VA) Public Schools; Rick Kaufman, Executive Director of Community Relations, Bloomington (MN) Public Schools; Gary Marx, APR, CAE, President, Center for Public Outreach, Inc., Vienna, VA; Montgomery County (MD) Public Schools; John Moscatelli, Public Relations and Advertising Department, College of Communication and Creative Arts, Rowan University, Glassboro, NJ; Amanda Morris, Director of School-Community Relations, Hilliard City Schools, Columbus, OH; Asi Nia-Schoenstein, Public Relations and Advertising Department, College of Communication and Creative Arts, Rowan University, Glassboro, NJ; Phi Delta Kappan, Bloomington, IN; Elise Shelton, Chief Communications Officer, Clarksville, Montgomery County (TN) School System; Mary Veres, Public Information Officer, Sunnyside Unified School District, Tucson, AZ. Thanks also to the reviewers of this edition: Tamara J. Williams from University of Nebraska at Omaha; Chandra Aleong from Delaware State University; Graham Weir from Lindenwood University.

—Edward H. Moore

BRIEF CONTENTS

CONTENTS

1

The Importance of Public Relations

This chapter reviews issues …

- For central administrators: The role public relations plays to offer a two-way link between the organization and its key constituencies. How research and planning aid decision-making by documenting community priorities and how public relations helps school leaders better understand key audiences while helping key audiences better understand and support the school system.

- For building and program administrators: The role public relations plays to offer a two-way link between school programs and services and the direct audiences they serve. How comprehensive communication planning helps schools and programs devise and disseminate key messages in line with the system's overarching communication objectives.

- For teachers, counselors and staff: How public relations can offer planning, materials, and support for the vital roles front-line educators play in communication with key constituents. The ways in which communication planning and development efforts can help professionals refine messages and tactics for communication that support student accomplishment and support school initiatives.

After completing this chapter you should be able to …

- Define the purpose and roles of public relations and communication in the educational organization.

- Demonstrate the benefits of planned and measured school communication to students, schools and the community.

- Outline the roles of communication in building parental and community partnerships.

- Establish the links between communication and the public understanding and support it fosters.

As new challenges continue to confront schools and educators, the importance of school–community relations and overall school public relations has grown rapidly. Consider some trends affecting school leaders daily:

Many states and local school systems today offer a broad array of choices for parents in determining where to send students to school, creating new demands for ongoing communication on program and quality issues between schools and parents, schools and prospective parents, and schools and communities overall. It was only in the 1980s that Minnesota started a school choice program. Today, the majority of states offer some form of charter school alternatives to traditional public-school systems. Many states now give parents options for choosing specific schools either within or outside of their home school systems, and home-schooling options exist in all 50 states.

Safety and security crises—such as violence issues, health concerns, environmental dangers and staff conduct—have challenged the reputations of schools and added new pressures on schools to communicate more effectively before, during, and after crisis situations.

As parents and taxpayers have become better informed and are armed with effective new ways for communicating and connecting with one another, they tend to increase their involvement in local education issues and to openly challenge many of the decisions being made by educational leaders.

For these reasons and more, many superintendents, other administrators, and teachers wish they had learned more about how to communicate effectively and about how to practice public relations when taking their administrative courses.

WHY SCHOOL PUBLIC RELATIONS?

In most communities, taxpayers are letting it be known that they care about the quality of education and its costs. They are demanding to be informed about and involved with key education issues. As a result, more and more of the school administrator's time is spent dealing with people and the administrative functions essential to building strong school communication and community relationships.

An administrator may provide excellent leadership for the school's curriculum or may be a financial wizard, but if an administrator cannot effectively communicate with the school board, parents, taxpayers, staff, and the news media—on a regular basis—his or her days in the district will be few.

News coverage frequently declares one of the following reasons for a superintendent's dismissal: "He couldn't communicate with the board," "Her comments alienated parents," or "He just didn't have a good feel for this community." Knowing the public and being able to keep abreast of the community's thinking are major requirements for today's successful administrator. Suggestions on how to accomplish these tasks are offered in Chapter 3.

Rich Bagin, executive director of the National School Public Relations Association (NSPRA), cites the following as the commonly found reasons that school and community relations fail:

1. Too often, educators equate communication with the dissemination of information. They fail to understand that communication is a two-way process that engages parents, taxpayers and communities in meaningful relationships.
2. School communication and engagement often are reactive to events and situations rather than planned efforts targeted at meeting specific objectives.
3. Leaders and front-line employees do not understand their specific communication roles, have little or no accountability for how they communicate, and receive little support to help them fulfill their communication roles.
4. Educators often have little communication training or experience and are not comfortable when issues have the potential to place their actions and decisions in the public or media spotlights.[1]

If school officials aren't convinced that they have a responsibility to communicate because communication helps people learn or because it builds confidence in the schools, they might want to consider another reason: to keep their jobs. More and more school systems now offer parents some opportunity to choose the school or programs their children will attend. This means that images and perceptions count more than ever for schools. Fair or not, accurate or not, schools that are perceived as being "good" will attract more students than schools that people do not seem to like. The point is that people working in schools that don't attract students will not have jobs. That sounds dramatic, but it probably will be the result because choice options continue to expand.

Why do people choose one school over another? What makes School A seem better than School B? Many people have different theories. Some feel that it is the overall image of the school projected by the school district newsletter and media coverage. Others feel that it is based on the test scores of graduates. Still others think that an aura, evolved over the years, continues, even though in reality the quality of that school has changed.

The reasons why people make school choices become important when considering the growing interest and action on school-choice options. Data compiled by the U.S. Department of Education's National Center for Education Statistics show that, "In 2012, the parents of 37 percent of all 1st- through 12th-grade students indicated that public school choice was available to them. Also in 2012, 13 percent of the students in traditional public schools were in a school chosen by their parents rather than an assigned school." The data also show that those in chosen public schools "had parents who were very satisfied with some elements of their children's education."[2]

INCREASING IMPORTANCE OF PUBLIC RELATIONS

With the increasing competition for students and funding, it's imperative that educational leaders be effective spokespersons for education. With only so many dollars available, the question facing legislators is whether those dollars should go for roads, bridges, health care, welfare, or education. Impressions are made daily by administrators—impressions that influence legislators' decisions about public education. While state and national associations can provide lobbying leadership, much also must be accomplished on a local level by school officials as they communicate in the community. Whether it's speaking in a classroom to explain how public education works (a neglected curriculum item in most

schools) or having breakfast with a local legislator, the school administrator constantly affects the public perception of education. Because administrators lead a fishbowl existence in the community, it's important that they understand and support ways of building confidence in public education.

Still, despite the increasing communication challenges facing schools and their leaders, many school systems continue to display a reluctance to commit dedicated staff and funds to the public relations function. The U.S. Census Bureau reports there are more than 14,000 public school systems in the U.S., but by comparison the National School Public Relations Association has just over 2,000 members in North America.[3]

Perhaps many school leaders feel that "public relations" carries a negative image inappropriate for tax-funded organizations—that it will be perceived as "spin" or "propaganda" to be used to cover up or obscure problems and not as an essential function to build the relationships and understanding vital to public support and student success.

Whether a school system chooses to call the function public relations, public information, community relations, or communications is relatively unimportant. The commitment to better planned, regular, two-way communications with all the audiences served by the schools is, however, important. One of the reasons more of a commitment has not been made may be the fact that so few school officials have been prepared to handle public relations responsibilities. In addition, education has in many cases continued its administrative organization with few changes in titles or responsibilities over the years.

The importance of communication in the overall school operation is being recognized by an increasing number of states, as more are requiring that candidates for administrative certification complete a course in the field of community relations. National organizations, such as the American Association of School Administrators (AASA), have recognized the growing importance of school–community relations by devoting resources and conference sessions to the topic. The 2017 AASA conference, for example, included a "Social Media Lounge" offering programs such as "Benefits of Utilizing Twitter as a Superintendent," "Using Social Media and Online

Tools for Collegial Cooperation and Personal Professional Development, and "Using Social Media to Effectively Engage Your Community" (https://web .archive.org/web/20170628075551/http://nce.aasa .org/wp-content/uploads/AASA-2017-NCE-Onsite-Guide.pdf). Other regional and state education associations are committing more and more sessions to the topic on a regular basis.

Clearly the commitment to school public relations function is essential. For communication success, however, schools need to commit to some of the basic tenets of public relations practice and its practitioners, including understanding that public relations.

Offers a Leadership Function

The practice of public relations is built on a foundation of two-way communication. Effective communication demands more than simply disseminating news and information. It is not just a mouthpiece communicating only school messages that school systems consider important to share. Effective communication also serves as the school system's eyes and ears—watching and listening to the many communities of the system. Of course, the communication function helps communities better understand the school system and its programs by disseminating information and messages in all manner of media. But the two-way aspect of true public relations also interprets the communities and their interests back to the school system and its leaders. In essence, to be effective the communication function needs to enable efforts by educational leaders to listen to and understand their constituencies in order to facilitate both decision-making and communication that will lead to understanding and support.

Acquiring feedback allows school officials to know how the community or staff will react to a decision. To effectively lead a school district, it is essential that leaders know and appreciate the thoughts, aspirations, and commitments of the community and that the community know and appreciate the thoughts, aspirations, and commitments of school leaders. There is a danger in seeing communication

as only a one-way function with school officials telling others what they think they need to know about schools.

When people are asked their opinion, they feel better about the person who asks for it, especially if it's made clear that the opinion will be considered. Whether it's using the key communicators, conducting surveys, or some other method recommended in Chapter 3, the need for feedback is vital to the leadership function of communication.

Builds Relationships and Seeks Consensus

For schools to serve students well, decisions about how schools function and operate need to enjoy support by those in the communities they serve. However, support is not possible without an understanding of the reasons behind the many decisions and actions school leaders are responsible for.

Communication supports this process by helping schools better understand the wants and needs of their many constituencies, and it also supports the process by helping outsiders better understand the facts and rationales behind decisions and actions.

This is a delicate balance that school leaders need to maintain. Some situations may call for bold leadership with efforts designed to inform the community and seek to change prevailing opinions. But other situations may call for the school system itself to change course—to adapt itself to the community's desires or demands.

Making the right decision on potential communication strategies depends upon careful and ongoing communication research. (For more on communication and community research, see Chapter 3.) Such research first helps school leaders to better understand the community and its prevailing attitudes. Such research also provides the foundation for creating a communication plan for the school system. But before a communication plan can be created the research first needs to be used to counsel school leaders on any changes the school system itself may need to make before attempting to successfully forge a consensus with its community.

Fosters Honesty, Transparency, and Ethical Behaviors

If two-way communication seeks to foster and support relationships between the school and its communities then it also must support the elements essential to establishing the trust relationships need to thrive: honesty, transparency, and ethical behavior.

Emotions often drive action. Getting people to care about school issues often involves helping them to develop an emotional connection to those issues and the schools they affect. But the connection people make and the actions they take as a result can be positive or negative for schools—depending upon the emotional connection they make. Those who trust school leadership and believe they have been dealt with honestly and ethically may be more open to school initiatives and to considering various points of view and recommendations. Those who do not trust the leadership and feel that leadership has been misleading or dishonest and is operating in ways that are less than ethical may not be as open-minded to messages from their schools.

Ironically, new media that have emerged in recent years have made it both easier and more difficult for schools to deal with transparency. New media now offer efficient and effective ways to quickly make tremendous amounts of information readily available to audiences. But at the same time these new media have created expectations among audiences that all information will be readily available, thus making schools who fail to effectively use new media appear to be hiding information.

These same new media have created highly connected communities. In such connected environments, transparency in communication is an essential ingredient in supporting accountability and building the sense of ownership and trust communities must hold before they will trust schools and their leadership.

Supports and Counsels the Total Organization

Along with being honest, transparent, and ethical when dealing with constituents, schools also must employ the same behaviors when dealing internally. Communication, and the research that drives and supports it, needs to counsel the organization when potential plans or programs may not be in the best interests of the communities that the schools seek to serve. Reaching consensus, then, may mean helping the school adapt to its communities as well as helping communities adapt to their schools.

This process is reflected in the evaluation the National School Public Relations Association (NSPRA) makes when it considers school communication programs for its Gold Medallion Award annually. The organization evaluates programs based on their research, planning/action, communication/implementation, and evaluation.[4] The planning/action phase, which follows research, gives the communication planner the ability to counsel the organization on any changes it may need to make before engaging in communication and seeking consensus with its community.

Seeks Community Partnerships Supporting School and Student Success

There is a significant amount of evidence demonstrating the tremendous positive effect that engaged families and communities have on student success. School communication is responsible for creating the atmosphere in which engagement becomes possible, and NSPRA's Communication Accountability Program (https://www.nspra.org/cap) has been collecting and disseminating this evidence for more than a decade.

Through two-way communication schools can build the kind of environment important to creating collaboration with the community overall and parents in particular—collaboration that will support student and school success.

Engagement between schools and their communities, however, depends on a foundation of understanding and trust, and planned school communication assures that such a foundation is created. Clearly, student and school well-being can be placed at risk when schools fail to effectively communicate and engage in ways that build working partnerships with the community.

Includes a Fiscally Responsible use of Taxpayer Resources and the Public Accountability Function for the School System Overall

As with any school function, school communication and the many activities needed to support it must be funded with public money. Communication investments, as a result, must be planned and evaluated in ways that document an appropriate return. Research helps to document key issues and audiences, and messages and tactics that can effectively be used to address those issues and audiences. Research and planning can establish the benchmarks and metrics by which communication investments ultimately will be judged.

Some metrics may involve communication-based outcomes—the amount of publicity generated, the level of awareness created, the number of subscribers to a social media feed and so on. But other outcomes might be tied to more bottom-line issues for the school system—the number of new student registrations generated, the increase in attendance at public meetings, the value of donations to a school foundation and so on.

Both types of measurements are critical to creating communication programming that is both fiscally responsible and accountable for the school system overall.

A PUBLIC RELATIONS PLAN IS ESSENTIAL

A plan must be developed for public relations or little will happen. Board members and administrators can commiserate for a long time about the need for a public relations program, but it won't happen unless someone develops a plan and makes a commitment to on-going communication.

NSPRA recommends that school communication activities be planned and guided by a written communication plan. The organization recommends the following:

- The public relations/communication efforts are planned on a systematic (often annual) basis to support the achievement of the organization's goals and objectives.
- The plan has the approval of the superintendent/chief executive officer.

- The plan focuses on meeting the goals of the organization and ultimately improving education, and, to the extent possible, enhancing student achievement.
- The plan identifies the needs of target publics and uses research data to identify key messages and strategies for delivering those messages.
- Communication plans for specific program changes or initiatives are developed in conjunction with the staff responsible for them.
- Communication plans identify the various publics who will be affected and the strategies for reaching them.
- To the extent possible, communication plans include measurable goals for behavior change or accomplishment, deadlines, responsibilities, resources, and strategies.
- Plans are reviewed regularly to ensure that communication efforts remain relevant and are on schedule, and are adjusted whenever necessary to reach planned goals or to deal with emerging needs and opportunities.[5]

Public Relations Addresses Many Needs

Some public relations activities may focus on addressing specific needs—celebrating a key anniversary, opening a new building, or launching a new fund-raising initiative, for example. But school communications overall should be driven by a comprehensive public relations plan that accommodates the need for over-arching and ongoing communication of a variety of messages in a range of situations to a wide array of audiences.

Communicating with external audiences is perhaps the function most commonly associated with public relations. Working with the news media to generate news coverage and positive publicity is another role that many also associate with the practice of public relations.

But along with these external communication functions, public relations also has a responsibility to communicate to and build working relationships with internal audiences such as employees. Communication efforts can be tied directly to issues of employee morale, productivity, and retention, all issues which can have important financial impacts on an organization. Employees need to be seen as ambassadors of the school in the community. What they say can make a significant impact on external audiences, and school leaders need to keep mind that workers—teachers and bus drivers, for example—are interacting with people in the community every single day.

Beyond seeking to inform others, public relations also has a role in influencing actions, and its communication efforts therefore also can play critical roles in helping to market schools and school services. From attracting new students to recruiting new employees, public relations plays a role in marketing a school system's many opportunities and options.

Public relations also plays a critically important role when schools are challenged by any of a number of crises that can erupt. Timely, accurate and open communication with internal and external audiences can help a school system effectively manage the many difficult issues a crisis can present. And effective public relations can support school leaders in maintaining their credibility and the community's confidence during times of crisis.

Even before a crisis strikes, however, public relations fulfills a role in helping school leaders identify potential issues and manage them before

they grow into controversies or crises that can threaten working relationships between the school and communities. By conducting communication research and collecting feedback from the school system's constituencies, public relations can interpret key audiences and issues to school leaders and support decision-making that aligns the needs of the school system with the needs of the community.

Along with counseling school leaders, public relations needs to play a role in helping all employees understand and fulfill their communication roles. People in all school functions have some level of public interaction and the way in which they handle these roles plays an important role in how others will view the school system and its commitment to serving the community. Public relations programs should offer activities to help all employees better understand the importance of these roles and they should offer training and support to help employees carry out their communication roles.

All of these activities reflect the role public relations should play in helping the school system to build the working relationships that are essential if a school system is to successfully and effectively serve its students and community.

One Expert's Point of View: Understanding the Role of Public Relations in Helping Schools and Students Achieve Their Best

Suzanne Sparks FitzGerald, Ph.D., APR, Fellow PRSA, is Professor and Chair of the Public Relations and Advertising Department at Rowan University in Glassboro, N.J. As part of its M.A. program in P.R. the Department offers a Certificate of Graduate Study in School Public Relations. Dr. FitzGerald has more than a decade of experience in corporate and marketing communications and more than 20 years as a professor at Rowan University. She serves as accreditation chair for the Philadelphia Chapter of the Public Relations Society of America and is co-author of the text *The PR Writer's Toolbox*. Dr. FitzGerald's research interests include credibility of PR and advertising and PR education.

Why is it so important that school leaders understand the role and importance of public relations?

Misunderstanding what public relations can and can't do for a school system can pose a tremendous threat. Public relations is not a function designed to whitewash problems or sweep bad news under the rug. In fact, using communication to mislead or hide facts will often make a bad situation much worse. But when properly understood and deployed, public relations offers tremendous potential in helping organizations meet their objectives and enjoy success. And

it also helps organizations avoid problems and crises by identifying them and addressing them before they become major issues. And public relations can help organizations navigate troubled waters when bad news does happen.

Communication happens in any organization all the time whether it's planned for or not. It's simply responsible management to plan activities for such an important function and to hold employees responsible for their performance in their communication roles. One might even argue that failing to properly plan and manage an organization's communication function is management malpractice.

Organizations such as the National School Public Relations Association (http://www.nspra.org) have many superintendents, principals and other administrators—as well as communication practitioners—among their members. The organization has developed a number of materials to help school leaders better understand, build, and manage the public relations function in school systems of all sizes and complexities.

Many educators have little if any formal communication training, so how can they be expected to manage public relations functions?

Two issues are important here. First, while many educators may not have formal communication training they do in fact have a great deal of communication experience. Teaching depends on excellent communication with students and colleagues, for example. A successful administrator must be a successful communicator to inspire staff members and motivate them to work towards a shared vision. So an initial step might be to look at where we are communicating now, how these existing communication skills might be expanded, and how they might be applied to wider audiences in the public relations function.

A second step, however, is to trust in the skill and advice of the person leading the public relations function. Most chief school administrators aren't attorneys but they rely on attorneys when they need legal advice. They aren't police officers but they rely on law enforcement officials for security insights. They aren't physicians but they know how to get insights on health issues affecting their schools. The same goes for communication issues. Part of the management function of public relations should be to counsel and support school leaders on communication issues. So the school leadership team needs to have someone leading the communication function who is trusted and respected. This is one reason why we also strongly recommend that the communication function report directly to the superintendent or chief school administrator. The counseling function only works when no filters or obstacles stand between the communication counselor and chief executives.

As part of this counseling role public relations sometimes is called the organization's conscience. What is meant by this?

Like people, organizations can sometimes make decisions or act in ways that are self-serving and harmful to others. It's not always done maliciously. Perhaps a decision maker is focused more on an action's benefit to the organization than on the harm that may be done elsewhere as a result. Or maybe the press of time leads to a decision that simply is made in haste without a careful assessment of all of its implications. But images and ultimately organizations suffer when bad decisions are made.

The public relations leader for an organization has an obligation to be constantly focused on the needs and wants of key constituencies and looking for ways that decisions and actions can be made in the mutual best interests of the organization and its constituencies. Communication flows in two directions. So while the public relations function is charged with interpreting the organization to its audiences the function at the same time should be interpreting those audiences to the organization. Some see this role as being a sort of conscience—an inner voice prepared to speak to the rightness or wrongness of a decision.

This all leads back to the idea that public relations seeks decisions and actions that mutually benefit the organization and its constituencies. In the long-run, one-sided relationships ultimately will fail.[6]

Questions

1. Explain what is meant by the two-way communication process and how public relations can use it to help strengthen school and community understanding and relations.

2. Why is it important to have a formal communication plan for a school district overall?

3. Explain the leadership function public relations should fulfill and why communication research is essential to that function.

4. Why is it important that the public relations plan address communication issues with employees as well as those in outside or external audiences?

Readings

Bagin, Don, and Anthony Fulginiti, *Practical Public Relations Theories & Practices That Make a Difference.* Dubuque, IA: Kendall Hunt, 2006.

Bagin, Rich, *Making Parent Communication Effective and Easy.* Rockville, MD: National School Public Relations Association, 2006.

Broom, Glenn, and Bei-Ling Sha, *Cutlip and Center's Effective Public Relations,* 11th ed. Boston, MA: Pearson Education, 2012.

National School Public Relations Association, *School Public Relations: Building Confidence in Education,* 2nd ed. Rockville, MD: Author, 2007.

Wilcox, Dennis L., and Glen T. Cameron, *Public Relations Strategies and Tactics,* 11th ed. Boston, MA: Pearson Education, 2014.

Endnotes

1. Adapted from personal correspondence in October 2013 with Rich Bagin, Executive Director, National School Public Relations Association, Rockville, MD. Used with permission.

2. National Center for Education Statistics, "Fast Facts: Public School Choice Programs." Retrieved August 9, 2017, at https://nces.ed.gov/fastfacts/display.asp?id=6.

3. Taken from personal correspondence in August 2017 with Rich Bagin, Executive Director, National School Public Relations Association, Rockville, MD.

4. NSPRA Gold Medallion Award Program. Retrieved August 15, 2017, at https://www.nspra.org/awards/gold-medallion.

5. Reprinted with permission from "Raising the Bar for School PR: New Standards for the School Public Relations Profession". Rockville, MD; National School Public Relations Association, 2002. Retrieved August 15, 2017 from https://www.nspra.org/files/docs/StandardsBooklet.pdf.

6. Adapted from personal correspondence August 27, 2017 with Suzanne Sparks FitzGerald, Professor and Chair, De-partment of Public Relations and Advertising, Rowan University, Glassboro, NJ. Used with permission.

2

Public Character of the School

This chapter reviews issues ...

■ For central administrators: Why the public character of the school demands a special obligation to foster engaged leadership. How public opinion, properly informed, can drive behavior offering significant benefits to students and schools. But how improperly informed public opinion can drive behavior harmful to schools.

■ For building and program administrators: How the public character of the school raises the need for understanding community attitudes and beliefs and accommodating them in everyday planning and decision-making. The ways in which opinions and resulting actions of those in the community can have a direct effect on the abilities of schools and programs to operate effectively.

■ For teachers, counselors and staff: How the public character of the school underscores the significance of engaging with parents and others invested in the success of students. The degrees to which opinions and resulting actions of those served by schools can have a direct impact on the ability to successfully serve students.

After completing this chapter you should be able to ...

■ Identify the characteristics of schools and educational organizations and how those features affect communication practice in schools.

■ Distinguish the features of attitudes, opinions, and public opinion.

■ Define what is meant by school–community relations.

■ Outline traditional public relations models.

From a communication perspective, the use of research, feedback, media, and messages to foster strong working relationships between the school and community would perhaps seem like little more than common-sense management and leadership mandates. After all, engaged communities grow from informed communities and engaged communities are more likely to understand the issues facing the school system and be more open to forging a consensus with others to work toward common goals supporting school and student success.

But the need for communication to support working relationships arises out of a legal need as well. The public character of the school and the legal framework within which it operates require an open flow of information between the school and the community as well as a consideration by school leaders of community views and interests. This process operates by understanding the role of public opinion in the shaping of educational policies and practices. It reflects an historical fact of the American way of life—a way that is characterized by constant change driven by a decision-making process in which individuals can exercise an influence on the nature and direction of change.

The position can be found in the applied definition of school and community relations that is presented in this chapter. The application of school communication practices should reflect the belief that sound and constructive relationships must be developed and maintained with the community by those who are responsible for public education if the school is to meet all of its many obligations to the cause, continuance, and preservation of democracy.

PUBLIC CHARACTER OF THE SCHOOL

While the fundamental nature of legal and communication issues affecting the management of school systems in the U.S. has remained basically unchanged for decades, tremendous shifts in communication practice and public opinion have ushered in many new challenges and opportunities for school leaders.

Emerging trends such as social media connecting and organizing communities more than ever, charges such as "fake news" chipping away at institutional credibility, and demands for more school-choice options, to name just a few, have placed schools under more and more pressure to meet the diverse demands of their communities.

One basic fact remains unchanged, however: In the face of these emerging trends as well as the continued involvement of the federal government in local and state educational affairs, it is evident in the legal structure of public school systems and in the laws regulating their operation that the power to manage schools still resides with the citizenry. At the state level, the people have the right to support or oppose legislation affecting the education of children, to work for the modification and repeal of existing laws, and to decide at the polls who shall represent them in the legislature.

This right exists at the local level as well, where citizens are elected or appointed to membership on the board of education and are expected to carry out the popular will when developing policy and practices to guide local schools. To ensure the public character of the board of education, state law typically prescribes that parents and citizens shall have the right to be heard at a regular meeting of the board or to file in writing their ideas regarding educational objectives, policies, and programs. Regular meetings must be open to the public, and no vote on school business can be taken in private by the board. The minutes of the board's meetings and records of transactions are public property and may be inspected at any time on request by a citizen. The failure of a school board and its individual members to abide by these and other regulations set forth in the law may result in dismissal of the board and prosecution of the members for misconduct in office.

In a sense, citizens in the community are part owners in the schools. They own stock, so to speak, in the schools, considering that it is, in fact, their taxes that support the schools. The dividends received from these investments include formal education for themselves and their children. Indirect benefits also accrue, such as a literate and well-prepared population and workforce serving the community, added value to real property in the community, added attractiveness of the community to individuals, businesses, and other organizations seeking a new place to live or work, and so on. The fact that the educational enterprise is built upon the concept of shared ownership further underscores the public character of the school.

Shared ownership, of course, also carries with it a responsibility for both citizens and school leaders. People must be supplied with accurate and adequate information about the school system if they are to form intelligent opinions and share their thinking with school leaders. To meaningfully participate as part-owners, citizens must have access to relevant facts, ideas, and options, and they must be able to evaluate them reasonably.

Citizens' beliefs and opinions can have a tremendous effect on the ability of the school system to function. Since opinions drive actions, community opinion can have a very real bottom-line impact on the school system, as citizen input and votes can elect board members, fix school-tax rates, pass or reject school funding initiatives, influence curriculum decision-making, and pass judgment on potential new services or other school offerings.

These bottom-line impacts underscore how important it is for school leaders to understand both the role of public attitudes in a democracy and the effects that role, when exercised, can have on schools and students as well as the community.

This issue also applies in situations where the community may be disengaged or apathetic toward local schools and their issues. If citizen engagement is essential to success in a democracy, then school leaders also need to be prepared to energize public interest and shape opinion in cases where it is lagging.

Disengaged communities will lead, over time, to disconnected leadership. The perception of school leaders will fall. The quality of education may suffer. Cries for alternatives and competition in school offerings will rise. And in some severe cases outside agencies might take over or even dissolve the local school system.

Clearly, the school leadership team needs to understand and appreciate the clear benefits of an engaged citizenry, how public attitudes and opinions drive actions, and the roles that school and community relations and communication can play in supporting this process.

THE MEANING OF PUBLIC OPINION

Public attitudes may be viewed as predispositions, thoughts, or feelings of persons toward something, such as an issue or a policy question that has not yet come into sharp focus. But prevailing attitudes can swiftly fuse into public opinion and prompt calls for action when emerging issues challenge traditional thinking. For example:

- In the early years of the country much education was private, but as the need for and benefits of universal education came into focus the demand for public education options emerged.
- Until the 1950s the federal role in local education was limited. But when the Soviets launched the first satellite and the nation became alarmed at the prospect of losing the space race, attention focused on the need for more federal aid to education. Demand grew for more foreign language teaching and science offerings in elementary and secondary schools, for example.
- More recently, the historic demands for public education options have been under pressure to reform as a new focus emerged on school and student performance accountability and the perceived benefits of competition in the school marketplace. Support for testing initiatives grew and demands for public funding of charter schools and other alternatives to traditional school systems increased.

Other characteristics are also ascribed to attitudes, the most common being their emotional tone. Attitudes are always accompanied by some positive or negative feeling, and the nature and intensity of this feeling influence an individual's perception of any new situation he or she encounters. For example, a beginning teacher who has had a series of unpleasant experiences with the principal might develop a dislike for principals in general despite the fact that another one under whom he or she is now working is sincere and thoughtful. To the teacher this new principal might have an ulterior motive of personal gain in acting decently. Such an attitude may persist for a long time, depending on the intensity of the negative feeling and the frequency of constructive acts on the part of the second principal. It is known that attitudes are, at least in part, the result of forces in each individual's environment—such as his or her physical needs, social needs, emotions, perceptions, motivations, and experiences—and that these in turn influence the individual's behavior. Interestingly enough, opinions are defined in a similar way.

Social scientists have not arrived at a standard definition of *attitudes* or *opinions*. Therefore, the terms are often used interchangeably. Yet it may be worthwhile to review some of the meanings connected with the term *public opinion*. Occasionally, *public opinion* is defined as any widespread belief or consensus arrived at by members of one or more groups, or as prevailing customs and traditions handed down by previous generations. The term is also frequently associated with the process of developing opinion instead of opinion itself, with fine distinctions drawn between judgments reached by logical methods of reasoning and judgments growing out of emotional states of mind. Attention may likewise be given to the quality of the opinions expressed or to the intensity of the opinions. No doubt these and other variations in the meaning of the term have a place in a detailed study and analysis of public opinion, but they are hardly suitable to guide the work of laypersons and professional school officials. As a working rule, we should think of public opinion as a collection of individual viewpoints held more or less in common by members of a group regarding some person, condition, or proposal. Generally, these points of view concern matters that are controversial or capable of causing controversy.

SCHOOL–COMMUNITY RELATIONS

In view of its background and status in U.S. society, the school has a definite responsibility to furnish taxpayers and parents with complete and accurate information regarding its needs and activities and to develop educational policies and programs that reflect popular interests and desires. How to implement this responsibility effectively is the problem of school–community relations.

The History

Although the necessity for keeping the public informed is as old as the school itself, nevertheless it was not until the beginning of the 1920s that a formal approach was made. This began with studies of publicity, especially newspaper publicity, and of the value such publicity had in keeping the school before the people and in acquainting them with what it was doing. During this period at least three books were published on the subject of school publicity,[1] as well as a scattering of articles in professional journals.

Within a few years the term *publicity* was replaced with the phrase *school public relations*, for at least two reasons. First, it was felt that the word *publicity* carried both positive and negative connotations. Second, the realization developed that a more inclusive concept than publicity was necessary for telling the story more fully and for reaching a wider audience. In the mid-1920s, Moehlman came out with the

first book in educational administration dealing with school public relations. He defined public school relations as an "organized factual informational service for the purpose of keeping the public informed of its educational program."[2] The book included chapters on public relations policy, the responsibilities of personnel, and the use of such media as newspapers, house organs, annual reports, school newspapers, and oral and written communications with parents. Attention was also given to the importance of social contacts, parent–teacher associations, school buildings, and appraisal of results.

These pioneering efforts were followed 11 years later with another book by Moehlman setting forth the doctrine of *social interpretation*. According to this doctrine, "Social interpretation may be considered as the activity whereby the institution is made aware of community conditions and needs and the factual information service whereby the people are kept continuously informed of the purpose, value, conditions, and needs of their educational program."[3] In other words, it is a two-way system of communication through which the community is translated to the school and the school to the community.

The objectives of a program in social interpretation, as set forth by Moehlman, are as follows: "The ultimate objective is to develop continuing public consciousness of the importance of educational process in a democratic social organization, to establish confidence in the functioning institution, to furnish adequate means to maintain its efficient operation, and to improve the partnership concept through active parental participation."[4]

School public relations at present represents an extension of the interpretive point of view. This extension takes into account a change in basic terminology, increased emphasis on communication, and greater citizen involvement and participation in the educational decision-making process. There is a movement now to eliminate the term *public relations* and to use instead the phrase *school–community relations* because the latter is more in keeping with current concepts concerning the involvement and participation of citizens in the educational decision-making process and is less subject to association with undesirable practices in promotion and persuasion for selfish ends.

It has been increasingly evident that the school in a dynamic, changing social order cannot adapt itself to change or make the necessary improvements in its program without involving citizens in its affairs. As pointed out by Sumption and Engstrom, "There must be a structured, systematic, and active participation on the part of the people of the community in the educational planning, policy making, problem solving, and evaluation of the school."[5] Through such involvement, citizens come to know the school firsthand. They are able to raise questions, obtain information, express ideas, consider proposals, and take positions on critical issues. They become part of the decision-making process that keeps up with social change and brings about educational change.

Citizen involvement ensures a better understanding of what the community wants for its children now and in the future. It likewise provides better opportunities for closer cooperation with local governmental agencies and community organizations that have an interest in education and public welfare. Generally, it helps to bring about increased use of community resources in the educational program, thereby integrating further the school and community.

Recent Definitions

Before stating what is meant by *school–community relations*, it might be well to examine some definitions of *public relations*.

Rex Harlow, the founder of the organization that eventually became the Public Relations Society of America (PRSA), discovered over 500 definitions of *public relations* from many sources. From all these he composed an 86-word definition that Grunig and Hunt reduced to "the management of communication between an organization and its publics."[6]

Cutlip, Center, and Broom later defined *public relations* this way:

> Public relations is the management function that establishes and maintains mutually beneficial relationships between an organization and the publics on whom its success or failure depends.[7]

Wilcox and Cameron cited this definition of *public relations* from the 1978 World Assembly of Public Relations, which was endorsed by 34 national public relations organizations:

> Public relations practice is the art and social science of analyzing trends, predicting their consequences, counseling organization leaders, and implementing planned programs of action which serve both the organization's and the public's interest.[8]

The PRSA noted "Public relations helps an organization and its publics to adapt mutually to each other."[9]

Many people consider that publicity, public information, promotion, and media relations are each exclusively public relations. Many practitioners, though, believe these activities are part of, but not exclusively, public relations. Being one-way communications, they lack the need of public relations to include two-way communications as an essential activity.

Leaders in school–community relations and the National School Public Relations Association (NSPRA) use parallel concepts in defining school–community relations.

NSPRA also substituted the word *educational* for *school* in its definition:

> Educational public relations is a planned, systematic management function, designed to help improve the programs and services of an educational organization. It relies on a comprehensive, two-way communication process involving both internal and external publics with the goal of stimulating better understanding of the role, objectives, accomplishments, and needs of the organization.
>
> Educational public relations programs assist in interpreting public attitudes, identify and help shape policies and procedures in the public interest, and carry on involvement and information activities which earn public support and understanding.[10]

Holliday defined school public–community relations as "a systematic function on all levels of a school system, established as a program to improve and maintain optimal levels of student achievement, and to build public support."[11] He contended that the two main purposes of a school–community relations program are to foster student achievement (through the establishment of a positive school climate, and parent and citizen involvement) and to build citizen knowledge and understanding leading to financial support.

Kindred defined public relations as:

> a process of communication between the school and the community for the purpose of increasing citizen understanding of educational needs and practices and encouraging intelligent citizen interest and cooperation in the work of improving the school.[12]

We now include two-way communication in this shorter definition: Educational public relations is management's systematic, continuous, two-way, honest communication between an educational organization and its publics.

Though other definitions might be quoted as a means of bringing out the various shades of meaning associated with the term *public relations*, the position taken here is that sound and constructive relationships between the school and the community are the outcomes of a dynamic process that combines the following ideas and practices:

- A way of life expressed daily by staff members in their personal relations with colleagues, students, parents, and people in the community
- A planned and continuing series of activities for communicating with both internal and external publics concerning the purposes, needs, programs, and accomplishments of the school
- A planned and continuing series of activities for determining what citizens think of the schools and the aspirations they hold for the education of their children
- The active involvement of citizens in the decision-making process of the school and school-initiated community outreach programs so that essential improvements may be made in the educational program and adjustments brought about to meet the climate of social change.

Perhaps another way of expressing the same concepts is to say that sound and constructive relations between the school and community are achieved through a process of exchanging information, ideas, and viewpoints out of which common understandings are developed and decisions are made concerning essential improvements in the educational program and adjustments to the climate of social change.

New on the public relations scene, because of numerous corporate scandals in the beginning of the twenty-first century, is the term *reputation management*. Seitel notes that after the scandals, public relations firms were quick to develop reputation management practices that would enhance corporate credibility. He goes on to define *reputation management* as "the ability to link credibility to business goals to increase advocacy, support, and increase profits."[13]

It should be noted that previous definitions of public relations did not include "honest communications" or "organizational credibility" because the authors assumed these characteristics already existed in the organization.

TRADITIONAL PUBLIC RELATIONS MODELS

Grunig and Hunt[14] developed four models of public relations: *press agentry–publicity, public information, two-way asymmetric,* and *two-way symmetric.* Each differs in the purpose and nature of communication. *Press agentry–publicity* is one-way communication with propaganda as its purpose. The purpose of *public information,* also one-way, is the dissemination of truthful information. Scientific persuasion is the purpose of the *two-way asymmetric* model, with mutual understanding being the intent of the *two-way symmetric* model. In the *two-way asymmetric* model, the communicator gets feedback from the public and then applies the latest communication and persuasion theories to persuade the public to accept the organization's point of view. On the other hand, in the *two-way symmetric* model, the communicator is a go-between for the organization and its public, trying through all methods of communication to have each side understand each other's point of view. If persuasion takes place either way, it's because of information flowing both ways between the organization and the public.

Grunig and Hunt estimate that 15 percent of organizations practice press agentry–publicity, 50 percent public information, 20 percent two-way asymmetric, and 15 percent two-way symmetric.[15] It would appear that many school districts use primarily the public information model, all one-way. Instead, they should be practicing the two-way symmetric model that develops mutual understanding with their communities.

On-going Programs and Relationships

Entirely too many school-communication programs are sporadic in nature, improperly conceived, poorly planned, and crudely executed. Often, they arise out a sudden need to spread information or respond to

a controversy. Such reactionary programming frequently appears self-serving, enjoys little or no credibility in the community, and generally ends up defeating its own purpose. If a school system wishes to engage in successful school–community relations programming, then it must be willing to commit to a comprehensive and continuing program. Such a program must be given resources to support planning that will determine how the school system's character, needs, and services may be interpreted best to the people, how the community's wishes and aspirations may be interpreted best to the school, and how citizen involvement may be included in the task of educational improvement and institutional and programmatic adjustment to social change.

One Expert's Point of View: Meeting the Demands of the Public Character of the School

Ethan Aronoff started his career as a social studies teacher and he went on to serve in both elected and appointed government positions, all of which required considerable commitment to engaging with multiple diverse constituencies and ongoing community relations activities. He served as Director of Human Services for Cumberland County (N.J.) helping to manage funding and programming for human service providers. He was executive director of the Millville (N.J.) YMCA for five years. He served two elected terms on the Millville (N.J.) City Commission. He has also participated on the planning board and an ad hoc master plan committee. He was a town manager in Maine and Massachusetts. Among his many volunteer board positions are the United Way (vice-chair), Millville Public Library (president), Shade Tree Commission (chair), Maine Audubon–Penobscot Valley Chapter (president), Kiwanis Club, Bayshore Discovery Project, and Citizens United to Protect the Maurice River and Its Tributaries.

The idea that informing the public is critical to our success as a democracy seems like a tall order to give to leaders. Is an institution's relationship with its communities really that serious?

It can be argued that it is an important part of how democracy functions. There is a quote often attributed to Thomas Jefferson that says "An educated citizenry is a vital requisite for our survival as a free people." Not that I want to edit Jefferson but I might tweak that a bit to say "An educated and engaged citizenry is vital... ." How included people feel with the basic institutions serving and supporting society is critical to the health of the democracy. And local school systems are a vital part of that infrastructure. Sure, there is a legal requirement to share information and serve the public interest. But the need to partner with the community and move forward in ways that meet

mutually beneficial needs is essential to long-term success. If our expectations are low we cannot expect much from the public or from public officials.

Some might argue that leadership is not about reading polls and bowing to public demands. Leadership, it might be argued, involves creating a vision and inspiring others to follow you on a journey to reach that vision. Are leaders of public institutions vision creators or poll readers?

There is nothing exclusive in either of those two descriptions. Of course, we are poll readers. Feedback is essential. We need to have a detailed understanding of public knowledge and beliefs and desires. This kind of insight provides the foundation for building any communication plan to support sound relationships with our communities. And only through these relationships can we create the kind of public discourse essential to moving things forward. But we also need to help others see and appreciate the many options out there. We need to help others see what the future can be and excite them about the ways in which, working together, it can become a reality. It's only when we function exclusively in one area or the other that leadership fails. Blindly following community whims may fail to exploit all that is possible. And blindly advancing a vision that few understand or appreciate will not create the kind of support that success demands.

Advances in technology and emerging media seemed to hinder this process in so many ways. Personal relationships have given way to digital partnerships. Specialized media and online communities have put audience segments in their own silos or echo chambers where they hear only things that reinforce their own beliefs. How do public leaders deal with such segmentation in society?

Talk to any communication expert about audience segmentation and he or she will tell you that this is nothing new. Knowing your audience has always been key. Communication researchers and planners have segmented audiences to better tailor messages and better target media long before today's new media came into play. In many ways today's online communication and online communities may have made this process even easier to deal with. The key here is for those leading public organizations to fully commit to the kind of communication research and planning needed to make sure communication investments will pay off. Messages need to be crafted in ways that grab audience attention, align a vision with their interests, point to a clear path for action. These messages need to be delivered through channels and by sources that people respect, find credible, and trust. We can't simply tell people what we think they should know using media that we think will work. Understanding communities is key to communicating in ways that will build relational capital. Committing to this process will kindle the strong sense of belonging and the capacity for cooperation that successful school and community relations need.[16]

Questions

1. List the bottom-line impacts that opinion-driven behavior by citizens in the community can have on schools and the positive and negative impacts this can have on schools and students.
2. Compare the various statements on public relations with those made by the National School Public Relations Association. How does public relations practice in general compare with its practice in schools?
3. Which of Grunig and Hunt's models of public relations should schools employ to be effective at supporting student and school success? Why might some of their models be more effective than others for school public relations planners and educational leaders?
4. What would you say to a person who wants to know the relationship between public opinion and public relations—and how can understanding public opinion contribute to school leadership success?

Readings

Bagin, Don, and Anthony Fulginiti, *Practical Public Relations Theories and Practices That Make a Difference.* Dubuque, IA: Kendall Hunt, 2006.

Bardes, Barbara A., and Robert W. Oldendick, *Public Opinion: Measuring the American Mind,* 5th ed. Lanham, MD: Rowman & Littlefield, 2016.

Broom, Glen M., and Bey-Ling Sha, *Cutlip & Center's Effective Public Relations,* 11th ed. Boston, MA: Pearson, 2013.

Ewen, Stuart, *PR! A Social History of Spin.* New York, NY: Basic Books, 1996.

Newsom, Doug, Judy VanSlyke Turk, and Dean Kruckeberg, *This Is PR: The Realities of Public Relations,* 11th ed. Belmont, CA: Wadsworth, 2012.

Sergiovanni, Thomas J., Martin Burlingame, Fred S. Coombs, and Paul W. Thurston, *Educational Governance and Administration,* 6th ed. Boston, MA: Allyn & Bacon, 2008.

Wilcox, Dennis L., and Glen T. Cameron, *Public Relations Strategies and Tactics,* 11th ed. Boston, MA: Pearson, 2014.

Endnotes

1. Rollo George Reynolds, *Newspaper Publicity for the Public Schools* (New York, NY: A. G. Seiler, 1922); Clyde R. Miller and Fred Charles, *Publicity and the Public Schools* (Boston, MA: Houghton Mifflin, 1924); and Harlan Cameron Hines and Robinson G. Jones, *Public School Publicity* (New York, NY: Macmillan, 1923).
2. Arthur B. Moehlman, *Public School Relations* (Chicago, IL: Rand McNally, 1927), p. 4.
3. Arthur B. Moehlman, *Social Interpretation* (New York, NY: Appleton-Century, 1938), p. 104.
4. Ibid., p. 106.
5. Merle R. Sumption and Yvonne Engstrom, *School Community Relations: A New Approach* (New York: McGraw-Hill, 1966), p. xi.
6. James E. Grunig and Todd Hunt, *Managing Public Relations* (New York, NY: Holt, Rinehart and Winston, 1984), p. 7, as cited in Todd Hunt and James E. Grunig, *Public Relations Techniques* (Fort Worth, TX: Harcourt Brace College, 1994), p. 6.
7. Scott M. Cutlip, Allen H. Center, and Glen M. Broom, *Effective Public Relations,* 8th ed. (Upper Saddle River, NJ: Prentice Hall, 2000), p. 6.
8. Dennis L. Wilcox and Glen T. Cameron, *Public Relations Strategies and Tactics,* 8th ed. (Boston, MA: Allyn & Bacon, 2006), p. 6.
9. "PRSA Official Statement on Public Relations." Retrieved August 28, 2014, from http://www.prsa. org/AboutPRSA/PublicRelationsDefined/Documents/Official%20Statement%20on%20Public%20 Relations.pdf.
10. *Raising the Bar for School PR: New Standards for the School Public Relations Profession* (Rockville, MD: National School Public Relations Association, 2002), p. 1, retrieved from http://www.nspra.org/files/docs/StandardsBooklet.pdf, October 2013.
11. Albert E. Holliday, "In Search of an Answer: What Is School Public Relations?" *Journal of Educational Public Relations 11* (2nd Quarter 1988), p. 12; and personal interview, January 28, 2003.
12. Leslie W. Kindred, *School Public Relations* (Upper Saddle River, NJ: Prentice Hall, 1957), p. 16.
13. Fraser P. Seitel, "What Is Reputation Management?" *O'Dwyer's PR Services Report,* August 2002, p. 31.
14. James E. Grunig and Todd Hunt, *Managing Public Relations* (New York, NY: Rinehart and Winston, 1984), pp. 21–23. Also see Todd Hunt and James E. Grunig, *Public Relations Techniques* (Fort Worth, TX: Harcourt Brace College Publishers, 1994), p. 9.
15. Ibid., Grunig and Hunt, p. 23.
16. Adapted from personal correspondence August 29, 2017 with Ethan Aronoff, President, Millville (N.J.) Public Library Board of Trustees. Used with permission.

3

Understanding the Community

This chapter reviews issues …

- For central administrators: The importance of using research-driven planning to understand diverse communities and drive overall communication efforts.
- For building and program administrators: How addressing the information needs of specific audience segments can enhance understanding of and support for schools and programs in the community.
- For teachers, counselors and staff: The ways in which over-arching communication research and planning can contribute to frontline efforts to communicate with students, clients, and their families and to reinforce the school system's communication efforts.

After completing this chapter you should be able to …

- Identify key community segments important to school–community relations planning and programming.
- Distinguish methods for community–audience assessment and identifying influential communicators.
- Recognize the characteristics of community power structures.
- Distinguish opinion research techniques commonly deployed in school–community relations programs.

Successful communication depends on having a thorough understanding of the community. To accomplish this, careful communication planning begins with comprehensive communication research. As a result, before investing in any formal communication activities school leaders need to carefully consider and study the audiences important to the school.

School leaders must understand the many segments that make up the school's community and they must appreciate the numerous complexities that diverse audiences can present to a communication effort. Also, while communication planning often is viewed as a systemwide effort, it's important to appreciate that information is shared— and reputations are affected—in school- and program-based community interactions along with systemwide interactions. School-communication planners also need to recognize that there is no over-arching "general public." Rather, any school's community consists of a diverse set of publics, with each often holding its own information needs, beliefs, and opinions.

To get started, communication research should compile the data and insight needed to help school leaders and communication planners consider:

- The characteristics of formal and informal power structures in the community that can influence how information is trusted and shared and how decisions are made, and the identification of individuals who may be key to influencing thought and action among various publics.
- The documentation of key channels through which individuals in the community seek and share information, ranging from formal channels such as traditional news media to less organized channels such as face-to-face conversations and even grapevine gossip.
- The level of information various audience segments have concerning their schools and school issues and the resulting opinions and expectations they hold concerning education.
- Opportunities for establishing better working relationships with different publics and the state of current relationships with individuals and groups both supportive of and opposed to the various educational efforts in the community.
- The information needs currently existing in the community and the best options to build better understanding and support among all publics.
- Recent economic, social, or other trends that have resulted in changes in the community and potential changes that may affect the community in the future.
- The various groups and organizations with an interest in community and school success.

Communities undergo constant change, so research to help school leaders understand their communities and drive their communication needs has to be ongoing. Communication research should be directed at the community's sociological characteristics, the nature and influence of its power structures, how trusted information flows through the community, and the ways in which people think and act concerning education and the programs provided by schools.

SOCIOLOGICAL INVENTORY

To plan an effective program, the district needs to know about the people who make up the community. The more that is known about them, the better the chances are of designing a program that will achieve its objectives. Therefore, it's recommended that school districts undertake a sociological inventory of their communities. But—and this is a major *but*—those inventories should not be so complex, time-expensive, and costly that by the time they're done people don't want to take the time to implement the findings. Too often some educators get wrapped up in the process and place that completed study on a shelf to do little more than wait for its successor. To conduct such a study and not interpret the findings and use the results would be a waste of time and money.

Choosing which items to include in such a study can help ensure the study's success. Some possible topics to include are the following: customs and traditions, historical background, material and human resources, age and gender distribution, educational achievement, organizations and groups, political structure, leadership, power alignments, religious affiliations, housing, racial and ethnic composition, economic life, transportation, communication, standards of living, health, and recreation. It would be extremely time-consuming and expensive to include all of the topics. To ensure the effectiveness of the study, school officials should choose the most important categories, focus on them, gather the information in a relatively short time, and then implement the study.

Among the topics that should get serious consideration are customs and traditions, population characteristics, existing communication channels, community groups, leadership, economic conditions, political structure, social tensions, and previous community efforts in the area.

Customs and Traditions

Customs and traditions are the common ideas, attitudes, and habits of people. They may be referred to as folkways, mores, or lifestyles. Significant in regulating conduct and in predicting behavior, they likewise exert an influence in the shaping of social action and in the determination of services rendered by community agencies.

One challenge in this part of the sociological inventory is identifying and defining the customs of groups in the community. This information is important to the school in guiding its relations with students, parents, and others. Nothing evokes a quicker reaction from parents and citizens than the adoption of policies and practices that run counter to their established attitudes, beliefs, and habits. This has been evident on occasions when, for example, new blocks of subject matter introduced into the curriculum caused students to think or act contrary to the convictions held by parents and relatives. Equally strong reactions are likely, for example, if the school calendar fails to accommodate religious holidays important to the community.

From another point of view, it is valuable to know how change takes place in group patterns of thought and action. What are the circumstances and forces that produce orderly change? Studies indicate that safe and rapid change occurs during periods of emergency when the need to make adjustments is immediate. Alterations in the physical features of a community, such as the construction of new highways, the improvement of housing, or the rezoning of land use, open the way for modifying social habits and customs. Significant changes are also possible when members of different groups are given opportunities to discuss and share in finding solutions to problems that have an effect on their ways of living.

A note of caution is in order here about stereotyping people and groups.

> Stereotyping is the process of assigning fixed labels or categories to things and people you encounter or, in the reverse of this process, placing things and people you encounter into fixed categories you have already established.[1]

It can be easy to do this with community groups such as senior citizens and young professionals, for example. Not all senior citizens are against spending for education or rigid in their thinking when it comes to educational issues. Nor do all young professionals aspire to send their children to private schools. When studying the characteristics of any population, it's important to remember that not all members of a particular demographic group, ethnic group, race, or religion hold the same attitudes, opinions, or voting patterns.

Population Characteristics

Population characteristics concerning educational attainment, age, sex, gainful occupation, race, creed, and nationality are important in developing an understanding of the community. Publications and services from the U.S. Census Bureau can provide useful information on population characteristics.

In looking at the educational attainments of the population, attention is directed to the years of formal education completed by adults. The amount of education may be classified as elementary, secondary, and college, unless the exact number of years is wanted. This information is useful in the preparation of printed materials. Vocabulary, style, and layout are fitted to the educational backgrounds of the audiences for whom they are intended. This information is also useful in estimating the best manner of transmitting ideas and factual information to the community so that attention and interest are generated. Another use of educational attainment information is constructing stratified samples of the population for purposes of opinion polling.

Age data should be broken down into convenient classifications and the implications carefully studied. For example, one community may expect an increase in school enrollments over the next five years, whereas another may just hold its own or suffer a loss. Age distribution may also suggest ideas concerning the future patterns of growth of the community. A fairly young adult population would almost certainly be more demanding of educational services and quality than a population of mostly middle-aged and older people. Similarly, the younger group would most likely support better financing of the school program, whereas the older groups might be more likely to resist an increase in educational expenditures. Thus, it is possible from age distribution to form working estimates of community reaction to various kinds of proposals.

In addition to educational achievement, age distribution and sex distribution are used as control factors in constructing stratified random samples of the population for purposes of opinion polling. Occupational information on gainfully employed adults may be organized according to the classification scheme[2] used in U.S. census reports. These data are useful in checking population stability, changing occupational opportunities, distribution of occupational classes, and employment outside the community. Findings influence the selection of program activities. The participation of citizens is also considered.

The study of population characteristics should be rounded out with data about race, religion, and nationality. These cultural factors may be important to gain an understanding of the community and some of the underlying causes of social tension and conflict. However, the meaning of the data may not always be clear unless the data are correlated with other information. It is well to treat the data statistically and to prepare summaries of the findings. These summaries should be used in the planning process, and copies of them should be distributed to key personnel within the system. At the same time, as much of the information as possible should be depicted on social base maps, with separate sections being blown up for use in individual attendance areas. Statistical summaries and social base maps often provide leads to the solution of everyday problems that are associated with school and community relations.

Communication Channels

Since the development of public opinion takes place through the exchange of ideas and information, it is necessary to know what communication channels are available in the community, how extensively they are used, and which ones are most effective for reaching different segments of the public. These questions are sometimes difficult to answer, but they can be worked out by persistent inquiry. It may be found that the public at large relies on the Internet, radio, television, and daily newspapers for most of its news and information, making the news media influential in shaping public opinion on some social issues. However, the investigation may reveal that members of special groups in the community receive information from a variety of other sources. These may include publications of clubs and organizations, religious organizations, labor unions, neighborhood publications and newspapers, and foreign-language newspapers and online news sources. On this last source of information, it is reasonable to assume that parents who speak and read a foreign language in the home may experience some difficulty in understanding student progress reports, school notices, and school news reported in traditional news sources. Where these conditions prevail, it would be advantageous for the school district to employ a number of bilingual home and school visitors, offer school materials in more than one language, and prepare news releases for foreign-language periodicals and newspapers.

The Internet, social media, and smartphone apps have added many new channels for information and notably increased the speed of communications. Websites and e-mail, and the proliferation of cell phones and text messaging, also allow immediate, two-way communication.

An unexpected benefit of this new technology is the reduced need for paper and physical files. E-mail and text messages can deliver information to many people with the press of a button. This saves time and the need to make copies to send by regular mail. Messages also can be retained for quick, on-demand access on school websites.

Community Groups

The American community is a composite of groups of people who are organized around special interests. Some of the groups have little or no influence on community affairs, but others have a great deal. Many are highly cooperative with those who hold similar interests, but a number are uncooperative. The variety is tremendous, and the numbers vary considerably from community to community. Informal groups that come into existence because of some common belief or cause may assume many different forms and often blend into a formal type of organization. No sociological inventory is complete without knowing the purposes and programs of these groups and the influence they exert on public opinion.

Although cooperation with community groups having an educational function to perform should be encouraged fully, care must be taken to prevent their possible exploitation of students. To some, cooperation means the right to insist that the school approve their requests and modify its program to achieve the ends for which they are working. To others, cooperation is nothing more than a guise for the privilege of disseminating self-serving information in the classroom, promoting product sales and services, and conducting contests for the sake of publicity.

On the other hand, some community organizations dominate school politics but are not concerned primarily with educational matters. Composed of small business groups, property and homeowners' associations, and civic improvement leagues for the most part, they take practically no day-to-day interest in such matters as dropout rates, standardized test scores, or the qualifications and selection of professional school personnel. Instead they are concerned about the overall impact of school policies and performance on the community, and they take a strong interest in school costs, especially tax increases and bond proposals.

Other community organizations are those known as special interest groups. Many of these are vehemently opposed to each other; even so, they all converge on schools and pressure them to accept their philosophical positions and to alter educational programs. Often they move, for example, to influence the school curriculum or to censor textbooks and library books or to challenge or support standardized testing programs. In any inventory of the community, school officials should attempt to identify special interest groups, become familiar with their philosophies, and perhaps anticipate and prepare for their contacts with the schools.

The extent to which individuals and families participate in the activities of organized groups, particularly those having to do with civic welfare, should be addressed in the course of the survey. The amount of participation is usually a rather reliable index of community spirit. Research in sociology shows that individuals and families who are active in organized group programs likewise take a strong interest in what happens to their community and that those who are inactive or take part occasionally show only slight interest in needed community improvements.

Leadership

The next aspect of the inventory concerns the status of leadership in the community. Leadership is a relational concept implying two things: the influencing agent and the persons who are influenced. In

other words, when persons are influenced to express organizational behavior on a matter of group concern, then leadership has occurred. Even though this concept may seem too simple and may represent a variance from others that could be cited, it nevertheless provides a feasible base for the examination of leadership and the leadership process.

At this point, it might be well to review a few findings from leadership studies without getting involved in too many details. Leadership is not related necessarily to social status or position in the community. An individual usually holds a position of leadership because his or her characteristics approximate the norms or goals of the group. It is equally true that leaders have traits that set them apart from their followers, but these traits may vary from one situation to another. However, all leaders usually have certain characteristics in common, such as special competence in dealing with a particular matter, wide acquaintanceship, easy accessibility, and contact with information sources outside of their immediate circle. Also, they are sometimes members of several community organizations and have more exposure than nonleaders to mass media. These characteristics are acknowledged as important, but they will not necessarily produce leadership. One school of thought sees leadership more as a consequence of an individual's occupying a certain kind of position in the social system, whereas another view holds that leadership is a situational matter requiring a particular issue and the exercise of influence on others.

In any event, the inventory task is that of identifying individuals who are recognized leaders of community groups and organizations and who have an influence on the attitudes and opinions of the members. Information should be obtained about their personal backgrounds, family connections, group affiliations, business interests, fraternal memberships, social and political convictions, special competencies, methods of operation, attitudes toward public education, and power in the community. Knowing their backgrounds is requisite to approaching group leaders on educational community problems and to determining their value in rendering particular services.

In working with leaders, it must be remembered that they are not always free to express their own ideas or to take independent action. Their behavior is dependent on the nature of their groups and the beliefs and opinions of the members. They may be especially sensitive to questions concerning patriotism, private property, economics, religion, politics, and respected conventions. They realize that any radical departure from the feelings and convictions of their followers on matters like these could quickly undermine their own security. Leadership, however, is a reciprocal arrangement in that group members depend on leaders to initiate ideas and execute plans of action. The leaders sense what members think and want, and so they can direct thought along lines that meet with acceptance. In doing this they play a powerful role in the determination of the attitudes and opinions held by their followers.

The study of leadership should extend to neighborhoods within elementary- and secondary-school attendance areas. Every neighborhood contains a number of men and women who are consulted by neighbors and friends whenever questions come up about the school and its relations with students and parents. Their opinions and judgments are important determinants of grassroots public opinion. It is vital to locate these individuals and to involve them in school activities. They become channels through which the school may be interpreted better on a neighborhood basis, and they can do much to win loyalty and support for institutional policies and practices.

Economic Conditions

An analysis of economic conditions will provide essential data for obtaining a better understanding of the community. Though a great deal of information about the economics of the community is available in governmental and business reports, an overview is needed. The overview should be limited to generalized findings on agricultural, commercial, industrial, and transportation activities and to employment, employment stability, and wage conditions. Related information on land use, property values, and tax rates should be considered. Such information is usually available in the school system's business office, which plays an important part in the planning of

the annual school district budget. If further data are wanted, attention should be directed to such items as production output, retail stores, levels of income, amount of savings, and standard of living. These details are relevant, as economic conditions determine in some measure the financial support available for public education. Moreover, these conditions affect public feelings toward the school and the means used for trying to bring about closer relations between the school and the community.

Political Structure

For generations, the public school has tried to uphold the idea of keeping politics out of education and education out of politics. It has done this on the assumption that the school as a nonpartisan, classless, and social institution should remain apart from the political life of the community. As meritorious as this may seem on the surface, the truth is that the school cannot and should not separate itself from the political scene.

More money is spent for education at state and local levels than for any other single function of government. This fact alone makes education a thoroughly political enterprise. The support received is the product of political struggles for the tax dollar. These struggles involve the interaction of special-interest groups, political leaders, members of legislative bodies, boards and departments of education, opinion leaders, professional educators, and others. Such items as formulas for the distribution of state aid to local districts, the assessment of property tax rates, and the location, size, and cost of school buildings are frequently matters of political conflict and resolution.

If educational leaders are to cope successfully with the problem of getting adequate public support, they need to acquire a sophisticated understanding of political realities. They should seek this understanding through a somewhat detailed study of the political structure and the political process within the local area. It is important that they know who makes political decisions, how these decisions are carried out, and what political instruments are available. In some matters, a similar type of study should be extended to state and even national levels.

Social Tensions

Social tensions and conflicts exist wherever people work and live together. Some are normal expressions of human behavior; others are indications of weakness in the social structure. These tensions are evident in the refusal of neighbors to speak to one another, sectional conflicts over the location of new school buildings, claims that the board of education is favoring the better residential part of the district, interracial confrontations, the formation of cliques within parent–teacher associations, and discrimination against minority groups.

The causes of social tensions may be nothing more than personality clashes, misunderstandings, spite, or petty annoyances, but they may also be associated with economic rivalry, cultural differences, social class competition, racial discrimination, religious conflict, and other major aspects of society. These tensions, no matter what the causes, are disruptive to life in the community and detrimental to the kind of consensus often needed for school success.

In the planning of a school–community relations program, the school must be fully aware of the causes of tension and the number of issues involved. If school leaders are not knowledgeable about these conditions, the program is likely to move in directions that will increase the tensions and deepen the cleavages that exist. Its real job is engagement that leads to consensus building—that is, trying to harmonize differences between individuals and groups in the community when the tensions militate against the operation of the school and the attainment of its objectives.

Previous Community Initiatives

A review of previous community initiatives—say, over the last 10 to 15 years—supplies useful leads for designing the school–community relations program. In this respect, it is important to know what kinds of projects were undertaken, who sponsored them, the degree to which they succeeded or failed, and the probable reasons for the outcome. With this information at hand, it is possible to determine specifics such as groups that offer the promise of working well together, types of projects that have a fairly good chance of succeeding, errors made in the past that should be avoided, the pattern of values held by the community regarding self-improvement, and the steps that must be taken in setting the stage for future school and community undertakings.

Sources of Information

If the superintendent of schools and members of the administrative team will start the survey by listing questions for which data are wanted, they will be pleasantly surprised to discover how much they know about the community. The answers they provide can then be supplemented from other sources of information. A valuable and readily accessible source is school records. The entry forms that children fill out when they first enroll in school contain information on family backgrounds. If used in accordance with the Family Educational Right to Privacy Act (also known as the Buckley Amendment), these records can provide important demographics of a specific segment of the community. When an annual or biennial census is taken in the district, the returns may supply similar information and other items not contained in the previous records. If supplemental data are wanted, they can easily be obtained by means of questionnaires administered to students. These sources furnish a good picture of home and family conditions in the community.

Numerous sources of printed materials, covering practically all aspects of the needed survey, also are available. City directories and telephone books contain the names of organized groups in the community. U.S. Census statistics include detailed information on population. If the community is too small for inclusion in the printed tracts, the information can be secured by writing the U.S. Census Bureau or logging onto its website: census.gov. Most social agencies maintain records that are useful on a number of points. Excellent data are available from the local chamber of commerce. City, county, and state historical societies and planning commissions have documentary materials that throw light on the growth of the community. A review of newspaper files tells an interesting story of happenings, traditional observances, community efforts, group tensions and conflicts, and outstanding leaders. Publications by the U.S. Department of Commerce are helpful in understanding the economic life of the community, and the publications of governmental planning boards often prove to be highly valuable sources of broad information. Online and published research resources may be used for biographical information, religious customs, traditional observances, and related items. The minutes of boards of education meetings are sometimes a rich source of data on leaders, group programs, tensions, sectional conflicts, and relations with the community.

Additional information may be gathered through personal interviews with prominent residents of the community. These individuals know many of the intimate details of social life that are seldom publicized. Although the reliability of their statements may be open to question, they can be cross-checked when a sufficient amount of information has been collected by this method. The success of these interviews will depend on how well they are planned and conducted.

An inventory should be made of what the instructional and noninstructional staff members know. Those who have lived for some years in the community may prove to be valuable sources of information, as these individuals may be asked to fill out questionnaires designed especially for the survey. Comparison of tabulated replies may be used to test the accuracy and completeness of their information.

POWER STRUCTURES

After completing the sociological inventory, attention should be turned to the power structure or structures and decision making in the community. The concern here is understanding the essential characteristics of the power structures, the areas in which they operate, and the effects of power decisions on educational policy and the school program.

In every community certain people exercise considerable control over decisions relating to social, economic, and political matters. They obtain this power for a variety of reasons, such as family background, financial status, political leadership, social influence, property ownership, or labor connections. Mostly, they are members of informal groups that sustain themselves through mutual interests. Because these relationships can be described as a structured way of influencing community decisions, they are identified as power structures.

A *power structure* is an interrelationship among individuals with vested interests who have the ability or authority to control other people, to obtain their conformity, or to command their services. They are accorded this power because of their involvement in the decision-making process and the influence they have on decisional outcomes.

General Characteristics

If the school is to deal intelligently with the power structure or structures in the community, it should have some knowledge of the characteristics peculiar to this form of organization. Power structures are controlled by people of influence who try to shape community decisions in ways that either protect or advance their own interests or both. Those who constitute the power structure may have few if any scruples about getting what they want. They are usually individuals with high intelligence and real leadership ability; otherwise it is doubtful that they would be able to command the status they enjoy.

Members of power structures are drawn from a wide cross-section of community life. They may be professional people, business executives, bankers, labor leaders, land speculators, newspaper publishers, or industrialists. Many of them make it a point to be associated with influential clubs and organizations, where they have numerous contacts with others of their kind and where they can use the membership to spread their propaganda and to mobilize popular support for policies and projects they favor. They do this very quietly and without thrusting themselves into the limelight. Typically, they use a secondary corps of influential individuals to handle matters for them and to report on the nature of public sentiment toward their proposals and the effectiveness of the strategies being employed.

Interestingly enough, power structure members are sincerely concerned with the well-being of the community, especially from an economic point of view. They know that they stand to gain as well if the community moves ahead and enjoys prosperity. It is not unusual for them to assist in bringing new industries into the community, to put pressure on politicians for modifications in the local tax structure, or to secure public funds for such items as urban redevelopment, a new highway, or a recreational area. However, when the public welfare on an issue does not coincide with their interests, they may take steps to swing the decision in their own favor.

Members of power structures find it advantageous to align themselves with political parties and holders of public offices. This allegiance gives them not only an opportunity to know what issues are under consideration but also an opportunity to influence the decisions that are made. For example, knowing some months in advance of the public announcement that a superhighway will be constructed around the borders of the community enables them to purchase land at reasonable prices and to locate motels, stores, gas stations, and other businesses from which large profits can be reaped.

Power structures influence decision making through a system of rewards and punishments. Rewards are given for going along with the wishes of the power group. These rewards may take the form of advancements to positions of higher social or economic status in the community, such as chairing of prestigious committees, and membership in socially prominent clubs and organizations. On the other side, punishment is meted out to those who do not comply with the wishes of the power group, and this may take the form of a loss of social position, occupational status, and economic welfare. Punitive measures include such examples as the failure to renew a business contract, refusal of membership in a prominent club, transfer to a position of lesser importance, or the reduction in purchase of goods and services.

Due to the lack of social responsibility on the part of power structure members, the community and its citizens pay a price for such individuals' influence on decision making. Instances are legion of sound social proposals that have been defeated because they ran contrary to the interests of the power structure, whereas socially undesirable proposals were adopted because they represented the wishes of this group. However, since power structures are an integral part of the American scene and influence decisions affecting public education, the school must learn to live with them and to neutralize some of their actions when necessary.

Many researchers have studied community power structures, and some have studied their relationships with schools. Smith studied community power structures, school board types, and superintendent leadership styles in North Carolina. She found that compatible relationships occur between school board types and community power structures and between school board types and superintendent styles. In contrast, she found that a compatible relationship did not exist between community power structures and superintendent styles.[3]

The Schools and Power Structures

How can a board of education and its professional leaders handle incursions of power structures into school matters? As suggested, an assessment must first be made of the structures existing in the community with reference to actions of participants in decision making and issue resolution.

Many opportunities are available for acquiring the necessary information to assess the current state of understanding and support a school system holds among its key audiences. Among them are continual scrutiny of stories carried in local newspapers, simplified content analysis of public documents, informal conversations with friends and colleagues, utilization of informative contacts through involvement in civic organizations and social activities, attendance at meetings where proposals are under consideration, and long-term observation of selected individuals connected with the power structure. Consistent collection and study of such information enable the board and its professional leaders to understand what they are dealing with and to note shifts taking place in the district's power picture. The National School Public Relations Association (NSPRA), for example, includes such analyses as part of its research and assessment efforts when conducting school–communication audits for school systems.[4]

Power structure members often take a direct interest in some phase of school operation. On occasion they will try to block proposed changes in curricular policies and programs when these represent a possible departure from the established way of doing things. They will profess a concern for school welfare and progress and will support a millage increase or a bond issue, but usually their interest centers on the financial side of the school, where decisions about the spending of money can result in a profit to them. They may try to influence the selection of school building sites or the placement of contracts for new and remodeled construction, for transportation of students, and for insurance. They likewise want a share in the thousands of dollars that are spent annually for supplies, equipment, and textual materials.

Perhaps the best protection the school has against power structure pressures on financial and other decisions is a well-planned and carefully implemented program in school and community relations. By taking parents and other citizens into complete confidence about the institution, its policies, its needs, its operating procedures, its problems, and its accomplishments, the school can develop sufficiently intelligent and supportive public opinion to offset the influence of the power wielders.

It has been apparent that properly organized citizen and advisory committees and groups of concerned parents have had a constructive effect on power groups. They have forced them to support needed school improvements in some instances and to withdraw power plays in others. They have demonstrated clearly that an enlightened public can become a force in society.

MEASURING PUBLIC OPINION

Measuring attitudes and opinions of taxpayers, parents, teachers, and students regarding education and the local school system is a third avenue through which community cooperation is accomplished. Sociological inventory and power structure analysis provide an informational framework within which the community relations program will be carried out. On the other hand, measurement of attitudes and opinions tells how people think and feel about the school system. It also tells what should be done to increase public understanding, support, and participation in the schools.

Opinion Research Techniques

Opinion research started in the field of marketing and soon spread to other walks of life. Its reliability has been demonstrated over and over again in predicting election results, ascertaining consumer wants,

determining audience reactions, modifying products, and forecasting trends in public thought and action. Schools have been somewhat slow to employ opinion research, despite its proven worth, in the planning and evaluating of their community relations programs. However, a noticeable gain has been observed in the number of school systems either undertaking their own studies of public opinion or hiring commercial firms to do this work for them. Increasingly, they are coming to realize the value of having precise knowledge of the opinions held by a specific group of people or those held by a representative cross-section of the population.

Opinion research is indispensable in planning, conducting, and evaluating the school–community relations program. It may be used to determine how people get their information about the schools, to learn how citizens judge the quality of their schools and the criteria they employ, to ascertain whether a proposed change will arouse controversy, to discover if a shift is taking place in public opinion, to find out how well the public understands the education program, to locate points of popular satisfaction and dissatisfaction with the school system, to identify problems that must be solved before increased cooperation and support can be expected, and to know the educational goals and aspirations of parents and citizens.

Opinion research can likewise reveal areas of improvement desired by citizens, their relative willingness to support financially the educational program, the nature of misinformation they possess, the motivations behind their defeat of a tax levy or a bond proposal, and the kind of information they want and how they want to get it.

As an extra dividend, opinion research actually stimulates the individuals who are contacted to form opinions about the subject being investigated. Individuals who have not thought seriously about the schools and school programs for some years are forced to do some thinking about them when their opinions are being sought in a research study. Moreover, they feel important for being asked their opinions.

When applied to staff members and students, opinion research discloses their attitudes toward the institution and the values they place on its policies and practices. The capable administrator uses this information to improve internal relationships and to make appropriate changes in the management of the school.

Types of Opinion Research

Opinion research comes under many names, scientific and unscientific, formal and informal, quantitative and qualitative, and probability and nonprobability. The name is determined by the manner in which the research is carried out. The results of unscientific, informal, or nonprobability opinion research cannot be projected with any statistical assurance onto the total group from which the sample is taken. On the other hand, the results from scientific, formal, or probability opinion research can be. The reason lies in how the respondents are selected to participate in the research. Only in the scientific, formal, or probability method is everybody in a population given an equal chance of being selected, that being the criterion used to determine if the results of a sample represent the thinking of a larger group.

Examples of unscientific opinion research methods are forums and conferences; advisory committees; some consumer panels; key communicators; mail surveys; newspaper, radio, TV, and magazine surveys; and some online surveys. Among the scientific methods are simple, systematic, stratified, and area or cluster surveys.

The following descriptions of selected opinion research methods—forums and conferences, advisory committees, consumer panels, key communicator programs, and public opinion surveys—are designed to acquaint school personnel with some of their options.

FORUMS AND CONFERENCES

Open forums are a method of soliciting frank discussion among a selected group of persons on some educational topic of current interest to taxpayers, parents, teachers, or students. The discussants are asked to state their views on topics, such as the construction of a middle school as a new unit in the structural arrangement of the school system, and the reasons for their views. After a specific period of time, people in the audience are invited to direct questions to the speakers or to express their own opinions. An attempt is then made to summarize the entire discussion and to estimate how those present stand on the question. Sometimes this estimate represents the judgment of the chairperson or the collective judgment of an evaluation committee. Sometimes it is based on a show of hands in response to specific questions asked by the chairperson or on the oral and written comments received shortly after the close of the meeting.

Open forums lend themselves well to audio or video presentations disseminated online or through traditional broadcast media. Such forums evoke wide interest if the issue under discussion is one of community concern and sufficient publicity is built up in advance. Interest is added when participants are known and carefully chosen. Open forums are used commonly in parent–teacher association meetings and in high school assemblies with students in charge. Open forums are difficult to defend on the basis of scientific appraisal of public opinion. They do, however, enable school officials to obtain rough but significant measures of how people think and to discover areas of their satisfaction or dissatisfaction. These forums have the added advantage at times of releasing tensions and enabling those who are interested to express themselves freely.

ADVISORY COMMITTEES

The advisory committee concept centers on the idea that a selected group of laypersons, representing a balanced cross-section of interest groups, can express the needs and reflect the opinions of the community. Meeting with school officials on a systemwide or individual-school basis, the members of the advisory committee are asked to suggest what should be done to solve the educational problems that are presented to them. Their recommendations are in no way binding and can be accepted or rejected. This method affords educators a practical method for evaluating group attitudes. Although it is always a danger to assume that the personal opinions of committee members are those of the group they represent, the danger lessens as experience is gained in using the method and as the personalities of participants are better understood. Moreover, this system familiarizes people with school problems and brings out their reactions before decisions are made. See Chapter 8 for more details.

CONSUMER PANELS

Consumer panels, also referred to as focus panels, are another approach to the measurement of public opinion. This procedure calls for the selection of a panel or jury of laypersons who are interviewed by trained members of the school staff. Usually, panel members are either selected to include representatives from organized interest groups, chosen in accordance with criteria for a stratified sample of the community, or tapped for expertise in a related field.

Two types of panels have a place in the measurement of opinion on matters involving public schools. One type is highly transitory and may be regarded as a one-shot affair. It is used for observing changes in opinions or behavior caused by a particular action or experiment entered into by the local district. As an example, let us say the system increases class size, or eliminates some extracurricular activities, or establishes experimentally a year-round school. An initial set of interviews is held before any of these changes occurs in order to record attitudes and opinions on the subject at the time. The interviews are held either individually or collectively with panel members. Then, after the change occurs, a second set of interviews is carried out to determine the effect of the change on members' opinions and behavior. Once this is done, the panel members are dismissed.

In the second type of panel, the members serve on a continuing basis. Interviews are held with them individually in order to elicit their opinions on a scheduled series of open-ended questions and to estimate the intensity of their attitudes and feelings. Interviews are conducted informally without reference to any printed set of questions, and the length of the interview is left to the discretion of the parties. When the interview is over, conversational highlights are recorded in private by the interviewer on prepared forms.

Research on the continuing type of panel indicates that such interviews reveal emotional tones in opinions; the nature and amount of information, as well as misinformation, about topics under discussion; the qualifications attached to stated opinions; the contradictions in expressions of beliefs; and some of the reasons underlying favorable and unfavorable points of view. It has been found that repeated interviews with properly selected panel members not only give a statistically reliable measure of opinion but also bring out causes for shifts in opinion. However, repeated interviews with the same individuals over a long time may produce mental sets that consciously or unconsciously bias their replies. To meet this problem, continuing panel operations can provide for the rotation of panel members, with a limit placed on the length of time to be served by any one person.

KEY COMMUNICATOR PROGRAM

Another method of getting opinion feedback from a community is through the key communicator program. It calls for identifying those people in a community who sit on top of a hypothetical pyramid of communications and asking them to pass along information from the schools to the community. Conversely, they are asked to relay information about the community to the school officials. They are usually invited to a luncheon or a get-together to talk informally about the schools. The program can be very effective in identifying and squelching rumors in a community. It can also provide a quick pulse of community thinking on major educational issues. Chapter 8 details the program.

PUBLIC OPINION SURVEYS

This method of opinion research can provide the most precise results of all of the preceding techniques if conducted properly. For this reason, schools and organizations are developing solid databases of community opinions through public opinion polls. Valid results will often silence vocal critics or vehement pressure groups, provide the basis for school officials to make a major decision that will be accepted by the community, and identify community values and priorities for educational programs.

Before surveying a community, a school should give some thought to the issues, the method of getting the information on a survey, the sampling technique, the construction and the wording of the questions, interview techniques, the design of the questionnaire, the use of data processing, and the handling of the results.

Methods of Getting the Information   The commonly used methods include the personal interview, the telephone interview, the mailed questionnaire, the automated telephone interview, online surveying, and the drop-off/pick-up questionnaire. In the last method, the survey instrument is delivered to a respondent's home or place of work and picked up a day or so later. Of all these methods, the best for comprehensive and usually valid results is the personal interview. The telephone interview is widely used, and the mail questionnaire provides proportionally the lowest returns. Table 3.1 shows the advantages and limitations of the methods.

TABLE 3.1	Advantages and Limitations of Six Methods of Surveying	
	Advantages	**Limitations**
Personal Interview	1. High percentage of returns 2. Information more likely to be correct than that obtained through other methods 3. Possibility of obtaining additional information 4. Clarification of respondent misunderstanding	1. Greater costs in transportation and personnel 2. Trained personnel required 3. Great amount of time needed 4. Guarded access apartments and communities 5. Safety of interviewers
Telephone Interview	1. Inexpensive 2. Short period of time needed to complete survey 3. No cost for transportation 4. Minimal training of personnel	1. Unlisted phones 2. Some families do not have phones 3. Easy for respondent to hang up 4. Answering machines 5. Caller identification devices
Drop-Off/Pick-Up Questionnaire	1. High returns in a short period of time 2. Clarification of respondent misunderstanding 3. Minimal training of personnel	1. Transportation cost 2. Need many volunteers or workers 3. Safety of interviewers
Mailed Questionnaire	1. Mailing costs cheaper than transportation costs 2. Possibility of reaching groups protected from solicitors and investigators 3. Increased candor among respondents	1. Low number of returns 2. Possibility of an irate citizen collecting many questionnaires from neighbors and answering all of them 3. Total population not represented by responses
Automated Telephone Questionnaire	1. Covers a wide area 2. Interviewers not needed 3. No mail or distribution costs	1. Expertise needed to format and record questionnaire 2. Representative sample difficult to obtain 3. Clarification of wording and meaning difficult to provide to respondents
Online Surveying (Web and E-mail)	1. Can be less expensive 2. Can be faster 3. Broad area reached 4. Automated tabulation 5. E-mail best for internal surveys or surveys among populations with defined e-mail addresses	1. Representative sample difficult to obtain 2. Response rates possibly influenced by familiarity with and trust in online initiatives 3. Creating and maintaining Web expertise needed 4. Internet access usually not universal among all households in a community 5. Population with Web and e-mail access possibly less common among some demographic groups

The Sampling Technique   If findings of a survey are to be used to make decisions on budgets, personnel, buildings, and programs, the results should be projectable to the entire community or population from which the sample was taken. This can be done if the sample is selected at random, but random sampling doesn't mean a haphazard selection of respondents. Standing outside a supermarket and selecting every tenth customer won't give you a random sample that will represent the thinking of the entire community.

A sample must represent a larger population if it is to be statistically valid. A sample is to a pollster what a model is to an architect. Each represents a larger entity within a certain degree of accuracy. A sample will represent a larger population if all the people in the population have an equal chance of being selected.

A properly selected sample of 400 respondents will give you answers that can be projected to a larger population within a predictable 5 percent error. This is true if the population is 4,000 people, 40,000, or 100,000 or more. *The size of the population generally does not determine the size of the sample.* Instead it depends on how closely you want the sample to represent the total population and how much time and money are available to do the survey. Table 3.2 gives the percentage of error regardless of the population size at the 95-times-out-of-100 and the 99-times-out-of-100 confidence levels. If you don't have to be sure 95 percent or 99 percent of the time that your tolerance or margin of error is plus or minus a given percentage, you can lower the confidence level. Table 3.3 provides sample sizes at various levels of confidence. If the population you want to survey is fewer than 400 or 500 people, it would be wise to survey everyone rather than take a sample. Attempt to get at least an 80 percent return in order to have the results represent the thinking of all 400 or 500 people.

TABLE 3.2	Sample Size for Two Levels of Confidence with Varying Degrees of Tolerance	
Tolerance of Error in Percentages (1 or 2)	95 times in 100	99 times in 100
0.5	38,400	66,000
0.7	19,592	33,673
1.0	9,600	16,500
1.5	4,267	7,333
2.0	2,400	4,125
2.5	1,536	2,640
3.0	1,067	1,833
3.5	784	1,347
4.0	600	1,031
4.5	474	815
5.0	384	660
6.0	267	458
7.0	196	337
8.0	150	288
9.0	119	204
10.0	96	165
15.0	45	74

TABLE 3.3	Sample Size Required to Achieve Desired Levels of Confidence and Tolerance of Error						
	LEVELS OF CONFIDENCE						
Tolerance of Error (In Percentages)	**50%**	**75%**	**80%**	**85%**	**90%**	**95%**	**99%**
1.0	1,140	3,307	4,096	5,184	6,766	9,600	16,500
2.0	285	827	1,024	1,296	1,692	2,400	4,125
3.0	127	358	456	576	752	1,067	1,833
4.0	72	207	256	324	423	600	1,031
5.0	46	133	164	208	271	385	664
7.5	21	59	73	93	121	171	296
10.0	12	34	41	52	68	96	165

Note: For example, if you wish to be 85% confident that your findings reflect the attitudes of your total population within ±5%, you must survey 208 people.

Simple probability sampling survey is basically the lottery system. It's like putting all the names of a population into a bowl and picking them out one at a time until the sample size is reached.

In a more practical way, let's say you want to pick a sample of 400 from a roster of 7,500 employees. Using a table of random numbers,[5] you would choose 400 numbers between 1 and 7,500, and they would be your respondents. Some computer programs will generate lists of random numbers. However, the program generally asks for a starting number, which must be chosen by chance. From a deck of cards, shuffle the ace through 10 and select a card. That's the first number of a four-digit starting number. Return that card to the ace-through-10 deck. Shuffle, and pick a second card. Do this four times, because 7,500 is a four-digit number. Give that four-digit number as the starting number to the computer to generate the remaining numbers of your sample.

Random digit dialing (RDD), a simple sampling technique, is used widely in telephone surveys. Using the table of random numbers, choose a four-digit number, combine it with the local three-digit exchange number and three-digit area code, and that's the first phone call made in a survey. For example, suppose you select the number 1816 from the table of random numbers, and the area code is 856 and the local exchange is 555. The first telephone number called would be 856-555-1816. The advantage of random digit dialing is that you can easily uncover unlisted numbers. One disadvantage is that not all the numbers you generate will be dwelling units. In addition, growing numbers of cell phone users, who often resist such unsolicited calls, can create issues for those using this technique. In addition, the overlapping of area codes and local exchange prefixes, now common in many areas, has made it more difficult to target specific communities or geographic areas.

By this method of sampling, the thinking of those interviewed will represent, with reasonable accuracy, the thinking of a larger population. This is a scientific probability: a (random) sample that can be defended statistically. Usually much criticism of a local survey is leveled at this sampling method.

To get a representative sample in a *systematic probability sampling survey*, you must work from a list of names (e.g., parents, students, employees, graduates, registered voters, or taxpayers). First, divide the number of people you wish to survey (400 gives you about a 5 percent error) into the total number of names on your list. Usually, this interval will be 10 or less unless your list is very large. Second, select a starting number by random from 1 to 10 because the interval is 10. This can be done by taking ten 3-by-5-inch cards and placing one number from 1 to 10 on each. Select one card. Using that as the starting number, select every tenth name after it as a person to be surveyed.

In *stratified probability surveying*, people are selected so that the sample in certain aspects is a small-scale model of the population it is designed to represent. For example, you may be interested in surveying registered voters. As in the systematic method, stratified sampling requires a list from which to work. In reviewing the list, you find that 75 percent of the registered voters did not vote in the last school election and 25 percent did. To stratify a sample of any size, you would choose 75 percent of it from among the nonvoters and 25 percent from the voters by using the interval method just described, thus giving every voter and nonvoter an equal chance of being selected. Assume that a sample of 400 respondents is sought. To stratify it as the total list of voters is divided, you would choose 300 respondents from the nonvoters (75 percent) and 100 from the voters (25 percent).

Area or *cluster probability surveying* is based on a previous subdivision of the population into areas, the selection of certain of these areas by using a random sampling technique, and the restriction of sampling units to these areas only. For example, the school district is divided into neighborhoods, and a random selection is made among neighborhoods. After sample neighborhoods have been chosen, households would be listed in each of them, and the required number of households would be selected, again using a random probability method. Details of this method can be found in several excellent textbooks and reference manuals on opinion research.

Of course, an unscientific or nonprobability sampling method is used in many cases. Thus, you must be careful what you do with the results. In this type of sampling, you cannot project the results to the entire population. For example, a school district sends a mailed questionnaire to all 11,000 households in a community, and 2,000 are returned. It would be unwise for the board or superintendent to make major decisions based on the answers on the 2,000 returned questionnaires. There is no way of knowing whether they represent the thinking of the entire 11,000 homes in the community. For the results to be valid, more than 8,000 questionnaires must have been returned. Such a large response to a mailed questionnaire is highly unlikely. Another unscientific sampling method is to have someone stand on a busy street corner and interview any 100 people passing by. The only thing you can do with the results is to say that this is what 100 people thought. Again, you have no way of knowing whether the sample represents the thinking of the entire community.

Some school districts may use the unscientific sampling method to start citizens thinking about the schools and to give them a way of voicing their thoughts about the schools. As a result, some citizens may become more interested and involved in the schools and may help solve some educational problems. For these reasons, unscientific sampling may be justified.

Construction and Wording of Questions   Open-ended and structured questions are the types used in surveying. The difference is that the structured or closed-ended questions have answers to choose from, and the open-ended questions do not. Structured questions are easier to tabulate; open-ended ones can provide information not anticipated.

A survey can be ruined not only by invalid sampling but also by the wording of the questions themselves. Here are some suggestions on how to word questions properly:

- *Be as concise as possible.*
- Use words and language that respondents understand. For example, a question such as "What is your attitude toward year-round schools?" is likely to be misunderstood. The phrase "year-round" may have different meanings to different people. Does it mean 45 weeks of school and 15 days off? Or does it mean two semesters of classes and a semester off? Or does it mean school every week of the year? Most citizens would be unable to answer this question with a valid response.
- Structure questions to provide you with the exact information, not the answers you desire. For example, in the question "How long have you lived here?" you may get answers such as "A long time," "Not too long," or "A good while." These answers are of little value. In such a question, list alternative answers, such as "Less than 1 year; 1 to 5 years; 6 to 10 years; More than 10 years."

- Avoid leading questions. An example of a leading question is "If your taxes were reduced, would you favor light industry locating in the school district?" The phrase "If your taxes were reduced" is leading. Many people will answer yes to any question that will indicate their taxes will be reduced.
- Avoid double-barreled questions. For example: "Do you work full- or part-time? Yes__ No__." If the respondents work full-time, how do they answer it?
- Avoid ambiguous questions. The question "Don't you think reading should be emphasized in high school?" is impossible to answer. What does a yes answer mean? "Yes, I don't think …" or "Yes, I do think… ."
- Pretest all questions on a small group similar to the one to be surveyed. (See Table 3.4 for examples of wording used in a Gallup poll.)

Interview Techniques   In cases in which you choose to conduct personal interviews either at the front door or over the phone, interviewers must be recruited and trained. Where can you get volunteer interviewers who will do a good job? One district used parents with children not yet in school to do a telephone survey. These parents were enthusiastic about doing something that extended their contacts beyond the home. Senior citizens, parent groups, college students, or community groups can also be helpful if they have proper training.

Each survey situation differs and dictates some variations, but some general rules of interviewing should be followed whether the personal interview or the telephone interview is used. Whatever the method, interviewers must strive for neutrality, avoiding any possibility of influencing the answers.

The following are major suggestions for interviewers:

- In face-to-face interviews, interviewers should dress similarly to those people being interviewed to foster better cooperation.
- Interviewers should become thoroughly familiar with the questionnaire, but should not memorize the questions.

- Interviewers should follow the wording of the questions exactly.
- Responses to open-ended questions should be recorded exactly as given.
- Interviewers should be friendly and show a genuine interest in the respondent without appearing to be meddling.

At least one training session is necessary for volunteer interviewers. In addition to some practice interviewing with each other, the volunteers should be briefed on the purpose of the survey, how the questionnaire was designed, why each question was included, how the interviewees were chosen, and how the data will be processed and analyzed.

Design of the Questionnaire   The design of the questionnaire helps respondents cooperate without feeling they are being exploited. First, they want to know how long the questionnaire is. If there are too many questions, respondents become frustrated and will not complete the questionnaire. If the copy is crowded and difficult to read, the respondent will give up quickly. If respondents have to work to find the place to check an answer, they will lose enthusiasm. A good rule to follow is to put all possible answers on the right side of the page near the end of the question. (This also will make the job of tabulating the results much easier.)

Whether it is a telephone interview, a mailed questionnaire, or a personal interview, the structure of the questionnaire is basically the same. Each should have an introduction, main section, and conclusion. The sections should include the following:

Introduction

- A brief description of the purpose of the survey
- The sponsor of the survey
- Instructions on how the questions are to be completed and returned if a written questionnaire is used
- Non-threatening questions

Main Section

- Opinion questions that deal with the basic problems the school is attempting to learn about
- Questions in a sequence to provide the respondent with a logical thought process

TABLE 3.4	Example of Wording in a Survey Question from the 45th Annual PDK/Gallup Poll

What do you think are the biggest problems that the public schools of your community must deal with?

	NATIONAL TOTALS		PUBLIC SCHOOL PARENTS
	'13 %	'03 %	'13 %
Lack of financial support	35	25	36
Lack of discipline	8	16	3
Overcrowded schools	7	14	11
Lack of parental support	5	3	8
Testing/regulations	4	1	4
Fighting	3	4	1
Difficulty getting good teachers	3	5	3
Use of drugs	3	9	3

Source: Retrieved from the Internet October 25, 2013, http://pdkintl.org/programs-resources/poll. Reprinted with permission of Phi Delta Kappa International, www.pdkintl.org, all rights reserved.

Conclusion

- Open-ended questions to get unanticipated information, such as "Are there any other thoughts you have on the East Bank School District?"
- Demographic questions (for example, age, gender, parent or nonparent, length of residency)
- A note of thanks

Use of Computers   Tabulating results by hand takes an inordinate amount of time and is prone to numerous mistakes. With the availability of computers, it is recommended that computers be used to process data from the results of a survey. This will provide a quick and accurate process for transferring information from numerous questionnaires to a report with total results. Also, computer data processing can quickly break out information by various demographics, such as the thinking of parents or nonparents, voting or nonvoting taxpayers, males or females, or any other demographic in the survey.

Handling the Results   If a decision is made to survey a community, a public announcement should be made through radio, TV, newspapers, and the school newsletter. The local citizens and staff need to be informed of the purpose of the survey, the approximate time when it will be conducted, the size of the sample, and that the results will be made public. In these ways, citizens are alerted to the possibility that an interviewer may call on them.

When the results are tabulated, they should be published. Otherwise, people will feel that something is being hidden. One of the surest ways of reducing credibility with the public is to hide the results of the survey.

A definite procedure should be followed in revealing the results of the survey. The sponsors (usually the board of education) of the survey should know the results first, followed by those who worked on the survey, employees, and students. Once the internal public is informed, release the results to the media in the form of a news release or news conference. Finally, the detailed answers to each question in the survey should be highlighted in a school newsletter or other external publications.

Provided that school officials construct and conduct surveys carefully, results will provide valuable information about the concerns and attitudes of citizens, and, in the long term, help schools continue to bridge the school–community gap.

Planning for Opinion Studies

Before detailed plans for making opinion studies are developed, the administrator should answer certain questions to his or her own satisfaction and that of the board of education. The questions that must be answered are the following:

EXACTLY WHAT IS THE PROBLEM TO BE STUDIED?

Too often individuals are carried away by their enthusiasm for something they believe is important without taking the time to consider just what the problem is and what kinds of facts are needed to solve it. This is evident in some of the questionnaires that school systems have devised for appraising the attitudes and opinions of parents and taxpayers.

The school administrator will strengthen his or her case and gain board support more readily if he or she has defined the problem and has outlined the exact points to be studied. This is illustrated in the work done by one superintendent who was faced with a steady barrage of criticism about the schools. An investigation of the problem brought out the fact that several individuals were openly declaring that the public had lost confidence in the educational program. With the permission of the board, the superintendent undertook a series of interviews with all persons known to be skeptical and antagonistic toward the schools. From these interviews he was able to determine the exact points around which most of the criticism revolved. He then formulated a statement of the problem and the points needing investigation. The board approved his statement in short order and then voted to approve the money for conducting an opinion survey. The administrator and board members wished to find out whether confidence in the schools had been destroyed and, specifically, what practices were under strongest protest. The results of the survey showed conclusively that the large majority of people believed in the worth of the instructional program and had faith in the competency of the administration. The results showed further that most of the opposition stemmed from a small but articulate minority who misunderstood many of the practices they were complaining about.

Too much emphasis cannot be placed on the advisability of formulating the problem for study in writing and attaching to this statement the reason why this information is required to solve the problem. This becomes not only a matter of record, when approved by the board of education, but also a guide to those who are charged with responsibility for making the study.

WHAT METHOD IS BEST TO OBTAIN THE DESIRED INFORMATION?

The choice of method depends on the problem and the information needed. Leaving financial consideration aside for the moment, the point is that one method or combination of methods may be more effective than another for obtaining certain types of data. For example, it would be wasteful to conduct an interview poll if the problem were one of trying to get a broad, general picture of how opinion was developing around a given issue. For this purpose, sufficient information could be collected economically and quickly through the open forum, the advisory committee, or the panel methods of measuring opinion. By the same token, none of these methods would suffice for obtaining an accurate measure of public understanding—say, concerning guidance services in the school. Actually, the methods brought into play do not have to be costly and complicated when all that is wanted is a general estimate of opinion.

HOW MUCH MONEY IS REQUIRED TO CONDUCT OPINION STUDIES?

The answer to this question varies with the nature of the studies made. Large citywide surveys can be expensive, costing thousands of dollars, and because of costs many administrators shy away from opinion studies without realizing that limited surveys can be conducted on restricted budgets. However, a preliminary or pilot study of opinion often yields satisfactory results and costs very little. Some survey organizations regularly make pilot studies before deciding whether or not it is necessary to engage in a large survey project. The argument on cost falls apart once administrators and school boards understand the need and value of knowing what the public thinks.

HOW MUCH TIME IS NEEDED TO COMPLETE A STUDY OF PUBLIC OPINION?

The amount of time will vary with the method employed. The time required is short for the open forum and advisory committee methods, somewhat longer for the panel method, and considerably longer for questionnaires and direct interviews. The last two methods, starting with a definition of the problem and ending with the publication of results, may consume several weeks. This length of time can be reduced with experience in polling procedure. One national polling organization is now able to conduct a nationwide survey and report the findings in less than a day. The significant thing is not how much time is required, but rather learning how to make opinion studies and putting the findings to work in building stronger relations with the community.

WHO SHOULD DO THE RESEARCH IN PUBLIC OPINION MEASUREMENT?

Typical school administrators do not have the background or training and experience for this research. They can familiarize themselves with the procedures involved and can learn to apply the more simple ones in their own communities, but they may not be competent to undertake direction of scientific polls. If they wish to undertake scientific polls, they should either employ outside experts or else subsidize the training of staff personnel. Although the more convenient alternative is to hire outside experts, this is difficult to sell to boards of education because of the cost involved. The better choice in the long run is to subsidize the training of staff personnel who are then available to conduct studies whenever they are needed. Staff personnel who take over this responsibility should be assisted at the beginning by an expert consultant who can show them shortcuts in procedures, eliminate confusion, and prevent serious errors.

HOW SHOULD THE FINDINGS BE USED?

The answers to this question will be governed by the nature of the findings. The findings may show that the superintendent should act at once to solve a pressing problem or that action by the board of education is necessary before anything can be done to clear up an unfavorable situation. They may confirm the soundness of present public relations procedures and the effectiveness of the program or point up the need for studying further a practice that is causing trouble. They may reflect a shift in public opinion calling for follow-up studies to chart direction. They may reveal problems for which immediate provision should be made in the public relations program. They may reveal many other things that are important in guiding relations with the community.

In general, the findings should be published in booklet form for distribution to staff personnel and citizens in the community. Such a publication serves to increase interest in and understanding of the educational program.

EVOLVING TECHNOLOGIES

The Internet and emerging computer technology have created new methods of surveying, other than the traditional personal, telephone, and mail surveys. These surveying techniques can include telephone and Internet-based surveys through websites, smartphone apps, and e-mail.

> *Telephone*—Two methods are used in this type of polling: in-call account and out-call account. In the first method, community members are contacted and asked to call a special number to respond to a recorded questionnaire. In the out-call account, a system initiates the poll by calling a predetermined set of phone numbers. The automatic system then asks each survey question, and the respondents press a number or speak to register their answers. Specialized companies can provide school districts with technical assistance and software to conduct these polls.

> *Online surveys*—Online surveys have become increasingly accepted options for school communication research. *The School PR Research Primer*, published by the National School Public Relations Association, notes:

>> E-mail and online surveys continue to grow in both popularity and acceptance among researchers. Although they have been used for some time, they were at first

considered suspect by some researchers—who perhaps lumped e-mail and online surveys in with the many informal polls and other unscientific "question-of-the-day" data collection efforts common on web sites. But properly designed and implemented, e-mail and online surveys can offer reliability and validity comparable to other survey methods.[6]

Most Web development programs now contain an option for creating, conducting, and tabulating these types of polls. A school district can compose a survey and post it on the Web or send e-mails and ask (by phone, e-mail, mail, etc.) a select universe to visit a certain Web address or reply to an e-mail to complete the questionnaire. Or the district can post the survey on a public page—their home page, for example—and just ask all visitors to fill it out. This latter type, though unscientific, is typical of the polls often promoted by TV news shows ("Visit our website to give us your opinion on the question of the day"). When respondents select themselves, the results are always unscientific.

The options of school communicators seeking to use online survey techniques continue to grow. A number of vendors, such as SurveyMonkey and Constant Contact, offer online surveying services and support. Online survey options are available in online storage and sharing services, such as Google Drive. Some vendors, such as K12 Insight, offer online survey services and support specifically for school systems.

Sampling in online polling can be both scientific and unscientific. Results are sometimes representative of the population from which the sample was taken. In the out-call, website, and e-mail methods, a representative sample is difficult but possible to get. This can be done by a panel of respondents preselected by chance. Lists of individual e-mail addresses for large populations, such as all tax-payers living within a school district, generally do not exist. As a result, e-mail surveys often are best used to query distinct populations easily reached by e-mail, such as staff members, parent groups, community organizations, business associations, and so on.

One Expert's Point of View: Understanding the Community

William J. Banach, Ed.D., is CEO of Banach, Banach & Cassidy, and is nationally recognized for his issues management and social forecasting programs. Dr. Banach has served as a local district, regional agency, and community college administrator.

He authored *The ABC Series*, four books focused on educational planning and marketing, the *Survey Research Primer*, and *The ABCs of Teacher-Parent Communication*. Dr. Banach's articles have appeared in more than 100 journals and magazines. He specializes in survey research, finance campaign planning, and marketing strategy.

With school budgets tight it would seem to make sense to invest limited funding directly into communication activities rather than communication research. Is this a good idea?

It is easy to forget that investing in communication research is, in fact, investing in communication. School leaders wouldn't commit to building a new school without research on population trends and community needs. They would not think about starting a new instructional program without investigating needs and assessing the success rate of the program. So why would schools even consider investing in communication programming before conducting the research essential to understanding what publics to address and which tools and messages to use to assure success? Jumping into communication activities without appropriate planning is like heading on a trip without a map. Spending public resources without proper research and planning guarantees less than optimal outcomes. Communication research is an integral part of the communication process. In fact, it is the first and most important step in the communication process.

Sometimes people may feel as if they've worked and lived in a community for many years and that planning research may simply turn up insights they already have. This would seem to make sense. So, what is the value in studying a community that we already know so much about?

There's little doubt that people who have lived and worked in a community for a long time can be a valuable resource. But they shouldn't be the only resource. Here's why: things change. And changes can only be effectively assessed when you analyze data and insights from a variety of sources and perspectives. This helps assure that you see the total picture, not just a small part of it, and underlines why a comprehensive study of the community and communication issues is essential.

Current school election research provides an example of how things change: 1. Parent turnout in school finance elections is down dramatically, often as low as 25 percent. 2. Absentee and early voting is increasing, so the outcome of the election may be decided long before the actual election date. 3. Older voters are an increasingly significant force in school finance elections, whether elections are successful or not. These changes clearly signal the need for a change in traditional, "proven" strategies and plans.

Everyone in the school system has a communication role. How can communication research be used to help employees at all levels succeed in their communication roles?

Everyone does have a communication role and almost everyone will need training and support to successfully address that role. Research can help identify the kinds of support that will be most effective. And, when shared with employees, the research can also help to build an understanding of informational needs in the community and how individual communication roles are essential in supporting school and student success. Just think of all the employees who are interacting with community members every single day. The teacher, the school-bus driver, the security worker at the front door, the secretary—all these people and more—may be the only point of contact many people in the community have with schools. They are important ambassadors for your school, and what they say and do positively or negatively affects public understanding and a school's reputation *every day.*[7]

Questions

1. As a school administrator or a school public relations director, you need to know the power structure of the community. What three types would you try to identify? How would you do that?

2. Suppose you need a quick study of public opinion in your community on an emerging school issue. What would be the pros and cons of conducting an online survey (where people are encouraged to visit your website to participate), an e-mail survey (where you e-mail your survey to local residents), or a traditional mail survey (where you mail your survey to selected households in the community)?

3. At a school board meeting, some citizens present the results of a public opinion poll and say that this is what the public thinks about a school issue. What questions would you ask to determine if the results of their survey are valid and represent the thinking of the community?

4. List the benefits that developments in online surveying options offer school communicators. How do these benefits compare to the limitations of online surveying methods?

Readings

Babbie, Earl R., *The Practice of Social Research,* 14th ed. Belmont, CA: Wadsworth Cengage Learning, 2015.

Bethlehem, Jelke, and Silvia Biffignandi, *Handbook of Web Surveys.* Hoboken, NJ: Wiley, 2012.

"The 49th Annual PDK/Gallup Poll," *Phi Delta Kappan* (September 2017).

Campbell, Gay, *Win at the Polls.* Rockville, MD: National School Public Relations Association, 2008.

Hughes, Larry W., and Don W. Hooper, *Public Relations for School Leaders.* Boston, MA: Pearson, 2000.

Moore, Edward H., *The School PR Research Primer.* Rockville, MD: National School Public Relations Association, 2008.

Tourangeau, Roger, Frederick G. Conrad, and Mick P. Couper, *The Science of Web Surveys.* New York, NY: Oxford University Press, 2013.

Endnotes

1. Richard L. Weaver II, *Understanding Interpersonal Communication,* 7th ed. (New York, NY: Longman, 1996), p. 61.
2. On the Internet, visit http://www.bls.gov/SOC for more information and available publications.
3. Beverly Jean Smith, "Community Power Structures, School Board Types and Superintendent Leadership Styles in North Carolina," doctoral dissertation, North Carolina State University, Raleigh, 1998.
4. On the Internet, visit http://www.nspra.org for more information on communication audits for schools.
5. Examples of tables of random numbers can be found online and in the back of many social research or statistical textbooks.
6. Edward H. Moore, *The School PR Research Primer* (Rockville, MD: National School Public Relations Association, 2008), p. 73. Reprinted with permission.
7. Adapted from personal correspondence September 8, 2017 with Dr. William J. Banach, CEO, Banach, Banach & Cassidy, Ray, MI. Used with permission.

4

Policies, Goals, and Strategies

This chapter reviews issues ...

- For central administrators: The critical roles communication policies play in providing clear support and direction for communication programming. The importance of developing objective-driven communication plans to guide tactics and activities.
- For building and program administrators: The roles that communication policies and planning can play for individual programs and schools as well as the school system overall.
- For teachers, counselors and staff: The importance of using communication research and planning to identify and guide individual roles in meeting communication objectives systemwide and for individual programs.

After completing this chapter you should be able to ...

- List the characteristics of policies, goals, and strategies that guide and influence school–community relations programming.
- Describe the importance of written policies on community relations and communication.
- Distinguish the components of school–community relations planning.
- Identify the connections between planning and success.

Developing an appropriate communication policy and determining attainable goals are early steps in creating and improving a school–community relations program. An appropriate policy describes the rationale for undertaking the program, expresses the system's commitment to open communication, and authorizes and charges the administration with responsibility for determining the means by which the policy will be implemented.

A communication plan then outlines realistic and valid goals, objectives, and strategies to effectively implement the communication policy. A communication plan also functions to provide the school–community relations program with direction and to establish a process for assessing communications accountability. The communication plan should offer a framework to properly evaluate the total program after given periods of time, such as one year or five years.

NATURE OF A POLICY

To understand the nature of a policy it would be well to start with actual examples. The following policy was adopted by the board of trustees in the Dallas, Texas, Independent School District:

Society has created public institutions to serve the best interests of its citizens. Those interests can only be met by an institution that incorporates the practice of public relations in its truest sense by operating in an open and sensitive manner.

The Board is committed to an ongoing public relations effort designed to help improve the programs and services of its schools. This effort will rely on a comprehensive two-way communications process involving both internal and external publics, with a goal of stimulating a better understanding of the role, objectives, accomplishments, and needs of the District.

Authority is hereby delegated to the General Superintendent to develop and implement public relations activities which assist in interpreting public attitudes, identify and shape policies and procedures in the public interest, and carry on involvement and information activities which earn public understanding and support. (Policy of Dallas, Texas, Independent School District.)

The Capistrano, California, Unified School District Policy on Community Relations is another example of a good policy:

The Governing Board appreciates the importance of community involvement and therefore shall strive to keep the community informed of developments within the school system in timely and understandable ways.

In order to gain the public support necessary to make our educational programs a success, the district shall establish a system of clear and directed communication. The district can maintain a positive public image by enhancing internal and external understanding and appreciation of school programs, and answering the challenge of those who would seek to undermine the American system of a full, high quality public education for all citizens.

The Superintendent or designee shall use all available means of communication to keep the public aware of the goals, programs, achievements and needs of the schools. Members of the community shall have opportunities to become involved in the schools and to express their interests and concerns.

The district encourages the dissemination of information to members of the media, and media representatives are encouraged to attend meetings of the Board of Trustees. (The Capistrano, California, Unified School District Policy.)

An examination of these school and public or community relations policies indicates that they include the following: the reasons for adopting the policy, the decision to do something or take some form of action for the reasons stated, the general means to be employed in carrying out the decision, and the delegation of authority for carrying out the policy. These elements make the policies sound.

In addition to overall policies on school and community relations, policies on specific communication activities should also be developed to help guide administrators and establish a district's commitment to such programs. The following policy, adopted by the Bloomington (Minnesota) Public Schools, is an example of that system's commitment to crisis communication:

DISTRICT CRISIS MANAGEMENT POLICY

I. Purpose

The district acknowledges the necessity of preparing a Crisis Management Plan in the event that, despite prevention efforts, a crisis or emergency should occur. Any disruptive event that threatens safety and security shall be considered a crisis. Crisis situations that could impact the district may or may not occur on school property and include, but are not limited to, suicide, death, acts of violence, trauma, natural disaster, threats of harm, and accident.

II. General Statement of Policy

To reduce the disruptive effects of a crisis, the superintendent and/or designee will develop a Crisis Management and Communications Plan. Development of the plan shall involve local emergency agencies, staff members, parents, students, community members, and other interested persons.

The plan shall include reasonable steps to ensure student and staff safety, and minimize property damage, such as:

- Written procedures for taking action in the event of a crisis.
- Written procedures for communicating with local law enforcement agencies, community emergency services, parents, students, staff, and media in the event of a crisis.
- A plan for crisis management training of all staff.
- Designation of specific management and reporting responsibilities of each staff member during a crisis.
- An outline of aftermath services for staff and students affected by trauma that addresses who will provide such services.
- An emergency intervention checklist to be widely distributed to employees and other appropriate persons for use in the event of a crisis.

The superintendent shall appoint a district-wide emergency management coordinator who shall work with the superintendent to develop the Crisis Management Plan, recruit and supervise a District and building level emergency response teams, coordinate in-service programs for teams and all staff members, serve as a liaison between central office and staff, and serve as a liaison between the district and local emergency agencies.

The coordinator shall be responsible for providing copies of current plans developed under this policy to local emergency agencies on a regular basis. (Reprinted with permission from Bloomington Public Schools.)

Advantage of Written Policies

Every board of education should have a carefully formulated statement of policy covering school and community relations. The policy should be in agreement with state school laws, the philosophy of the institution, and the traditions and opinions of people in the community. It should consist of a plan of action in which the purposes and general means for their attainment are described in written form or else in a statement in which the decision to act and the rationale for it are spelled out clearly.

Purpose is the crucial element in a policy statement because it tells why the policy has been developed and sets the goal to be accomplished. In this respect, the school–community relations policy should emphasize the development and continuance of a strong partnership between the school and the community. By bringing individuals and groups into a dynamic team, ideas can be exchanged, problems examined, practices reviewed, and decisions reached that will enrich the quality and increase popular support of public education.

Practical experience has shown that a number of advantages may be gained when a school system formulates and adopts a policy having the characteristics just described. These advantages are as follows:

- Policy facilitates the orientation of new board members regarding relations between the school and the community.
- Policy facilitates a similar orientation for new employees, both professional and nonprofessional, in the school system.
- Policy acquaints the public with the position of the school and encourages citizen involvement in educational affairs.
- Policy provides a reasonable guarantee that there will be consistency and continuity in the decisions that are made under it.
- Policy informs superintendents what they may expect from the board and what the board may expect from them.

- Policy creates the need for developing a detailed program in order to implement it.
- Policy provides a legal reason for the allocation of funds and facilities in order to make the policy work.
- Policy establishes an essential division between policymaking and policy administration.

The policy should be printed, with copies available for all members of the staff and for any resident of the community.

Policy Styles

For the most part, four styles are followed in the makeup of a policy statement: (1) Provisions of the policy statement may be set down in broad, flexible language and the details of its administration left to the discretion of the superintendent and his or her staff; (2) the policy statement may include the rationale or purposes for the decision and the aspects, parameters, or limits within which the program is to be designed; (3) rules and regulations or procedures may be attached to the policy statement and thereby become an integral part of it; or (4) the policy may take the form of a resolution on which the board will take legal action.

Policy Development

The development of a school–community relations policy starts with a determination of the end to be served by the policy. This means simply asking why the policy is necessary. The answer to this question may be nothing more than a vague feeling of concern about the nature of the interaction between the school and the community, or it may arise quite naturally from the pressures of outside groups who are seeking change in the school program. The need for a policy might also be indicated by the complaints of parents, the defeat of a bond issue or millage proposal, or the treatment of the schools in the press. No matter how it arises, there must be first an understanding and determination of the reason or reasons why a policy should be developed.

Once the need for a policy has been reviewed with the board of education and the board has authorized the superintendent to work out the details and present them in writing, the door is open for establishing this task as a cooperative undertaking. Under the leadership of the superintendent or a member of his or her immediate staff, invitations can be extended to a cross-section of individuals who have an interest in the proposed policy or who will be affected by it later. They can be asked to serve on a committee for developing the policy, knowing that their recommendations will be subject to board of education acceptance, rejection, or modification.

The members of such a committee might consist of representatives of the board of education, administrators, teachers, parents, and other community residents. The committee should be large enough to produce a rich reservoir of pertinent ideas and information and small enough to permit a suitable arrangement for getting the job done. Not only should the committee have well-balanced representation, but it should also be made up of individuals who are seriously and constructively concerned with the promotion of public education.

The work of the committee calls for the gathering of information, ideas, and opinions about the needs and conditions to be met under the policy. It also calls for the determination of an appropriate rationale or statement of purposes as well as a decision to act that is in keeping with the rationale or purposes. The committee may decide to outline the general means for implementing the policy decision or to define the essential elements constituting the framework for a detailed program in school–community relations. In whatever way the committee handles the content and style of the policy statement, the results should be expressed in writing and transmitted by the superintendent to the board of education for review and decision.

Distribution

After a policy statement has been adopted by the board of education, it should be made available on the school district's website. It also might be printed in an attractive leaflet or flyer for distribution to key internal and external audiences. Copies should go to all employees of the school system, to parents of all students in the system, and to a selected cross-section of people in the community. In this way, the nature of the policy has a good chance of becoming common knowledge among the special publics in the community relations program.

Appraisal

In addition to the legislating of a policy in school and community relations, the board of education has a responsibility for appraising its effectiveness. It should require periodic reports from the superintendent in order to determine, first, whether the policy is being carried out as intended and, if so, whether the results are satisfactory. In accordance with the findings on these points, the board can decide to continue, amend, or repeal the policy.

GOALS AND STRATEGIES

With a sound school–community relations policy approved by the board of education, a school district dedicated to effective communication programming moves on to determining goals sought and to selecting strategies to be employed in trying to reach them. Some districts are mandated by law to develop a strategic plan for a given period of time, perhaps five years. Part of this plan should cover internal and external communications and community relations. Moreover, community members should be on committees involved in developing a school district's strategic plan. This approach is considered the conventional approach to planning.

The Conventional Approach

The use of the conventional approach in communication program planning involves a number of important considerations and a logical sequence of procedures. While an overall communication plan considers the communication needs of the total school system, individual communication plans might be developed to supplement this plan and to serve the specific communication needs of individual schools and programs. Such individual communication plans should also work to reinforce the goals and messages of the overall communication program. In all cases, communication plans should be developed in line with the same procedures.

PROGRAM GOALS

Goals are expected results, such as what an organization wants its public to know, feel, or do about itself. Not only do they reflect the viewpoint of the policy statement, but they also reaffirm the position taken in the stated philosophy and expected results of the school system.

Bagin and Gallagher give an example of program goals found in various school systems:

1. To develop intelligent public understanding of the school in all aspects of its operation
2. To determine how the public feels about the school and what it wishes the school to accomplish
3. To secure adequate financial support for a sound educational program
4. To help citizens feel a more direct responsibility for the quality of education the school provides
5. To earn the goodwill, respect, and confidence of the public in professional personnel and services of the institution
6. To bring about public realization of the need for change and what must be done to facilitate essential progress
7. To involve citizens in the work of the school and the solving of educational problems
8. To promote a genuine spirit of cooperation between the school and community in sharing leadership for the improvement of community life[1]

USING COMMUNITY DATA

At this point in the conventional planning process, attention should be directed at the findings of the sociological inventory, the analysis of the power structure, and the measurements of prevailing opinions and beliefs of various special publics regarding the schools and the educational program. These findings and their interpretation make it possible to block out areas in need of new and of continued treatment. For example, the data might show what additional information people would like to have about certain aspects of administration, special services, or instructional practices. They might indicate the channels through which communication can be carried on more successfully with given publics. Certainly, they can help to delineate areas of most concern to taxpayers and to parents. Long-term and short-term goals can be readily identified and the need for priorities established. It is likewise possible that the data may disclose what values people in the community hold, who makes certain kinds of decisions, and what the educational expectations of citizens are. Data that serve to identify these and other matters of concern are invaluable in working out an efficient and effective school–community relations program.

It is advisable to put in precise written style all of the needs, problems, gaps, and so forth that the data reveal. The more precisely the objectives are stated, the better will be the decisions made subsequently about strategies and the means to be used for dealing with them.

MODIFYING THE GOALS

The findings may also indicate that some of the stated goals are unrealistic and for practical reasons should be modified. For example, if apathy and ignorance are dominant characteristics of the population in regard to the school system and its educational policies, this condition will have to be changed before a working partnership can be established with the community. The findings may instead show that it would be more desirable to focus attention on the need for guidance, remedial reading, or corrective physical education than try to interpret the work of the board and the administrators to the public. By relating the findings to the goals, it is possible to determine what modifications, if any, should be made before strategies and means are considered.

At the same time, a distinction should be made between long- and short-term goals. Long-term goals are those that require continued effort over a period of time, perhaps several years, before they can be achieved. Such a goal might be gaining acceptance and understanding of an innovative program some months before a transition from the old to the new takes place. Short-term goals, on the other hand, are those calling for immediate action, such as apprising parents of the necessity for changing the bus schedule at the beginning of the next month, or conducting a three-month campaign for an increase in the tax rate.

Short-term goals can be reached and disposed of in a relatively brief period.

STRATEGIES AND MEANS

After the goals have been defined and accepted, thought should be given to the strategies to be followed for achieving them. Those who are doing the planning need not only to identify what has to be done but also to select the best possible way of doing it. For example, perhaps the broad line of action should be that of improving face-to-face relationships between school personnel and lay citizens in order to step up the dissemination of school information and correct some of the current misunderstandings about educational policies and practices. The implementation of this strategy would then call for a fairly long-range and continuous effort employing such techniques as internal publications, simulated parent–teacher conferences, interpretation of pupil records, and establishment of parent advisory committees.

If the goal is one of securing additional financial support in order to bring the educational program in line with the times, alternative strategies may be considered, such as working through community leaders, working through a special citizen advisory committee, making the problem exclusively that of the parent–teacher association, or singling out special publics for continuing exposure to the importance of additional support in terms of pupil and community welfare. The alternative selected or the combination of strategies to be used would dictate the techniques or means that offer the most promise of reaching the goal.

The strategies and means available are influenced by the nature of the audience, the availability of funds and facilities, and the competence of personnel. For instance, an annual report in tabloid newspaper form might be good strategy in one community where the appeal of this kind of format is high, and poor strategy in another area where the appeal is low. If there is not enough money to make a broadside attack on a problem of hostile attitudes toward administrative personnel and distrust of the board of education, it may be necessary to tailor the activities to available resources or abandon the project entirely. Furthermore, school systems do not always have individuals with the knowledge and experience required to use sophisticated devices and equipment for communicating ideas and information to selected audiences. All of these considerations play a vital part in the determination of the strategies and means that are to be employed.

VARIATIONS OF THE CONVENTIONAL APPROACH
Public relations planners have further refined the conventional approach by giving added detail to the process. Anthony Fulginiti, an authority in public relations planning, divides it into two main sections: conceptualization and operationalization.[2] He further divides these sections into specific areas. For example, under conceptualization he includes goals, objectives, strategies, and tactics. Operationalization includes tasks, activities, agents, cost, and time.

Fulginiti's first step in planning is situation analysis, which he divides into three parts: Learning, Thinking, and Planning. Tucked into all three of these activities is the need to conceptualize a challenge and to operationalize activities to meet that challenge.

In the Learning stage, the school public relations counselor learns as much as possible about the issues through three specific activities:

- *Recording the issues' history.* Use this history as a benchmark to improve the situation, to avoid pitfalls, and to make certain everyone's collective impression of the issues is the same.
- *Collecting additional issues data.* Time and activity change the facts of issues. Counselors use files, records, databases, emails, reports, and similar sources. At times, it might be necessary to conduct additional research to update the issues.
- *Describing the issues as they actually exist.* This is the all-important "real state" analysis, in which the counselor specifically describes and draws the starting line for the project.

In the real state analysis, the planner would interview members of the school district's top administrative team to gain their insights about their own district and like districts. Following this, the planner would interview experts and authorities about the issues. Then she or he would interview potential target audience members of the proposed plan.

In the Thinking phase, the counselor pictures the issues as they should be. The planner describes the general ambition of the district from the viewpoints of the school board, superintendent, staff, community advisory committee, and other stakeholders, presumably in a symmetric process in which many with a vested interest in the district have a seat at the planning table. Five activities comprise the work in this phase:

- Identifying all important audiences or publics
- Fashioning messages appropriate for each audience
- Picking channels appropriate to the messages to carry them to the audience
- Calculating competition to the plan or constraints in audiences who might not support the district's activities
- Estimating resources necessary to do the job

After completing these two phases, the school planner moves to complete the conceptual part of the plan—the Planning phase. In this phase, the planner specifies goals, objectives, strategies, tactics, and measurement of achievement.

Conceptualization Goal—an expected result that may or may not be attained. As the purpose of the plan, it is a target toward which the organization or school district is moving. It's often referred to as the desired outcome of a plan of action.

Example: Persuade the public to accept the board's decision on grade reconfiguration.

Objective—a specific, measurable subdivision of a goal; a benchmark that measures progress toward a goal. Objectives must be attained collectively for a goal to be reached. An objective tells what is to be accomplished.

Fulginiti and the Public Relations Society of America contend,

> Objectives must: (a) address the desired communication or **behavioral outcome**; (b) designate the **public or publics** among whom the behavioral outcome is to be recognized; (c) specify the expected **level of attainment** or accomplishment; and (d) identify the **time frame** in which those attainments or accomplishments are to occur.[3]

Example: To have 75 percent (level) of the parents (public) testify (behavior) by the end of the year (time frame) to the educational soundness of the board's decision to reconfigure the grade program.

Strategy—"The thoughtful, planned general approach to the tactics ultimately undertaken. Strategies do not indicate specific action to be taken to achieve objectives."[4]

Example: Provide opportunity for parents to personally investigate the merits of a grade reconfiguration.

Tactic—a specific way used to implement a strategy. It is the "how" of planning. The available money, other resources, and the scope of the job govern the number of tactics.

Example: Arrange tours of the school district using the new grade reconfiguration.

In creating a school plan, it's important for communication planners to convert the elements of the daily public relations practices they are familiar with into the elements of a new plan. Here is an easy conversion table:

Public Relations Practice Elements	**Public Relations Plan Elements**
Issues	Goals
Audiences	Objectives
Messages	Strategies
Channels	Tactics

By following this conversion table, the school public relations counselor will make an efficient plan, which conveniently becomes a recognizable bridge to the other members of the school family.

Operationalization—To be truly operational, Fulginiti emphasizes that the plan should be divided into tasks and activities, with time, agent, and cost applied to each.

Example:

Task—Identify all the parents who will tour the district.

Activities—Draft a letter inviting the parents on the tour. Have the letter typed, duplicated, and mailed.

Agent—Person responsible for carrying out an activity.

Cost—Where possible, list the cost of an activity.

Time—Give the dates on which the activity is to be carried out.

When all these are determined, Fulginiti develops a chart for all parts of the plan, but primarily the operational section. Across the top of the chart (Figure 4.1), he lists Activity, Agent, Cost, and Time. Underneath each word, he enters the appropriate information. Across the top of another page, he lists the numbers 1 through 31 for each day of a month. Down the left side, he places the number of the activity. Adjacent to it, he puts an "x" or a horizontal bar under the days when the activity is to take place.

Fulginiti's approach to planning emphasizes the need for research at every step of the process to ensure that the strategies, tactics, tasks, and activities taken are going to be productive. When his approach is followed, the final plan is very detailed, well thought out, and ready to be followed over a number of days or months. Fulginiti's process is excellent for short-term planning or for doing projects within a total school public relations program. In addition, his techniques can be effective even if used in developing a total comprehensive community or public relations plan for a school district.[5]

COMMUNITY RELATIONS PLANNING

Every strategic plan should include an internal and external communication plan. If it doesn't, the person in charge of public relations needs to do one for her or his office, as well as for the district. Some strategic plans may imply the need for communications, but they do not outline specific communication activities between the administrator and the staff, students, and the community. All employees have a role in communicating internally and externally. Moreover, how well they communicate should be a required part of their periodic evaluation.

In the 1960s and 1970s, management by objectives (MBO) was popular with companies and organizations. Some educators adapted it to schools. Others tailored it and came up with a method that was better suited to their situations.

Activity		Agent	Cost	Time
1.1.1.1	Draft a letter inviting parents on the tour	Tom	- - - -	Jan. 3
1.1.1.2	Have letter typed & duplicated	Harry	- - - -	Jan. 4–5
1.1.1.3	Address and stuff envelopes	Dick	- - - -	Jan. 4–5
1.1.1.4	Mail letters	Mailroom	$320	Jan. 6

Activity	Month January
	1 2 3 4 5 6 7 8 9 10 11 12 13 14 15 16 17 18 19 20 21 22 23 24 25 26 27 28 29 30 31
1.1.1.1	X
1.1.1.2	X X
1.1.1.3	X X
1.1.1.4	X

FIGURE 4.1   Examples of Format in Public Relations Planning.

The basic concept of MBO is still valid: (1) determining objectives, (2) planning methods and processes to reach the objectives, and (3) implementing the plan. Some planning consultants claim strategic planning has now moved two or three steps beyond MBO.

Whatever the case may be, a wise school district should develop a districtwide community relations program. It should be an explicit part of a strategic plan, if the district has one. If no such plan exists, the district still should develop an internal and external communication plan.

In such a plan, usually the superintendent develops his or her own internal and external communication objectives. They, in turn, become a part of each administrator's communication plan on which she or he is evaluated.

The district should have a computer procedure or a form for all professional employees to use to list their goals and objectives and email or send them to their immediate supervisor prior to a conference, if one is needed to agree on the goals and objectives. This facilitates the task of defining what the individual will try to accomplish within the scope of her or his responsibilities and authority. Thus, instead of a district community–public relations plan being

developed exclusively by the communications coordinator with objectives and activities, all administrators have responsibility in school communications and community relations.

Figure 4.2 provides some of the typical information that can be used or adapted to help school or program administrators evaluate their communication activities. It covers activities in some of the primary ways in which information is disseminated to and collected from key audiences. Figure 4.3 presents an acceptable format for stating goals and objectives. It is also followed by many planners in business and industry. In this example, the objectives are essentially quantified. To facilitate measurement and evaluation, objectives are usually stated in terms such as percentages, amounts, weights, ratios, numbers, time, and volume. If quantification has been tried without success, a descriptive statement is used that points out the circumstances that will result when the objective has been reached.

Usually, specific objectives fall into four broad types. The first type is known as *routine objectives*, or those that recur annually. A second type is called the *problem-solving objective*. This type deals with a particular problem that it tries to eliminate or at least to explain. Generally, these objectives are different each

How frequently are school (or program) publications distributed to parents?

___ Weekly
___ Monthly
___ Quarterly
___ Other: _____

How often is the school (or program) website updated with new information?

___ Immediately: As soon as information is available
___ At least once a week
___ At least once a month
___ Irregularly/Infrequently
___ Not sure

How quickly do you or your staff respond to questions or concerns from parents and others?

___ Within 24 hours
___ Within 48 hours
___ Within one week
___ Not sure (no policy or not tracked)

Parents and community members have opportunities to share ideas and concerns about the school (or program) through (check all that apply):

___ Regular community meetings/forums
___ School (program) open house events
___ Parent–teacher organization
___ Advisory committees
___ School-based management
___ Online or telephone feedback programs
___ Other: _____

Volunteer programs for the school include:

___ Senior citizen projects or activities
___ Business and/or community partnerships
___ Parent projects or activities
___ Other: _____

Training or in-service activities on communication roles and responsibilities are conducted for staff:

___ At least once a year
___ About every two years
___ Never
___ Not sure

When was the last time you surveyed parents or other key constituencies to assess their opinion about communication by your school (program)?

___ Within the past year
___ Within the past two years
___ More than two years ago
___ Never surveyed
___ Not sure

FIGURE 4.2 Example of an Instrument for Evaluating Communication Activities.
This instrument shows some of the typical information than can be used or adapted to help school or program administrators evaluate their communication activities.

year. A third type is referred to as the *creative objective*. Here the focus is on a new and different approach to something that may produce a new or expanded result. The last type is the *personal objective*. This represents effort that leads to the improvement of professional or managerial skills—career growth.

Each of these objectives is then followed by the steps to be taken in accomplishing the objective.

PLANNING CHECKLIST

Good planning is nothing more than a way of determining where to go and how to get there in the most efficient and effective manner possible. However, sometimes a yardstick is needed to measure the plan before it is finalized and put into action. In this way

discrepancies may be discovered, omissions noted, and other weaknesses brought to the surface. Such a yardstick is the checklist suggested here. Although this checklist is quite comprehensive, it does not include the principles of communication; they are given in Chapter 6. Aside from these principles, the checklist summarizes the points made in the discussion thus far of the planning process:

- Program planning represents a process for implementing a legally adopted policy in school–community relations.
- The larger goals and specific objectives of the program are consistent with the philosophy of the school system and the laws of the state.
- The larger goals and specific objectives are stated in measurable terms to the extent possible.

Goal	Objectives	Activities	Evaluation
To develop a program of cooperation with community groups within the school district	1. To identify *all* community groups	1. Obtain group names from Chamber of Commerce. 2. Contact local libraries for list of groups. 3. Review telephone and online listings for group names.	Tabulation
	2. To gather information about *each* group	1. Contact each group. 2. Get title, address, phone number, and names of officers. 3. Request information on structure and purpose of each group. 4. Categorize groups according to the nature of each. 5. Put information from #2, #3, and #4 in computer file.	Tabulation of completed group files
	3. To meet with 50% of the groups this school year	1. Invite six community group residents or leaders to lunch each week. 2. Prepare school district handouts for luncheon meetings. 3. Prepare agenda for each meeting. 4. Get feedback on how the school district can better cooperate with the groups.	Tabulation of number of acceptances

FIGURE 4.3   An example of a partial school–community relations program.

- The strategies selected for attaining the objectives call for the involvement of members of various special publics when such involvement is feasible.
- A distinction is made in the plan between short- and long-term objectives.
- The objectives of the school–community relations program reflect an assessment of need or the gap discovered between what is and what should be.
- The program is planned and tailored to the nature of the school and the community with which it is identified.
- The communication channels selected for disseminating various kinds of information are appropriate for the audiences involved.
- The program calls for a continuing audit of the results it produces.
- Each individual having responsibility in the program knows exactly what he or she is trying to accomplish.
- The plan includes guides for resolving issues of emotional and intellectual concern to members of the community.
- Provision is made in the plan for long-range, in-service education of the staff to the extent needed.
- Program strategies and activities are adapted to available human resources, funds, and facilities.

One Expert's Point of View: Effective Public Relations Planning Contributes to Communication, School and Student Success

School communication leader Susan Hardy Brooks sees school communication planning as critical to both program and personal success. Hardy Brooks has counseled executives and organizations on a range of leadership, *strategic planning, management, marketing, public relations, and communications issues for more than 30 years. As Assistant Vice-President at Schnake Turnbo Frank PR, a regional PR and management consulting firm* *with offices in Oklahoma City and Tulsa, she provided strategic counsel to several education clients as well as clients in the private, public, and nonprofit sectors. She specializes in strategic planning, branding, process improvement, and market research. Hardy Brooks now serves as Chief Communication Officer for the Cooperative Council for Oklahoma School Administration in Oklahoma City.*

What is the role of school public relations planning in the ultimate success of students, the schools that serve them, and the administrators who lead them?

Effective communication is crucial to the success of any endeavor. In order for students, schools, and administrators to succeed, a plan for communicating effectively needs to be in place. Without a school public relations plan, there are countless opportunities for communication to break down between administrators, teachers, students, parents, and the taxpayers that support the schools. Most school districts would never consider running a school without a curriculum plan.

I believe a communications plan is equally important for the ultimate success of students, schools, and administrators.

What are the connections between sound strategic planning and sound public relations planning?

There is a strong and necessary connection between the two. It is always important for the public relations plan to be developed to support the overall strategic planning goals and initiatives of the school district. Most school districts today have strategic plans that guide the overall priorities of the district. If a public relations plan is built without consideration of the district's goals, it is difficult to place much credibility or importance on the work of the public relations staff.

Process is another strong connection between strategic planning and public relations planning. Although there are a variety of approaches to planning, most include the basic steps of research, analysis, plan development—including goals, tactics, responsibilities—and evaluation or measurement. A good public relations plan has all of these elements.

Schools talk a lot about accountability in many areas—but you rarely hear about accountability for communication and public relations. How should schools and their leaders be held accountable for performance and success when it comes to communication and public relations?

Communications and public relations effectiveness should be measured by how it contributes to the achievement of the district's strategic mission and goals. Incremental or tactical measures such as the number of "likes" on the district's Facebook page, or the number of responses generated by an earned media campaign are helpful, but they don't really demonstrate how communication is motivating behavior that moves the needle toward achieving district goals. School-communication professionals have to be able to make the case that their work directly impacts the district's success.

Many school public relations professionals believe that the public relations director should be a part of the management team or executive cabinet. Do you agree—and what would you counsel superintendents about including the public relations leader on this team?

I absolutely believe that the public relations director should be a part of the leadership team. It is a lot easier to make the case if the public relations professional understands the big picture and is able to demonstrate how his or her counsel contributes at a strategic level. There are public relations implications for most of the big plans and decisions a leadership team makes. If the public relations professional is not at the table from the beginning and influencing decisions, it is often too late to correct the course later in the process.

However, I have talked with superintendents who have included their PR person on the leadership team, but become frustrated because they aren't getting any benefit from including them. In other words, the public relations person takes a passive role in the meetings, listening but not contributing much to the discussion. If you have a seat at the table, it is important to provide communications counsel, discuss the implications of decisions on internal and external audiences, and spot trends and issues that warrant the team's attention.

What would you tell aspiring public relations leaders about what they need to do to be considered and accepted as part of the top-management team?

Be proactive rather than reactive. Be strategic rather than tactical. Lead communications rather than simply fulfill requests. Anticipate issues and trends that will impact the district and offer strategic solutions.

The superintendent may have a narrow view about what the public relations professional's role is within the district (media relations, collateral development, and event planning). The challenge is to teach the superintendent and others on the leadership team about the value of research, strategy, and counsel when it comes to achieving the district's goals.

The best time to negotiate for a seat at the table is when you are interviewing for the job. On two different occasions in my career, I made reporting directly to the superintendent and being a part of the leadership team conditions for my employment. If you are early in your school-communication career and not in a position to negotiate for a leadership role, earn your way there over time. You can demonstrate leadership regardless of your title or place on the organizational chart.[6] ∎

Questions

1. You are a school administrator. A school board member says to you, "There's no need for a written policy on school–community relations. We have good relations with the citizens of the community." What points would you make to show the importance of a written policy on school communication?

2. Why is a formal communication plan important to a school–community relations program, its effectiveness, and accountability for communication results?

3. Explain the importance of having the communications director as part of the district's leadership team. What should a communications director be expected to contribute as a member of the leadership team?

Readings

Austin, Erica, and Bruce Pinkleton, *Strategic Communication Management: Planning and Managing Effective Communication Programs,* 3rd ed. New York, NY: Routledge, 2015.

Bagin, Don, and Anthony Fulginiti, *Practical Public Relations Theories and Practices That Make a Difference.* Dubuque, IA: Kendall Hunt, 2006.

Broom, Glen M., and Bey-Ling Sha, *Effective Public Relations,* 11th ed. Upper Saddle River, NJ: Pearson Prentice Hall, 2012.

Hughes, Larry W., and Don W. Hooper, *Public Relations for School Leaders.* Boston, MA: Pearson, 2000.

Sergiovanni, Thomas J., Martin Burlingame, Fred S. Coombs, and Paul W. Thurston, *Educational Governance and Administration,* 6th ed. Boston, MA: Pearson, 2008.

Wilcox, Dennis L., and Glen T. Cameron, *Public Relations Strategies and Tactics,* 11th ed. Boston, MA: Pearson, 2014.

Endnotes

1. Don Bagin and Donald R. Gallagher, *The School and Community Relations*, 8th ed. (Boston, MA: Allyn & Bacon, 2005), p. 43.

2. Taken from correspondence in July 2006 with Anthony J. Fulginiti, Fellow/APR PRSA, Professor, Public Relations/Advertising Department, College of Communication, Rowan University, Glassboro, NJ. Also, from an unpublished paper, "Conventions for Program Terminology Use," *Public Relations Society of America Accreditation Program* (New York, NY: The Society, 1992), p. 7.

3. Ibid.
4. Ibid.
5. Ibid.
6. Adapted from correspondence in November 2013 with Susan Hardy Brooks, Schnake Turnbo Frank PR, Oklahoma City, OK. Copyright © 2013 by Susan Hardy Brooks. Used with permission.

5

Administering the Program

This chapter reviews issues ...

- For central administrators: The important distinctions in communication roles and responsibilities for school boards and employee segments. The appropriate ways in which the communication director should work with administrators and other personnel while managing the communication function.
- For building and program administrators: The ways in which the communication director and the communication program can help to support building- and program-level communication needs.
- For teachers, counselors, and staff: How the communication program can aid frontline personnel in identifying their communication responsibilities and preparing to successfully fulfill their communication roles.

After completing this chapter you should be able to ...

- Distinguish the key organizational and administrative structures that characterize successful programs.
- Identify the roles boards play in contributing to school–community relations success.
- Identify the roles administrators play in contributing to school–community relations success.
- Define the standards for education public relations practitioners.
- Outline methods for delivering training and support to staff to foster the development of skills essential to their communication roles.

Setting up a school–community relations program means paying attention to organization and determining who is responsible for what. What is the role of the board of education? What do the superintendent and the administrative team need to do? How about the person appointed to be in charge of the operation? What kind of organizational plan will be developed? Which administrators and supervisors are responsible for which parts of the program? How much money will be allocated to the school–community relations effort? An important component must be clearly outlined: the role of teachers and support staff.

THE BOARD OF EDUCATION

Board members must constantly remember that the schools are owned by the people: taxpayers. The community expects the children sent to the schools to learn effectively, and the community members pay the bills to keep the schools running. In most districts, people elect representatives to govern the schools they own. They should, therefore, be kept informed on a regular basis about how money is being spent and how effective the education being provided is.

How people feel, what they believe, and how they act toward the school, its officers, proposals, and programs can be summed up in the term *public opinion*. Public opinion is that intangible but powerful force in American life that influences all that is done in public affairs. A school board must know something about the nature of public opinion in order to run a good school system. If it fails to adequately inform the public to build understanding before acting, criticism often follows. If it moves too far ahead of public opinion, it invites opposition. If board members confuse their own interests with those of the public, they can stir up resentment and conflict.

Every school board constantly faces the task of trying to satisfy all the people and groups in the community. This can never be done. Nonetheless, the board can be better prepared for reactions of various constituencies if it constantly measures public opinion and anticipates those reactions. Board members must recognize that the board is always subject to criticism by diverse elements of the population.

Many people see the schools personified in the board members themselves. Because the board is the governing body, the public often judges the school system on the manner in which the board conducts itself. Therefore, in its relations with the public, a board has a number of important responsibilities.

Policy

The first thing that must be done before a program can be built is for a board to adopt a community relations policy. It is essential that this be put into writing and made available to the public and the profession; it puts a board on record as wanting to make education a collaboration between the school and the community.

A policy is the basis for the superintendent and his or her staff to work out the details of the program for the board's approval. The policy statement can be short and somewhat simple. It should say what should be done and reasons for doing it. A clear-cut statement of this kind reduces the chances of misunderstanding, puts up a restraint against impulsive action, and serves as a guide in decision making. (Chapter 4 provides details on community relations policy development.)

Modeling Communication Externally

The board of education sets a better tone for the system when it consults with interested citizens and representatives of community groups on problems facing the schools. Interested citizens have much to contribute to the solution of problems facing a board. Although a board can gain much from hearing the views of citizens, it is in no way bound by them. Moreover, those whose opinions are sought usually become strong and loyal supporters of the system. Good ideas and suggestions can also be obtained from groups that have interests in recreation, safety, health, library services, special services, citizenship training, and the like. Consulting these people makes them partners in the job of education and helps to build many bridges of goodwill and understanding.

In daily contacts with people, the individual board members are both listeners and ambassadors of the school system. They have wonderful opportunities at family gatherings, through church activities, in fraternal orders, and in everyday business to talk constructively about the needs of the schools, the work of the teachers, and the hopes for the future. Through what they say and the way they say it, they can build a desire in people for better education for children (see Figure 5.1).

Modeling Communication Internally

The attitudes and actions of the school board affect the attitudes and actions of employees in the school system. The board should take an interest in the welfare of staff members and meet their needs before they become demands. It should recognize the outstanding work of employees, who want recognition for jobs well done. Recognition makes them feel more important, more willing to work harder, and

The following criteria (developed by the National School Public Relations Association) should be evident in any organization that is working to develop and achieve a strategic and comprehensive public relations program.

Governing Board: The governing board of the organization understands and models its policy-setting responsibilities on actions that are in the best interests of students and their learning.

— The board has adopted and ensures periodic review of a mission, goals, and objectives that have been developed with stakeholder involvement.

— The board has a code of conduct that includes modeling respect, civility, and integrity.

— Board members work with the superintendent and staff in relationships that are built on mutual trust and respect.

— The board understands and practices its role of setting clear policy direction and helps build a culture that supports the staff in its role in implementing and administering those policies.

— The board seeks input from organization stakeholders before developing policy and clearly communicates its actions and the reasons for them.

FIGURE 5.1   School–Community Relations and the School Board.

Source: Reprinted with permission from *Raising the Bar for School PR: New Standards for the School Publication Profession*, a publication of the National School Public Relations Association (www.nspra.org), 15948 Derwood Road, Rockville, MD 20855.

more loyal to the school system. Recognition can be given through letters of commendation, newspaper publicity, periodic banquets, release from teaching for special assignments, and so forth. The board should also invite teachers to give presentations on their work at public board meetings. In other words, it should show a real interest in the work being done by employees.

The board of education sets a better tone for the system when it consults with employees on problems facing the schools. Employees like to be consulted. They appreciate knowing that interest is taken in their ideas and that they are important to the school system. Personnel studies in industry have shown that production increases when workers are taken into the confidence of management and feel that they have some part in decisions that are made. Those districts that have a history of consulting with employees on workload, sick leave, retirement, supply and equipment needs, discipline, curriculum revision, hiring of personnel, and so forth have found staff morale high, an improved educational program, and fewer and less severe confrontations with employees. With this relationship of staff to administration, everybody is better able to get down to the business of educating the children of a community.

Relationship to Parents

Board members often receive complaints about the school from parents. The manner in which they handle these complaints has a great deal to do with the effectiveness of the school administration. Some board members attempt to answer a complaint themselves without directing it to the appropriate administrator, or they may bypass the superintendent and go directly to the teacher or principal involved. Both of these approaches should be avoided. When a complaint is received from a parent, a board member should always ask if the parent has contacted the principal of the school or the superintendent.

It is wise for each board to develop and adopt a policy on how complaints are to be handled in a school system. Once adopted, this policy should be distributed to all parents and publicized in newspapers and at parent–teacher meetings. In this way parents will know to whom to complain, and board members will understand their role in handling complaints.

Relationship with the Administration

The separation of responsibility between the school board and the administration is not always recognized by the board. Some members have the mistaken belief that it is their duty to actually administer the schools. Some boards spend time dealing with administrative details that should be the responsibility of the superintendent. When boards attempt to manage the schools, they fail to give the necessary attention to their major responsibility: seeing that the schools are run properly.

Communication Influences Board Effectiveness

School communication is an essential factor in school board effectiveness, according to the National School Public Relations Association (NSPRA).

According to NSPRA Vice President at Large–School Boards Focus Tom Gentzel (Executive Director, Pennsylvania School Boards Association) and NSPRA Associate Director Karen H. Kleinz, successful school boards:

- Take responsibility for communicating with and engaging their communities.

- Recognize communication as an important management function and hold their administration accountable.
- Develop a strategic communication plan tied to their district's mission, goals, and objectives.
- Speak with one clear voice on behalf of the students and schools.
- Establish a culture of effective, two-way communication and engagement with all stakeholders.
- Demonstrate accountability through effective school governance

standards supported by effective communication.

Source: Adapted from *The Communication Factor in Board Effectiveness: Responsible Communication Builds Strong Relationships.* Retrieved from www.nspra.org/files/docs/sixtipsforsmart-schoolboards.pdf. Copyright 2008 by the National School Public Relations Association (www.nspra. org), 15948 Derwood Road, Rockville, MD 20855. Reprinted with permission.

Some boards consider themselves a group of administrators, with the professional staff as its servants. This is a very poor attitude, and it results in a lack of cooperation with the administrative staff when the closest cooperative consideration of issues and problems by the board and the superintendent and his or her staff is necessary. The board and the administration must work in separate areas cooperatively if a school system is to function properly.

THE SUPERINTENDENT'S ROLE

Current conditions in community life have added new meaning to the superintendent's role as the leader in building constructive bridges between the school as a social institution and the people who own and support it. Traditionally, the superintendent's role has centered on such activities as working with the parent–teacher association, establishing rapport with civic groups, becoming involved in community improvement projects, encouraging citizen participation on school study committees, supervising the preparation and publication of news stories and literature concerning various phases of the educational program, handling the more serious complaints and criticisms of school policies and practices, and trying generally to bring the school and community into a

closer and more harmonious relationship. Although these are desirable activities that have a place in any school–community relations program, they are not broad enough in concept to prepare for problems arising from the growth and expansion of the educational enterprise and the changes occurring in social, political, and economic life.

In both large and small school systems, the superintendent must be an effective communicator supported by a planned communication program. Consider: The superintendent is faced today with strong demands from organized groups often advocating for special interests. Among other things, such groups want a larger and more decisive voice in policy determination, including such matters as more functional curricular offerings, improved food services for undernourished children, better racial representation among administrative and instructional personnel, expansion of special services in child and family welfare, lower costs for education, accountability for the educational outcomes produced in students, and increased community use of school facilities. Lined up opposite each demand are powerful and influential groups maintaining a diametrically different position.

Under such circumstances superintendents become mediating agents in matters relating to public education. They must try to reconcile individual and social values, negotiate conflicts between personal and professional interests, and divert the influence of groups into constructive channels. This role calls for a high level of social insight and considerable skill in dealing with people. In reality, superintendents are cast by circumstance into the role of educational diplomats and must spend much of their time dealing with individuals and groups whose influence and power help to shape the quality of educational opportunity in the community.

While carrying out their role as educational diplomats, superintendents must likewise attend to the responsibilities of the office on the more formalized aspects of the school–community relations program. In this regard they are central to developing and putting into practice the several strategies and activities called for in the program. Even though they delegate a substantial part of their responsibility to members of their administrative team, nevertheless they set the tone of the program, stimulate the effort that goes into it, and make the critical decisions it requires. *Unless they show dynamic leadership in pointing the way and setting the pace, it is doubtful the program will be successful.*

As program leaders, they have certain functions to discharge. Their all-pervasive function as heads of their school systems is that of maintaining, facilitating, and improving the educational opportunity for all children and youth in their districts. Correlative to that end are their functions in community relations, decision making, communicating, influencing, coordinating, and evaluating.

Translated into specific types of action, these functions fall into such performance patterns as the following:

- Developing a basic policy for encouraging and expanding constructive relationships between the school and the community
- Assuming initiative in the planning of processes and procedures for keeping the board, staff, and public well informed on school matters
- Helping all personnel connected with the school system become sensitive to the meaning and importance of their contacts in the community
- Ensuring the establishment and maintenance of open communication channels within the school system and between the system and the public

- Developing the structure and working relationships essential to the discharge of community relations responsibilities by administrative staff members and others
- Working with key groups and influential individuals in the community on significant educational policies and problems
- Seeing that key groups and influential individuals are supplied with facts and information that will challenge them to act on behalf of education
- Taking leadership in providing the opportunities required for districtwide involvement of citizens in programs for educational improvement
- Putting board and staff members in contact with groups and individuals whom they are most likely to influence on behalf of better education and with whom a two-way system of communication may be developed
- Seeing that the evaluative aspects of the school–community relations program are carried out and that findings and their interpretations are submitted for review by the board of education
- Bringing together members of the administrative system and utilizing their experience, knowledge, perceptions, and skills in decision making with regard to various facets of the school–community relations program.

These performance patterns vary among superintendents depending largely on district size and outside pressures. In smaller districts that lack specialized personnel, a superintendent may assume almost total responsibility for technical aspects of the program. He or she may prepare news releases, pamphlets, parent newsletters, radio scripts, details of open-house events, and direction of bond and millage campaigns, among others. Though the acceptance of such responsibilities is commendable, usually the more important aspects of community relations are either overlooked or disregarded. These include the development of basic policy, goal definition, and balanced program execution. In larger districts, outside pressures sometimes build to a point where the superintendent delegates his or her principal administrative tasks to a deputy and devotes his or her time almost exclusively to the demands of the situation.

THE ADMINISTRATIVE TEAM

The superintendency has become complicated enough that those who hold the position depend on the services of specialists in meeting their leadership responsibilities. In fact, the superintendency may be viewed today as more of a team arrangement than a single position. However, there are no standard patterns concerning the composition of the team. It varies with the interests and special abilities of the superintendent, competencies of his or her staff, and community pressures on the school system.

In large school systems the team may consist of the superintendent, deputy superintendent, associate superintendents, and district superintendents, with heads of divisions and principals being invited to meetings from time to time. The larger administrative staff, including principals, may be organized into a number of smaller groups for discussion of problems and exchange of ideas on a scheduled basis. In other districts, the team may be made up of the superintendent; directors of instruction, student personnel services, business management, staff personnel, research, planning, and school–community relations; and a representative sampling of school principals.

The team performs two important functions. First, it provides a superintendent with information and ideas that enable him or her to keep the school and community program in proper perspective and to generalize about the larger aspects of it. Second, it brings the expertise of members to bear on the development of program details and operational procedures.

In addition to their role as perceptive generalists, superintendents may serve on the team as specialists in one or more administrative task areas. It is common to find superintendents wearing the cloak of building specialists, business specialists, community relations specialists, or instructional specialists. In some instances they retain the same specialties they had prior to becoming heads of their school systems. Occasionally, they are forced to assume a specialist's role because of the system's size or the lack of qualified personnel. However, as team members they usually pursue a specialty that is appropriate to their training and experience.

DIRECTOR OF SCHOOL–COMMUNITY RELATIONS

Directors of school–community relations are members of the administrative team in many school systems. They are members because of the strategic position they hold and the nature of their assignment. This will be evident in the discussion that follows regarding their status at present and the qualifications required for fulfilling their role successfully.

Title of Position

Directors of school–community relations have a variety of position titles. The titles used most frequently are director, specialist, coordinator, or manager of communications; director, specialist, officer, or coordinator of public information; director of community relations; and public relations director. In addition to these titles, there is a smattering of additional titles, such as publication specialist or coordinator, director of public affairs, director of community services, and marketing specialist.

These titles represent a shift in concept that has taken place over the years from such terms as *public relations* to *community relations* or *community services, communications, and information.*

Administrative Level

The position of director of school–community relations varies somewhat in terms of the administrative level at which it is placed. Only the largest school systems designate this officer as an assistant or associate superintendent with line authority. Usually the person holds a staff position and in many instances his or her title carries the word *director, coordinator, officer,* or *specialist.*[1] As a staff member, the officer reports directly to the superintendent, though in some school districts he or she reports to some other administrator, such as an assistant superintendent, an associate superintendent, or a deputy superintendent.

With the public becoming more sensitive to educational costs and to what goes on in schools, it's imperative that the public relations person be a member of the superintendent's cabinet. He or she can help the district administrators understand how a decision will be perceived by the public. Likewise, if the public relations person is to explain, defend, or interpret school district policies properly to the public, he or she must be involved in their development from conception to birth. In addition, this person, with an understanding of citizen attitudes, must be part of the cabinet if the group is to understand thoroughly the feelings of the community.

Size of System

The question frequently arises as to how large a system should be in terms of student enrollment to justify the employment of a full-time director of school–community relations. One generally accepted rule of thumb is that a full-time director should be employed when student enrollment is in excess of 5,000. But many school districts with fewer students have a full-time director of school–community relations. Size of the school system, however, is just one criterion for such a decision. The needs of the community and the school system should be carefully considered when assessing appropriate staffing and resources for school–community relations programming.

A number of school districts have given the full-time director all the responsibilities that are directly or indirectly related to communications. Aside from the usual public and community relations duties, these responsibilities also can include managing employee communications, community education, adult education, school district foundation, district graphics and design, publication and online content editing for district schools and programs, and communication training for employees, among other responsibilities. To meet such responsibilities some offices of communications employ 20 to 30 people.

In districts that do not group all communications responsibilities in one office, the decision to hire a qualified person to head the school–community relations program is contingent on factors other than student enrollment. Some of these factors probably are the financial condition of the district, the nature of existing community relations problems, and the board members' and superintendent's conceptualization of program requirements.

Functions and Responsibilities

Directors of school–community relations have to perform six basic functions when trying to reach the objectives of the program. One or two more could be added, but their addition would depend on how the position is viewed by the board of education and the superintendent of schools. The term *function* describes something that is done to facilitate the realization of the objectives for which the program is designed. The functions of the director are *research*, *advisement*, *planning*, *coordination*, *communication*, and *evaluation*. They make up the structure or system within which the details of the program are selected and carried out. From this point of view, these functions are the constants of the program—they do not change. What makes one program different from another is not the functions but rather the activities or variables that come under them. For example, advising the school board and superintendent should be a permanent task of directors, but the nature and subjects of their advisement may differ markedly from one system to another. The same is true regarding evaluation of program results. Here the function remains constant, but the way it is implemented may range considerably in what is done and how carefully it is done.

There are several reasons why directors' activities vary among school systems. In some districts the perception of their role by superiors is broad and balanced, and in others it is narrow and restrictive. Often district size influences the nature and scope of their activities. In small districts, for example, little or nothing may be done with the research function. Sometimes in larger school systems some of their activities will be handled by line personnel or even the superintendent. The amount of money available for community relations is a strong determinant of how directors spend their time and what they do. The nature of their work is likewise influenced by the kinds of problems facing the district and the image of the school system held by residents of the community.

Against the background of functions, school systems throughout the United States have worked out statements describing the responsibilities of full-time directors of school–community relations. These statements represent not only the conceptualization of their role in a particular school system but also the nature and scope of the program they are expected to develop and put into practice. School-communication professional organizations such as the National

School Public Relations Association (http://www
.nspra.org) can provide current examples of such
statements and descriptions for school districts of
various sizes. Typically, such statements cover such
areas as:

Communication Leadership

- Research community and communication
  issues relevant to school and community relations programming.
- Manage the development, implementation, and
  ongoing evaluation of communication plans
  supporting the district's strategic goals and
  objectives.
- Provide regular insight and counsel on communication issues to the superintendent and other
  administrators.
- Direct regular reviews of and recommend
  changes to communication policies and
  procedures.
- Assure the effective coordination and communication of the school system's key messages in
  all online, print, and multimedia communication activities.

Communication Programming

- Supervise the development and production
  of publications and communication products,
  including brochures, calendars, booklets,
  handbooks, newsletters, and video and audio
  programming.
- Oversee the content, design, and management
  of district and school-based websites and social
  media programming.
- Direct special events and community activities
  throughout the district, while enhancing school
  and community relationships.

Media Relations and Publicity

- Serve as the primary contact and spokesperson for news media covering school activities, announcements, special events, and other
  developments.
- Direct activities to identify and produce positive news stories for district programs and
  accomplishments in the news media.

Other activities

- Support the communication and related fundraising efforts of the district's education
  foundation.
- Support the communication needs of the district's school–business partnership programs
  and community education programs.
- Serve as a principal point of contact for parents
  and community members with questions and
  special requests made by telephone, in-person,
  and online.
- Develop training and support for school staff
  in media relations, online, interpersonal, crises,
  and other communication procedures.

In systems that employ a part-time director of
school–community relations, the position is given a
range of titles. In many instances, this individual is
a central office administrator who reports directly to
the superintendent of schools.

The responsibilities assigned to the part-time
director are associated mostly with the use of online
and mass communication. They include handling the
development of online content and information, collecting news and preparing news releases, writing
community newsletters and staff newsletters as well
as leaflets and brochures, developing video and audio
material for community relations projects, managing
social media efforts, producing speeches and reports,
and performing editorial services for members of the
central office staff. In addition, the part-time director may be responsible for handling citizen inquiries
and complaints, a speakers' bureau, and millage and
bond campaigns. Some part-time directors prepare
the superintendent's annual report, establish contacts
with civic groups, disseminate information on federal
and state projects, and direct special-event undertakings, such as American Education Week activities or
school open-house events.

Professional Qualifications

More and more school systems have established
formal requirements for the position of director of
school–community relations. One school district has
as its requirements: graduation from a four-year college with a specialization in English and participation

in specialized workshops, seminars, and conferences pertaining to community education programs and school public relations. Course work in journalism and graphic arts is desirable but not required. Besides education, the director must have administrative ability, a broad knowledge of the school district and community, leadership skills to administer the community education program, an ability to establish effective relations with sources of information and public news media, an ability to compose interesting news and feature stories about school topics, an understanding of the role of public relations in the school setting, an ability to organize effective procedures for dealing with requests for facility use, and editorial skills. The position also includes responsibilities of board secretary and director of community education, with related required qualifications.

Perhaps the most complete statement of standards for educational public relations professionals is the following one adopted and published by the National School Public Relations Association (www.nspra.org):

STANDARDS FOR EDUCATIONAL PUBLIC RELATIONS PROFESSIONALS

A skilled school public relations professional performs essential communication functions to help improve the programs and services of an educational organization. While qualifications can vary depending on the sophistication of the work required, all practitioners should meet certain minimum standards.

General Standards

An understanding of and commitment to the role and social responsibility of public relations and communications for all educational institutions, organizations, and agencies in a democratic society.

A commitment to improving educational opportunities for all.

A commitment to professional performance and ethical behavior as described in the National School Public Relations Association's Ethics for Educational Public Relations (see https://www.nspra.org/code-ethics) .

Professional Preparation

A bachelor's degree from an accredited university or—for department leaders—experience in the field is a minimum requirement.

Abilities and Aptitudes

A comprehensive working knowledge of internal and external public relations and communications programs for an educational organization.

A mastery of communication skills.

An understanding of the importance of two-way communications between an organization's staff and its many publics and audiences, and the ability to carry it out.

A thorough knowledge and understanding of communications theory and research.

An ability to provide expertise and advice to top management.

Professional Growth and Development

Standards for professional growth and development require that educational public relations and communications professionals continue to refine their skills and expand their knowledge by:

Maintaining membership and participation in the National School Public Relations Association and other professional public relations associations and societies.

Pursuing professional accreditation.

Participation in public relations seminars, conferences, workshops, and institutes.

Pursuing additional study beyond a bachelor's degree.

Reading, researching, writing, speaking, and consulting in education, public relations, and communications.[2]

Communication Specialists

Except in small school systems where it would be difficult to justify the expense, directors of community relations need the services of one or more trained communication specialists. Without such help it is virtually impossible for them to undertake a comprehensive program or to achieve established objectives. They must instead eliminate all but the most critical parts of the program and then concentrate their efforts on those activities that they handle best. A glance at the nature of programs in school systems having only a director indicates that attention centers principally on such things as preparation and dissemination of online and social media content, preparation and release of news stories, development of newsletters and pamphlets, and maintenance of relationships with some community groups.

Where directors have the right to employ professional staff, practice shows that they usually select individuals with a background of preparation and experience in editing, writing, and use of online and mass media. Many come from communication backgrounds, including journalism, public relations, or broadcasting. Some, however, have specialties in commercial art or graphic and digital design. If the system is large enough, the office of director may be divided into sections, such as an information section, online and publications section, community relations section, and community education section, with a supervisor placed in charge of each one. A substantial portion of the director's time then goes into the administration of these sections.

Many school systems, however, depend on a one-person communication office to direct and implement their communication programming. In such cases, it is essential for the lone communication director to build a network of support with other school-communication executives. Organizations such as the National School Public Relations Association (http://www.nspra.org) can be helpful in building such a professional network. Single-person communication programs also have a special need to maximize the impact of the limited time and resources they can bring to the overall communication function. To do this, the communication director should work to make sure the school and community understand the role of and priorities for communications in the school system. He or she should take care to avoid being seen as just the school system's web person, or newsletter person, or media spokesperson, to make sure all of the functions of a comprehensive

communication effort are appreciated. Clearly, effective time management is important to success in such situations.

PLANS OF ORGANIZATION

In general, three plans of organization are used to place responsibility for community relations activities and to facilitate the operation of the program. They may be described as centralized, decentralized, and coordinated plans.

Centralized Plan

A centralized plan is one in which responsibility for the program is centered almost entirely in the chief administrative officer and his or her immediate line and staff associates. Those who support this plan of organization point out that the superintendent is the person best known to the people of the community and is looked to for leadership in matters affecting the welfare of children. Superintendents are expected to supply information on the conditions, needs, and practices of the schools. They enjoy many contacts with important citizens that enable them to keep their fingers on the pulse of public opinion. As a result, they know when it is opportune to propose new policies and suggest changes in older ones. Specific assignments can be made and responsibility fixed more easily in the plan. Moreover, the staff is readily available for consultation. The example set by superintendents and their associates can have a wholesome influence on all employees in the system, who may show more interest in their own relations with the public.

Thus, in a small school system the superintendent engages in a variety of activities for interpreting the work of the school and earning the goodwill of the public. For example, he or she may give talks before many groups, join different organizations, participate in community affairs, supply news copy, prepare printed materials, and handle complaints received in the system. He or she may also consult with teachers on community problems and urge them to improve their relations with students, parents, and other citizens.

In larger systems, superintendents delegate much of this responsibility to other persons. Usually they will delegate it either to an assistant superintendent in the line of authority or to a director of school–community relations with staff status. The program operates at the top of the system, with comparatively slight attention being given to individual building principals and their staffs. Instead of focusing on the personal side of community relations as an essential part of the total program, emphasis is placed heavily on community group relations, relationships with the community power structure, contacts with commercial media, and the preparation of materials for media distribution.

Although this type of centralized arrangement is found in many large school systems, it has serious weaknesses. The most serious is the fact that good community relations can never be achieved solely through the office of the superintendent and his or her immediate associates. They may do excellent work through their personal contacts in the community and through the preparation and distribution of online and printed materials, but these activities are scarcely effective enough to offset the negative influence of unsatisfactory relationships between individual building personnel and students, parents, graduates, and others.

Decentralized Plan

In a decentralized plan, responsibility for the program is centered almost entirely in the building principal and the individual school is regarded as the natural unit for community relations. This is a common plan in many school systems today. There is justification for it. As an educational leader, the building principal is in a strong position to foster friendly relations with the school's publics on a neighborhood and area basis. Principals are close to the people and have a more intimate understanding of their needs and interests than do the administrative and supervisory officials at the top of the system. Principals can work with the instructional and noninstructional staff in establishing need for the program and conduct in-service training through the everyday situations that arise in the school. Excellent digital and traditional communication tactics are available for keeping parents informed and educating staff in the service area about instructional aims and practices. Through the principal's efforts, the building can become a community center of activities carried on for the improvement of community living.

Though the decentralized plan is excellent in many respects, it is open to criticism in others. It usually means a neglect of community relations by central administrative officials and a failure on their part to reinforce the efforts of school principals and their staffs. Without central administrative leadership and direction, some principals are incapable of developing sound programs or they are unwilling to take the initiative. Nor does this plan function successfully in systems replete with dissension among staff and with strong conflict between staff and administration.

Coordinated Plan

A coordinated plan is one in which community relations responsibilities of central administrative officers and building principals are fitted together into an articulated unit. The work of those at the top is planned to complement and reinforce that of the principals and their staffs. Each knows what is expected of the other. Central administrators, especially the director of school–community relations, serve as resource persons in assisting the principal and members of his or her staff. The administrator's advice and special knowledge may be requested in such matters as preparing effective online and printed materials for parents, resolving complaints and criticisms, gathering and writing news stories, and appraising the effectiveness of certain program activities. In many phases of the individual building program, central administrators are expected not only to perform advisory functions but also to share responsibility with the principal and his or her staff. They may share responsibility, for example, in arranging contacts with the news media, selecting a representative panel of citizens for advisory purposes, and assessing the nature of public opinion on particular issues in the attendance area served by the individual school.

In the coordinated plan, the building principals have broad discretionary powers. However, they must use them within the structure of the district's philosophy and objectives of education and its policy on community relations. In their leadership role, they involve teachers and other staff members in program planning and operation, beginning with the identification of needs through the evaluation and dissemination of results. In making special assignments, they try to gear them to the interests and competencies of staff members. In their role as communicators, the principals explain all facets of the program to building personnel and interpret the educational enterprise and its problems to students, parents, people in the school system, and residents in the immediate attendance area.

In some large secondary schools today, the principal is assisted in his or her work by either a full- or part-time community relations specialist. This person may act as a liaison with community groups, handle news media contacts, prepare news stories and spot news announcements, edit internal and external publications, involve parents and others as resource persons for classes and committees, prepare and direct tours and observations for visitors, organize special advisory groups, and serve as a clearing agent for inquiries.

If the coordinated plan is organized carefully and the division of responsibilities is understood clearly, it offers an excellent opportunity for developing a comprehensive and well-balanced program that should produce satisfactory results.

RESPONSIBILITIES OF OTHER TEAM MEMBERS

Other central administrative team members, in addition to the superintendent and the director of community relations, have definite responsibilities in the community relations program. These members include assistant superintendents, district superintendents, and directors of special divisions and departments. Their community relations responsibilities cover the reception and treatment of office visitors, the effect of team activities on the community and district employees, the proper handling of online and telephone inquiries, the effective management of email, online, and mail correspondence, and the maintenance of satisfactory contacts with professional and noncertificated personnel within the system. They also serve in a resource capacity to building principals, as in the coordinated plan of organization. Through contacts with business leaders and others in the community, they have many chances to interpret the school and to create channels for a two-way flow and exchange of ideas and information.

These administrative members are expected in some systems to prepare their own interpretive materials, using the services of the community relations director's staff and special offices of the school system, such as online and computer-based graphics and editing services. They are also expected to furnish information requested by the community relations director and to apprise him or her of any significant happenings that come to their attention. In a number of districts, they are assigned responsibility for specific program activities, such as producing television and other video content, sociological studies, special events, and the preparation and application of evaluative instruments.

BUDGETARY PROVISIONS

How much money should a school system spend for public relations personnel, services, and media? Administrators and school board members frequently ask this question. They want to know approximately what their school system will have to pay for a good public relations program. No method has been discovered for calculating this figure, nor is there likely to be one in the future. The cost will naturally vary with the amount of work to be done and the willingness of the system to do it. Therefore, the only practical answer to the question is to first build the program and then determine how much money must be appropriated to operate it.

Determining how much money a program will cost is not easy because many of the activities are interwoven with regular services. However, many methods have been advocated for arriving at a cost figure. One is to take a fixed percentage of the total school budget—say, one-half of 1 percent (0.5 percent)—and allocate this amount of money for program operation. Another is the project-appropriation method, whereby the budget is based on the estimated cost of the projects planned for the year. A third method is followed in systems having a public relations office with a director in charge. The budget is restricted to this office alone and worked out in the same way as the budgets for research, student personnel, accounting, adult education, and similar departments performing special services. Still another method is to make a careful analysis of the program for the year and estimate how much money the board of education must provide. The amount needed can be presented in a separate budget statement, or it can be included in the budgets of the several departments and units of the system having responsibilities in the program.

A problem in public relations budgeting is determining just what should be included. So many activities in a school district can be considered public or community relations activities, such as any external correspondence, report cards, design and printing of stationery, communication technology costs for all offices, board meetings, appearance of buildings and transportation equipment, special events, community education, adult education, and so forth. Obviously, in many districts budgeting for these activities can't be included totally under the school–community relations section of a school budget. In some larger districts it may well be.

More specifically, the budgets of many school–community relations offices would include such considerations as salaries, technology costs, postage, stationery, office supplies, printing and publications, graphic supplies, memberships in organizations, travel, conferences, subscriptions to professional publications and local papers, and equipment such as cameras, audio-visual items, computers, and printers. Outside services, such as graphics and artwork; photography and stock photographs; mailing services; online design, management, and hosting services; and media and online-content monitoring services might be included as well. If any special event is the total responsibility of the school–community relations office, it should also be included in the department's budget.

STAFF MEMBERS

Unfortunately, many school systems have no organized community relations program. In these situations, some employees sense a responsibility to relate to the public and in many cases do a good job. This group unfortunately is in the minority. Even in districts in which there is a community relations program, there are often staff members who do not know what to do because they haven't been informed by their supervising administrator. If staff members knew exactly what was expected of them, they would

undoubtedly carry out their part of a community relations program. Too often a plan is implemented at the administrative level and much lip service is given to it as well as a low priority, and it never becomes a functional reality. Staff members who are enthusiastic about relating the school story to the public are not involved in the plan or given an outline of their responsibilities and duties. Other staff members may be inadvertently creating a poor image for the school because they lack an understanding of good community relations techniques. A community relations workshop or other in-service training will help all employees understand their community relations role in the school and provide them with information and methods of relating to the public. An assertive administrator not only sees to it that employees understand their community relations role and responsibility but also gives them assistance and direction in carrying out the role.

GENERAL COMMUNITY RELATIONS RESPONSIBILITIES

Regardless of the position held in a school system, all employees have at least three general community relations obligations or responsibilities: do a good job in carrying out daily work, know the school system, and know the community. Prior to being hired, prospective employees should be apprised of these obligations.

Do a Good Job

It is not uncommon for school employees to feel that what they are doing often goes unnoticed. In tandem with that, it is important to consider the number of students who observe what school employees do each day and relate their observations to their parents or friends. Students are quick to notice how school employees are carrying out their daily work, particularly in the case of teachers.

Someone once said that a good school–community relations program begins in the classroom. It might be added that an effective community relations program is also maintained there. If teachers are doing a poor job of teaching, the image of that school in the community will likewise be poor. Teachers have an obligation to do the best possible job of teaching. Essentially this is what schools are all about, and the public understands this very clearly.

Noninstructional personnel, as members of the educational team, should be aware of the effect their daily performance has on the image of the school in the community. Students who visit the school office can quickly see if office workers are performing their duties well and efficiently. The bus driver who drives carelessly, the custodian who does not clean the building well, and the cafeteria worker who delays the food line are all known in many homes in the community, and they cause many local citizens to think poorly of the school.

Know the School System

Responsible administrators should keep employees informed about the school system by providing them with information or sources of information. Each employee, in turn, should make an effort to learn more about his or her place of employment. Unfortunately, this is not always the case. Either out of apathy or by design, employees make very little effort to learn more about their school district; they do not realize that to many people in the community, they are the only contact with the school. Citizens look to the employees for many answers to questions about the school. When an employee is unable or unwilling to provide information to a citizen about the school district, the image of the school suffers.

Know the Community

The third general obligation all school employees have is to know the community in which they are working. This responsibility falls primarily on teachers. Usually, the noninstructional employees are residents of the community with a reasonable, although not necessarily thorough, understanding of the local area.

Teachers sometimes obtain positions in a district and make little effort to understand or become knowledgeable about the community. Often they live in another area and feel they have no need to be familiar with the community that supports the school. The days are gone or are numbered when teachers are required to live in the district in which they teach, but this does not excuse them from the responsibility of knowing something about the community and becoming active in it.

SPECIFIC COMMUNITY RELATIONS RESPONSIBILITIES

No community relations program or plan of organization will function successfully until employees know exactly what they are expected to do and understand the limits of their authority. Although the general community relations responsibilities usually apply to all employees in all school districts, specific responsibilities may differ between one system and another. Those described here may be tailored to the needs of a particular school system.

Teacher

The teacher is a frontline interpreter of the school system through daily contacts with members of its different publics, particularly the students. In this capacity teachers have a number of specific community relations responsibilities:

Do as good a job of teaching as possible. The backbone of any community relations program is the teaching job done in the classroom.

Work constantly for good relations with students, parents, and people in the community. Student success depends upon active parental and community involvement. Such involvement is fostered by the sound, working relationships teachers build with students, parents and people in the community.

Work cooperatively with colleagues. Few school systems can attain or hold the confidence of the community if there is internal discord. Successful schools and teachers have learned that they must live in some degree of harmony if they are to gain the support of the community and maintain educational effectiveness.

Participate in community affairs. It is important that the teacher voluntarily take an active person-to-person role in the community if the school–community relations program is to be effective. By virtue of background, education, and experiences, he or she should be able to make a contribution to the community.

Work closely with the director of community relations. If a school system employs a director of community relations, he or she, working through principals, can be a great help to the teachers. Usually, the director brings to the position a background that enables him or her to see the community relations value of classroom activities, which may be overlooked by the teacher. Therefore, the director of community relations needs to be informed of the activities the teachers are planning over an extended period of time to make a judgment on their community relations value.

Cooperate in the development of an individual community relations program for a school. Even though a school system may develop a total community relations program, each school is responsible for developing whatever part is unique to the individual building. This possibly calls for a committee of administrators, teachers, parents, and even students to suggest activities that will help the school and the community understand each other better. However, some school principals may choose a method other than a committee to develop a community relations program.

Specialists

Specialists are those professionals in the school whose services in no way affect class size. Usually included among specialists are subject specialists, counselors, school psychologists, home visitors or social workers, librarians, nurses, doctors and dentists, and tax collectors. Many of their community relations responsibilities parallel those of the teachers. Others are unique.

Subject specialists. This group includes the coordinators and staff members who have specialized in a subject area such as music, art, languages, and so forth. Their community relations responsibilities include those of a teacher plus the responsibility of keeping their colleagues and students informed of the activities and developments in their subject field.

Counselors. Like teachers, the guidance counselors work closely with students, parents, other staff members, and the community. They have a major responsibility in making sure that the relationship with these various publics continues to result in better education for the students and continued support of the schools.

School psychologists. Psychologists' relations with the various publics are similar to those of a guidance counselor; likewise, many of the responsibilities are the same. Much of what has been suggested in the way of activities to promote confidence and understanding of the school applies to school psychologists.

Home visitors or social workers. Many school systems are fortunate to have a home visitor. Often, this person is the only contact between the home and the school—a fact that emphasizes the importance of his or her community relations role and personal qualifications.

Librarians. The librarians bear an important responsibility for the success of a school–community relations program. They have contacts with students, parents, and the community and work closely with colleagues in making sure that students are provided a good education. What they do in establishing and maintaining good relations with these groups is instrumental in building the image of the school that is conveyed to the community.

Nurses. In the course of the school year, many students come in contact with the school nurse. This, of course, means that there are many occasions for direct or indirect contact with homes and colleagues. The importance of the nurses in school–community relations is apparent in the skill with which they perform their duties and the manner in which they work with students, parents, colleagues, and the community.

Doctors and dentists. Often these medical professionals, because they are usually part-time employees, don't consider themselves part of the school team. Yet their level of competency in treating students and their contacts with parents and the community are bound to have an effect on the school–community relations program.

In the community, these professionals have contacts with colleagues and patients that give them an opportunity to interpret and explain the schools. This means that school administrators have an obligation to provide the school doctors and dentists with helpful information about the schools. Conversely, these professionals should keep the schools informed of information, community attitudes, and opinions toward local education.

Tax collectors. Schools must work closely with these professionals to keep them informed about the schools. They come face-to-face with many taxpayers who are critical of the schools. Tax collectors who understand the school district and its needs, goals, programs, and procedures can deter many critics. In fact, they can provide citizens with a significant amount of positive information about the schools. This requires school officials to maintain a structured program to keep tax collectors informed through workshops, meetings, and literature.

Support Personnel

This group of employees typically includes the clerical personnel, maintenance and facilities personnel, transportation workers, and food-service workers. They all have a measurable influence on the school–community relations program, yet they are sometimes overlooked by school officials.

Clerical personnel. In a real sense these employees are on the front line of the school–community relations program. They are often the first contact the parents and the community have with the school. What they say, the tone they convey, and the courtesy they extend all contribute to the attitude and opinions formed by the public about the schools. The sheer number of contacts with the public each week puts clerical workers in an instrumental position for developing good or ill will for the schools. It cannot be stressed enough how important these employees are to the effectiveness of the school–community relations program both internally and externally.

Maintenance and facilities personnel. Opinion about a school is often formed from two impressions—the appearance of a building and the personnel associated with the school. Often overlooked in a community relations program are the maintenance workers: custodians, groundskeepers, and mechanics. Their influence is felt primarily in the housekeeping and the general appearance of the building and grounds.

If they take pride in what they do and in keeping the building clean and maintained properly, this will reflect favorably on the school. Well-kept buildings and grounds say something to the public about the school system: that tax money is being spent wisely, management is effective, and public property is maintained properly.

Transportation workers. In many districts, bus drivers—after teachers—constitute the second largest group of school employees. Their contacts are primarily with students, parents, and the community. It is with these groups that their important community relations responsibilities lie.

Food-service workers. These employees also hold a strategic position in carrying out a school–community relations program. Many students carry home impressions of the cafeteria that influence parents' attitudes toward the school. An adequate selection of food, a diverse and popular menu, and reasonable prices impress children. Cafeteria workers have the responsibility of being courteous, treating students with respect, and serving them efficiently.

PROFESSIONAL DEVELOPMENT

Provision for professional development of communication skills is part of a good community relations program. Staff members must possess the knowledge and skills required to meet their responsibilities. Training may be given either through direct instruction or indirectly through a series of devices. The nature of the training and its supporting budget should be determined by the experiences of the staff and the demands of the local program.

Direct Training

The more usual and successful types of direct training are as follows:

Orientation programs. These are designed to acquaint the new staff members with the school system and to help them make a satisfactory adjustment. During this training, their attention is directed to the community relations objectives and activities of the school system and the responsibilities they must meet. A staff member who has gone through a good orientation program is better equipped to interpret the schools and to build wholesome relations with the public.

Instructional courses. These are formal courses taught by competent instructors from both inside and outside of the school system. They may be offered online or in traditional face-to-face formats and are used to train personnel for work done in all branches of the system. Courses in radio, television, video, editing, interviewing, news reporting, opinion polling, online communication, social media communication, and e-mail correspondence make it possible for interested staff members to receive technical training and to qualify themselves to work with special communication media. Other courses of a more generalized nature may also be organized and offered in connection with the community relations program.

Workshops. The workshop method of training is regarded as an excellent means for increasing staff efficiency. It is built around problems that grow out of daily experiences, or it may be used for planning purposes. Held during the school year, the summer months, or both, the workshops meet in small groups with consultants to exchange ideas and to pool thinking. Groups may be set up to deal with such matters as home visits, open-house programs, oral and written expression, relations with parents, lay advisory committees, news reporting, and the like.

Clinics. This word is sometimes applied to short, intensive training programs for experienced personnel in specialized fields of service. For example, a clinic might be held for teachers who are responsible for gathering and reporting news stories. The purpose of the clinic might be to review their work and to find out how it could be improved, or it might be to propose a new system of reporting and acquaint teachers with the procedures.

Special meetings. From time to time the staff may be called together for special meetings devoted to community relations. Matters of current interest can be taken up with the entire group and points emphasized that are in need of immediate attention. Such meetings are more effective for disseminating and imparting important information than are written communications. The response to these meetings is favorable when good instructional techniques are employed in the presentation of materials.

Preschool conferences. As the title suggests, preschool conferences are held before the official opening of school in the fall. Anywhere from three days to two weeks are set aside for the conferences. During this time, the staff can work without interruption on the program for the year. They may be assisted by consultants and resource persons. The results more than justify the time expended.

Faculty meetings. Time can be set aside in regular faculty meetings for in-service training in community relations. The agenda should be planned cooperatively by the staff and administration and restricted to topics in which there is a mutual interest. More will be achieved when subject matter is presented with the aid of films, videos, PowerPoint presentations, charts, graphs, printed materials, demonstrations, objects, and panel discussions.

Executive luncheon meetings. Executives need training just as much as do other staff members in the school system. This training can be carried on through a series of monthly luncheon meetings. The conference method of discussion, using carefully prepared material, is effective in dealing with problems that need attention and in presenting new ideas for consideration. Not enough has been done to stimulate the growth of executive personnel in school systems generally.

Indirect Training

Indirect training is accomplished through the use of instructive devices. The following are some of these devices:

Handbooks. Two types of handbooks contribute to the training of personnel in service. One supplies information that should be known by staff members in order to intelligently discuss the school with the public. The other outlines the responsibilities of each person in the program and how they should be handled. Both may be revised annually and distributed for ready reference and reading.

Internal publications and web-based resources. These may take the form of a magazine, bulletin, newsletter, or material and resources available on the school system's intranet or other online communication system. They are prepared for employees of the school system. Published and updated regularly, they keep users and readers informed of what is happening in the system and offer many practical suggestions for better community relations. Sometimes they contain a citation column for bestowing recognition on those who have performed outstanding services.

External publications. All staff members should have access to copies of every external publication, including the annual report of the superintendent to the board of education. They should know how the schools are being interpreted to people in the community and the nature of the publications distributed. The information contained in these publications is essential to their own work of telling the school story.

Checklists and rating scales. These devices cause staff members to look at themselves and evaluate their own practices. Used sparingly, they can be valuable aids in the training program.[3]

Subscriptions to publications. A number of worthwhile national publications on school–community relations are available at a reasonable price to distribute to employees. The National School Public Relations Association in Rockville, Maryland, publishes many of them.[4]

One Expert's Point of View: Boards and the Communication Program

David Hackney started his career as a newspaper reporter for the Philadelphia Evening Bulletin and went on to serve in senior communication leadership positions at various corporations, including Exelon, Campbell Soup, and Sunoco. He served as a board member for a number of non-profit organizations, including Camden (NJ) County College, the Arden Theatre Company, Philabundance, and others. Hackney also has taught graduate and undergraduate classes in public relations and public opinion at Rowan University for more than 25 years.

Why does a board member have a critical role when it comes to communication between the school and its community?

Internally, employees will almost always look upward for leadership and vision. Externally, customers and others in the community also will look at what an organization is saying and doing when forming the opinions that are the framework for a reputation. This means that chief executives and the boards they work with have a tremendous effect on the ability of an organization to succeed. This is true in the corporate world and perhaps even more so in the non-profit world of education and other community organizations. An uncommunicative, closed, seemingly uncaring board will create the image that organization overall is the same. Eventually frontline employees will adopt these behaviors too. But an open, responsive, inclusive board will create a whole different and much more positive image and organization.

Tracking public opinion is important to effective leadership, but isn't leadership more than simply doing what the public wants?

To be successful the board and an organization's leaders must participate in an on-going balancing act. Sure, at times there will be a need to follow public will. But at other times the organization will need to lead an unwilling or unsupportive public into new territory. Both scenarios depend on a proactive communication program, fueled by solid research, and focused on building understanding, support, and consensus.

What are some ways in which a board member can best support the organization's chief executive and its communication director on communication issues?

Board members need to have a clear understanding of their role in setting policy and the role of management in processing and implementing policy. This is why many organizations offer training and development activities for board members on their roles, just as they offer support to employees on succeeding in their roles. Board members should also always appreciate the tremendous weight that their words and actions carry. No matter how divisive an issue or situation might be, board members have an obligation to represent themselves and their organizations as honest and dignified communicators.[5]

Questions

1. You have been asked to give a workshop to new school board members on their role in school–community relations. What points would you cover in your presentation?
2. At a conference for superintendents, you are asked to give a presentation on the importance of the superintendent in a successful school–community relations program. What would you say to attendees, especially the skeptical ones?
3. Why is it important that directors of school public relations have direct access to the superintendents and be members of their cabinets?
4. Why is it important that good communication be practiced by all school system employees? List three categories of frontline school employees and the specific communication challenges they face.

Readings

Bagin, Don, and Anthony Fulginiti, *Practical Public Relations Theories and Practices That Make a Difference.* Dubuque, IA: Kendall Hunt, 2006.

Broom, Glen M., and Bey-Ling Sha, *Effective Public Relations*, 11th ed. Upper Saddle River, NJ: Prentice Hall, 2012.

Hendrix, Jerry A., *Public Relations Cases*, 9th ed. Belmont, CA: Cengage Learning, 2012.

National School Public Relations Association, *School Public Relations: Building Confidence in Education*, 2nd ed. Rockville, MD: Author, 2007.

National School Public Relations Association, *Communication E-Kit for Superintendents*. Rockville, MD: Author, 2013.

National School Public Relations Association, "Communications Needs of School Superintendents; Related Perceptions of School-Communications Staff," *Network*. Rockville, MD: Author, January 2007.

National School Public Relations Association, "How Strong Communications Help Superintendents Get and Keep Their Jobs," *Network*. Rockville, MD: Author, February 2007.

National School Public Relations Association, "Characteristics of Effective Superintendents?" *Network*. Rockville, MD: Author, September 2007.

National School Public Relations Association, "What Leading Superintendents Say about Communication," *Network*. Rockville, MD: Author, November 2007.

Sergiovanni, Thomas J., Paul Kelleher, Martha McCarthy, and Fred Wirt, *Educational Governance and Administration*, 6th ed. Boston, MA: Pearson, 2008.

Wilcox, Dennis L., and Glen T. Cameron, *Public Relations Strategies and Tactics*, 11th ed. Boston, MA: Pearson, 2014.

Endnotes

1. 2009 *Network Directory Issue* (Rockville, MD: National School Public Relations Association, January 2009).

2. *Raising the Bar for School PR: New Standards for the School Public Relations Profession* (Rockville, MD: National School Public Relations Association, 2002), pp. 3–4. Reproduced with permission. Also see www.nspra.org.

3. The National School Public Relations Association, 15948 Derwood Road, Rockville, MD 20855, has examples of these.

4. Ibid.

5. Adapted from correspondence October 3, 2017 with David Hackney, College of Communication and Creative Arts, Rowan University, Glassboro, NJ. Used with permisssion.

6

The Communication Process

This chapter reviews issues ...

- For central administrators: The practical applications of communication theory in developing and delivering effective, persuasive messages in school communication.
- For building and program administrators: The elements of communication and communication theory to be considered when assessing and designing effective, programmatic school community relations strategies and tactics.
- For teachers, counselors and staff: How communication theory and processes can be effectively applied in direct communication with audiences.

After completing this chapter you should be able to ...

- Identify the key components of the communication process.
- Outline the role of communication in changing attitudes and opinions.
- Distinguish the roles media play in school communication.
- Outline the issues that influence the ability of communication to persuade.

In building a school–community relations program, close attention should be given to the communication process. Although some kind of communication takes place in all walks of life, effective communication doesn't just happen. It is the result of carefully planning the kind of information that needs to be disseminated, the particular audience that is to be reached, and the choice of tools that are best fitted for the job. The job itself is that of bringing about understanding, gaining acceptance, and stimulating supportive action for ideas or proposals.

Communication is not just telling or hearing something. In the true sense of the word, it means communion or a mutual sharing of ideas and feelings. It comes from the Latin *communicare*, meaning "to share" or "to make common." In this setting then, communication is the giving and receiving or sharing of anything. This is accomplished through the use of language, which may be spoken or written, or the use of symbolism, or variations of sound or light, or some other such mode. Usually, the word *communication* brings to mind the sending or receiving of a letter, a telephone call linking one speaker with one listener, a conversation between friends, the publication of a newspaper, a radio or television broadcast, or an e-mail message.

In any event, communication is a cooperative enterprise requiring the mutual interchange of ideas and information, and out of which understanding develops and action is taken. Communication can also be regarded as a tool for drawing people and their viewpoints closer together, and thus improving the quality of the relationship they enjoy. As the sociologist Charles Horton Cooley pointed out more than a century ago, communication is actually "the mechanism through which human relations exist and develop."[1]

From this point of view, the nature and importance of the communication process in a school–community relations program will be discussed with reference to the elements of communication, communication and persuasion, the media's role in communication, words and messages, and crisis communication.

ELEMENTS OF COMMUNICATION

In communication theory, five elements are identified in the transmission of a message. Figure 6.1 identifies them as the source or sender of information, the message form used by the source (encoder), a channel that carries the message, the decoder who perceives and interprets the common language, and a receiver who reacts to the message after conceptualizing it.

This simple pattern of message transmission has just as much application to a complex city newspaper that puts messages into print and sends them to thousands of readers as it does to the encoding, sending, and decoding of a letter from one friend to another.

Source of Information

The source of information may be a person or a group of persons who possess certain ideas, feelings, and needs, as well as a reason for wanting to engage in communication. In selecting the source as the starting place for a message, it should be remembered that the source has been influenced by messages received earlier and by perceptions made in the past. In reality, the source is the human brain—a highly developed internal communication mechanism that is able to combine concepts stored there, and so to create ideas, establish purposes for communication, and decide how a message will be transmitted.

The Message Encoder

The information furnished by the source must be put in message form before being sent to a particular person or audience. Here a number of factors come into play. They are important determinants of message effectiveness and may be summed up briefly as follows:

- Although language is the principal tool in coding a message, there are times when a body movement, a facial gesture, an unusual noise, or some other sign will convey just as much meaning to the receiver of the message.

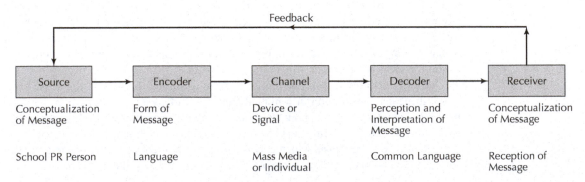

FIGURE 6.1 A Common Communication Model with Examples of Components.

- Senders must understand their messages themselves before they can make them understood by their receivers.
- To impart information or feelings, the sender and receiver should know not only what the words, phrases, or other signs mean, but both should be able to interpret these elements in the same way.
- Unless a message can be decoded easily and accurately, there is a danger that the receiver's attention will shift to something else that appears to offer an equal or greater reward for less effort.
- A message is received more readily when it contains one or more cues or suggestions that appeal to the receiver's needs and interests. Such cues or suggestions become an inducement for decoding and accepting the message.
- Once the source determines what ideas the message should convey, he or she can decide how to express them in a form that will appeal to the receiver.
- The use of symbols in a message makes it possible to compress and simplify complex information. When such symbols as the Red Cross, a school building, or the American flag are used, they stand for concepts that people readily understand and grasp.
- Most encoded messages contain a number of parallel messages. When a message is delivered orally, the words, those that are emphasized, the rate of delivery, the pauses, and the facial expressions are all interpreted along with the content of the message.

From this list it is evident that effective encoding calls for a message form that is appropriate for the particular situation, place, and audience.

The Channel

When a message has been coded, the sender must select a channel that will carry it to the person or audience for whom it is intended. The channel may be a word-of-mouth conversation; an oral presentation on radio or television; a written document in the form of a letter or a memorandum; printed matter such as a newspaper, book, magazine, or brochure; or a combination of words and pictures through the medium of motion pictures, videos, e-mail messages, and the like. These are merely some of the more commonly used channels in message transmission.

At the same time, it is essential that the sender know which of these channels are available in the community, how extensively they are used, and how effective each is in reaching various audiences. One channel, for example, might be better than another for message delivery to a foreign-language-speaking segment of the population, whereas a different one could be used with good results for keeping professional persons in the community informed about critical school problems.

Channels that are selected for message transmission should be free from distracting elements that discourage audience attention, such as printed pages of a brochure in which the type is smudgy and hard to read, or flashy graphics and pop-up items on a web page, or distracting background noises in a video production. Such distractions can quickly terminate communication possibilities.

The Message Decoder

Assuming that the transmission channel is working satisfactorily, the question then arises of whether the decoder is able to decode the message accurately. This means interpreting the sign or the way in which the message is coded. If the message is coded in written English, will the decoder understand the vocabulary? Does his or her background of knowledge and experience enable him or her to comprehend quickly and correctly a reference, for example, to a system of open education, a nongraded curricular arrangement, or a minicourse? Unless the reference kindles the same meaning in the mind of the reader as in the mind of the writer, the attempt at communication may be only partly successful, and it may even be totally unsuccessful.

The matter of interpreting the words of a message is further complicated by the fact that the same words have different meanings for different people. Generally, words have two kinds of meaning: (1) a denotative or dictionary meaning that has more-or-less universal acceptance and (2) a connotative meaning—a meaning that is read into the words because of the reader's background and experience. For example, the word *school* denotes a place where children go for an education under the direction of qualified teachers. To some individuals this may connote a place where many happy hours were spent, whereas to others it may connote just the opposite, depending on the individual's experiences while attending school.

Sometimes the people who are the decoders will not take the time to review the message carefully unless they feel that it relates to things of interest to them or that their efforts will be rewarded in some way. In view of the many messages that confront one daily, the problem of getting an individual to select and decode those about the local school system is difficult. Suppose, for example, that the letter carrier just delivered a brochure about school taxes for the coming year and also a popular magazine that the resident thoroughly enjoys reading. If the size, title, color, format, and so on of the brochure lack appeal, it will probably be set aside in favor of the magazine. However, if the brochure creates curiosity regarding the tax situation, reinforces the individual's concern over mounting educational costs, or suggests that the recipient stands to gain something, the individual may be motivated sufficiently to examine this particular message.

Furthermore, the decoder is more apt to decode a message that calls for the least amount of effort. A six-page brochure on school guidance services that is made up largely of clear photos with clever captions will attract and hold the receiver's attention more than one on the same subject that consists of six pages of small print. This example illustrates what is referred to in communication theory as Schramm's "fraction of selection" theory. The expectation of reward is divided by the effort required. Thus, a person will select a particular communication, in all probability, if it promises more reward or if it seems to require less effort to decode than competing messages.

The Receiver

When the message reaches the receiver, who is usually the decoder, it is expressed in some kind of shorthand—letters, drawings, photographs, tables, sounds, and so on. If this shorthand is something that the receiver has learned in the past, he or she

will respond accordingly. His or her responses will indicate the meaning that the shorthand has for him or her. Although these responses are the products of experience, but they are modified at times by the receiver's physical and mental state. For example, a picture of an attractive tray of desserts will be more appealing to the hungry receiver than to one who has just finished dinner.

Besides translating the shorthand into meaning, receivers' responses will determine what they will do about the message. The action they take may be based on things they have learned in the past. The word *war* in a message, for example, may call forth strong feelings of antagonism against the idea of destroying human life. This type of response may cause people to start encoding a message in reply—one that expresses their reactions. Thus, each person in the communication process may be both an encoder and a decoder. On the other hand, the decoder may regard the message as being unimportant or may decide not to reply to it, with the result that the process stops there. However, most individuals are constantly decoding signs, reading meaning into them, and then sending back their reactions. Graphically, the flow is shown in Figure 6.1. Table 6.2 shows how sources of information often evolve during a persuasion cycle.

The return message from the decoder or receiver is known as feedback. It tells the sender or source how his or her message is being interpreted. This occurs almost at once in a face-to-face conversation, where verbal responses along with body gestures such as a nod of the head, a facial expression, or eye focusing shows the receiver's responses. In the light of these responses, the encoder or sender may modify future messages.

The feedback situation is somewhat different when messages are carried through mass communication media such as newspapers, television programs, books, or recordings. It is true that the recipients of these messages are individuals, but these individuals supply little or no direct feedback, and only occasionally will they express reactions through telephone calls, letters, or e-mails to the sender. The type of feedback to the sender is usually in the form of a refusal to do something—subscribers discontinue taking the newspaper, listeners and viewers turn to another station, and consumers stop buying the

TABLE 6.1	Persuasive Efforts Begin with Clear Audience Analysis	
Type	**Description**	**Example**
Adoption	You attempt to get the reader to adopt an idea or plan.	The PTA urges every resident to get out and vote YES to support two new schools in the district.
Continuance	You want the audience to continue a behavior.	We urge every resident to continue their support and vote YES next Tuesday to support school expansion.
Discontinuance	You want the audience to stop doing something.	Residents need to reverse the failed bond referenda and support a plan to infuse the district with much needed funds.
Deterrence	You want to convince the audience *not* to do something.	Residents have voted against the last two bond referenda to infuse needed funds into our school system. Next Tuesday, let's reverse that trend and vote YES for school expansion.

Source: Adapted from *PR Writer's Toolbox: Blueprints for Success* (Kendall Hunt Publishing Co.), copyright 2012 by Joseph Basso, Randy Hines, and Suzanne FitzGerald. Reprinted with permission.

TABLE 6.2	As audience members move through a persuasion cycle, the channels they use to seek out information generally evolve.
Audience Stage	**Communication Channels**
Audience members have little or no awareness of an issue, product, or service.	Mass print and online channels, including publicity and news coverage, are sources of general information.
Audience members are aware of an issue, product or service and interest is beginning to develop.	Use of mass print and online channels continues, but direct communication in print and online (letters, emails, brochures, etc.) become more effective as do meetings and special events offering information, insight, and analysis.
Audience members are interested in an issue, product or service and are beginning to consider commitment to it.	Face-to-face communication with informed individuals and influencers offering opinion and endorsement becomes effective, reinforced by on-going direct communication activities.

product. This is a compelling reason why so much consumer research is conducted by business organizations. It is the only way available for finding out what programs are watched on television, or what homemakers like about a particular product, or how readers are reacting to given advertisements.

COMMUNICATION AND PERSUASION

A primary purpose behind the communication process is trying to change attitudes and opinions through the use of persuasive messages. In school–community relations this purpose is frequently referred to as that of trying to bring about *informed public consent*. The procedures for achieving this involve the preparation and presentation by the school of messages containing information, ideas, or proposals that the public who receives them considers and then decides what action, if any, it is going to take. In a two-way communication flow, the process is reversed, with school personnel analyzing and evaluating suggestions and ideas received from people in the community and subsequently deciding what course of action to follow.

The problem of trying to get individuals to learn new ideas and adopt new behaviors through the use of persuasive messages has been the subject of much research. This research has centered on the stages people go through; the characteristics of the sender, the message, and the receiver; and the results. Some of the findings appear to have practical application in a school–community relations program.

How People Accept or Reject a New Idea, Product, or Innovation

Many studies have been conducted on the adoption or rejection of a new idea, product, or innovation. Known as the *diffusion process*, this communication theory generated much interest in the 1930–1960 period. Many of the studies are relevant today. The diffusion generalizations in the 1950s have since generated some 4,000 empirical studies.

In the 1950s a group of rural sociologists developed a standard diffusion model with five stages: awareness, interest, evaluation, trial, and adoption.

> *Awareness*—This stage introduces a person to a new idea, practice, or product. Little or nothing is known about it other than general information.
>
> *Interest*—This is sometimes known as the information stage, in which an individual becomes interested in learning more about the idea, practice, or product. He or she will actively seek additional information.
>
> *Evaluation*—An individual weighs the merits of the idea, product, or practice and attempts to determine if it is good for him or her.
>
> *Trial*—The person tries the product, idea, or practice a little.
>
> *Adoption*—The individual decides that the idea, product, or practice is good enough for full-scale use.

According to Lionberger and to Rogers,[2] these stages or phases of the diffusion process do not follow a linear sequence. They are not discrete, nor are they experienced by all people.

Mass media play the leading role in the *awareness* and *interest* stages, and friends and neighbors are most influential in the *evaluation*, *trial*, and *adoption* stages. In the first two stages, information flows one way, but in the last three stages two-way

communication is dominant where attitude change starts taking place.

Message development and audience analysis also play key roles. Basso, Hines, and FitzGerald writing in *PR Writer's Toolbox: Blueprints for Success* identify adoption, continuance, discontinuance, and deterrence as the message types linked to direction of persuasive changes.[3] Table 6.1 lists the factors and examples for each.

Everett Rogers renamed the stages: (1) knowledge—the individual learns of the innovation and gains information about it; (2) persuasion—the individual forms a positive or negative attitude toward the innovation; (3) decision—the person makes a choice to adopt or reject the innovation; (4) implementation—the person puts the innovation into use; (5) confirmation—the person seeks reinforcement for the decision already made.[4]

In a similar marketing model, Topor[5] emphasizes that people are influenced more in decision making by face-to-face contact than by mass media.

> *Awareness*—Bringing an institution to the attention of an audience
>
> *Comprehension*—Developing an understanding of the appeal of an institution
>
> *Conviction*—Matching individual interests to institution offerings
>
> *Commitment*—Assisting in the decision process

Like Lionberger's diffusion process, Topor's marketing model shows that information flows primarily one way in the first two stages, but in the last two stages two-way communication is dominant, whereby a commitment is made. It would appear, then, from both of these models that for the greatest persuasion to take place, a two-way person-to-person communication process must exist.

In other words, the mass media serve to inform the public and to make people aware of a situation or an idea. When it comes to accepting or rejecting a new idea, people are apt to confer with a neighbor or friend whose judgment they respect. The classic diffusion model also included the idea that individual differences cause people to adopt innovations at different times utilizing varying amounts and sources of information. Five categories of adopters were conceptualized: innovators (first 2.5 percent), early adopters (next 13.5 percent), early majority (34 percent), late majority (34 percent), and late adopters or laggards (last 16 percent).[6] (Chapter 13 gives additional material on the diffusion of information.)

Too often school districts flood the mass media with news releases and public service announcements, thinking such announcements will be enough to persuade citizens to accept a new idea or change in the schools. However, school district personnel should be aware that, if attitude change is to take place, they must develop some additional communication approaches to reach citizens on a person-to-person basis. They need to communicate with those people to whom citizens turn to get opinions during the last three stages of the diffusion process. One answer is a key communicator program, which is explained in Chapter 8.

Confidence in the Source

The persuasiveness of a communication is greater when certain things are known about the communicator. This is usually the case if the sender has gained a reputation for being honest and direct, is a highly respected person among associates, is thought to be well informed on the subject of the message, or shares a common background or set of experiences with his or her listeners.

A message is also likely to receive favorable attention when it is sent by persons in positions of leadership. Such a person could be the president of a school board, a superintendent of schools, or a civic-minded industrialist.

Some additional research findings are interesting with regard to source credibility. For example, a physically attractive source is generally more persuasive than an unattractive source, regardless of the gender of the receiver. Furthermore, if receivers see the sender to be similar to themselves in experiences, opinions, and background, they are more apt to accept the message. Some researchers define source credibility as expertness and claim that it is related more to attitude change than to the source's attractiveness or similarity to the intended audience. However, in order for the expertise to be persuasive, Oskamp[7] claims that special conditions are needed: (1) The

area of expertise must be related to the issue or topic being presented, and (2) before the message is to be delivered the expertise must be made known to the audience. In general, researchers suggest that people will often accept or reject message conclusions based on source credibility without paying much attention to the supporting arguments.

In certain unusual situations, researchers have discovered an interesting relation between the source credibility and the passage of time. They found that receivers remember the context of a message from a noncredible communicator, think about it, and sometimes later accept the message after they have forgotten where it came from. This phenomenon is known as the *sleeper effect*. In brief, then, the tie between the source of a message and the content of a message is not the same in perception as in memory.

Support of Personal Views

Much research has been done on attitude change when the receiver of a communication is exposed to a message that agrees or disagrees with his or her point of view. Among the more important findings are these:

- People tend to read, watch, and listen to communications that are in agreement with their beliefs and interests.
- When people receive a message containing a point of view or information that casts doubt on their position, they either disregard or distort the message in order to confirm their existing attitudes and opinions. Actually, they hear or read only what they expect to hear or read, not what the message says.
- In some instances, exposure to such material leads to receivers restructuring the message so that the content agrees with their predisposition or at least so that it is made tolerable. In other words, receivers end up perceiving the message as though it reflected their own point of view.
- People remember the content of a message that supports what they believe much better than they remember material that is antagonistic to their convictions.
- Information and ideas about a subject receive the most attention from those who are most

interested in it or those whose minds are most firmly made up beforehand. Those who have no interest in the subject pay little or no attention to communications regarding it.

- When a discussion of an issue reaches the stage of controversy, those taking part in it are apt to ignore additional information unless it happens to agree with their attitudes and convictions. At this point it is usually too late for further information to influence them; in fact, too much information may produce a negative reaction.
- In an area where few opinions have been formed, the chances are rather good that a well-devised communication will accomplish its goal. In an area, however, where opinions are fixed and strongly defended, the chance of achieving attitude change is only slight. Where this is the case, it is better to take existing attitudes and try to redirect them slightly.

Benefit to Receiver

Messages can be persuasive when they deal with the receiver's needs or appeal to his or her self-interest. It is only natural to look more sharply at the content of a communication from which one can gain something. A communication could, for example, request that one serve as chairperson of a committee that is highly regarded by the members of one's group, or it could contain an offer to finance a research project in which one has a strong interest. In much the same way, citizens respond favorably to school communications that explain the services children receive from the tax dollar. Although indirect, this type of benefit makes citizens feel that a worthwhile return is being received from their investment.

Sometimes a message is persuasive because it is received when the individual has a predisposition to change. Suppose, for example, that the receiver has been active in an independent citizen movement to upgrade instruction in the schools and feels that this activity is no longer satisfying. As a result, he or she may have become predisposed to change. Then a message is received describing the value of citizen involvement in the formulation of educational policies under the auspices of the board of education. The receiver's new predisposition to change may cause a positive reaction to similar communications rejected on prior occasions.

Group Influences

Research studies have turned up a series of findings about group influence on the receiver's acceptance or rejection of a message. To begin with, a message is more likely to stimulate a favorable response if the content of it relates clearly to group values and beliefs. Group values and beliefs are those established by the family, friends, coworkers, and organizations to which the receiver belongs or would like to belong. On the other hand, if the content is in disagreement with group norms, it will probably be rejected unless it undergoes substantial change. It is difficult to persuade the receiver to believe in something or to do anything that runs counter to the value system of his or her groups.

This raises the question of what individuals receive in return for conforming to the standards and beliefs of a group. Research on this question shows that they get two returns for conformity: First, they identify more closely with the group and enhance their acceptance as members, and second, they receive some ready-made interpretations of experience and consequently find it easier to meet the daily pressures of life and its accompanying problems.

It has also been found that receivers cannot be persuaded easily if their acceptance of a message will cause them to lose face among their peers. In speculating on this possibility, the sender should scrutinize all available alternatives before transmitting the message and should word it accordingly.

There are other ways in which the individual is influenced by people's judgment. For example, an individual who will go along with the position of a speaker when the position appears acceptable to the majority of the audience may be less likely to agree with it when he or she senses a discrepancy between the speaker's position and that of the audience. It has also been observed that an individual responds to appeals in a crowd that he or she would scarcely consider, let alone accept, apart from the group. Thus, it is sometimes possible to convince an individual to accept a point of view in private, even though later he or she will deny it when reacting with a crowd.

Research has also found that opinions individuals have made known to others are more difficult to change than those they hold privately. Also, group discussion and decision making (audience participation) help to overcome resistance to persuasion.

Presentation of Issues

In presenting issues to an audience, the question has come up of which method is more effective to use: a one-sided or a two-sided message—in other words, to present only your position, or to present both yours and the opposite one. Research results indicate that the answer varies with the conditions and circumstances under which the presentation takes place. The following are some of the important findings and should be regarded as guidelines in school–community relations:

- Presenting only one side of an argument often causes the audience to feel that it is being talked down to by the speaker. Those who are well informed on the subject and those who think they are resent this type of treatment.
- If it appears that an audience is unfriendly and skeptical about the integrity of the speaker, as well as rather well informed on some aspects of the subject, the presentation should be carefully balanced and highly objective.
- When a group is initially exposed to a two-sided communication, such as the pros and cons of constructing a new school building, it is more likely to resist propaganda to which it is subsequently exposed.
- Persons with little information or background on an issue can be influenced by a one-sided message if the content is limited to arguments favoring the communicator's position.
- Persons with high intellectual ability and a good educational background tend to be more influenced by a two-sided message.
- When audience members are well informed on an issue, more persuasion is accomplished by reviewing both sides of the matter; but when they are poorly informed, a one-sided presentation is more effective.
- A one-sided message is more apt to influence persons who were initially inclined to support the position being advocated, but a two-sided communication is more influential for those who were opposed at the beginning.
- More attitude change occurs when the desirable features of a proposed change are presented first and the undesirable second.
- When different communicators present two sides of an issue successively, the side presented first has no real advantage. However, when a single communicator presents both sides, the material presented first seems to have more impact on the audience than that presented subsequently.
- In controversial situations, messages that offer some reasonable conclusion to an issue are more likely to be persuasive than if the audience is left to make up its own mind.
- When conflicting information is important to the audience, failure to divulge such information may be regarded as an indication that the communicator has not looked at the other side carefully enough.
- Research has yielded conflicting findings on the matter of whether the opening or closing of a message should contain the more important content. When the weaker points are presented first, an interested audience looks forward to what is coming later, whereas an apathetic audience is more likely to be aroused when the important points are presented at the beginning.
- Research findings lack agreement on the effectiveness of emotional versus rational appeals. Sometimes messages containing one type of appeal are more persuasive than the other type. Appeal effectiveness of either emotional or rational messages seems to depend on the issue under consideration as well as on the composition of the audience.

Fear-Arousal Messages

Are people persuaded to change their attitudes and behaviors because a message arouses fear and insecurity? Much of the research in fear-arousal messages confirms that as these messages increase from low to moderate levels, attitude and behavior changes increase. However, as the messages progress from a moderate to a stronger level, persuasion is less apt to take place. Apparently, strong fear evokes ego defenses that block attitude change.

In some studies it has been found that when an audience is exposed to conflicting messages on the same issue, the use of a strong threat appeal tends to be less persuasive than the use of a minimal one in bringing about attitude change. However, if the communicator wants the audience to remember the threat and nothing else, then a strong appeal may prove to be persuasive.

Therefore, it should be recognized in school–community relations that fear-arousal messages, either direct or indirect, will not evoke acceptance or help to gain the support required in providing a sound educational program. Messages that help people in the community to see reasonable and feasible solutions to educational problems are more effective in gaining support for needed school programs.

Repeating the Message

Advertisers have known for many years that repeating a message through a variety of media helps to achieve persuasion. The principle of repetition applies equally to school-devised messages. For example, in a rapidly growing community in which pre-kindergarten programs are just starting, it might be necessary to let parents know of their availability and their advantages in early childhood education. By carefully selecting the timing of releases on the subject, a direct mailing of brochures could be made over a three-week period. At the same time, both straight news and feature stories could be prepared for newspapers, and announcements and messages could be distributed over social media and other online sources, as well as radio and television news programs.

Scheduling the announcements about pre-kindergartens in close succession and through different information channels not only strengthens the impact of the initial exposure to the message but also converges a variety of announcements on the audience from more than one direction. Repetition with variation promotes better message understanding and acceptance.

However, a qualifying note should be emphasized here. Repetition of a message can have an attitude enhancement effect only if the content (stimulus) is positive or neutral. If it is negative, the opposite effect will take place.

Personality Variables

The personality of the receiver has a dramatic effect on how the message is processed. Research indicates that people with low self-esteem are predisposed to attitude change when exposed to persuasive messages. This is particularly true if the messages are simple and poorly substantiated. Conversely, high-self-esteem individuals are more often persuaded with complex, but well-substantiated, messages. Experts in attitude change also indicate that individuals with chronically high levels of anxiety and aggressiveness usually resist persuasion.

Further Findings about Persuasion

The following are further findings about persuasion in messages that try to effect attitude change and stimulate behavioral action:

- There is usually better assurance that an audience will comprehend more clearly the nature of a message when it contains a stated conclusion. However, this concept does not always work successfully. A suspicious audience may view the stated conclusion as a deception, whereas an informed audience may regard it as an insult to its intelligence.
- When a message suggests a pattern of action for the satisfaction of particular needs and interests, the suggested pattern should generally be in agreement with the norms and beliefs of the group to which the receiver belongs.
- In trying to validate the information received in a message, broadly educated people are likely to seek out recognized authorities, whereas less well-educated people are likely to turn to their friends and neighbors.
- With reference to matters of taste, individuals who read good books usually listen to good radio programs, whereas those who read light books or none at all listen to light radio programs. This principle of selective exposure applies to a variety of life situations.

- The communicator can influence attitudes or behavior only when the message is accompanied by the possibility of equally valuable changes in the surrounding situation. For example, a parent may pay slight attention to a school web page on homework when a child is doing satisfactory work, but the parent may read it carefully when the child's marks drop sharply.

- Attention may be drawn to communications containing important information through the use of indicators. *Indicators* are devices that suggest that the message may be valuable to the receiver. Common indicators are highlighted links on web pages; boxed stories in newspapers; large headlines over a news story; tones of voice that indicate urgency, sincerity, or fright; colors; and various symbols.

- Face-to-face conversation with a trusted friend who knows a new program from personal experience—let's say, in reading instruction—has almost the same influential quality as an actual visit to a school and an observation of the program in operation.

- Effective communication calls for the use of several different communication channels. It has been found that some channels may call the receiver's attention to an issue, others to the alternatives that are open, and still others may convince him or her that a choice is a sound one. Some channels may be useful in helping him or her to carry out a decision.

MEDIA'S ROLE IN COMMUNICATION

Much of the communication that takes place between school personnel and people in the community is through the media—radio, television, newspapers, newsletters, magazines, and online. These media are commonly thought of as vehicles or means for transmitting identical messages to many individuals at the same time. For instance, several thousand people may read a feature story in the newspaper both in print and online, describing a special school program in child care for high school students. An equal number may see on a television program the floor plans and site arrangements for a proposed school facility. Many may receive a leaflet about mathematics or listen to a speaker give an illustrated lecture on competitive sports and character development.

Unlike a small group of parents discussing a proposed change in the school lunch schedule or members of the parent–teacher association listening to a talk on teenage health problems, those who constitute a mass communication audience have practically no contact with each other. One person may be looking at a television program on a travelogue through Ontario without knowing whether anyone else in the house next door or on the same street is looking at that program.

However, each person who is independently viewing such a program, reading a news magazine, hearing a radio broadcast, and so on is connected with various groups in the community, such as family, close friends, fellow workers, members of a community organization, or a religious congregation. This fact is important in mass communication because the real impact of messages transmitted by means of the media is produced through the dissemination of ideas and information by individual receivers in small-group situations.

A brochure on the teaching of science in the schools, a news story about the president of the school board, or a television interview with an outstanding teacher may be the subject of conversation over the dinner table, among friends on Facebook, among business associates, or at a social gathering in the neighborhood. What is reported by the individual receiver is then reinterpreted by the group, and the outcome is translated into group opinion and possibly group action. Thus it would seem that an important outcome of mass communication is the influence of the individual receiver in message distribution and opinion development among members of his or her group.

In addition to this, other outcomes are associated with the use of the media. First is that mass communication makes it possible to deliver a message to large numbers of people in a relatively short period. For example, a newspaper story on a proposed annual school budget may be read by a fairly high percentage of citizens in the community the same day that it is posted or printed. Moreover, each reader receives the story in identical form, thereby minimizing the element of distortion that often characterizes message distribution on a person-to-person basis. Second, the media are most effective in creating awareness on the part of message receivers. The media serve as agencies through which information about an innovation, such as a change in the traditional conduct of a school board meeting, is brought to popular attention. Third, research findings consistently indicate that the media serve generally as a means of reinforcement rather than of change. People select messages that they want to see and hear—messages that confirm preexisting beliefs and attitudes. Fourth, most people who learn about an innovation or an event through one medium—for example, the local newspaper—are likely to learn about it through other channels as well. Fifth, there is evidence that frequent repetition of a message helps it to gain acceptance, providing, however, that it is repeated in various ways. The identical repetition of a communication tends to annoy people and can reduce the chances of its being regarded favorably.

Certain limitations are connected with message transmission through the media because of the diverse nature of the audience. In face-to-face communication, the encoder is able to observe the way a communication is being received and to modify it if the receiver's reaction suggests this need. On the other hand, in mass communication the sender is dealing with large groups and many classes of people. Thus, if a school pamphlet is published for general distribution in the community, careful attention must be given to its readability; otherwise, it may be pitched above the level of reading appeal and understanding of many of the people who receive it. In view of this limitation and the corresponding lack of feedback, it is advisable to appeal more often to important publics rather than to the general public. This means that a subject can be treated differently for different audiences that make up the several special publics of the school. For example, a leaflet on the financial needs of the school district could be written and designed one way for businesspeople in the community, another way for parents of elementary-school children, and still another way for senior citizens.

It should also be noted that readers, listeners, and viewers have been exposed to thousands of media communications and are therefore able to distinguish between those that are attractive in appearance and skillful in design and those that lack these qualities. This exposure to good techniques causes people to demand excellence in all publications and programs without being conscious of their reasons for doing so. Parents may not expect a school newsletter to look like a report distributed by a large corporation to its stockholders, but they expect it to have an attractive flag, good page layout, readable type, interesting illustrations, and timely news. Skill in handling the media is no guarantee of establishing communication with all receivers, but it does make it much more likely.

WORDS AND MESSAGES

Successful communication is tied closely to the way in which words are employed in messages. Although a large body of research studies on this subject is available, only the more pertinent findings will be reviewed here. If used correctly, these findings should improve the meaning and acceptance of school messages intended for various community audiences.

Words are tools for fashioning messages. When used properly, they enable the message receiver to interpret accurately the purpose and meaning that the sender had in mind. The achievement of this outcome calls for a thorough knowledge of word usage and its application in communications for specific audiences.

Research indicates that several measures of word usage must be taken into account by message encoders. To begin, senders cannot tell other people something they themselves do not understand. They must know precisely what they want to say and then make the message easy for the receivers to comprehend. However, in making the message easy to comprehend, senders must be sensitive to the fact that word meaning varies with individuals and environmental conditions. The word *football*, for example, has a different connotation in England than it does in the United States. The word *dog* to a canine enthusiast may refer to a friendly, loyal animal, whereas to a person bitten by one the word may represent an unfriendly, vicious animal. In this respect, words can play on an individual's feelings and tap his or her memory as well.

It is likewise necessary to know the meanings of words that are brought into play by self-interest groups. Each group uses words and phrases peculiar to the goals the group stands for in American life. Bankers talk about prime interest rates, physicians about preventive medicine, educators about curriculum and instruction, and workers about fringe benefits and union contracts. Knowing the meaning of words that are used by self-interest groups enables the message writer or speaker to select those that will be received favorably and understood.

The meaning of a word is influenced by the context in which it appears. For example, the word *rare* has a different connotation when it refers to a sense of humor than it has when used to describe a piece of meat. For another example, take the words *progressive* and *education*. When used separately in a sentence, they are regarded as positive words with acceptable meanings. However, if combined into the term *progressive education*, they acquire another sense and to some people become negative words that convey emotional overtones. In short, the meaning and reaction to a word can be changed by placing it in another context.

The number of syllables used also appears to have some effect on the readability of printed material. It has been found that words with as many as four or five syllables add to reading difficulty. For this reason, reading specialists advocate the substitution of words with fewer syllables whenever possible. The longer the physical length of a word, the less chance there is of its being understood.

Somewhat similar is the pronunciation problem created by the use of words unfamiliar to the reader. Instead of focusing on what a word means in the message, attention is diverted to the question of how to pronounce it. The reader is often required to spend some time analyzing a word before he or she is able to say it correctly. If too many words in the message are unfamiliar, the pronunciation block may become large enough to destroy the message. However, in the case of uncertainty in the mind of the reader about the status of a word, the word can be clarified casually. For example, it could be said in a school publication that "we want to *correlate* or *pull closer together* our English and social studies in the middle-school program."

CRISIS COMMUNICATIONS

Unfortunately, many school districts fail to engage in planned, ongoing communication and communicate only when they are in a crisis. They find themselves in a reactive situation that keeps them in a defensive position. Communication during a crisis is extremely difficult without a track record of ongoing communication and planning.

Ongoing communication will build the trust and relationships between the school and community that can be relied upon to mitigate the kind of difficult situation a crisis or other controversy can present. Such relational capital can be accrued with sound communications over time and thus be available to serve the organization when needed. Organizations that fail to develop such relational capital in advance of crises and controversies may find that their crisis communication is seen as self-serving and met with suspicion.

Sadly, many school districts believe that when a crisis arrives, they can eliminate it with some strong public relations. However, the communications and public relations should have taken place before the crisis. Kennedy addresses this point by stating,

> Particularly in today's climate, public relations must be more than crisis communications. It must be more than press releases or egg-on-face statements from officials. Real communication must be constant and personal, blunting the need for any criticisms before they can arise.[8]

In this way, the severity of a crisis can be reduced. Once into a crisis, a district has to ride it out by communicating the best way it can. What it needs in a crisis is trust and credibility, which can be best established with prior communications and public relations, and with much planning.

The National School Public Relations Association has compiled a comprehensive school crisis manual that provides procedures and policies, tips on dealing with the media, and ways to communicate with staff.[9] (See Chapter 9 on crisis planning and handling violence.)

One Expert's Point of View: The Communication Process

Joseph Basso, Ph.D., is a Professor in the Department of Public Relations and Advertising at Rowan University. Dr. Basso is the author of the PR Writer's Toolbox: Blueprints for Success. *He also serves as a consultant on business writing and organizational planning issues.*

Why should we think about communication as a process rather than a single act?

Successful communication generally seeks a behavioral outcome. We want people to do something as a result of our communication. Getting a behavioral outcome, however, generally involves a process that accommodates information needs along the decision-making progression. Think about the last time you made an important decision on something—buying a new car or choosing where to go on vacation, for example. We rarely make these kinds of decisions in a split-second. These decisions are made as part of a process—a process where we become aware of something, seek out more information about it, talk with others about it, consider our options, and then eventually decide. Communication programming needs to facilitate this process.

How important is developing the right messages to the communication process?

It is critical. Consider the concept that people often respond to or even actively seek out information that reinforces their existing viewpoint. If you want to modify or change that viewpoint you will need messaging that appreciates this behavior. This means messages may need to be constructed in ways that appeal to an audience's existing attitude as part of a process that then introduces new information that then seeks to change opinions and behavior. Effective messages must do more than just present facts. Messages need to build a context or a frame of reference for audience members that will allow them to consider, accept, and act on those facts.

Feedback is cited as an important part of the communication process. Can feedback take forms other than formal research?

Absolutely. Sometimes people might think of feedback only as the structured process of collecting insights and data through formal research. But successful communicators seek feedback in informal ways all of the time. This process is no different than a classroom teacher who senses a class is getting bored and then adjusts his or her teaching to capture the students' attention again. A good teacher is alert to students' response just as a good communicator is responsive to audience response. In face-to-face communication this might involve watching body language or assessing questions. In other forms of communication, this might involve tracking web traffic or event sign-ups. Finding ways to judge ongoing audience reactions to communication can help to spot what's working and what's not working as a program is implemented and help us to either reinforce or adjust communication to boost effectiveness.[10] ∎

Questions

1. Identify a current issue in your local school system. How would you craft a continuance message on this issue, and how would you craft a discontinuance message on the issue? Specify when it might be appropriate to use each message.

2. How can the values of the sender (source) and the receiver affect the fidelity of the communication process?

3. What are the implications for school communicators in assessing the values of the sender when selecting spokespersons for particular issues confronting a school system?

4. If some school board members were to say that you need to work only with the mass media to get school messages across to the community, what would you say to them about that point of view, and how would you counsel them on communication approaches?

Readings

Bagin, Don, and Anthony Fulginiti, *Practical Public Relations Theories & Practices That Make a Difference.* Dubuque, IA: Kendall Hunt, 2006.

Basso, Joseph, Randy Hines, and Suzanne FitzGerald, *PR Writer's Toolbox: Blueprints for Success*, 2nd ed. Dubuque, IA: Kendall Hunt, 2013.

Cialdini, Robert B., *Influence: Science and Practice*, 5th ed. Boston, MA: Pearson, 2008.

DeVito, Joseph A., *The Interpersonal Communication Book,* 14th ed. Boston, MA: Pearson, 2015.

Dilenschneider, Robert L., *The Corporate Communication Bible.* Boston, MA: New Millennium, 2004.

National School Public Relations Association, *School Public Relations,* 2nd ed. Rockville, MD: Author, 2007.

Newsom, Doug, Judy VanSlyke Turk, and Dean Kruckeberg, *This Is PR*, 11th ed. Belmont, CA: Cengage Wadsworth, 2012.

Wilcox, Dennis L., Glen T. Cameron, Philip H. Ault, and Warren K. Agee, *Public Relations Strategies and Tactics*, 11th ed. Boston, MA: Pearson, 2014.

Endnotes

1. Charles Horton Cooley, *Social Organization* (New York: Charles Scribner's Sons, 1909), p. 61.

2. Herbert F. Lionberger, *Adoption of New Ideas and Practices* (Ames, IA: Iowa State University Press, 1960), p. 3, and Everett M. Rogers, *Diffusion of Innovations*, 4th ed. (New York, NY: Free Press, 1995), p. 160.

3. Joseph Basso, Randy Hines, and Suzanne FitzGerald, *PR Writer's Toolbox: Blueprints for Success* (Dubuque, IA: Kendall Hunt, 2013), p. 103.

4. Everett M. Rogers, *Diffusion of Innovations*, 4th ed. (New York, NY: Free Press, 1995), p. 202.

5. Robert S. Topor, *Institutional Image: How to Define, Improve, Market It* (Washington, DC: Council for Advancement and Support of Education, 1986), p. 55.

6. Eric A. Abbott and J. Paul Yarbrough, "Re-Thinking the Role of Information in Diffusion Theory: An Historical Analysis with an Empirical Test." Paper submitted to Communication Theory and Methodology Division, Association for Education in Journalism and Mass Communication, for its annual convention, New Orleans, LA, 1999, p. 6.

7. Stuart Oskamp, *Attitudes and Opinions* (Upper Saddle River, NJ: Prentice Hall, 1991), p. 217.

8. Jack L. Kennedy, "Building Positives Must Start with Educators," *Journal of Educational Relations*, 16, no. 4 (November 1995), p. 24. Copyright © 1995 by Rowman & Littlefield Publishers, Inc.

9. Rick Kaufman, *The Complete Crisis Communication Management Manual* (Rockville, MD: National School Public Relations Association, 2009).

10. Adapted from correspondence October 11, 2017 with Joseph Basso, Ph.D.; Professor; College of Communication and Creative Arts; Rowan University; Glassboro, NJ. Used with permission.

7

Communicating with Internal Publics

This chapter reviews issues...

- For central administrators: The roles of communication with internal publics to both disseminate information and build engaged, productive and supportive employees and students.
- For building and program administrators: The ways in which communication with internal audiences can help to support school and program objectives through an involved workforce and student body.
- For teachers, counselors, and staff: How internal communication and working relationships among individuals can be important to fostering school and student success.

After completing this chapter you should be able to...

- Demonstrate how internal communication contributes to and supports the success of school—community relations programming.
- Identify essential internal audience segments and distinguish how each contributes to school—community relations efforts.
- Describe the role of human relations in developing productive working relationships with internal audiences.
- Outline methods for communicating with key internal audiences.

Internal communication has become increasingly important to school boards and administrators as a vital part of comprehensive school—community relations programs. In the past it was not uncommon for school systems, in developing a community relations program, to concern themselves exclusively with ways and means of communicating with their external publics. Rarely did they think of structuring a program of effective two-way communication with their internal publics: the employees and students. This has changed as the age of involvement has spread throughout society, including education.

Internal publics, particularly employees, began to see themselves in a different role—one that called for a more active part in the total planning of the educational program along with their professional and personal welfare—and school systems began to realize that good relations with and among internal publics were a necessary part of good public relations. Just as a successful school system depends on trusting, working relationships with its various community audiences, a school system also needs solid relationships with those internal to the organization.

WHY INTERNAL COMMUNICATIONS?

School administrators and boards are coming to understand the importance of good internal communications. This awareness has been brought about in an age of school choice and increasing competition for limited public resources by the need to gain continued public support of education. School boards and administrators can no longer get that support alone; they must enlist the help of employees, and doing so requires a structured internal communication program.

School districts, then, see three reasons why a good internal communication program is important: (1) A good external communication program cannot survive without it; (2) constructive ideas will be suggested by employees because someone is listening and informing them; and (3) human needs, such as recognition and a sense of belonging, will be met, thus making employees more productive.

SCHOOL BOARD ACTIONS

In analyzing the causes of good and poor relations within a system, it is advisable to start with the board of education or board of trustees. This body sets the climate of the school system through the exercise of its authority, the conduct of its business, and the relationships it maintains with administrators and staff members.

Board Authority

A local school board is given broad discretionary powers: both the right and the authority under state law to manage the school system. What matters is the manner in which the board of education exercises this authority. If it refuses to listen to the advice of the chief executive officer, shows indifference to the welfare of the employees, usurps the functions of the administrator, rules on matters about which it is uninformed, issues unreasonable orders, makes political appointments, tries to summarily dismiss teachers, or engages in other undesirable practices, it soon creates unfavorable working conditions and lowers the morale of employees. The result is that the school employees no longer feel a loyalty to the system and do not hesitate to say what they think about the board of education and the policies with which they are forced to comply. And no external community relations programming, no matter how well planned and funded, can reasonably be expected to reach its objectives when competing with negative commentary emerging from the organization's own internal audiences.

The Conduct of Board Business

The board of education is legally required to conduct its business in regular meetings and in special meetings called from time to time. All meetings are open with the exception of executive sessions. In some states the decisions reached in executive sessions are not binding until voted on in an open meeting.

Whether a board adheres to the proper conduct of its business exerts a direct influence on public and employee attitudes. A well-organized meeting in which sincere efforts are made to serve the school community will inspire employees with confidence, respect, and trust; a poorly managed, perfunctory, and discordant meeting will leave a residue of discontent.

Relations with the Superintendent

School board relations with the superintendent deserve special consideration in any discussion of internal affairs. In many systems, the board of education is organized into a series of standing committees. Each committee is made responsible for some area of the school program. There may be committees on personnel, buildings and grounds, transportation, finance, public relations, instruction, and welfare.

This system is used to expedite board business and to divide the amount of work carried by members. However, it has potential weaknesses that could influence the effectiveness of internal communication and should, therefore, be recognized:

- The executive officer is required to report to committees instead of taking up problems with the whole board of education.
- These committees become policymaking bodies because their recommendations are, as a rule, accepted by the board without much question.
- Members of the board may have but slight understanding of the system aside from the specific areas in which they work on committee assignments.
- There can be a tendency for committees to encroach on the administrative function of the superintendent.

Complaints received by board members from teachers, parents, and people in the community are another cause of poor relationships if they are handled incorrectly. Sound administration requires that all complaints directed to board members be referred to the superintendent of schools and cleared through him or her with members of the staff. If satisfaction is not received by the complaining party, before any official action is taken the board can request the superintendent to report the facts and tell what he or she has done. Instead of following this procedure, or one comparable to it, some board members assume responsibility for settling complaints themselves. They not only take over the authority of the superintendent but also undermine his or her prestige in the school and community. The incorrect handling of complaints is a fertile breeding ground for discord in the relationship of the board and the superintendent.

The kind of interest that board members show in education problems is another potential issue between board members and the superintendent that can affect the ability to communicate effectively. As a professional adviser to the board and the educational leader of the school system, it is up to the superintendent to keep the board informed of current problems and to recommend courses of action for meeting existing needs. Although superintendents do not expect the board to approve all of their recommendations, they do expect that the members will consider suggestions with a fair degree of impartiality. If board members are casual or indifferent about a superintendent's recommendations, or if their decisions are made for personal, business, or political reasons, the superintendent is left with the alternative of either protesting vigorously or going along with the board for his or her own security. In the long run, superintendents who play the game for their own security may enjoy smoother relations with the board, but their leadership role in the school system and the community may be forfeited.

Adverse relations may also develop from the kind of methods employed by the superintendents in dealing with boards. For instance, superintendents may withhold vital information to protect themselves, or they may initiate important policies without consulting the board beforehand. Some superintendents destroy goodwill by assuming an attitude of intellectual superiority and by insisting on the right to decide all educational policies. A few may try to elicit community pressure to get what they want and, failing this, to engage in a whispering campaign to defeat members who are up for reelection.

Board relations with staff personnel are carried on mostly through the superintendent. He or she is expected to advise the board on staff problems and to recommend policies.

ADMINISTRATION—EMPLOYEE RELATIONS

Relationships between the board of education and the superintendent of schools have a positive or a negative effect on relationships between the superintendent and the employees. A superintendent who enjoys good relations with the board is more likely to look upon his or her job as an opportunity to build a better school system. Employees catch the spirit of the superintendent and welcome the leadership provided. A different reaction takes place when the superintendent is forced to contend with an unpleasant board relationship or an environment, for example, where the board's vision for the school system does not appear to be aligned with the superintendent's vision for the school system.

The use of the word *superintendent* in this chapter pertains to school districts other than large city or county districts. In larger school districts, where the superintendent often is far removed from district-wide employees, the suggestions in this chapter might apply to regional, cluster, or deputy superintendents.

Primary relations between administration and employees start with the superintendent and flow down a line of authority to the assistant superintendent, directors of special departments, supervisors, and building principals, according to the size of the system. The superintendent is the one who sets the overall pattern of relationships, because of his or her position as chief executive officer. Under proper administrative conditions, success or failure is bound up closely with the willingness of the employees to support the superintendent's policies. In systems where desirable administration—employee relations are found, the superintendent is usually a capable executive who possesses a dynamic and pleasing personality, a deep respect for human values, and an ability to work democratically with people. His or her policies follow a clearly defined philosophy of education and management and include recognition of staff achievements, opportunities for growth in service, staff participation in policy and program development, fair and consistent treatment, satisfactory working conditions, and a sincere concern for staff welfare. What a school system has in the way of organization, administrative procedures, instruction, plant, and esprit de corps is due largely to the policies, leadership, courage, and vision of the superintendent.

Except in small school systems, the superintendent must rely on subordinate administrative and supervisory officers to promote desirable staff relations. Poor subordinates, however, may do much to impede his or her leadership and efforts to build a unified school system. They can misinterpret policies and badly manage excellent programs. Their individual struggles for prestige and power may divide staff loyalties and set up competing factions. Unless superintendents have capable and reliable subordinates, they may find themselves heading a mediocre and strife-torn system.

Aside from the superintendent, perhaps the most important administrative officers are the building principals. They may be in more direct and regular contact with the staff than their immediate superiors. The attitudes and actions of principals often determine the way in which many teachers and other school personnel think and feel and talk about the school system.

Human Relations in Improving Employee Relations

The day has long since passed when school administration could be considered as purely a technical skill of developing a budget, constructing and maintaining school plants, assigning teachers, accounting for students, and operating school support services. All these are necessary and vital to the operation of a school or a school system. However, another skill, the human skill, must be considered in any discussion of good school administration, particularly where internal relations are concerned.

Sergiovanni, Kelleher, McCarthy, and Wirt contend, "*Human skill* refers to the school administrator's ability to work effectively and efficiently with others on a one-to-one basis and in group settings. The skill requires considerable self-understanding and acceptance as well as appreciation, empathy, and consideration for others."[1]

Running through studies in all areas of administration is a consensus that, although technical skills cannot be disregarded, human skills are vital. The relationship that should exist between human and technical skills has been outlined by Sergiovanni et al.:

> Human skills seem equally important to administrative and supervisory roles throughout the school hierarchy. Regardless of position, all administrators work through others; that is, they use human skills to achieve goals.[2]

School administrators, therefore, must focus attention on acquiring skills to deal with human problems. A necessary requirement for an administrator to develop skills in human relations is a positive attitude toward the supreme worth of all individuals. Not only must this attitude be present in the administrators, but it must be evident and manifested in their behavior. It is not enough for them to state that they believe in democratic administration and total involvement of their staffs and employees; they must verify this philosophy in their day-to-day relations with their employees by showing a regard for others and by generating goodwill among school employees. Good human relations is a matter of using good common sense in administration, which in turn will generate mutual respect and goodwill.

In a successful school system, the spirit of goodwill is a pervasive feeling that emanates from the board of education, the chief school administrator, and the administrative and supervisory staff. Educators may think they are practicing good human relations if they provide their employees with good salaries, comfortable work areas, release time, social functions, free coffee, and reserved parking spaces. Important as these features are in the total picture of good employee relations, if such benefits are provided out of a spirit of paternalism to make the employees more compliant, they will not bring about the desired result of good human relations. Employees must perceive that administrators and supervisors are being sincere and honest with them if goodwill and mutual respect are to develop in a school system.

Administrators must train themselves to be sensitive to the importance of communicating through their own behavior and action. If this behavior belies what they say, they will invariably have difficulty in maintaining good human relations. In taking action or making a decision, administrators must anticipate how their employees will perceive the matter. Take, for example, the superintendent who informed the staff that the budget was to be cut and no additional hiring was to take place. In the meantime, the superintendent, preoccupied with an additional assignment from the board of education, hired an additional secretary. The new workload may have warranted the hiring of an additional person, but the school personnel perceived it differently as they had slashed their own budget and denied themselves services. To them the superintendent's behavior destroyed the sincerity of what had been said and served to reduce the superintendent's chances of improving relations with them.

Ultimately, good human relations will lead to better employee relations because of job satisfaction. A problem in education is that a number of administrators make the assumption that the factors that contribute to job satisfaction also contribute to job dissatisfaction. According to Herzberg,[3]

these are two separate sets of factors. He includes under satisfiers (motivational needs) such factors as achievement, recognition, work itself, responsibility, advancement, and growth. Under dissatisfiers (hygienic needs) he lists policy and administration; salary; work conditions; interpersonal relations with supervisors, peers, and subordinates; status; security; supervision; and personal life. If these hygienic needs are met, employee dissatisfaction is prevented rather than having an impact on employee satisfaction with work. The hygienic needs relate to the condition of the work, whereas the motivational needs relate to the work itself. Herzberg reasoned that because the factors causing satisfaction are different from those causing dissatisfaction, the two feelings cannot simply be treated as opposites of one another. The opposite of satisfaction is not dissatisfaction but *no* satisfaction. Similarly, the opposite of dissatisfaction is *no* dissatisfaction.

In order for the employee to move from the hygienic needs to the motivational needs, where morale and productivity improve, the hygienic needs must be reasonably met.

In relating Herzberg's theory to education, Sergiovanni and Carver note:

> It must be remembered, however, that in general providing of hygienic needs prevents decreases in performance but will not increase performance. The motivation to work beyond what is necessary to meet minimum requirements comes from the satisfier set—achievement and recognition, for example. According to the theory, these are the motivators. This concept is of fundamental importance, for the theory suggests that it is a mistaken notion to assume that school executives can buy teacher motivation through concessions across the collective-bargaining table or in similar ways. The bargaining process as we presently know it is largely limited to hygienic concerns.[4]

Relations Among Teachers

Relations among teachers should be evaluated for the effect they have on public opinion. Poor relations have resulted in serious damage to school systems and to the status of professional employees in the community. Teachers have undermined support and respect for the school system by criticizing the work of colleagues to students, parents, and the public. Some teachers have openly opposed school policies—as well as newer educational practices and legislative proposals aimed at improving their own welfare—in news and social media.

The reasons for poor relations among teachers can be traced to a variety of causes. The more typical reasons are a lack of administrative leadership, instructional practices, unethical conduct, division of responsibility, and the formation of cliques.

Lack of Administrative Leadership

Unity among staff personnel is difficult to produce without strong administrative leadership. Lack of such leadership diverts attention from problems of teaching and learning and brings into prominence petty differences and personal irritations common to any group of people. This in turn leads to rivalry, clique formation, destructive criticism, disagreement, and quarreling. These human weaknesses are less significant and destructive in a school system in which the administrative leader brings teachers together to share ideas, to identify instructional problems, to pool resources, to define acceptable goals, and to coordinate their services.

Instructional Practices

Instructional practices in any good school should be guided by a definite statement of the philosophy and objectives of teaching. When there is no definite agreement on such philosophy and objectives, friction may develop between teachers and may leave parents confused as to what kind of education their children are receiving. One teacher may believe that children grow best in a democratic institution with as much freedom as they can manage successfully, whereas another teacher may believe that children should be kept under strict control and be told exactly what to do. One teacher may give home assignments as an aid to subject-matter mastery, and another may think that home assignments are unnecessary. One may employ a methodology of recitation, drill, and testing; another may build instruction around problems and projects involving many different types of learning activities.

Differences in instructional practices can be a serious cause of poor relations among teachers.

Unethical Conduct

Unethical conduct creates friction among teachers, and examples are numerous. For instance, a teacher may attribute the weaknesses of a class to poor instruction by the previous teacher and make this opinion known to students and parents. Sometimes parents are told that their children do not read well thanks to the methods used by the second-grade teacher, or that their children will pay an educational penalty later on because certain members of the staff are not upholding desirable achievement standards. Teachers who show initiative and imagination, who experiment with newer methods, and who try different curricular arrangements may be ridiculed by some colleagues for their efforts. Any teacher who is the target of unfair criticism and abuse by colleagues is bound to feel resentful.

Malicious gossiping and spreading rumors are other forms of unethical conduct that induce strained relations among faculty members. These unfair practices can disrupt harmony among staff members and cause much unnecessary suffering. Teachers cannot work together efficiently and present a solid front to the public when they are beset by malicious gossip and rumors.

Division of Responsibility

Disturbances often may arise over the division of responsibility among teachers. A heavy classroom schedule will be accepted without too much complaint, provided some teachers do not receive fewer classes, smaller sections, and fewer preparations than others. Sponsorship of extracurricular activities may elicit vigorous protest from those who are assigned such difficult, time-consuming activities as newspapers, yearbooks, and dramatics, for which no allowance is made in workload. Resentment over unfair division of responsibility becomes acute when there is a reasonable suspicion that favoritism has been shown to some members of the staff. The resentment is directed as much at these members as at the administrative officers who are responsible for staff assignments.

Formation of Cliques

Cliques are small, exclusive groups of individuals who band together for their own shared interests. They may keep to themselves as much as possible. In an individual school, members of the various departments or other groups may remain apart from their colleagues, feeling that they have little in common with the rest of the faculty.

Cliques thrive mostly in schools where nothing is done to involve the staff in the study of common problems and where administrators remain in the background. The influence of such cliques can be modified when the causes are known and suitable measures worked out for diverting attention to instructional improvements.

RELATIONS WITH NONINSTRUCTIONAL PERSONNEL

School administrators and boards of education sometimes forget that noninstructional personnel are also critical frontline interpreters of the school to the outside community. For example, custodians, secretaries, clerks, bus drivers, food-service workers, and maintenance personnel have many contacts in the community with friends and neighbors and through membership in religious, fraternal, and social groups. Their attitudes toward the institution and its personnel are just as important as those of teachers in influencing the community overall. When noninstructional personnel are dissatisfied with their jobs and do not get along well with staff members, the reasons are usually associated with poor communication, internal politics, job definition, or recognition. Much of the trouble between instructional and noninstructional personnel could be avoided through the technique of job definition so that each individual understands what is expected of him or her. When responsibilities are not well specified, the result is often disagreement over who does what. Examples: The custodian claims that the teacher should have children pick up stray pieces of paper on the floor before they are dismissed. The teacher blames the custodian for leaving the window shades uneven or not arranging seats in proper order. Clerks disparage teachers for requests to photocopy materials needed for classroom use.

Noninstructional staff personnel want acknowledgment and proper recognition for outstanding service just as much as teachers, but they seldom receive any. Instead, they may be treated unfairly by some teachers. Conflicts involving noninstructional personnel would be reduced and almost eliminated if friendly attitudes were shown toward them and they were accorded deserved recognition. Better relations have been promoted in schools where these workers are actively engaged in the school's operation, invited to faculty meetings and serving on staff committees dealing with matters in which they have an interest.

IMPROVEMENT OF STAFF RELATIONS

The improvement of staff relations starts with the board of education. Through its actions in conducting meetings, showing an intelligent concern for instructional problems, extending fair treatment to administrative staff personnel, and maintaining a strict division of labor between policy decision and policy execution, the board of education can inspire confidence and build a real feeling of security that will permeate the entire school system.

Given this condition, the superintendent and those who assist him or her have an excellent opportunity to foster good staff relations and to make progress toward the achievement of educational goals. The extent to which they succeed will depend on their collegiality, understanding, integrity, and skill in working with people.

In a small school system, the superintendent is the person responsible for establishing cooperative relations with and among members of the staff, largely through leadership in everyday affairs that involve close personal relations. As a school system increases in size, opportunities for personal relations between the superintendent and the staff become fewer. It then becomes the function of the superintendent to establish the climate for good relations through personal contact with representatives from various groups in the school system. Along with this, the superintendent must instruct his or her intermediary assistants and supervisory personnel that they are responsible for close personal relationships with each employee under their supervision. Of this group, none is quite so important as the individual principal. Unless he or she seeks to achieve good employee relations, efforts on the part of the superintendent at the district level might be diffused and therefore ineffective.

More is needed to effect wholesome internal relations between members of the staff and the administration than merely a spirit of personal leadership by those in charge of a school system. Practices and structures must be in place that contribute to the development of good relations.

Studies of internal communications and staff morale frequently reveal that managers and administrators mistakenly assume they know what each employee wants from his or her job. Managers generally rate good pay, job security, promotion, and growth among the top items they believe employees desire. Employees, however, frequently express other key desires: doing interesting work, receiving appreciation for jobs well done, and having a sense of involvement in the workplace.

There can be a communication disconnect between supervisors and employees when it comes to job recognition. Heathfield notes that numerous studies have documented that employees often seek more than financial rewards for work performed while supervisors see money as the key motivator employees seek. Recognition from employers for work done well often is an important motivational aspect cited by employees, while research has found that supervisors often cite money as a more important motivator for employees.[5] Sirota, Mischkind, and Meltzer claim there are three basic goals of people at work: They want to be treated fairly, have a sense of accomplishment from work, and have camaraderie.[6]

In another study cited in the late Pat Jackson's *pr reporter*,[7] "Ability to have a 'balanced' lifestyle blending with time off for friends and family" was the number-one priority of public relations employees. Conversely, the managers of the public relations firms ranked it number eight on their understanding of employees' priorities. The employees' number-one priority ranked above "financial compensation," which managers thought they had desired most.

It would seem, then, that managers and school administrators tend to communicate from a value perspective that is different from that of school employees. In reality, what the school administrator thinks is important to the employee is not. If morale is to be improved and internal communications accomplished, the school administrator must attempt to understand the work environment needs and wants of employees and communicate from that perspective.

Perhaps one way of approaching the problem is through a structured internal communications program that encompasses participatory management approaches fostering good employee feedback and involvement. Some components of a functional internal communications program are discussed in the following sections.

One-on-One Conferences

The purpose of these conferences is to enable the administrator to learn the values and priorities of each employee regarding the job assigned. In addition, the employee learns what the administrator and the school district think is important for the organization.

One technique used during a conference is to provide the employee and the administrator with a sheet of paper each. The employee is asked to list what is important to him or her to get the job done. Simultaneously, the administrator lists on a sheet of paper what he or she feels the employee considers important to complete assigned duties. They then compare the lists, discuss the differences, and see how the employee's values do or do not mesh with the school's values. The second phase of this process reverses the first phase. The administrator lists what he or she feels is important to get the job done. At the same time, the employee lists on a separate sheet of paper what he or she thinks the administrator considers important to carry out his or her duties. Perceptions are then discussed, with a better understanding of each other's values resulting.

An administrator might have a conference with each employee to learn his or her workplace values. Usually, those things that the employee feels are important to getting his or her job done are things that can be influenced or changed by the administrator—for example, getting sufficient supplies in a timely fashion, being able to post student work on walls, having a parking space, or getting proper furniture in a room. When administrators can effect changes, they should do so; when they can't because of legal, budgetary, or policy reasons, they should communicate that to the employee.

Once the administrator understands these workplace values of employees, he or she can communicate messages that address what employees feel is important. Otherwise, employees will tend not to listen to what is communicated.

Internal Advisory Committees

Regardless of the size of the school system, employees want some contact with the chief school administrator other than through the usual administrative channels or over a bargaining table. They want to be able to express their concerns, to have some direct impact on policy development, and to suggest ideas that will improve the overall effectiveness of the school system. Many employees feel that in order to be heard they must communicate with all levels of administration, particularly the top level. The traditional procedure of communicating through one's immediate superior is viewed by many employees as a deliberate move to keep them silent and under control. It also is often true that a step-by-step procedure of communicating upward through the levels of administration tends to stifle employee initiative and creativity.

Some foresighted school administrators, recognizing the need to communicate with employees and to involve them in the overall planning of the school system, have created a superintendent's advisory committee. The committee is designed not only to hear what members of the internal community have to say but also to help inform employees of the many activities of the school district. A number of models have proved functional. One is in the form of a *general advisory committee* with membership from all constituencies of the school system. Another model is that of *special advisory committees* according to positions—one for the faculty (teachers, counselors, and librarians) and another for classified employees (office workers, transportation personnel, cafeteria workers, and the maintenance force). Normally, if a general advisory committee is organized, there is little need for special advisory committees, and vice versa.

The effectiveness of advisory committees depends a great deal on the attitude of superintendents and their ability to orchestrate the whole communication process that develops. If, in creating an advisory committee, their attitude is to talk "at" the representatives and not "with" them, the committee, as a one-way communication vehicle, will eventually become ineffective. However, the committee can be helpful to the entire educational program if superintendents perceive issues from the viewpoint of an administrator and an employee, if they are sensitive to the importance employees might place on an issue, if they can effect change where change is possible and offer a rationale where change is not possible, and if they keep the committee informed.

Many times a concern of a committee may seem to be insignificant to the superintendent although it is of major concern to the committee. Often it is an item that can be changed or corrected by a simple memo or phone call from the superintendent. For example, getting their supplies on a Monday rather than on a Friday may be vital to teachers, yet the superintendent may not be aware of a problem related to that. Furthermore, his or her administrative staff may not be aware of the problem either. An advisory committee, then, may be one of the few ways such an overall problem of the staff can be revealed.

There are times that the superintendent will have to reject the advice of the committee and say no to a requested change in procedure, and it should be understood by the committee members that this will happen. In these cases, the superintendent should give the rationale for saying no. Committee members may not agree with this decision, but with an explanation they will understand better how the decision was reached.

Particularly important is the committee's ability to help the superintendent communicate with the other employees. If a new program is being launched, details can be relayed to the committee for further dissemination. The details of the annual budget can be passed along to the employees through the committee as one of a number of ways of keeping the employees informed of the activities of the school system.

Over a period of time the superintendent should be able to begin anticipating sensitive areas among employees from the issues discussed at the advisory committee meetings. In turn, he or she may be able to effect change or develop a communication strategy that can eliminate a possible crisis or confrontation with employees.

Encouraging Suggestions

One of the quickest ways to find out how good morale is in the schools is to ask employees this question: "If you had an idea to improve the schools and it would cost nothing to implement it, would you suggest it?" In some school districts that we worked with, 80 percent of the employees said that they would. In others, only 10 percent said they would suggest the idea. This is a quick way to find out how people feel about where they work. The following are examples of easy ways to let the staff know that you're noticing they're doing a good job:

- One hospital started a CIA ("Caught in the Act") card. Employees were given these cards to distribute to other employees who they saw doing something special for other employees or for patients. Each card would be worth a free lunch in the cafeteria.
- A publishing company gave each employee 10 coupons, again to distribute to employees they saw doing something especially well; 1 coupon was worth a free lunch, 2 were worth a dinner, and 10 were worth a night at a local casino. If funding is not available for such initiatives, perhaps a local company would be willing to sponsor and pay for such an undertaking.
- A school system offered a monthly recognition and preferred parking spot for an employee nominated for outstanding customer service. Nominations were made by all employees and the recognized employee was chosen by the vote of a committee comprised of employees and administrators.

Recognition of Accomplishments

Another policy of far-reaching importance in building good relations is that of recognizing the outstanding accomplishments—both in the school and in the community–of individuals and groups. All individuals, no matter what kind of work they do, are psychologically so constructed that they must know whether their labors are being appreciated by those above them in the line of authority. They may not be willing to do their best or to expend extra effort if what they do is taken for granted. Studies of morale among workers

in industry have borne out this point, but for some unexplainable reason little has been done about it by some administrators. Yet it can be accomplished rather easily, with a letter praising an employee, a note of thanks, a pleasant telephone call, or a congratulatory note.

Involvement in Planning

Administrators interested in fostering good internal communications would be wise to involve all employees in the planning processes for the entire school district. It would seem that each employee has enough expertise to benefit the school district by serving on a planning committee or task force on—for example—curriculum, long-range goals, finances, buildings, athletics, or community relations. Employees asked to serve on such planning committees or task forces will feel a sense of belonging and be honored that they are invited to help improve the school district. Their interest in working for the schools should increase once they have a chance to be heard and possibly effect needed changes. In addition, this upward communication from the employees as a result of serving on planning committees or task forces has another benefit: Many new ideas are generated that ultimately will help the instructional program either directly or indirectly.

Aside from involving employees in general district planning, some school officials have found it helpful to involve employees in designing activities for their own positions. This type of planning requires the employees to develop goals, objectives, and activities for their own positions. Once these are developed, the employee meets with his or her administrator and negotiates a final plan, usually for a year. This type of planning requires communications between the employee and administrator in order to agree on a plan and to monitor the progress periodically and gives the employee a chance to have a voice in his or her professional activities.

Improvement Teams and Quality Circles

The quality circles concept was developed in Japan in the 1960s. American corporations became enamored with it and copied it in their quality improvement efforts. With new names such as *quality teams* or *improvement teams*, quality circles have been tailored to focus also on the improvement of the whole system rather than exclusively on one specific area. Although these new-fashioned quality circles continue to emphasize the *achievement* of quality, they now include *maintaining* quality once it's reached. Educators, then, would be wise to examine the original concept as a way to improve not only internal communications but also the instructional and operational processes in the school system.

In the original concept, a quality or improvement circle is composed of 7 to 10 people who do similar work. They meet voluntarily on a regular basis to identify and analyze sources of problems, to recommend solutions to the administration, and, where possible, to implement solutions. Each group has a leader or facilitator to keep the discussion from digressing from the prescribed agenda. The leaders might be educators from outside the district until facilitators can be trained from among administrators and employees within the school district.

Improvement circle meetings have a definite structure to them with an agenda, a conducive meeting place, and limited guidelines for functioning. In many cases the agenda is determined by the circle ahead of time and includes such items as pay, insurance, benefits, personalities, or grievances. Likewise, meetings do not interfere with the negotiation process. Meetings are scheduled for conference rooms with the necessary supplies and equipment to enhance productive discussions and analyses of problems.

The improvement circle process consists of six major steps: problem identification, problem selection, problem analysis, recommended solutions, management review, and recommendations for implementation.

Important in the improvement circle process is the selection of the problems to be addressed. Members develop lists of problems related directly to their jobs that they consider of major importance to carry out their work in an efficient manner. Noncircle members such as other employees and administrators are contacted for problems the circle can discuss. Circle members then compile a list of the problems, put them in some order of priority, and begin to address them.

The circle members are the ones who select the problems to be worked on. No pressure or guidance from outside the circle should be permitted. Once a problem is analyzed and a solution is determined, a formal presentation is made to the appropriate administrator. Acceptance of the recommendation by the administration is a strong motivation for the circle members to address the next problem on their list.

The improvement circle process cultivates better internal communications by meeting the employee's basic need for a feeling of belonging, providing for employee feedback of creative ideas and suggestions, encouraging all employees to focus on the primary purpose of helping students learn better, and establishing an environment of communication between the administration and employees.

Staff Development

The administration of a school district communicates with employees more, perhaps, by actions than by words. What is done often has more of an impact than what is said. Programs established to benefit employees are important in this respect. One that says to employees "You're important" is a staff development program that helps employees improve professionally.

A staff development program provides employees with professional direction, permits them to attend conferences and workshops in their field, reimburses them for courses taken, and provides salary increments for professional development. Such a program not only makes them better employees but also communicates that the district does care about its employees. Ultimately, such efforts with employees should also have a positive effect on the students, parents and others with whom employees interact.

Many districts overlook the support and service employees in a staff development program. Maintenance personnel, custodians, office workers, bus drivers, food-service workers, and other noninstructional employees are motivated to do a better job when provided a formal program to improve their skills and better understand their roles in contributing to school and student success. A staff development program, obviously, will not motivate every employee to improve, but if functioning properly, it will communicate a positive message to all employees that the district wants to help them professionally. Many, if not most, will respond.

Orientation of New Employees

A well-structured orientation program for new employees is essential for developing good staff relations at the outset. Employees new to a school system can fail to become engaged with the organization and co-workers if they are not properly familiarized with the school or are not told what is expected of them. Successful programs have included a meeting with the district's central office personnel to learn about the characteristics of the system and to be informed of the procedures for pay, medical benefits, purchasing, and housing availability in the area. Afterward, new employees meet with the administrators and other employees of their assigned department or building. Often they are assigned a mentor from the current staff to be with them during orientation. Generally, the mentor is from the same department in which the new staff member will be working and therefore can be readily available to help and to answer questions that come up. New employees who are made to feel welcome and are helped in adjusting to their new duties will probably be better employees as well as better ambassadors for the school system.

Internal Publications, Websites, E-Mail, and Social Media

A school district can lose face with its employees when they constantly learn about happenings in the district from an outside source, usually through the news media. Occasionally, this is unavoidable. Nevertheless, the superintendent and his or her administrative staff must be continually sensitive to the need of the employees to be kept informed as soon as possible of activities in the district. Many districts can inform their employees via e-mail and the district's websites and social media accounts.

One very popular type of publication summarizes the actions of the board of education. Many districts attempt to have a brief write-up of board meetings in the hands of the employees prior to public discussion in the local news media. However, in some systems this is impossible since the meeting may be broadcast on TV or radio. Still, there are many details that can be supplied to the employees, such as the appointment of personnel or the letting of bids. The summary can be promptly e-mailed to employees, or inexpensively duplicated or printed internally.

An employee newsletter (either print or online) is another popular medium for communicating with employees. The format of internal publications can range from a formal newsletter with photos to a fact sheet highlighting general activities of the school system. Whether in print or online, these publications are most effective when written in clear, simple language that avoids educational jargon—as many of a school system's employees are noneducators.

Many school systems overlook the importance of distributing publications designed for external audiences to internal audiences as well. Examples include a community newsletter, a pamphlet welcoming new parents, and a calendar of school activities. School employees feel more a part of the educational team if they have access to copies of external publications that the school sends to the community.

Other popular internal publications that can be disseminated online or through printed versions are curriculum newsletters, a personnel publication that notifies employees of vacant positions in the district, a substitute teacher handbook, general information brochures, an internal professional publication that contains articles written by employees, and written summaries of important internal meetings.

COMMUNICATING DURING NEGOTIATIONS AND STRIKES

Unfortunately, the image the public has of a school district when a work action or strike occurs is not a pleasant one. Much of the image has to do with the messages coming from both sides. Many citizens can't understand how "educated" people can adhere to an emotional rhetoric that points an accusing finger at the other side. Nor can they understand why, in the negotiating process, time is wasted by both sides starting from extreme positions, knowing that ultimately both sides will have to compromise with a moderate position. "Why," they ask, "couldn't they start with reasonable demands and positions, cut the rhetoric, reduce the emotionalism, and get the children back to school?"

This public image of schools is unfortunate because this is the very public whose confidence in the schools is needed for continued support. That confidence has not been as high as it should have been in recent years, caused in part by strikes; the long, drawn-out negotiations process; poor communications with the public; and poor internal communications.

Mistakenly, many school systems believe that negotiation procedures are confined to a period of haggling over demands laid on the table by both sides. However, more is involved. It is the overall picture of what takes place throughout the year that has a decisive impact on the negotiating sessions.

It must be emphasized that good employee relations are achieved and less severe bargaining sessions experienced when teachers and noninstructional employees are consulted by the board of education and the administration on questions relating to their welfare and their working conditions. Their recommendations may not always be accepted, but this is less important than the right to make their wants known. School employees are willing to go along with a policy or a program when they understand the facts behind it, even though the policy runs contrary to their opinions.

Many of the demands placed on the bargaining table by employees are concerns that employees may have expressed to the administration, and they were ignored as being insignificant. Take, for example, a request by teachers that a desk and a chair be available in each classroom. This furniture had been missing for some time despite the fact that it was requested for three years in a row. The administration felt it was insignificant, didn't have the money for new furniture, and therefore ignored it. Ultimately, the request for the furniture became a demand at the next collective bargaining session. It didn't have to be, and in addition it made the negotiations on other items more testy because of the lack of trust by the teachers. Through special or general advisory committees, the school administration should be identifying such concerns and meeting them where legitimate. This can reduce the time needed for negotiations.

Experts contend that good communication is the key to keeping the school district together during negotiations and strikes. Bad communication can cause confusion and diminish the school system in the eyes of the public, the media, and the employees. It is vital that all three of these publics be kept informed. Public statements should be objective and be made jointly or by either side. They should outline the issues being covered but not the biased position of each side. The statements should be totally factual, free of emotion, and not slanted to make one side or the other look good or bad.

Important, too, is the need for one spokesperson for each side. For the school district that could be the communication specialist, the chief negotiator, or the president of the board of education. Otherwise, if various members of either side make public statements, confusion and inaccuracies result. Experts believe the superintendent should not be the spokesperson because after negotiations or a strike he or she has to unite the employees and the district to get back to educating children.

Whenever financial figures are presented, particularly in salary increments and percentages of pay increases, they should be given with background information explaining how they were determined. Otherwise both sides may accuse the other side of lying because inaccurate figures are revealed. In reality, often both sides may be accurate, but they are not explaining how they arrived at the final data. For example, the employees may say they are being offered a 6 percent increase, and the school district says the employees are getting a 10 percent increase. They are both correct if they explain how they determined the percentage. The employees are not including a scheduled increment as part of the overall increase and the school district is.

Communication between the school district and its employees is vital during negotiations or a strike. Many districts make weak attempts to communicate internally at such times, feeling the employees' organization or union will provide that service to the employees. School districts must not abdicate this responsibility. Otherwise, the employees may not understand fully the position of the school district on issues.

Not to be overlooked is communication with students, particularly at the secondary level. Some educators feel that it is important to communicate with students once a strike occurs. Perhaps it would be wise to communicate prior to the strike. Any communications should be factual, stating issues and the school district's position. Care should be taken not to portray teachers or any other employees as being at fault in a strike. Otherwise, when the strike is over, student respect for the teachers may be difficult to restore.

The National School Public Relations Association (www.nspra.org) other resources providing detailed advice detailed advice on managing communications during negotiations and strikes.

COMMUNICATING WITH STUDENTS

A universal question asked in many homes each evening across the nation is "What did you learn in school today?" The answer to such a question is important, of course, but perhaps just as important is the emphasis such a question places on the student as a communications link between the school and the home. An impressive number of parents and others in every community form their judgments of a school system from the comments that are made about it by students. They hear the students discuss their teachers, talk about homework assignments, express opinions on the value of what they do in classes, evaluate the fairness of rules and regulations, and describe experiences they had with school staff members.

No school can expect to enjoy the confidence and support of parents unless the comments of most students are favorable to the system. Much may be done in the name of community relations, but what a school system does may be neutralized if the day-to-day relationship with students is unsatisfactory.

The Student as an Individual

All students from kindergarten through grade 12 want their school to care about them. They want their teachers and principal to convey interest in them as individuals. How well the school fosters an "I-care-for-you" feeling with its students will go a long way in helping the individual develop a healthy attitude toward learning and a positive approach when he or she discusses the school in the community.

Often the organizational nature of the school system tends to foster an impersonal relationship between the school and the student. Consider the cool, impersonal nature of a student number, a form letter, a locker number, or an online grade report. Necessary as they may be to the proper functioning of a complex school system, these impersonal relationships cannot stand alone as the only recognition of the student. They tend to reduce all students to a common denominator, whereas the students want to be treated as individuals. Needed, then, are programs and teaching methods that raise the students' self-image and recognize their human dignity.

Respect for Personality

It has long been an accepted belief in a democracy that respect should be shown for the worth and dignity of the individual. Effective teachers subscribe to this belief because they know that it leaves its mark on the behavior of students and satisfies a human need for security. Teachers show this respect by treating serious breaches of conduct in private and by working quietly with pupils who present problems of social adjustment. Honest mistakes made by students are acknowledged pleasantly, and suggestions are offered for overcoming these mistakes in the future.

Allowance is provided in the learning process for individual differences, and tasks are assigned that can be handled successfully. In order to encourage continued work, a wise teacher acknowledges a sincere effort on the part of the students. Such teachers are not hesitant to help students to understand their own weaknesses and natural limitations, but the help is given without undermining self-confidence or injuring the student's status in the group. The common amenities of social life are practiced, and departures from them are not permitted. Students come to feel that they are individuals in their own right and that they are each contributing to the group. Teachers who show respect for personality in these and other ways stimulate better learning and enjoy the cooperation and goodwill of the learners.

Discipline

The handling of discipline plays a major role in establishing satisfactory or unsatisfactory relations with students. Effective teachers regard good discipline as a condition that is essential to good learning. When students become restless, inattentive, or disruptive, teachers examine their own practices to find out if they are responsible before they reprimand the students. Experience has taught them that most students do not become restless and disruptive in the classroom when activities move along at a brisk pace, when they are being challenged, and when learning is made exciting.

Moreover, competent teachers understand the normal behavior of students at different stages of growth and development and make allowance for these in their planning. They are able to prevent situations from arising that would call for disciplinary action. Their knowledge of child growth and development equips them to make distinctions between normal behavior and symptoms of maladjustment and to refer students who show the latter to trained counselors.

Less experienced teachers can make mistakes in disciplinary action, thereby placing a strain on their relations with students. One mistake is that of employing punishment freely for slight infractions of rules or failure to meet achievement standards.

Students want their teachers to be consistent in discipline. They want to know the rules and discuss them for relevancy and purpose. Students don't like teachers to make study a punishment by imposing extra work. Students also don't respect teachers who lose their temper; these teachers then lose their ability to solve discipline problems in a professional way. On the other hand, students respect teachers who admit they are wrong if they have treated a student unjustly.

INSTRUCTIONAL PRACTICES

Relations with students are changed for better or worse by the instructional practices of the teacher. Among the more crucial features are homework assignments, marks and marking systems, examinations, and guidance procedures.

Homework Assignments

Schools have traditionally followed a policy of giving students assignments of homework. A few schools do not believe in homework; nevertheless, there are those who do believe that the assignments are educationally beneficial to pupils. This policy has been generally accepted by young people and their parents.

Continuing support of the homework policy may be damaged by the introduction of such questionable practices as requiring so much homework that time is taken from children for rest and relaxation, allowing assignments to pile up unevenly, engaging children in dull and worthless copy exercises,

failing to explain clearly what is expected, assigning problems that are too difficult for students, and committing the sin of not correcting and returning assignments turned in by students.

School officials should give high priority to establishing a regulation that requires consistency of assignments by all teachers. A student and his or her parents may have difficulty understanding how and why each teacher has a different set of homework rules. Thus, standardized regulations can serve to reduce criticism over the nature and amount of work involved in assignments. If criticism does arise, school officials should check its validity. It may be discovered that teachers are beginning to introduce practices that should be corrected before more serious trouble is encountered.

A parent who takes an interest in homework knows whether or not assignments are worthwhile and reasonable and may feel aggrieved if school officials try to defend poor practices. One solution would be to invite students and parents to meet periodically with faculty members and review the whole question. This is an excellent means of preventing problems and of bringing pupils and parents closer to teachers.

Grades and Grading Systems

Grades and grading systems should be included in any examination of instructional practices because of the effect they have on student attitudes and feelings toward teachers. So much importance is attached to grades in connection with promotion, graduation, and college admission that it is natural for students to be concerned. Because their welfare is tied up in grades and grading systems, students want to know how teachers evaluate tests, written work, and special assignments and whether or not their methods are fair and impartial.

Teachers who establish fine interaction with students take full advantage of this interest. They devote as much time as necessary to the clear enumeration and discussion of factors that enter into the evaluation of tests and work submitted by students and the explanation of how these factors are weighed in arriving at the judgments expressed in terms of percentage or letter grades. Teachers are receptive to suggestions made by students for modifying and improving the grading system, recognizing that students will believe more fully in the fairness of the system if they have had a hand in devising it. These teachers recommend that the whole subject of grading be studied by members of the faculty under the direction of the principal. They are convinced from the remarks students make during their conversations with them that some standardization should prevail among the different teachers in the school. Consistency promotes confidence and faith in the grading system.

Teachers who are concerned about their interactions with students try to eliminate the tension that too great a stress on grades inevitably produces. This can be particularly challenging as online grading portals give instant access to and create an overwhelming focus on grades for both students and parents or guardians. Teachers often do not want grades to be regarded as the end products of learning or the principal cause for motivating achievement. Teachers want students to look on grades and grading systems as convenient and helpful tools for understanding their own strengths and weaknesses and for guiding their efforts toward self-improvement. It has been their experience that student growth and development take place more rapidly when the progress of the learner, rather than the satisfaction of academic standards, is made the point of attention.

Standardized Tests and Examinations

Tests and exams have always been a part of education but the growth of standardized testing has created many new challenges for school communication programs. While standardized tests would seem to offer what many in the community seek—data tracking student performance and teaching effectiveness—such tests often are not readily accepted by the community.

In its report, "Communication Planning and Strategic Tactics for Releasing High-Stakes Test Scores," the National School Public Relations Association acknowledges the role that school communication programs have played in helping communities better understand the purposed of testing programs and the results they produce. The organization urges communication about testing should begin well before it's time to release test scores to help communities

better understand the roles of such tests in helping both schools and communities assess education in the community.[8]

Regular coursework examinations are generally accepted by students as a necessary part of instruction and learning. To them, examinations are a challenge that affords them the opportunity to determine how well they are doing in their classwork and where they need to improve. Seldom do students object to taking examinations that cover material they have studied. Their attitude toward examinations changes when practices are introduced that they think are unfair. Included among these practices are administering examinations for disciplinary purposes, inconsistency among teachers in methods of scoring, test items foreign to the material studied, too much concern for test results instead of their diagnostic value, and criticism for poor outcomes without attempting to discover the causes.

Guidance Procedures

Although the teacher plays a major role in guidance and counseling, the student's attitude toward the school often is affected by the guidance specialist. This member of the educational team must ensure that he or she does not convey the feeling that guidance is inquisitiveness but, rather, a kind of caring about the student. Many times when students feel they can no longer communicate with their teachers, they will expect the guidance counselor to be a good listener and one who can get a message to their teachers on their behalf. If a counselor can maintain a human approach from day to day and can provide a tangible link between the students and their school, he or she can then be of help in addressing many student needs.

Students are quick to detect the overzealousness of some counselors in getting as many students as possible into college. This is particularly true of the student who is not interested in college but rather in career education. Too often entire guidance departments have conveyed a "We-are-only-interested-in-college-bound-students" image. Consequently, many students who are not college-bound can see very little help coming from such counselors. It is incumbent upon guidance departments to extend themselves to the pupils, individually or as a group, rather than to take the position of waiting until students walk into the guidance office. Guidance counselors can project a constructive image through orientation programs with entering students and through planned programs of meeting all students in small, informal discussion groups. Counselors can also improve their image by clarifying their role with the instructional staff and by placing equal emphasis on career and college education.

RELATIONS OUTSIDE THE CLASSROOM

Students have numerous contacts with instructional and noninstructional personnel outside the classroom. These points of contact should be considered as a means of increasing friendliness and cooperation between students and members of the staff.

Library

The library is one point of contact where students form definite opinions of schools. The nature of their opinions varies with the personality of the individual in charge and the services they receive. A librarian who greets pupils with a smile, chats cheerfully, and tries to understand their needs sets an entirely different tone from one who gives short answers, shows impatience, and demands observance of minor regulations. In some schools, the library is associated with the instructional media or instructional resource center in which a number of learning devices and resources are housed. This arrangement increases student—librarian contacts and makes the librarian's role even more important.

Medical Centers

The protection of a child's health is now an established part of the school program. School board policies and state laws require that students be examined periodically by physicians, nurses, dentists, and other specialists and that they receive first-aid treatment and care for sudden illness.

How medical personnel handle their contacts with students and parents is important in building good community relations. Nothing wins praise more

quickly than the tactful and efficient administration of medical services and a high degree of personal interest in children needing corrective and remedial attention. Unless medical personnel are sensitive to their legal parameters and their community relations opportunities, they may handle child and parent contacts poorly.

School Office

It is surprising how many times in a school year students have occasion to visit the school office. Every time they enter the office they have contact with staff members. If they receive courteous treatment and their business is handled efficiently, the office ranks high in their estimation. However, if the students feel, for instance, that secretaries think of themselves as assistant principals, they do not welcome students, or they make them wait unnecessarily to see the principal, pupils' feelings about the office staff weaken good internal communications.

Cafeteria

School cafeterias exist for the benefit of students and the convenience of staff members, not for the accumulation of profits. In this respect, they may be thought of as service agencies having the function of preparing and distributing wholesome meals. The extent to which they fulfill this function determines how they are appraised by students. Perhaps no other agency outside the classroom undergoes a more careful scrutiny than does the food-service and nutrition program.

It would be beneficial to all concerned if the director of food services made efforts to communicate with the students, discussing the various aspects of food preparation and explaining why certain food can or cannot be served. Often, in establishing communications with students the food-service director will uncover helpful suggestions for improving the food service.

Physical Plant

Relations between students and custodial personnel who are responsible for the physical conditions of the building and grounds should be examined. Although these men and women who perform cleaning and maintenance services have no direct jurisdiction over students, they sometimes assume this authority and treat students who disobey their orders with shouts, abusive language, and even rough handling. Resentment against abusive treatment may be expressed by marking walls, plugging lavatory facilities, and scattering paper on floors. This condition is disruptive of the unity sought in a school and should be prevented.

The possibilities for conflict between students and custodial personnel can be reduced and usually eliminated if thought is given to the problem. The solution should start with the employment of individuals who have social intelligence. The limits of their authority should be defined clearly and procedures outlined for reporting students who violate regulations. Such personnel should be made to feel a responsibility for the success of the school and should realize it is their job to earn the goodwill and respect of students.

Transportation

In school districts that have their own transportation fleet, the bus drivers are in a unique position to influence students' thinking. Students do not regard bus drivers in quite the same way as they do other members of the staff, and they talk freely in the driver's presence about their teachers and the school. In the course of a year, a driver can learn a great deal about the school and how students appraise it. Competent bus drivers who regard themselves as members of the staff can be exceedingly helpful in correcting students' false statements and explaining reasons for policies and practices students do not like. Drivers are in a special position to listen to their complaints, discuss their problems, and bring out facts students might not consider. Drivers' services in interpreting the school to students and reporting their attitudes to the principal can be invaluable.

STUDENTS AND INTERNAL COMMUNITY RELATIONS

The school itself consists of many internal publics, and the students constitute the most important internal group. As such, students should be given a chance to become involved in the entire internal educational community by making suggestions and participating in school planning. This is particularly true in the secondary school, where students want to be considered as contributing members of the school family.

Until recently educators traditionally used a one-way method of communicating with the students, either from the principal to the student or from the teacher to the student. Announcements were made over the loudspeaker in homerooms, at assembly programs, by written memo, or in the classroom through lectures. The students were to be "seen and not heard." They were talked "to" and not "with," for in the judgment of many educators they had very little to offer by way of suggestions about their school programs or their school life. Out of such an environment student activism emerged, and the traditional method of communicating with students was revealed as lacking effectiveness. In fact, this one-way method contributed greatly to the rise of student militancy, since students were neither kept informed nor given answers to legitimate questions, and they were also denied an opportunity to contribute ideas to the school.

One of the most effective methods of communicating with students, particularly at the junior and senior high-school levels, is a two-way structure enabling them to express opinions, make suggestions, and offer constructive criticism on various aspects of school. At the same time, they learn more about school policies and procedures, staff duties, and responsibilities. Such two-way communications can be accomplished through student advisory committees, student opinion surveys, student town meetings, and ombudspersons.

Student Advisory Committees

Some schools have developed excellent programs of two-way communications with students at the secondary level by restructuring the student council and perhaps even changing and formalizing its name—for example, Student Advisory Group or Student Advisory Committee. Successful administrators will see to it that all students are eligible for election to the group regardless of grades or discipline problems. Good administrators know that they must structure some type of student advisory group to hear the voices of all students. Here is where the democratic system must work at its best. The principal meets with the students periodically, listens to their suggestions, and grants their wishes when common sense dictates that they should be granted. He or she always explains the reasons for decisions. These committees become a two-way communications process whereby student leaders come to understand the problems of the principal, and the principal comes closer to the student body.

The student advisory committee does have many good ideas and is often helpful to the principal in a time of crisis. Its members can squelch rumors among its constituency and in turn reduce inflammatory rumors in the community. The key to success for this type of communication is the credibility of the principal, who naturally must "tell it like it is" and be truthful with the students.

Student Opinion Surveys

Student advisory committees do provide some amount of feedback from the students. However, a sound internal community relations program also calls for direct information from the students concerning their feelings about the school. One of the most common ways of getting this direct feedback is through a survey or questionnaire.

Some schools have developed a functional student opinion survey for high school students. It asks student opinions about report card grades, class procedures, extracurricular activities, changes in school plant and procedures, courses, weaknesses, rules and regulations, student government, counseling, teacher attitude, and study halls, among other topics.

When students participate in such a survey, they assume that the results will be shared with them or some action will be taken by the school to implement suggestions. If the survey is filed away and nothing is done with the information, the school's credibility with students is weakened. A major consideration, therefore, in planning a student survey is the disposition of the findings. Prior to administering the survey, students should be informed that a summary of the results will be shared with them, and valid suggestions will be implemented.

Student Town Meetings

Student town meetings can be in the form of a student assembly in which all students have an opportunity to participate. Such assemblies are similar to the traditional assembly programs except that there is no performer or guest speaker or musical program. Instead, it is the students' town meeting, in which teachers and administrators ask for student thoughts, criticisms, and ideas. Some meetings are held after school hours for the entire student body, or they can be held during school hours in small groups on the grade level or in each classroom.

Ombudspersons

The concept of the ombudsperson has merit in a school if an administrator is committed to developing feedback from students about the school procedures, staff, programs, or facilities. Students can confide in the ombudsperson without fear of retaliation. Often students are reluctant to talk to teachers or counselors for fear they will be reported to the principal or other school officials. The ombudsperson then becomes a communicator, facilitating the circular flow of information between school officials and students. Whoever fills this position must gain the confidence of students to make the system function.

STUDENT UNREST

When student activism erupts into unrest or violence, unfavorable publicity generally results for the school. Citizens begin pointing an accusing finger at the local educational system or begin classifying all students as an unappreciative new generation. When student unrest has reached the point of actual violence, it is usually too late to resolve the crisis immediately. Instead, school officials have to weather the situation until emotions become less charged.

Why Students Rebel

Frustration is the primary reason for most student unhappiness and unrest. Although frustration is part of life and cannot be eliminated entirely, it should be avoided when it has the potential to pierce the very heart of a student's self-esteem and personal dignity. Many times teachers and administrators nurture frustration by showing a lack of understanding or respect for the students as individuals; by applying rigid rules without considering circumstances; by not providing an opportunity for every child to experience success in the classroom; by not permitting students to be heard; by overburdening students with demands beyond their ability; by not providing good channels of communication with school officials and with other student groups; or by not seeking student input at various decision-making levels of the school system, particularly in junior and senior high schools.

Students are looking for well-defined channels in a school through which their influences can be felt. When there are no such channels or when these are not clearly defined, frustration often sets in, and a protest is not uncommon. The students' protest is an attempt to prove their importance and to say that they want to participate. They want to be heard and to present their ideas and suggestions. If students are given an opportunity to be heard and to be involved and if the school officials and the staff can convey the idea that they do care about the students, unrest and destructive activism can be minimized.

Channels of Influence

Much of what has been presented in this chapter has been addressed to the idea of providing channels of influence for students. Many of the ideas presented, if implemented, could alleviate or prevent student unrest. However, three additional areas are relevant: diversity committees, student involvement in the community, and student communications. These are all helpful in minimizing student unrest.

DIVERSITY COMMITTEES

Poor communication among students themselves, ironically, can be a source of student unrest. This can surface as racial or ethnic conflict or conflict between cliques or "in" groups and "out" groups. Much of the conflict spills into the school from society itself, where ethnic groups have drawn battle lines for years. All students want to be recognized by school officials and by other students. They want to be recognized for what they are, their customs, their ethnic backgrounds, and their culture. As long as student groups within a school cannot relate these cultural and ethnic characteristics to one another or do not have an opportunity to learn about another ethnic group, the chances are great for misunderstanding and for rumors to develop and fester.

When potentially abrasive situations are possible among diverse groups in a school system, ample time during the day should be provided for students to come together in a meaningful way for solving their problems. A diversity subcommittee of the student government can often serve as a functional group to provide constructive dialogue between two factions and to serve as a logical vehicle to develop meaningful understanding of different customs and cultures. Often these diversity or human relations committees with representatives from each class and each diverse group can identify racial problems, suggest solutions, hold forums for all responsible opinions, advise curriculum committees on including the history of various ethnic groups, advise school officials on racial matters, and hold discussion sessions between diverse groups so that each comes to understand the other better.

In its publication, *Diversity Communications Toolkit*, the National School Public Relations Association notes:

> The issue of diversity engagement is not some other school district's issue. Large or small; urban, suburban or rural; with or without a public relations staff or plan, the issues of diversity engagement are present in every school district in America.
>
> The challenges that school districts face can surface in any area where students and families are different from the dominant culture: based on disability, sexual orientation, gender, religion, nationality, language, race or ethnicity and many other differences.
>
> Because of these differences, traditional public relations (PR) approaches may not be most effective.
>
> As an example, any research conducted to develop communications strategies should be adjusted to fit the best communication methods for each community.[9]

STUDENT INVOLVEMENT IN THE COMMUNITY

In many schools, students' thirst for action goes beyond the talking and listening stages, particularly when the issues are social and political injustices in society. Students' concern for their fellow humans often takes the form of direct action to alleviate human suffering in the areas of poverty, ignorance, hunger, pollution, housing, or health. They become frustrated when action is not taken; consequently, they may become restless and strike out at the academic establishment because they cannot gain a sense of satisfaction by working for their ideals.

Student interest in solving political and social problems can be a positive force, especially in secondary school. Authorities on student activism claim that one of the best ways of meeting students' thirst for action is for the school to offer meaningful and worthwhile activities for community involvement and service. Such activities can include many school-coordinated community service programs, such as fund-raising campaigns for less fortunate citizens, suggested proposals to eliminate pollution and to protect the environment, tutoring programs for migrant workers' children, work in hospitals and nursing homes, public opinion surveying, recreation programs in housing projects, voluntary work with welfare agencies, and other activities that show a concern for human welfare and justice.

Not only do community activities channel student unrest toward constructive outlets, but such activities also relate the students' education more directly to social and political problems of concern to them. Furthermore, student concern and involvement in the community often help improve communication among students, between students and teachers and administrators, and between the school and the community. Not to be overlooked is the amount of goodwill generated by such community service. The aid of faculty members and community advisers is often needed to coordinate student involvement in the community.

In addition, when the classroom is extended beyond the walls of the building, the community becomes a laboratory for learning. Students have an opportunity to brush against reality, develop further sensitivities to social needs and problems, and acquire a deeper sense of civic responsibility. The community by-products of students' study and involvement in the community are increased public confidence in the abilities of these young people, a better understanding of the educational program, and a willingness to support the school system more generously.

STUDENT COMMUNICATIONS

Schools have learned that students will make their views known even when the school officials haven't asked for them. If students are not given an opportunity to express themselves in a school paper, particularly in secondary schools, they will often resort to an underground press and social media. Such activities have been nightmares for those administrators who have not provided students with a channel for self-expression. The delicate task of school officials in this matter lies somewhere between permitting absolute freedom of expression and a totally censored publication that does not represent student thinking. A middle road is needed, giving expression to students' ideas but in words that are acceptable to the community.

Some school systems have established a school communications committee that is helpful in setting guidelines of responsible communication and in developing a relevant learning experience for students in school publications and other communication activities. The committee is made up of students, faculty members, parents, and citizens from the community, some of whom may be members of the local media or adults with experience in journalism and communication. Such a committee can be helpful as an advisory group to the principal or to a school board if necessary. With the presence of students and laypersons on the committee, dissident students are more apt to accept the committee's recommendations and suggestions as not coming directly from the principal. Such a committee will eliminate the feeling on the part of students that all school communications are under the thumb of the school administration or faculty adviser.

One Expert's Point of View:
Understanding Internal Audiences

Sandy Cokeley, APR, is CEO of SCoPE School surveys (www.scopeschoolsurveys.com) and an experienced school public relations practitioner, counselor, and planner with a background in both private- and public-sector communications programming. As Director of Quality and Community Relations for the Pearl River (NY) School District, she worked with the district's leadership team on communication and continuous improvement efforts that led the district to be named one of the first Malcolm Baldrige National Quality Award recipients. Cokeley is co-author of the book "Malcolm and Me: How to Use the Baldrige Process to Improve Your School" and a contributor to the book "School Public Relations: Building Confidence in Education." She is past president of both the New York State and the National School Public Relations Associations (NSPRA).

It's often argued that research shows that engaged communities lead to greater student achievement and success. If this is the case, why should we focus our limited resources on internal audiences when it seems that external constituencies matter more?

While the research supports the link between engaged families and student success, this does not mean districts ignore internal communications. The responsibility for effectively communicating with and engaging parents, families and community members does not reside solely in the district's public relations office or the leadership suite. Each and every member of the district staff plays a part in how they interact with all stakeholders.

External audiences look to faculty and staff they interact with regularly for information and opinions. There are times when teachers, bus drivers or other employees who work with parents and others regularly will have far more influence than the superintendent, board president, or other school leaders.

More important is the connection between internal communication and employee engagement. Research also tells us that engaged employees perform at higher levels and are less likely to seek different employment. Having stable, informed, and engaged staff who feel valued are the big end-game goals for internal communications. The bottom line: effective internal communication supports student achievement through meaningful employee relations and the exponential strong relationships it builds with all stakeholders.

Teachers and other employees have a job to do. They're busy and they may see public relations needs as beyond the scope of what their jobs are. How can the school system and the communications program help teachers and others better understand and fulfill their communications roles?

There is no question that part of any comprehensive communication effort needs to focus on helping internal audiences build the understanding and skills they need to excel in communications in their work. In fact, when properly supported in these roles, teachers and others often report their job performance improves and becomes less stressful as they are able to address specific needs, concerns, and controversies with proven communication tactics that work.

No two districts will have the same internal audiences and communication needs. While the specific strategies and tactics districts deploy will vary, essential to the program is supporting the expectation that all employees are responsible for communication through district policy and making that expectation clear from their first day of employment with the district.

What role does the district's leadership play in building internal communication relationships and expectations for communication success districtwide?

In much the same way that outside audiences may look to your employees for insights and information on your schools, employees will look to and watch school leaders for insights and information on communication expectations and behaviors. Open, honest, and transparent communication and action by district leaders, including meaningful two-way communications with faculty and staff, will set a standard that others in the organization will follow. On the other hand, perceptions of disregard, secrecy, or duplicity in communication will impact morale, employee behavior, and ultimately the district's image and brand.

Expectations for ethical decision-making or instructional excellence are set at the top. Expectations for communication excellence, respectful interactions, and productive relationship-building are set at the top as well. Just as teachers and front-line staff need support in understanding and fulfilling their communications roles, the senior leadership team also needs counsel and support from the communication leader on their invaluable roles in contributing to school—communication success.[10]

Questions

1. The top administrator in your school district, speaking to principals, states, "Just remember that teachers and other employees care about two things: their salaries and benefits." If you were secure in your position, what would you counsel this administrator privately about this statement? What suggestions would you make to the administrator regarding sharing information about what employees want on the job?

2. You've just been named public relations director for a fairly large school district. You have discovered that the 2,000-student high school is fraught with a lack of staff morale. What would you do to try to improve staff morale?

3. The difference between one school district and another in terms of quality is frequently the number and quality of ideas being generated by employees. What three techniques would you share to encourage employees to suggest ideas that would improve the schools?

4. List some of the reasons why school communicators might want to focus less on traditional public relations approaches for diverse audiences and perhaps more on developing communication strategies designed to fit the best communication methods for each community.

5. Why is it important that support staff (secretaries, custodians, bus drivers, etc.) know their roles in the public relations process overall and their interactions with students in particular? How can these internal audiences influence a school system's external public relations efforts?

Readings

Bagin, Don, and Anthony Fulginiti, *Practical Relations Theories and Practices That Make a Difference.* Dubuque, IA: Kendall Hunt, 2006.

Belilos, Claire, *Understanding Employee Drives and Motivation—The First Step towards Motivation at Work.* Vancouver, BC: CHIC Hospitality Consulting Services, 2003. www.easytraining.com/motivation.htm.

Broom, Glen M., and Bey-Ling Sha, *Effective Public Relations,* 11th ed. Upper Saddle River, NJ: Prentice Hall, 2012.

Hughes, Larry W., and Don W. Hooper, *Public Relations for School Leaders.* Boston, MA: Pearson, 2000.

National School Public Relations Association, *School Public Relations,* 2nd ed. Rockville, MD: Author, 2007.

National School Puwblic Relations Association, *Diversity Communications Toolkit.* Rockville, MD: Author, 2013.

National School Public Relations Association, *Communication Planning and Strategic Tactics for Releasing High-Stakes Test Scores.* Rockville, MD: Author, 2016.

Weaver, Richard L., II, and Saundra Hybels, *Communicating Effectively,* 11th ed. New York, NY: McGraw-Hill, 2014.

Wilcox, Dennis L., and Glen T. Cameron, *Public Relations Strategies and Tactics,* 11th ed. Boston, MA: Pearson, 2014.

Videos

Frederick County (VA) Public Schools: Convocation Program – Bus Karaoke
https://youtu.be/eJrOer3AH68

Granite (UT) Schools: New School Year
https://youtu.be/xAkl7yUCvC0

Plano (TX) ISD: Bond Election: Overview Video
https://youtu.be/kwMOd0qX8-s

Clarksville-Montgomery County (TN) School System: Welcome back CMCSS students and staff!
https://youtu.be/M9y7jd_ZCTI

Clarksville-Montgomery County (TN) School System: Because of You
https://youtu.be/A4fq1b9RVrI

Atlanta Speech School: Communicating with Students
https://youtu.be/VxyxywShewI

Endnotes

1. Thomas J. Sergiovanni, Paul Kelleher, Martha M. McCarthy, and Frederick M. Wirt, *Educational Governance and Administration*, 5th ed. (Boston, MA: Allyn & Bacon, 2004), p. 71.

2. Ibid.

3. NetMBA Business Knowledge Center, "Herzberg's Motivation-Hygiene Theory (Two Factor Theory)." Retrieved September 1, 2014, from http://www.net-mba.com/mgmt/ob/motivation/herzberg.

4. Thomas J. Sergiovanni and Fred O. Carver, *The New School Executive, A Theory of Administration*, 2nd ed. (New York, NY: Harper and Row, 1980), p. 104. Also see Thomas J. Sergiovanni, *The Principalship, A Reflective Practice Perspective*, 2nd ed. (Boston, MA: Allyn & Bacon, 1991), pp. 242–243; and Thomas J. Sergiovanni, *Moral Leadership: Getting to the Heart of School Improvement* (San Francisco: Jossey-Bass, 1992), pp. 59–60.

5. Taken from Susan M. Heathfield, "What People Want from Work: Motivation." Retrieved September 2, 2014, from http://humanresources.about.com/od/rewardrecognition/a/needs_work.htm.

6. David Sirota, Louis A. Mischkind, and Michael Irwin Meltzer, *The Enthusiastic Employee* (Philadelphia, PA: Wharton School Publishing, 2005).

7. Pat Jackson, *pr reporter*, vol. 39, no. 20 (May 13, 1996), p. 1.

8. National School Public Relations Association, *Communication Planning and Strategic Tactics for Releasing High-Stakes Test Scores* (Rockville, MD: Author, 2016), p. 14.

9. Reprinted with permission from National School Public Relations Association, *Diversity Communications Toolkit* (Rockville, MD: Author, 2013), p. 5.

10. Adapted from correspondence October 26, 2017 with Sandy Cokeley, CEO, SCOPE School Surveys (www.scopeschoolsurveys.com). Used with permission.

8

Communicating with External Publics

This chapter reviews issues . . .

- For central administrators: The key external audiences essential to building understanding and support through comprehensive school and community relations programming.
- For building and program administrators: The roles that building and program leaders should fulfill when assessing the needs of and working with key community constituencies.
- For teachers, counselors and staff: How parents and other external audiences prefer to communicate and how strong communication can build the kind of meaningful interactions that support student success.

After completing this chapter you should be able to . . .

- Identify roles external communication plays in successful school–community relations programs.
- Identify key external audiences and distinguish how each contributes to school–community relations efforts.
- List specific tactics deployed in external communication programming.
- Define a key communicators program, and identify the steps in developing a key communicators program.

The discussion of school communication with external audiences should begin with an assessment of communication and relationships with internal audiences. Simply put, a school system cannot expect to enjoy external public relations success unless it enjoys strong relationships with its internal audiences. Teachers and students are powerful, credible communicators throughout the community on school issues, and if they are expressing support and enthusiasm for schools their words will be influential in reinforcing a school system's communication initiatives. If, however, these internal audiences are expressing doubt or derision about school issues then their words will forcefully undercut the school's formal communication efforts.

It's also important to consider the effects that online and social media have had on current-day school communication efforts. Such media have, in one respect, made it easier and less expensive for schools to rapidly communicate with external audiences. Maintaining social media accounts and updating websites, for example, can be far less expensive and certainly timelier in reaching audiences than more traditional methods such as publishing school newsletters or generating news stories through local newspapers and broadcast media. But newer trends in media have also changed audience expectations about school information and communication. Increasingly audience members expect to have information available on demand and may view the lack of available information as a reason to be suspicious of school motives or question leadership's competence on important issues.

Communication technology has been rapidly adopted and now is routinely used by most audiences both in the community and in schools. And schools that fail to use communication technology successfully risk damaging the effectiveness and efficiency of school communications and losing the confidence of those in the community.

In its "Rubrics of Practice and Suggested Measures" the National School Public Relations Association argues that external communication efforts should be research-based with "communication effectiveness embedded across district and building operations." Typical outcomes include multiple and varied communication strategies that use a host of tactics and media to reach targeted audiences.[1]

The school research organization SCoPE (School Communication Performance Evaluation) School Surveys (www.scopeschoolsurveys.com) uses surveys and detailed analyses to help schools plan and then evaluate communication efforts among three key overall internal and external audiences:

– Faculty and Staff
– Parents and Families
– Community.[2]

Sandy Cokeley, CEO of SCoPE School Surveys writes, "As professional communicators, the majority of us are most comfortable in the C-Communications phase of the RACE (Research – Analyze and Plan – Communicate – Evaluate) Model. C-Communicate is where we get to do all of the fun stuff like grabby tweets, inspiring videos, and cool logos. Our sad reality, though, is that if we don't do E-Evaluate, we cannot be certain that they worked.

"As important as E-Evaluate is, many of us avoid it or give it glancing attention at best. While our reasons vary, one many of us fall prey to is not knowing how to set realistic targets. We get confused between measuring the success of the program or the tool, i.e., how many "likes" for the post, versus what the program or tool was supposed to accomplish – did it change knowledge levels, attitudes, or behaviors.

"Determining if it changed knowledge levels, attitudes or behaviors requires us knowing what those levels were before we implemented our plan. In the world of performance management, we call this baseline data. Our starting point, our baseline, is considered part of our R-Research step: where our audiences are now versus where we would like them to be."[3]

EXTERNAL AUDIENCES

Initial planning research is key to identifying, segmenting, and understanding important external audiences that school communications should address. This research also is key to help communication planners determine each audience's specific information needs, which media would be most effective in reaching these audiences and what specific messages would be successful in getting their attention and prompting action.

Typical external audiences identified in planning research might include parents, taxpayers, service and civic organizations, key communicators, and news media.

Parents

The bottom line for any school–community relations program is to help students succeed, and students have a better chance to succeed when parents are involved in the schools.

The National School Public Relations Association cites research it has collected and reviewed to conclude that "The research clearly underscores one straightforward concept: Students simply do better when parents and the community are involved with schools." The group notes evidence showing higher test scores, lower remediation rates, and higher graduation rates when parents and the community engage with schools.[4] Consequently, a school–community relations program should incorporate the concept of a partnership between the school and the parents.

The school-parent relationship is built upon ongoing and open communication, including the free and continual exchange of information between parents and teachers and the involvement of parents in school affairs. This two-way exchange of information enables teachers to acquire a knowledge about their students that they otherwise might not have. Teachers engaged with parents can gain a better understanding of challenges facing parents, experiences influencing children, and situations that have been determinants of their behavior. They learn how parents think and act, what their attitudes are toward life, and what they want for their children. With a working teacher–parent relationship and clear communication, teachers can better understand students and be able to specifically consider and address student needs affecting instruction and learning.

Parents also acquire valuable information from their contacts with teachers—information that is useful with their children at home. Some parents may know relatively little about their children's school experiences and what teachers must contend with in directing their growth. Parents are able to better understand their children's needs from analyses of test results, school records, behavior reports, classwork and homework. These insights can help to support productive conversations between teachers and parents on how much progress their children have made and how much more they could make with support at home. Parents can reach agreements with teachers on plans for attaining common objectives.

Of course, a successful partnership between teachers and students involves more than exchanging information with parents and acquainting them with the school. It includes cooperative work on problems that affect children and advance the cause of education. Nothing else produces in parents a better understanding of the school and a deeper sense of responsibility for its progress.

Despite such beneficial outcomes, some administrators and teachers may oppose the parents-as-partners concept. They may fear that parent participation may lead to serious interference with their rights and duties. Or, they may not believe that parents are qualified to decide what education is best for children or to discuss technical matters of curriculum building and instructional procedures.

But teachers must recognize that parents are well qualified to make contributions for the advancement of education. Parents can productively discuss the purpose of education and many of the specific outcomes they would like for their children. In addition, knowledge in specialized areas possessed by many parents makes them valuable resource persons for committees engaged in ways to help foster school success. Parents can offer talents and experiences that can be drawn upon for the enrichment of curricular and cocurricular activities. Many parents are highly competent in problem-solving procedures and the formulation of policies that reflect the wishes of the people. They can be of enormous value in helping to chart the course of education while leaving the technical details to professionally trained educators.

Also, parents—perhaps like no other group of citizens in the community—exert a strong influence on public opinion, and only through a broad sense of favorable opinion can the school expect to make significant progress.

SPECIAL ROLES OF PARENTS

Clearly, parents should not be seen as a single audience and research can help school communication planners identify segments of the parent audience that might require special planning to meet any unique information needs or communication preferences. Such segments might, for example, include parents of:

- pre-K students
- elementary-school students
- middle-school students
- high-school students
- students with special needs
- students from out-of-district communities

- students attending vocational or other program outside of the district
- students from families with specific language or other communication needs.

School-communication efforts must also recognize audiences beyond parents, especially considering that in most communities the majority of households in the community do not have students in school. The trend of increasing numbers of households with no children living at home has been significant. According to the U.S. Census Bureau, between 1970 and 2012, the share of households that were married couples with children under 18 dropped from 40 percent to 20 percent.[5]

BUILDING RELATIONSHIPS

Initiating closer contacts with parents begins the process of building working relationships between schools in general and teachers in particular. This often involves addressing the question of what activities are most appropriate to interest parents in engaging with school faculty, administrators, other staff, and other parents. There are numerous ways of starting a school–community relations program that will appeal to parents—a program that will bring parents into the school, so they will become acquainted with teachers and staff and meet other parents. Such efforts will help parents learn more about the school and its services and to take a direct interest in various phases of instruction.

Identifying parent representatives for each grade level is one common means for accomplishing this purpose. Either the principal appoints the parents, or they elect their own representatives in each grade to promote good relations with teachers. Periodic meetings are held to discuss school issues and practices. A typical meeting agenda might, for example, call for a consideration of students' difficulties in a subject area, and include questions concerning social development, personal habits, or health concerns. Parents decide on the discussion topics in consultation with teachers and the principal and should include items of concern to both parties. Handled skillfully, such a program can be highly effective in bringing together parents and teachers each year.

Another system, the invitational visitation technique, is a practice that provides a venue for introducing school and parents to one another in a productive environment. Generally, a certain number of parents, usually five or six, are invited by the principal to spend time visiting classes, having lunch, and observing student activities in the school. The principal may select parents at random, have parent–teacher associations and community-interest groups name some, and draw other names from a preferred list. A new group of parents is brought in each week for as many weeks as the principal and teachers decide is effective. These visitors are given a copy of an evaluation sheet and asked to use it for guiding and grading their observations. The evaluation contains questions about, for example, what parents think of the way discipline is handled, whether or not they would change the methods of teaching, and how valuable they consider the learning activities to be. Each of these questions is discussed in conference with the principal and one or two teachers at the close of the visitation. The conference provides an excellent opportunity to clarify observations and to further interpret the work of the school. In addition, recaps of the visits (including photos or video) can be included on the school's website or covered in school online or print newsletters. Such extensions can help to spread information about the visits to other interested parents and staff.

A variation on this technique is that of convening committees of parents, from time to time, to meet with the principal and gather and discuss feedback about the school. The danger inherent in this approach is that the negative side may be overemphasized at the expense of practices deserving commendation. The technique has some merit when parents are asked what they like most about the school and how they think the school could be improved. Concern with improvement is a constructive lead that directs thinking to problems needing solution and offers opportunities for involving and sharing responsibility with parents. Often principals can get constructive leads for improvement by inviting six or eight citizens to lunch or inviting businesspeople to breakfast.

Most parents respond favorably to personal invitations from teachers and students asking them to attend some school event. The event may be a room exhibit where they can see their own children's work, a classroom play, an open-house program, a special lecture, a luncheon prepared by students, or a discussion on school parties.

The use of checklists has also proved helpful in bringing about closer cooperation between parents and teachers. One type of checklist that deserves attention covers the joint responsibilities of home and school. Statements are set forth describing what both the school and the home can do to further the growth and development of students. Parents are asked to check those items that apply to their own practices as well as to the school practices and to confer with teachers on the results. This sort of instrument suggests possibilities that parents may never have realized before and lets them know that the school wants to work cooperatively. Another type of checklist represents an inventory of contributions parents can make to the educational program. They are invited to check those items they are willing to contribute, such as speaking to a class about a trip to a foreign country; explaining their occupation; demonstrating a hobby; lending books, pictures, and objects to the school; or serving as volunteers on student field trips. The information compiled from these checklists enables teachers to enrich the learning process and to involve parents voluntarily in the actual work of the school.

Another good suggestion is for the principal to write the parents of new students in junior and senior high school, inviting them to visit the school at any time and to confer freely with teachers. A similar effort can be made in the elementary schools by brief, friendly phone calls from teachers to parents of new children in their classrooms. Letters sent to parents of secondary-school students are sometimes accompanied by a bulletin or handbook containing information parents want, for example, on grades, attendance, homework, health requirements, college entrance requirements, food services, extracurricular activities, and expenses.

Many other means to promote closer cooperation with parents have been used successfully. The following are some examples:

- Hosting teas or coffee klatches for parents of preschool children
- Having night sessions so that parents may attend classes
- Opening the gymnasium and other school facilities to the parents for recreational purposes

- Sponsoring online meetings or bagged lunch events where parents can chat with the principals, teachers, or specialists on topics of interest
- Offering a monitored online or email feedback service where parents can ask questions or raise concerns and get a quick reply
- Having a telephone tended in the evening for questions from parents or citizens
- Inviting parents to observe their children in activities related to classwork
- Arranging meetings in the school library for advising parents on books they may wish to purchase for their children
- Asking parents to help with seasonal celebrations or similar events for elementary-school students.

BACK-TO-SCHOOL VISITS AND CONFERENCES

Schools move closer to a realization of partnership when they adopt policies providing for parent visits and conferences with teachers as a regular part of the educational program. Such policies establish friendly relations, minimize misunderstanding, and promote lay–professional cooperation.

The initial problem of motivating parents to visit the school can be addressed rather easily when the program is thoroughly publicized and reinforced and promoted as a critical way that parents can contribute to student success. It's also important that the school take the initiative in arranging the visits. Parents are often reluctant to take it upon themselves to contact the school and ask if they may visit the classrooms. Once parents learn of the visitation policy through the mass media and from parents who have visited the school, their reluctance and shyness give way to natural curiosity. They are interested in seeing how their children behave in the classroom, what the teachers are like and how they handle their students, whether methods of teaching are much different than when they were in school, and how their own youngsters compare with others of similar age.

A welcoming visitation policy can also be extremely helpful in establishing a liaison with not only parents but others in the community who do not currently have students in the school. These individuals might include parents of private and parochial school students, parents of preschoolers, or parents considering moving into the district's community. It also might attract interest from nonparents looking for ways in which they can support the schools, or those simply looking to learn more about the school and its services.

Planned parent conferences traditionally have been a valuable method of clearing up sources of misunderstanding and of interpreting the instructional programs. Such conferences continue as an accepted and important practice in many school systems. In some instances, regular conferences supplement or have even replaced the report card. Teachers discuss the student's progress in more detail and respond to parental concerns directly. Parents are able to get a more complete picture of their child's progress, including a review of his or her grades, test scores, interest inventories, participation in extracurricular activities, and anecdotal records. In addition, the teacher can share with the parents his or her observations of the student's work habits, behavior, attitude toward learning, and relations with others.

Annual back-to-school type programs and visits are another important way for the principal, teachers, and other school staff to showcase school achievements, activities, and programs while getting to meet parents in a collegial setting. It's important that such programs be carefully planned so as to not overload visiting parents with too much information, and to allow time for parents to react to information and raise questions to help better understand information that is being shared.

Any program that brings parents and school staff together requires careful planning and support for the communication demands such activities will place on teachers. Some teachers may benefit from training on how to communicate effectively and how to communicate in difficult or stressed situations. Even the best teacher may be challenged in tense situations, and it is not uncommon for a parent to become emotional or even aggressive when expressing what may be unreasonable opinions about a school or teacher. In such cases, a teacher needs to be confident in his or her abilities and options to listen actively and respond in ways that will address the person's real concerns while not escalating an already difficult situation.

Good conference procedure depends on the teachers who are well prepared to listen attentively

and understandingly; to sift facts; to determine the nature and limits of any conflict; to correct misunderstandings without engaging in arguments; to use simple language free from ambiguity, jargon, and emotional coloration; to seek other support when needed; and to present clear issues to which thought should be directed. Conferences should end on a constructive note and culminate, if possible, in a mutual plan of action on behalf of the students. A record should be made of each conference and filed for future reference.

COMMUNICATION MATERIALS

The most common type of printed material for communicating regularly with parents is the report card. While online grade portals now offer students and parents regular updates on student progress, the traditional grade report, issued several times a year, continues to be an important platform to inform parents about how their children stand in subject achievement.

Another means of written communication used by many schools is the monthly or quarterly newsletter or bulletin, emailed or mailed to parents and to citizens of the community or sent home with students. The purpose of this publication is to keep parents and citizens informed on such features as instructional practices, outstanding professional activities, lunch menus, fiscal matters, and special problems facing the school system.

Increasingly, school systems issue annual publications, such as handbooks and calendars, for parents to provide a ready reference for answering questions that are commonly asked. Opening usually with a friendly foreword by the superintendent explaining the purposes of the handbook, such publications supply information on the school system, the board of education, entrance requirements, attendance regulations, school hours, methods of contacting the school, appointment procedures, emergency school closings, student personnel services, transportation, curriculum offerings, and taxes; they also include a directory of the schools in the system. Such publications may be disseminated online or in print and in some districts both online and print versions may be made available.

In some districts, individual schools may manage their own online communication programming and disseminate their own newsletters, bulletins, handbooks, and calendars. Whether done at the building level, district level, or both, such publications play an important role in keeping parents informed and reinforcing solid parent–school relationships.

NOTES TO PARENTS

Emails, letters, and personal notes from teachers can improve relationships between home and school. Sometimes emails and letters may be limited to reporting only negative information—unsatisfactory work or disciplinary problems, for example. It's important to balance such communications by sharing good news—when students do well on classwork or make important contributions to the school, for example. Parents who receive these letters feel pleased and grateful for the information.

Schools may also issue letters and notices for general distribution to parents on such topics as opening and closing dates of school, health concerns, new policies and regulations, procedures for emergency school closings, use of school facilities, bus schedules, and open houses or other school events. These notices are important tactics for conveying basic information and creating favorable impressions of the school. But close attention should be paid to the messages contained in the announcement with careful thought given to the action expected after parents read the message. A message seeking only to inform parents of a new school rule might contain a very different message from a letter informing parents of the rule and asking them to explain it to students and encourage compliance with it. In either case, the vocabulary, tone, and readability of the message play important parts in making sure parents both notice and read it.

OTHER OPPORTUNITIES FOR PARENT ENGAGEMENT

The suggestions made thus far for parent involvement tend to establish closer relationships between home and school and to set a foundation for parent participation in school affairs. Leadership for parent participation should come from administrators and teachers. But schools have also found other methods that can be useful in engaging parents and strengthening their working relationships with teachers and other school staff members.

Study and discussion groups have grown rapidly as more parents have expressed interest in becoming more involved in schools. Such groups represent an increasingly popular concern for childhood education and a desire on the part of community members to know more about the schools their children attend. Organized at times at the request of parents, such groups are known by a variety of titles, including, for example, parent–teacher study groups, parent–teacher discussion clubs, grade and homeroom councils, parent study councils, or parent workshops.

Study and discussion groups provide a forum for dialogue on key education interests and issues. *Example:* A group might focus on policies and practices of the school systems and the methods by which parents and teachers can work together. *Another example:* A group might focus on discussing current uses of technology in instruction with parents who wish to know more about using technology at home to reinforce learning experiences.

Work connected with the study and improvement of curriculum at all levels affords rich opportunities for parent participation. Parents can take an active and constructive role in helping the school define the purposes of education, the objectives for specific fields, and courses of study. Parents have advised or served effectively on faculty committees concerned with the adequacy of the curriculum, revision offerings, and introduction of changes that could not be attempted without their support. They have served as resource persons, because of their specialties, in the preparation of instructional units, and have worked with teachers in the selection of materials and technology to enhance course content.

Parents can make worthwhile contributions to classwork and other learning activities. They can speak on topics about which they possess firsthand information. They can share rare books, objects, audio and video material, historical collections, and other such artifacts. They can assist on field trips and take part in follow-up activities. Such expertise and willingness to volunteer might also be used in conjunction with extracurricular activities. Parents in the community may possess talent and technical knowledge that can be used to enhance extracurricular activities. For example, parents might be willing to assist students and teachers in designing simple costumes for dramatic productions or building stage scenery. They might respond to invitations to participate in plays, musicals, assembly programs, and athletic games, to act as judges for contests, or help to organize and attend parties, dances, celebrations or other social events.

Taxpayers

While parents may be a prime audience for all school communications programs it's important to also recognize that the majority of the households in many school communities may have no children enrolled in the local system. While they may lack such a direct connection with the school system, the non-parent taxpayers are expected to pay for the school enterprise and they will, as a result, view themselves as important stakeholders in the community's schools.

The non-parent taxpayer audience can be especially challenging for school communicators since they can often fail to see why school issues have relevance to them. Still, the success of schools and students offer many beneficial outcomes to a community overall and research can contribute to helping these audiences better understand these issues.

COMMUNICATING TESTING PROGRAMS AND RESULTS

Nearly all states for years have used testing programs to measure student and school performance. The news media, as well as many parents and other community members, have come to expect the scores and explanations from local school leaders.

But despite this long history of testing, which dates to nearly the time when the first public schools were being formed, schools and communities still have problems communicating when it comes to testing programs and their results.

One problem is that far too few schools build communication plans around testing programs and too often communicate only when scores are released. If scores are high districts proclaim the progress local students are making. When scores are less than good schools are left to explain what went wrong and what will be done to address the "problem" of poor scores.

When testing programs aren't carefully explained—in advance of scores being released—concern over the tests themselves can begin to build among parents and other audiences. Parents—and even some teachers—may complain about privacy concerns or too much of an emphasis on testing and too little emphasis on the individual.

On top of this, many educators often agree that scores alone generally have little meaning. The news media or others may misuse them in ways that pit one school system against another. Direct comparisons can be difficult to justify and, some might argue, are at times a misuse of the data. Scores need to be presented in the appropriate context and in ways that interpret their meaning considering past programming and plans moving forward.

STRATEGIES FOR TALKING ABOUT TESTS AND SCORES

When developing communication plans and messages related to test numbers, efforts should:

- Not overlook the district's ongoing efforts and progress made on continuous improvement.
- Offer the experts and resources needed to give parents, the community, and the news media the insights they will need to fully understand the testing program and its results.
- Avoid pressures to draw instant conclusions or make unfair comparisons when reporting and discussing test results.
- Look for ways to help others understand the numbers in a full context of what's working and what needs to be done to bolster strengths and address areas that need improvement. In other words, highlight good news but don't fail to also recognize opportunities for growth.

Despite a significant amount of data and resources on testing developed by schools, testing organizations, and government agencies designed to help others understand testing programs, confusion and concerns about testing remain in many local communities. As with other issues, the dissemination of information alone often is not enough to raise the level of understanding needed to build public support.

The National School Public Relations Association (www.nspra.org) has developed a number of resources to help schools better communicate testing issues to their communities, including, for example, its publication *Communication Planning and Strategic Tactics for Releasing High-Stakes Test Scores*.

Just as with parents, non-parent taxpayer audiences need to be more carefully segmented by research into groups that will enhance the prospects of communication success. Such segments might include:

- Senior citizens, many of whom may be politically and socially active in the community but have little or no recent connection to local schools or appreciation for current school issues or initiatives.

- Business officials, who may see themselves as community leaders with vested interests in community success but who may not see a clear connection to schools or enjoy a clear understanding of how school success ties to community success.

- Faith and religious leaders, who serve as important sources of information for many in the community and who often have a keen interest in obtaining information and insight to help them better understand and interpret school issues for their own constituencies.

- Social workers, healthcare providers, police, and firefighters and other first responders, all of whom have direct relationships with many students and their families and carry a shared interest in school and community success.

- New community residents, who are at a critical point at which first impressions about local schools can lead to enduring positive or negative viewpoints.

WORKING WITH SENIORS

School public relations professionals have many reasons for becoming involved with older adults. Here are three:

- The United States now has a growing population of people over age 65.
- Among tax-paying households in many school districts, a majority of households do not have children in school. This suggests that it's important to maintain good relations with older adults, who often represent a significant number of such households.
- Among older adults, many are registered voters and their voting participation is high, including participation in school budget and bond elections.

The majority of older adults want the best educational programs for their community and its children. However, many older people don't have easy ways in which to connect or learn about the students, teachers, administrators, or services in their local schools. Thus, older people often end up voting against an unfamiliar and impersonal brick building. However, school officials can change this negative attitude by reaching out to local older adults in personal ways to build working relationships and the mutual understanding that can result.

Intergenerational programming—getting people of various ages engaged with one another in school activities and events—has emerged as a key public relations strategy.

Today, students and older adults seldom get together on an ongoing basis to socialize, pass on traditions and values, and solve local problems. During the 1960s, individuals began to see the need for intergenerational activities. Among them were teachers, who, on their own, began to develop ways in which they could bring the generations together. Another group, the American Association of Retired Persons (AARP), founded in 1958, has approximately 40 million members and offers many services to its members, including intergenerational resource material.

FOCUSING ON INTERGENERATIONAL EFFORTS

One successful way to bring the generations together is with an intergenerational conference: Different age groups come together to confront the myths and stereotypes about each other, to suggest ways to improve the relationship, and to initiate an intergenerational club to ensure ongoing activities. To start an intergenerational club, the school invites the same number of students and older adults to participate in the four-hour program at the school. Participants follow an agenda, which includes an icebreaker, word associations, slides, videotapes, discussion groups, a working lunch, group reports, a survey, and the start of the club. A proclamation by the office of the mayor or governor recognizing the event as "Intergenerational Day at Blank School" adds publicity clout.

The establishment of an intergenerational club flows naturally from the conference. The club connects the school with the community in a special way. The purpose of the club is to cultivate a group of retired volunteers and students to work within the school and community and to provide social settings for students and older adults to exchange ideas and pass on traditions and values.

FOCUSING ON FINANCE

Many older adults haven't been in a school in years and have little positive contact with students, teachers, and administrators. They feel disconnected from their schools; they only remember the way it was. As a result, young and old have misinformation and negative attitudes about one another. Most senior citizens, however, indicate that they want students to receive a good education.

In one New Jersey school district with many senior voters, the budget and a referendum were placed on the same ballot. The referendum was defeated but the budget passed, thanks in large measure to the support of senior members of the intergenerational club. Superintendents of various schools indicate that the senior citizen members of the clubs are positive, articulate key communicators of school programs in the community.

FOCUSING ON GRANDPARENTS

The 2010 U.S. Census report indicated that the United States is continuing to become a nation of grandparents. The census data show that nearly 5 million children (7 percent) under age 18 live in grandparent-headed households—an increase from 4.5 million living in grandparent-headed households in 2000. Obviously school-community relations efforts need to plan for and address the needs of this important and growing school audience. AARP has developed special resources and information to help families with this issue.[6]

COMMUNICATING WITH DIVERSE CULTURES

With the world getting smaller because of instant communications and rapid transportation, people outside the United States are learning more about our freedom and quality of life. They like it and want to be part of it. They want to migrate here and become citizens. Such migration affects all aspects of a school district and, especially, communications.

Most immigrants value education and quickly enroll their children in our schools. This underscores the importance of school administrators and teachers understanding the cultures of the diverse groups in a district. Before they can do that, they must understand a major barrier to cross-cultural communication: ethnocentrism. This phenomenon is defined as an unconscious tendency to view and judge people by one's own customs and standards. It is imperative that school personnel view objectively customs or beliefs that differ from their own.

Closely related to and emanating from ethnocentrism are cultural absolutes. Groups with such absolute values believe "The way we do things is the correct way. Anybody who does things differently is wrong." These "absoluters" judge different cultures from their own set of values, not understanding that other cultures or ethnic groups may have a different value structure.

Multiethnic diversity exists in most communities. Here are some suggested activities:

- Develop a school policy on working with diverse groups.
- Identify the various ethnic groups in the district.
- Learn who the key communicators are in these groups and meet with them. They can be identified by contacting churches, community groups, governmental agencies, and bilingual aides or employees.
- Ask the key communicators to relate information about the schools to their groups.
- If functional, create an advisory committee within each diverse group. If school employees are from that group, have them work with the school administrators when meeting with this committee. This helps make the committee members more comfortable and bridges the cultural gap between the school and the group.
- Hold workshops to train teachers and aides on how to work with children from different cultures and how to communicate with their parents. Have the key communicators from the groups meet with school personnel and explain thoroughly their culture. They need to explain

not only the surface culture, such as their dress, food, holidays, and music, but also the deeper aspects, such as values, family structure, education, work habits, and religious beliefs.

- Print publications in the language spoken by each of the diverse groups if it is not English.
- Work with the ethnic media who service these diverse groups.
- Provide a school bus to transport parents of immigrant students to school for back-to-school night. If one of their own group works for the school district, have that person ride with them to serve as translator and to make them comfortable when meeting with school officials.
- Teach all students to respect all languages, cultures, and people. It is especially important that they understand that the lives of the immigrant students are extremely complex. This is true because they have experienced many changes in their lives all at once.
- Understand that an effective method of communicating with these parents in many situations is conversing in their native language in their home. While personal contact often works well, communicating in their native language through letters or over the telephone also can work well, depending on the issues being addressed.[7]
- Believe that immigrant students can succeed academically if they are given the proper support.
- Consider the resources of governmental agencies and organizations such as the Intercultural Development Research Association (idra.org) and National School Public Relations Association (nspra.org).

SERVICE, CIVIC AND NEWS ORGANIZATIONS

Service and civic groups and organizations, as well as their leaders, contribute to community success in specific ways and may also have unique information and communication interests and behaviors. They can be key to reaching many audience segments that make up non-parent community audiences. Some of these organizations may need guidance in better understanding the school system and how the school's needs coincide with their own interests in community success. Research should focus on helping school-communication planners identify and assess the needs for a variety of group types, which might include:

- Civic organizations, including service clubs, such as Lions, Kiwanis, Rotary, Exchange, Jaycees, and Optimists. Many of these groups concern themselves with issues related to education, health, social welfare, better government, recreation, and so on. Other such organizations might include those with more patriotic, political, or fraternal interests, such as the League of Women Voters, American Legion, Sons and Daughters of the American Revolution, and Veterans of Foreign Wars.
- Cultural groups, including those with interests in the fields of art, music, architecture, horticulture, literature, drama, or race relations.

- Economic groups, including chambers of commerce, labor unions, farm organizations, manufacturers' and business associations, real estate boards, merchants' associations, and others of a specialized character.
- Government groups and agencies, including local, county, state, and federal government organizations whose interests may have an impact on the local school system. These agencies might include those offering or regulating services in health, recreation, law enforcement, safety, family life, child care, housing, and so on.
- Professional groups, such as those serving practitioners in law, medicine, dentistry, pharmacy, architecture, and engineering. Such organizations often take an interest in educational efforts and may cooperate with administrators and teachers on matters related to their special fields.
- Senior citizen organizations, serving the needs of the growing retired community. Many of these organizations are open to programs in which retired citizens are asked to help in schools or in devising programs to help seniors engage in school events and activities.
- Social service agencies, many of which operate in the fields of health, recreation, child care,

and family life. Because these agencies are concerned with many social issues vital to schools as well as families, these groups can often be important school and community partners.

– Youth organizations, which, like schools, also share an interest in serving the needs of young people. Some of the groups may even operate within the school as part of the extracurricular activities program, and may be staffed with teachers and administrators who volunteer their services.

KEY COMMUNICATORS

Citizens often do not accept or reject an idea until they talk with residents of the community whose opinion and judgment they respect. These key people or opinion leaders in a community must be identified so that they may be informed about the schools, learn quickly what the community is thinking, and get the public involved in the schools. Importantly, such opinion leaders may or may not be part of the community's formal power structure. Opinion leaders often do hold positions of leadership among community groups and organizations. But they may also come from the ranks of those in the community who are respected and consulted by many community members but are not part of the community's formal power structure.

The concept of key communicators is probably not an innovative one for some school officials. Many educators have applied the ideas behind the key communicator approach in their schools. But school leaders seeking an ongoing, beneficial relationship with opinion leaders should seek to formalize such programming as part of their communication program.

Benefits of Key Communicators

Being person-to-person in nature, the program enables school officials to get the pulse of the community with quick texts, emails or phone calls to key communicators. Likewise, rumors can be quelled when they are sparked. Because key communicators have developed a solid rapport with school officials, they can help the community gain and maintain confidence in the school. Perhaps above all, a positive school story can also be spread. The key communicators, then, serve as gatekeepers of information to and from the community.

Prior to making major decisions, school officials are often interested in the community's feelings about an issue. Such decisions could include the change of attendance boundaries, a tax increase, the closing of a school, or the moving of administrators or teachers within a district. Many cases are documented in which school officials, insensitive to community feelings, had to reverse a decision when citizens protested vehemently. One way of getting an early pulse of a community on an issue is through an organized key communicator program.

A major benefit of having a key communicator program is the squelching of rumors. Too often in almost every community rumors get out of hand. In many cases, such rumors, although unfounded, have resulted in severe problems for the school. Rumors about drug use, violence, racial problems, school closings, and the like get started with no foundation. Usually, these rumors could have been quickly ended in their early stages with a key communicator program.

Likewise, through a program with personal contact and phone conversations with school officials, the key communicators come to know them as people rather than distant figureheads. The mutual understanding and trust developed between school officials and key communicators can then be extended by the key communicators to the community as they discuss and share school information with others, correcting or adjusting misperceptions or misunderstandings that have previously existed throughout the community.

Newspapers, radio, and television cannot cover many positive activities of schools. By nature, they tend to highlight the negative happenings. By having the key communicators in the community and schools, and sending them brief informative messages, more good-news activities can be shared with the community from sources they know and trust. This is not to say that key communicators shouldn't be given negative news. They should—schools must level with them. Candor ultimately will help in establishing credibility with the group.

Identifying Key Communicators: Any person who talks to large numbers of people should be considered for key communicator designation. Persons who are believed and trusted by their audiences should be asked to serve. They need not have the usual power-structure status that educators frequently seek for school help. They may be citizens who sit on top of a hypothetical pyramid of communication in a community, such as barbers, beauticians, bartenders, small business owners and managers, doctors, dentists, letter carriers, or other people to whom citizens turn and ask "What do you think about . . . ?"

It's important to identify key communicators who will talk to all the different segments of the community.

Starting a Program

If a superintendent decides to begin such a program, ordinarily a list of people would be compiled by various employees independently. The community's demographics would be assessed to ensure that various groups would have a representative on the list. The names obtained from employees would be reviewed and the key communicators chosen. Usually the same names appear on many lists. Key people can also be identified by the local chamber of commerce, or county and city directories.

The superintendent then sends a letter to all selectees advising of their selection and explaining the purpose of the key communicator program: to help improve schools through better communications. If the invitation, both written and by phone, comes from the superintendent's office, the affirmative responses will be greater. A personal phone call from the superintendent usually elicits a higher acceptance rate than a phone call from an assistant or a letter alone.

Once the list of key communicators is compiled, the superintendent, with a personal phone call, invites six or so different key communicators at a time to lunch in a school cafeteria until all have met with the superintendent. At the lunch or any get-together, the tone is informal. No formal agenda is prepared, and the time pressures of all involved are respected. This means that the meeting is held to 60 or 75 minutes at the most. The guests should feel free to raise questions or to join a discussion. Often visitors will be seeking information that the superintendent has assumed they know. This is a confidence-building session that allows people to see that the chief executive is a person who cares about children, understands that problems exist, seems to be doing the best possible job to solve them, and is receptive to ideas and encourages questions and suggestions. People are asked to call when they hear a rumor and are told that they will be apprised of information about the schools when a problem, a challenge, or a need exists.

Perhaps once a year the entire group of key communicators will be called together for a meeting (for example, to consider a budget or bond issue or to discuss test score results). This enables the group to see that other people in the community care enough about the school to give time to help communicate.

Such a program can also operate on the building or program level, with principals or program directors following steps similar to those outlined above. Such building- or program-level key communicator efforts are focused on audiences and issues more directly tied to the schools or programs they serve, and they can be especially helpful at meeting communication needs in larger or more complex school systems.

Number of Key Communicators

The number of key communicators varies from district to district. Some small districts might use only 15 or 20. But the number might run as high as 250 to 300 in a large school system. The exact number, however, is not the key. If, for instance, a person feels slighted and wants to be a member, add him or her. Every person can help in some way. It is unusual that a person who gets involved in the schools in this way does not aid the school's program either directly or indirectly.

NEWS MEDIA

While news organizations might be seen as a means to the end of generating good news coverage or managing bad news stories, the news media and the people who work for them should be considered an external audience when researching and planning communication programming.

Like any other external audience, the media representatives have their own information needs and preferences which should be accommodated in communication planning. The continuing evolution of online news reporting also is shifting some of the traditional needs of news organizations. Newspaper reporters, for example, might now also be filing stories for the newspaper's online website or smartphone app, meaning he or she also may want to do video or audio interviews to be used in reporting. On the other hand, TV and radio reporters might want access to print documents or photographs to supplement their online reporting as well.

Shifting deadlines also have changed the traditional ways in which schools worked with news media audiences. Media organizations now often have ongoing deadlines as stories may be released online at any time during the day or night, meaning that school communications offices that once sought to accommodate daily deadlines now need to be prepared to accommodate information requests at any time.

Changes in media staffing also should be analyzed in planning research so communication plans can accommodate any special needs. At one time it was common to have dedicated education reporters at many media but today school officials may find themselves dealing with reporters and editors covering many topics and organizations and with little in-depth knowledge of many educational or school issues. Their intent is still to produce meaningful, accurate coverage but school communicators may need to plan to offer more detailed background information on issues as part of the reporting process.

ACTIVITIES

Many communication efforts aimed at external audiences of course will be deployed through mediated communications, using the media of the school system itself (websites, social media, newsletters, and so on) or the media of news reporting organizations (newspapers, TV broadcasters, online news sites, and so on).

But the many activities the school system engages in throughout the community should be seen as communication opportunities and properly considered in planning research and communication programming.

Whenever community members witness a school athletic event, read a student publication, or watch a student performance, their impressions are conveyed by word of mouth to friends and acquaintances throughout the community.

The cumulative effect of favorable reactions to such face-to-face interactions over time may influence, more than is realized, the attitudes and opinions of citizens toward the school system.

There is not much doubt about the value of student activities and accomplishments in cultivating and strengthening relations with the community. Some schools overlook these public relations opportunities connected with such routine events as commencement, plays, musicals, athletic contests, and service projects, and others emphasize the publicity side of these events and lose sight of their educational worth to students. Clearly, activities through which students are presented to the public should be a logical part of the instructional program and should fit in with its educational objectives. Unless this principle is respected, there is always a danger of exploiting students for publicity purposes. But properly planned and presented, such activities can play a legitimate and influential role in helping external audiences develop a fuller appreciation of student and school activities and accomplishments.

Although public entertainment by students is hardly a function of the school, nevertheless there are sound educational reasons for having students present enjoyable and entertaining programs. The mere knowledge that they will appear before the public adds incentive and zest to the work they are doing in school.

At the same time, the institution has an excellent means at its disposal for acquainting adults with different phases of instruction and demonstrating the nature and quality of the result. Such public presentations might include:

Musical Programs

Aside from athletics, perhaps no activity has caught the interest of the public more than music. In many communities, taxpayers are perfectly willing to have their boards of education start music instruction in the elementary grades and to provide instruments to students during these early years. School systems do a great deal to further musical understanding and appreciation through a school band, orchestra, glee club, and chorus. Although these activities may be carried on before or after school or during a club period, many schools include them in the regular program of studies.

Opportunities to present the musical accomplishments of students are numerous. Musical activities can be scheduled in connection with other events, such as assemblies, commencement exercises, and dramatic productions. The band can play at athletic contests and take part in civic celebrations. Invitations can be accepted by all musical organizations to appear before interested clubs and societies in the community and to put on radio and television programs when there is no conflict with regular studies. Video of student performances can be made available on school district websites and other appropriate online sites serving the community.

Shows and Theater Productions

Shows and other productions in the form of plays, talent shows, pageants, and musicals rank high on the list of events that bring people into the school and that are sought by groups in the community. Here again, audiences will share their good impressions with friends and neighbors throughout the community.

Dramatic productions also may make it possible to involve parents and interested citizens on a volunteer basis in the schools. These individuals can help make costumes, properties, and stage sets. In some instances, they can also take part in programs.

Art and Creative Exhibits

The display of student art and other creative work is another way to highlight student achievement while bringing schools and the community closer together. Many schools present student work in school facilities, but such displays often can also be extended into the community with exhibits in local community centers, government buildings, and shopping centers.

Assembly Programs

Regular and special assembly programs are another avenue for presenting the students and educating the public about the affairs of the school. These programs may be built around everyday happenings in class and extracurricular activities or around the observance of special days, weeks, and anniversaries. The programs for these assemblies may be developed by students or undertaken jointly with outside groups and organizations. A number of groups and organizations in the community always welcome the chance to share in programs of this character. To extend the reach of such efforts throughout the community, assembly programming can be broadcast on local cable TV outlets, livestreamed online, or recorded for viewing later on the school's website.

Regular assembly programs have appeal for parents, particularly when their own children are participants and the programs deal with topics related to their interests. The opportunity should never be overlooked to invite prominent citizens to take part

in programs. They might administer oaths to incoming student officers, chair a discussion, or speak on a vital subject. Like parents, they will hold the school in higher esteem after experiencing well-organized assembly programs.

Field Trips

Field trips to places of interest in the community or well beyond the community are an excellent device for bringing notice to the school and for explaining some aspects of the educational program. A merchant, for example, who takes students on a guided tour of his or her business shares an important learning experience with teachers and students. Trip activities can be covered in school media, may be of interest to local news media, and might be reported or blogged on by students or faculty participating in the trips.

Athletic Events

For many citizens the most common contact with a school is through its athletic teams. These citizens may know very little about the school's instructional program because the American tradition has been to highlight a school through its athletic teams. This sometimes can be seen in the amount of local newspaper coverage devoted to school sports events versus the amount given to other school activities. Also, it can be seen in the number of people who attend an athletic function, compared with those attending another type of school function. It seems that many communities want a rather comprehensive athletic program in their schools, particularly in their high schools. When a school attempts to suspend its sports program, public outcry and sentiment often demand the return of athletics even if it means a rise in taxes.

Adults who view athletic contests often admire the fine precision with which a team makes a play and the resourcefulness shown by its members in the face of stiff competition. They observe the physical stamina of players and the products of character-building experiences, such as cooperation, fair play, and courage. They go away from these contests with many impressions of the school and the contributions it makes to students. Unfortunately, attention can sometimes be directed away from the educational side of participation in contests by the premium attached to having winning teams. Some adults may seem more interested in enhancing the reputation of the school itself than in the welfare of students. Pressure can be exhorted on boards of education and school officials to replace unsuccessful coaches and to overlook eligibility requirements.

On the other hand, community members also may judge the value of the educational program by the appearance of the team, how well it is organized, and the planning that has taken place before the team appeared before the public. Since athletic teams may be the major image of the school in the community, it is wise for an administrator to ensure that a team is properly coached and organized and that it follows acceptable rules of conduct and fair play.

Commencement

Commencement programs make it possible for students to highlight for themselves and their parents the meaning and value of an education. The traditional commencement program of a few remarks by class officers and by the principal, followed by a main speaker, is sometimes replaced by a different type of graduation exercise. In this latter type of ceremony, members of the class being honored take over responsibility for most of the program. They may give short talks explaining what they have studied and accomplished in school, introduce honor students, present awards to outstanding classmates, or dramatize in play and pageant form some of their school experiences.

During the week of commencement, demonstrations and exhibits of classwork may be arranged for public inspection and an open house held for tours of the building. Such exercises are interesting to parents and families, and they also can provide meaningful insight into the school and its products. Commencement is an appropriate time to invite leading citizens and distinguished graduates to the school. Their names can be printed in the program, and they can be honored from the stage.

Business Partnerships, Work–Study, and Internship Programs

Business partnerships, work–study, and internship programs provide other opportunities for students to represent their school in the community. These programs may call for a student to attend classes for only part of the day and to work in a job related to his or her courses of study for the rest of the day. These positions may be in business, industry, law, or public service.

Work–study students and interns come in direct contact with members of the community. The impression they make or the information they pass along about their school, whether good or bad, often will be interpreted as gospel by the public.

The community relations aspect of such programs that can easily be overlooked is the need for the student to be properly informed and prepared to represent the school and to be observed and supervised properly by the school. Also, it is wise to take time and give these students some information and facts about their school district in case questions are asked.

Close cooperation with employers obviously is needed if the school wishes to place the students in the most educationally beneficial positions. Such cooperation is also needed if the employer is to understand that all students are not alike. Many employers are inclined to judge the school by the performance of one student. Directors and advisors of work–study and internship programs should work closely and communicate constantly with both employers and students to assure a mutually beneficial experience.

Accomplishments

The achievements and successes of students and graduates have a receptive audience in any community. People are naturally curious and interested to learn what students are accomplishing and how well their school experiences have prepared them for life. If the school wants citizens to value its program and acknowledge the competencies of its staff, it must continually report on what students are achieving and alert the community to the recognition, awards, and honors students and graduates have earned.

Students who receive college scholarships and win awards for outstanding accomplishments should be recognized. Citizens are more interested than ever before in high-level attainment and the recognition it brings to the school and community.

In addition to scholarship and award winners, recognition should be given to the students in every school who are engaged in many important service activities or other significant endeavors to benefit the community and the people who live in it.

The news media are aware of community interest in student achievements and accomplishments and often assign a prominent place to stories of outstanding student achievement. This publicity can be supplemented by honoring winners at special assemblies, introducing them at service club and civic organization meetings, and acknowledging parents for their contributions to the success of these students.

SPECIAL INTEREST GROUPS

Special interest organizations with a focus on local schools and educational issues often form in the community. Such organizations may have the ability to significantly strengthen or weaken school-community relationships, and how school leaders interact with and accommodate the needs and requests of these organizations is important to the school and communication relations program overall.

While these organizations may be structured in various ways and organized under a variety of names, they may be broadly classified in these types: parent–teacher or home-and-school associations, neighborhood associations, citizen advisory groups, and alumni groups.

Parent Associations

A local home-and-school or parent–teacher association may be described as a voluntary organization whose membership consists of the parents of children who attend a particular school or school system. Teachers from that school system may also be involved with or even members of such groups. There are many types of parent organizations, each with a name that attempts to indicate its primary purpose for existing. Some educators classify the various types of parent–teacher groups as individual school associations, homeroom and grade councils, school and parent councils, home and school associations, and so on.

Such groups have no legal authority to make policy decisions or to administer educational programs. Their primary purposes often include promoting student welfare in the home, school, and community. Local associations are usually organized around individual schools or separate divisions of the educational system—that is, elementary, middle, junior high, and senior high schools. Where junior and senior high schools are housed together or the elementary and secondary programs are in the same building, a single association may serve the combined unit.

Typically, the membership of local associations consists of parents, teachers, and administrative and supervisory officials of the individual school and school system. Invitation to membership may also be extended by local associations to interested citizens in the community whether or not they have children in school.

Community-wide associations also are often formed where there are several building units. Each unit sends representatives to a central group whose activities are governed by a constitution and set of bylaws. The same idea has been carried out on a county and regional basis in rural and semirural areas. The larger association speaks for the entire membership on important issues that cut across the school system, and this larger grouping makes it possible to share experiences and develop better programs.

Apart from the direct benefits to students and the community of parent–teacher cooperation, the overall influence such groups can exert on community relations outcomes must be considered when assessing the importance of local associations.

Good school-and-community relationships start when parents and teachers come to know one another and to talk about what they want for young people. Through these conversations, parents soon learn to know the school, to understand what teachers are trying to do for children, and to appreciate instructional conditions and problems. At the same time, teachers and administrators are made aware of the needs, interests, and attitudes of people in the community and the responsibility they have for adjusting the school program to local conditions. This is a two-way process and the backbone, in many respects, of a sound program in school and community relations.

Neighborhood Associations

Neighborhood associations can be found in many school districts, particularly those serving larger cities and towns. Generally, they operate within definite geographic boundaries and are deeply interested in local school and education issues. In addition, they are interested in housing, recreation, and community improvements—many of which may have school connections. These groups offer the schools another excellent method of establishing and maintaining good community relations.

Citizen Advisory Committees

Citizen advisory committees provide additional opportunities to engage residents with schools and to acquaint community members with important, local educational programs and issues. As the name implies, these committees are composed of community members who study educational needs and problems and then recommend to school authorities actions they believe should be considered.

One reason for school-sponsored advisory committees is the desire of boards of education and superintendents to collaborate as fully as possible with members of the community on critical issues. The boards and school leaders realize that the responsibility of long-range planning for better schools is a public one and that the advisory committee is an excellent means for sharing this responsibility. Through this committee they can acquaint a representative body of the community with the conditions and problems of public education, share ideas and information, and work toward meeting common goals.

Sometimes advisory groups may be formed by school boards and superintendents to meet a specific, pressing problem or an emergency that has emerged. This is not always the most appropriate time to form an advisory committee. By the time a crisis is reached, public attitudes already have been formed, and the public may view an attempt to form an advisory committee as a ploy on the part of the board of education to substantiate its position.

Whenever possible, forward-looking boards and school leaders should form advisory committees well in advance of a potential crisis or controversy. Such forward-looking actions clearly can be facilitated by meaningful communication and community research that seeks to identify audiences in the community and potential issues important to them.

MEMBER SELECTION

Different methods are used and various factors considered in the selection of citizens for membership on school-sponsored advisory committees. Essentially, there are three primary methods of selection: by school leaders or the board of education, by requests to community interest groups for representatives, and by asking people in the schools and in the community to suggest names.

Whether one or a combination of methods is employed for selecting members, the advisory committee should be as representative of the community as possible. Representation can best be ensured when population factors are considered in drawing up membership for the committee and when criteria for the individual qualifications of members are determined. The term of office for advisory committee members should be stated in the formal policies of the board of education.

GROUP SIZE

An advisory committee should be large enough to represent the community adequately and small enough to encourage productive and efficient working relationships among its members. Size may be affected by the nature of the school district and the issues being studied as well as the responsibilities assigned to the committee. Many advisory groups have fewer than 5 members, but the optimum size often falls somewhere between 15 and 25. Where a large committee is organized to increase citizen participation in schools for example, an executive body of 10 to 15 members may be established to plan and coordinate the activities of the several subcommittees into which the advisory group is broken. An intelligent use of subcommittees makes it possible to widen the scope of the advisory committee program and to tap the talents and interests of many citizens. The number of subcommittees depends on the amount of work brought before the advisory group and the number of people who are involved.

LEADERSHIP AND MEETINGS

During the initial meetings of a new advisory group, an appropriate school district leader (the superintendent or the president of the board of education for example) should act as chairperson until he or she is satisfied that the members have learned to know one another well enough to elect their own officers. The officers should be a chairperson, vice chairperson, and secretary, and each should hold office for a period of one year.

Meetings should be held monthly during the school year, and more often if necessary, and should last no longer than two hours. Longer meetings often undermine productivity and discourage attendance. Special subcommittees may meet more frequently than once a month if they have definite assignments to finish within fixed time limits.

It is not uncommon for school-sponsored advisory committees to include administrators and teachers. These school representatives usually have *ex officio* status with no voting power. They attend all meetings, provide leadership in planning study projects, keep the board informed of activities and developments, and assist in numerous other ways. School staff members can sometimes tend to dominate because of their in-depth knowledge of the school system and issues under review. As a result, they may assume more responsibility than they should. An advisory committee is likely to function better, therefore, when administrators and teachers are not actual members but cooperate in other ways with the committee.

A brief written report should be filed with the school board immediately after the advisory committee has completed its study. A joint meeting with the school board should then be held after board members have had an opportunity to review the report. Subsequently, the board's reactions to the report should be sent to the committee along with an expression of appreciation for the work that was done.

Alumni Groups

One community group that is often overlooked by educators interested in good community relations is graduates of a school. Former students often are eager to accept invitations to attend school functions and events. Relations with this group should be founded on a continuing interest in the welfare of both former and current students. Services to facilitate relationships with former students often include:

- Sponsoring social events allowing graduates to meet current faculty and students.
- Sending congratulatory letters or other notices to former students for achievements and notable works.

- Maintaining contact information and basic professional and personal information to maintain contact between the school and graduates as well as graduates themselves.
- Producing online and published materials to promote engagement with the schools by graduates, to highlight achievements of graduates, and to keep graduates informed of current school accomplishments.

Although it would be advisable to have a formal group coordinate activity with graduates, a school system can sponsor these activities without having a formal alumni association.

PROTEST AND PRESSURE GROUPS

Pressure groups generally are described as organizations that seek to influence education or government policy or legislation. Some pressure groups might be created to prohibit the school system from taking a planned course of action or to force it to take a particular course of action.

When citizens become dissatisfied with the school system and the officials in charge of it, they often form pressure groups. Often, they take a name that includes the word *citizens* or *taxpayers*, sometimes combined with the word *concerned*, to inform the public that this is a group that wishes to confront the school system on some issue or issues. These groups often place a heavy reliance on communicating issues and garnering support through online media as well as publicizing their viewpoints and information through traditional news media.

Expressions of dissatisfaction that have brought about the formation of pressure groups include the desire to reduce school spending and taxes, anger over a proposed building or other school expansion program, suspicion or other concern with a school system's testing program, concern over student performance and school accountability for it, and many other issues.

Pressure groups can grow out of meetings called by one or more civic groups for the purpose of discussing means for increasing public concern and interest in the schools. Sometimes the initiative for organizing pressure groups may even come from parent–teacher associations. Such groups may emerge when it seems advisable to have a wider representation of taxpayers involved in the study of a problem, because a broad-based committee would carry more weight with the board of education and the general public, or out of frustration with what is perceived as a lack of interest or concern by school officials in current interactions.

Common in many school districts is a pressure group that is extremely small in membership, yet is quite vocal, often giving the impression of being larger than it is. This type of group is often the work of one person who, under the guise of a large organization, continually attempts to make the public look with disfavor on the school system. To have the public think that he or she speaks for a large group of citizens, social media, online media and news media are flooded with position papers, news releases, charges, and criticisms against the school district. This is the type of person who gives the organization an emotional title and appears at most school board meetings, contending representation of a group while in fact representing only himself or herself. Often such persons represent what might be considered an extreme point of view. However, it is important to know that they generally are sincere in their viewpoints even though the views may not be in the mainstream of thinking about local schools and issues.

Handling Group Pressure

One of the best ways of handling group pressure is to detect it before it gets too intense. Often strong feelings can be identified by key communicators and confronted before they spread through the community.

Another way of handling group pressure is to monitor and assess the community and its feelings continually. Surveys of community members will help to document what are and are not issues of serious concern to the majority of residents.

Getting and keeping the community involved in the schools is another important way to manage the potential of outside pressure on the school system. This involvement can be done through citizen advisory groups for such potentially controversial areas as long-term goal setting, sensitive programs, school closings, declining enrollment, and communications

with the public. With citizens being involved in the schools and helping with their own expertise, a better understanding of the schools can be transmitted to the community. Keeping the public and the employees informed is another important step in managing the impact of group pressure on the school system. An informed public tends to support schools, provided the community believes that school officials make logical and sound educational decisions in the community's best interests.

OPPORTUNITIES FOR COOPERATION

It is apparent from the preceding description of types of community groups and organizations that many hold interests in common with the school. These groups are part of the school's public, and they offer numerous opportunities for interpreting the needs, programs, and problems of the institution. Their concern and cooperation should be enlisted to such an extent that they assume a responsibility to work for the support and advancement of education in the community.

Policy on Cooperation

Good community relations means that the community is pleased with the educational services that the tax dollar has purchased. Although this statement is simple, the procedure for bringing about this result is complicated—complicated because the school must deal with many segments of the public and satisfy a wide diversity of opinion on education.

As a matter of policy, the local board of education must recognize that the school has an obligation to promote intelligent understanding of what it is doing and win goodwill from as many groups as possible, regardless of the size of the group or the sex or age of its members. People who belong to community groups are paying the school bills, and they are entitled to know what services the schools offer and why, as well as the problems that confront them.

The local policy on cooperation with groups should provide that every person connected with the school system gets into the act, from the president of the board of education to the worker in the cafeteria. They should get into it by joining organized groups and sharing in their activities, by being invited to assist in the program of the school whenever possible, and by taking full advantage of opportunities for cooperative action related to school and community welfare.

To work successfully with groups, school personnel must know, for example, something of the fears, ambitions, and frustrations of parents in their relationship to the school. They must recognize that childless couples and career women may be heavy taxpayers who represent a sizable segment of the population and that these individuals should not be neglected in enlisting support for the school.

Furthermore, school leaders must be aware that older members of the community can interpret the modern school experience only in the light of their own experiences unless they are informed differently. It is important to help this group to understand the impact on schools made by population shifts, expanding government regulations, and emerging student needs, and to fathom the demands of a curriculum expanded to meet individual needs of children and the tremendous cost of education that accompanies these changes.

The policy must be one of interpreting the school program to all groups in the community and inviting their cooperation in the tremendous task of advancing the cause and quality of public education in our democratic society.

Community Involvement

Clearly, educators cannot be guided by a philosophy that proclaims, "We know best and we will tell the public how schools should be run." Parents, grandparents, seniors, and organized groups will be offended if the school arbitrarily makes decisions that directly affect them. In a sense, they want to become involved and want to know the rationale before school decisions are made.

The idea of involving citizens in schools can be frightening to some educators. This is understandable, but one fact should be kept in mind: A fully informed public is more likely to support schools and their leadership. The public can be partly informed through the news media and special publications. But schools must also get citizens involved in their programs in order for educators to understand people's attitudes toward the schools and to learn what the citizens want to know about the schools.

Even in smaller communities, the school system is a large and complex organization which can too easily become isolated from the community. Also, citizens and parents in the community are better educated than ever before—and enjoy greater access to news and information than ever before—— often making them less likely to automatically accepted decisions and actions.

Engaging on Goals

One way of involving the community is in educational planning and goal setting for schools. By working on goals, citizens can better understand the role of the school and provide the board of education with an accurate reflection of community opinion regarding those goals.

Successful programs involving the community in determining goals emphasize that a total commitment by all involved is a necessity. School board members must believe in the program and back it 100 percent. Likewise, administrators must be committed to it and become active in the goal process.

Generally, a program is initiated by the passage of a formal resolution at a school board meeting. It gets off to a better start if the resolution is passed unanimously by the board. In addition to authorizing the program, the board resolution also authorizes any necessary funds and offers the support of the board in providing personnel, facilities, and supplies needed to carry out the program.

Important also is a well-formed plan of action. Initial planning for the program should include the setting of a time frame and the appointment of a project director. The plan of action generally calls for the selection of an advisory committee. The guidelines on selection of members for such a committee have been outlined previously in this chapter.

A study of successful programs involving the community in determining and ranking goals suggests these additional considerations:

1. Since each district is unique, it should develop a program that will best suit its community.
2. The size of the school district and the amount of participation by citizens should determine

whether the goal process should be performed on a district-wide or school-to-school basis.

3. Almost anyone who wants to become involved in the goal process should be accepted.
4. Board members, administrators, and committee members should attend a goal conference, or a consultant should conduct an in-service workshop for them.
5. The whole goal process should be publicized thoroughly throughout the program.
6. Information should be published in different languages if non-English-speaking people live in the community.
7. A structured program for internal and external communication is vital.
8. All points of view should be given an opportunity to be considered throughout the goal process.
9. When the statement of the goals is finalized, the board of education should accept it as soon as possible. If there is a difference between the board and the advisory committee, it should be discussed and resolved.
10. The board of education should publicize and disseminate the agreed-upon goals and formally thank the advisory committee members for their dedication and service.[8]

MEETING CRITICISM AND ATTACKS

The problem of trying to develop wholesome relations with community groups is complicated further by unfair criticism of and attacks on schools. Condemnations of public education made by misinformed citizens and special-interest groups have been responsible for weakening popular confidence in the work of the instructional program and in the competency of professional personnel. Unless checked, these unfair criticisms threaten to destroy some of the fundamental principles underlying the free school system in this country. Boards of education, administrators, and teachers can't simply ignore the seriousness of the problem and hope that these forces will expend themselves in time. Careful measures must be taken to counteract any destructive tendencies of unfair attacks and to foster solution-focused working relationships. Addressing the complex issue of criticism and attacks

must start with a definite understanding of what the criticisms and attacks target and how they may be met.

Role of Criticism in Public Education

Since the nature of criticism is usually unfavorable or fault-finding, the tendency may be to overlook or suppress it. This is a mistake. For one thing, neglected criticism grows and becomes exaggerated. On the other hand, some criticism is inevitable and when used wisely can be valuable to a school.

First, criticism can be used to measure unrest in the community. A community with low morale may focus on its schools. For example, communities suffering from disorganizing influences—such as unemployment, political upheaval, religious bickering, or other negative factors—often will involve the schools in their problems.

Criticism can also measure interest. When people want to help, they are often interested in the neglected and inadequate aspects of the school system. This type of criticism is well intentioned, though often unenlightened and vague. The critic in this type of situation is also different from other critics.

Critics sometimes tell schools things that other people hesitate to mention. Constant involvement in a situation may produce "blind spots," and educators are as subject to this difficulty as other people. Sometimes only the frankness of a critic can motivate further evaluation and action. Instead of avoiding critics, we should realize that their barbs and frankness can add perspective to the management of a school. As long as there are human beings working in the school system, there is a need for criticism and evaluation. The possibility that mistakes will be subject to public discussion should keep schools dynamic, flexible, and subject to change.

Types of Critics

The art of meeting critics hinges on the capacity to identify the different types of critics. Following are some general categories into which most of them can be classified. It must be remembered that these categories are general and they do overlap. It should also be remembered that a particular critic may be reclassified as times and situations change.

The most bothersome are the *hostile critics*. They suffer from uncontrolled feelings of hostility.

Instead of becoming upset or angry with the real cause of their feelings, they take it out on the schools. Psychologists call such attacks "misplaced hostility." Earmarks of the hostile critic are fairly uniform but vary in degree. The hostile critics can be identified by the following characteristics:

They are unduly emotional. Hostile critics are angry but also full of other emotions. They are irate, highly incensed, and easily insulted.

They are personal in their complaints. Complaints from hostile critics are almost always in terms of personal happenings. They or their children have usually been insulted or neglected. They demand immediate action and punishment of the alleged offender.

They classify people by status. Hostile critics appeal to personal privileges. Because they live in a certain neighborhood or know the mayor or the board member, they feel they should have preferential treatment.

They have a deep sense of right and wrong. For hostile critics, there is only one right answer. They usually have the "right" answer before contacting the schools. Their thoughts and actions are rigid and allow for few exceptions.

They are suspicious by nature. Hostile critics are extremists and demand investigations. They suspect that the nation is going to the dogs and that there are subversives around every corner. The most radical of them pester police stations and the Federal Bureau of Investigation.

Less dramatic are the *uninformed critics.* However, in terms of numbers and influence, they are important. They, too, have identifiable characteristics:

They are indifferent. Uninformed critics are usually uninterested in school programs and activities. Their visits to the schools are few. Unless someone talks about schools when they are around, they are not bothered by what is going on in the classroom.

They repeat criticism rather than create it. After uninformed critics hear or read about the schools, they willingly repeat what they have heard or read—it is seldom that this type of critic has firsthand information.

They tend to be negative. Because other interests are more important to uninformed critics, they are willing to believe criticism. For example, if this criticism substantiates their position about taxes, they are likely to pay attention to what they hear or read.

They accept explanations and facts. Since uninformed critics are not emotionally or intellectually committed to a point of view, they are responsive to facts and explanations from the schools that make sense to them.

Professional critics are self-appointed or work for particular organizations interested in low taxes or some particular brand of education. They are motivated by the desire for fame and feelings of self-righteousness for saving education from "professional" educators. Such critics have some of the following characteristics:

They are intelligent and astute. Professional critics could be of great help to education. It is unwise to underestimate their influence. Their supporters are usually few in number, although their actual strength is difficult to determine because many of them are hidden behind some front organization.

They profess friendship for and support of education. Professional critics mingle with school people. Sometimes they are people who left the teaching profession because of various dissatisfactions. They study education and can speak highly of it when it serves their personal purposes.

They sponsor organizations and resolutions. Professional critics seek strength and recognition through organized fronts. They have impressive letterheads and do considerable corresponding with newspapers and other groups.

Finally, there are those who can be considered *enlightened critics.* They are friends of the school but avoid or reject any suggestion that they are rubber stamps for school officials. These critics can be identified as follows:

Friendly. Enlightened critics have no axes to grind. They know many school people. They are proud of their associations in education.

Educated on school subjects. Facts and information are important to enlightened critics. They criticize after studying a situation.

Specific. Criticism from enlightened critics is usually spelled out in detail. They ask questions more than they give answers. They know what they are talking about and expect to receive specific replies.

What Can Be Accomplished

An opportunity to meet the critic should seldom be refused. Before each meeting, however, the educator must have some general idea of what broad goals might be achieved. Ideally, the critic would listen to the educator's explanation and be converted, but this is not very likely.

Conversion to one's point of view seems to be a worthwhile goal in community relations, but practically speaking it is too often an impossible one. Conversion implies very often that the other point of view is wrong or valueless. Such an implication is not likely to win friends or influence critics. This is particularly true for hostile critics, whose very criticism develops out of insecurity and confusion. The more they are attacked, directly or indirectly, the more they will defend their position.

The school representative will find the creation of *understanding* his or her fundamental goal. Understanding is based on facts and explanations. This type of approach will evoke favorable responses from many, particularly uninformed critics. It can also make professional critics use care in what they say. Critics who comprehend what the school is trying to do will usually support a well-organized, purposeful program. They may say that if they were responsible for a program it would be somewhat different, but these critics usually do not want such responsibility and, providing they understand what is happening in the classroom, would rather just accept the school's programs.

In such contacts, schools must seek to develop a sense of respect for educators and educational programs. No matter how committed to a point of view a person may be, he or she is capable of recognizing, understanding, considering, and studying a situation. The critic can also realize when an educator is well informed about the situation and has facts to justify his or her conclusions. All this should be accomplished without the hope or expectation of the actual conversion of this type of critic, although hostility can be minimized.

The greatest gain from facing critics is the development of understanding—not necessarily conversion. Sometimes the only practical goal is that of developing respect. If understanding and respect are achieved, there is every reason to believe that better support of the schools will follow.

Facing a Critic

All critics should have at least one interview with a designated school representative. This interview will be one of two types: Either it will involve people who seek out a school representative, or it will involve people who are asked to attend a conference because of their verbal or published statements about the school.

When someone asks to speak with a school representative, the representative's main task during the first meeting is to listen and to ask questions. He or she should get a detailed description of the complaints and find out what happened, when it happened, and who was involved, as understood by the complainant.

If criticism focuses on policy and practices, find out what the person knows about school policies. Seek the source of his or her information. While this questioning is taking place, try to gain some insight into his or her motivation. A word of caution is in order: Be wary of questions that may be perceived as demanding or accusatory. Questions that ask for further information and specific examples are least likely to offend. It is also helpful to arrange any meeting to be as non-intimidating as possible. For example, it is always helpful if the school official is not sitting behind a desk when talking with a critic. The desk can signify authority and create a barrier between participants, which the critic may resent.

It is helpful to know if the critic is speaking for himself or herself, his or her family, his or her neighborhood, or an organized group, or if he or she is there to repeat random comments picked up somewhere. It also helps to know if the criticism is local or part of a national reaction. Is it continuing or the result of a particular situation? Is it hearsay or factual? Getting details about the critic and the criticism in the first interview is more important than giving answers.

Whether explanations should be given during the first interview is a matter of judgment. There is considerable satisfaction in receiving immediate answers, and time may be saved. On the other hand, some people call only to raise concerns and are satisfied after doing so. Attempts at explanations many only upset them further. An advantage of a second interview is that it allows time for feelings to settle and new perspectives to develop. The situation might correct itself in the meantime.

The temptation to defend the schools or their representatives should be avoided while one is listening to complaints. This may be difficult, particularly when the attack seems unjustified. It should be remembered that defense often implies some degree of fault and that there may be no reason to assume such a position. Furthermore, defensiveness sometimes handicaps the school representative in his or her efforts to develop understanding, respect, and support.

The stronger the disagreement, the more important it is that the communication be honest and effective. Don't assume that the other person understands what you say or write. Occasionally, ask the critic to check his or her understanding against yours. Likewise, be sure you understand what he or she is trying to communicate. Listen to everything a critic says before you begin to formulate your answer or question.

Preparation should be made for the second interview. Tentative goals should be outlined, and then the appropriate techniques should be chosen. Facts, explanations, and clarifications organized around the criticism should be assembled.

If this second meeting is a personal interview, the critic should be invited to the school office. Home visits are to be discouraged because of the potential distractions in the home. The visitor should first be given an opportunity to revise his or her story or to state a new conclusion. Time, as indicated, may have erased the complaint, or he or she may have been satisfied after telling the story. In such cases, school representatives can thank complainants for their interest in the school and tell them that their interests and services will be useful to the school in the future.

If the critic is not satisfied, the conference should proceed. The essence of the conference should be communication, so that some form of understanding may be reached. The school representative need no longer assume a passive role.

In presenting the school story, be mindful of the time involved. Long interviews may defeat your purpose. Emphasize your points but avoid repeating them. Assume that the critics are capable of asking for clarification if they don't understand what you are presenting. Remember that in interviews it is necessary to extend to others what you are seeking from them. That is, if you want understanding, show understanding. If you disagree, either at the beginning or at the end, you should still show respect for the critic's point of view. Also remember that the more you disagree, the more important it is to maintain further contact.

Focusing the Answer

Personal attention to a critic calls for answers tailored to his or her particular needs. Clichés and generalized explanations repeated over and over may temporarily satisfy many critics, but they do very little to build genuine understanding and support for the schools. To help focus answers, the following suggestions are offered:

Measure the understanding your critic displays. It is better to overestimate the critic's knowledge and understanding than to underestimate them. However, errors in either direction should be avoided. Although an individual may not know too much about the professional aspects of education, he or she may be well informed and motivated to learn even more.

Evaluate the emotional climate when the complaint is made. Hostile critics often are not seeking answers—they want to raise concerns and release tensions. Appeals to reason are not likely to succeed, at least in the beginning. Understanding through listening and patience are usually good antidotes to emotion. You can give reasonable answers later.

Make use of personal interests and needs. People will try to understand what concerns them. Application of this truism will do much to focus your answers. Members of the chamber of commerce, for example, might be more interested than others in comparative costs, school-to-work issues, and classroom productivity. Members of other groups will be more interested in classroom activities, educational programs, and philosophies. There is no reason to believe, however, that other interests cannot be developed in people or that such interests do not already exist. Eventually, the public can learn to think in terms of school and student needs.

Include illustrations and examples in your answers. People tend to think in concrete terms. A person is not likely to think philosophically when playing the role of a critic.

Avoid side issues and exceptions. Admittedly, education is complex and interrelated. However, we are faced with the challenge of giving simple answers. Side issues and exceptions only complicate matters when we are trying to create understanding.

Don't give the history and background of problems unless requested. As interesting as the total story is to you, it can't be assumed that other people will want to listen to the details. Keep your focus on the problems or criticisms expressed by the critic.

Avoid long answers; they can create hostility and destroy interest. The fact that officials, including educators, have been accused of being "long-winded" should encourage cautiousness.

Avoid professional jargon. Even if such terminology is understood, its effectiveness is limited and can in fact create an atmosphere of exclusion when used.

Follow-up Work with Critics

Your answer to critics may satisfy them and the case can be considered closed. However, a dynamic community relations program does not stop at this point. Many critics can become friends and supporters of the schools. Criticism should be the beginning of the relationship, not the end. This is particularly true for the uninformed critic and the enlightened critic.

After the final interview, there is need for follow-up work—a phone call, a letter, or a visit to ask if everything is still in order. There might also be an opportunity to tell the critics how the school has offered time and effort to resolve their complaints. Let them know their interest in the school is important.

Other follow-up efforts to engage critics in the educational process might also be helpful. Critics might be used on committees, for example. They can be called on to answer questionnaires. They might be invited to dedications and other special events. It's important to remember that they can serve as barometers of opinion in their particular segment of the community.

Public Meetings

Using public meetings (instead of a personal interview) to face and answer criticism is full of dangers.

The attraction that public meetings hold for some critics always opens up the possibility of useless talk and wasted time. Unless meetings are carefully organized, there is no way to control purposeless speeches. If they are controlled, you run the danger of being accused of railroading the meeting. Prestige and vanity also become involved in public meetings. Sometimes useless and undesirable commitments are made in public. Because they are made publicly, it becomes more difficult to persuade people to change their evaluations and opinions.

Decisions can seldom be made during such meetings, and therefore those meetings are likely to be dull and disappointing to some of the audience. This does not mean they are not useful. Public meetings can be constructive if they are called and designed for specific purposes. A meeting organized to clarify issues and impart information can be productive. The basic requirements are good speakers, effective visual aids, and prepared speeches. People can also be brought together for purposes of debate. In such instances, respected and reasonable leaders should be invited to present the issues. Questions from the floor should be submitted in writing.

Another technique is the small-group discussion. Issues can be presented in a general meeting and then discussed in small groups with trained leaders. After discussion, summaries are prepared and given to the whole group and to interested citizens.

In rare instances, where feelings are particularly intense and widespread, meetings can be called just to blow off steam. When this is done, there should be little attempt to develop understanding or make decisions. About all that can be hoped for is order. This type of meeting may clear the air, but there is also the risk that feelings will become more intense.

Minimizing Criticism

Although criticism cannot be avoided, it can be minimized. Because schools are handy targets for misplaced hostility, part of a community relations program should be devoted to the development of skills and policies that prevent such attacks. Following are some suggestions for avoiding criticism:

- *Never ask for advice unless you are able to use it.* There are a number of reasons for this policy. First, people usually guard their own opinions. They want approval of them. To be invited to offer an opinion and have it completely rejected creates a defensiveness in a person that often is expressed negatively toward the person who requested it. Second, if it is really approval you want, instead of advice, the intelligent person can distinguish the difference. It is an insult for you to use subterfuge to gain anyone's approval.
- *Avoid telling half-truths.* Even if the complete story is not entirely favorable, it is better to give all the facts. By doing so, you show that the school position is one of strength—and a strong program can afford to expose its weaknesses. This policy also avoids the danger of a hostile critic revealing something to the community. Such exposés are embarrassing and sometimes even damaging. The public should never be led to feel that the school officials don't trust them. Usually it is better to let all the facts of a situation be available and risk criticism than to try to conceal unfavorable facts, only to have them become known later. As long as the schools are public, the public will want to know the entire story.

- *Be consistent.* It is usually best to have one person make all important policy announcements. Other statements and clarifications should refer to the official announcement. Written releases always serve as a record in case of misquotations or misunderstandings. A briefing of the employees will help avoid conflicting reports. Besides their public relations value, staff briefings also contribute to good morale.
- *Anticipate criticism from certain decisions.* Educators often make decisions without looking over the horizon to public reaction. Some unpopular decisions must be made, but many poor decisions are made that cause unnecessary criticism.

Teamwork Needed

Although the responsibility of meeting the critic is delegated to particular individuals, the ultimate success of any program depends on the entire personnel of a school or a school district.

Complaints will be made to everyone. Each person who receives a complaint should evaluate it and then deal with it if it is something that can be settled immediately and if it is within his or her jurisdiction. Other types of complaints should be referred to the central office. The same principles of understanding and listening are applicable whether you resolve the complaint or refer it. Criticism resolved on the spot should be summarized periodically and reported to the responsible department.

In return, the central office staff should report back to the teacher or person making the referral. If the criticism is received by someone in the central office, it is important for morale and teamwork that any individuals involved be informed. When advisable, the critic should be referred to the individual involved. Occasionally, a summary of this aspect of community relations should be given to the entire staff.

Community relations leaders within the school should constantly train, advise, and support the staff on positive ways of working with critics, and alert them to effective community relations techniques. In other words, effective communication on all levels is the key to teamwork in facing criticism.

COMMUNICATION DURING NEGOTIATIONS AND A STRIKE

Communications during negotiations and work actions obviously can be critical to the immediate issue but they also are important in preserving the health of school–community relationships long term—well after the work issues have been resolved. Negotiations and work-issue communications can be emotional and upsetting if not properly managed and can, therefore, result in damage to existing school-and-community relationships that could take considerable time to correct.

School districts should plan for communications during negotiations or a strike or other work action. If poorly prepared, schools can be outmaneuvered by employee groups with well-orchestrated communication programs. Local citizens may receive basically one side of the issues and then may perceive their elected school officials as being uncaring and unreasonable. Thus, a school district must have a communication plan with administrative and communication procedures set up weeks or months in advance of negotiations to eliminate the confusion and chaos that can result when a crisis occurs.

The importance of a communications plan can be seen in the impact a strike and the subsequent settlement have on a community. A strike means students' education will be interrupted. Parents, especially working parents, must make arrangements to have their children cared for if classes are canceled; local services, such as police, traffic, and transportation, have to be rearranged if a strike occurs; and the confidence the community has in its school officials and, ultimately, its support of the schools are at stake. Ultimately, all citizens will have to finance the settlement. School leaders who handle themselves well during negotiations and a strike will help to indicate that they have integrity, reasonableness, and the leadership qualities to continue with the stewardship of the community's children and tax dollars.

Communication Suggestions

Communications experts have suggested the following thoughts for school districts involved in negotiations and a strike:

- Communications should begin as soon as negotiations begin.
- The school district should refrain from partisan statements and stick to transmitting facts.
- The school district should have one spokesperson, probably the chief negotiator, with advice from the communication specialist.
- The objective is a settlement; it is not to make the employees look bad with a propaganda campaign.
- Overreaction by school officials to an employee group's remarks can cause the community to respond emotionally by supporting "underdog" employees.
- Public charges and counter-charges tend to delay settlements by diverting attention from issues to personalities.
- The communication specialist should be close to the negotiating team but not on it. In this way he or she can learn and understand issues and actions at the bargaining table. Likewise, the specialist can advise the district spokesperson on working with the media, the content of public statements, and suggested written materials.

Informing the Community

The primary source of information about negotiations and a strike will often be the news media as well as the school's own online and social media. Employee organizations, with the help of state and national affiliations, are usually well prepared to use such media to their communication advantage. School districts must confront this with a well-organized plan that emphasizes facts rather than emotions and recriminations. (Chapter 11 provides guidelines on working with the news media, many of which are useful when communicating during negotiations or work actions.)

Informing Parents and the Community

The media are important sources of information for parents and the community during negotiations and a strike. However, they should not be considered the only methods of communicating with the external publics. The key communicator program outlined previously in this chapter can be most effective in getting and keeping the community informed and in learning what the feelings of citizens are toward issues in negotiations and toward the strike. A word of caution is in order: The key communicators program should be established long before a crisis, or those participating in it may think they are being manipulated.

Communication Plan

A school district should start planning for next year's negotiations as soon as this year's settlement has been completed. A valuable step in such planning is to identify employee wants that can be met prior to negotiations. Many of these are minor wants, such as a need for a piece of furniture in a classroom, a parking space, or secretarial help. If ignored, they can be part of major demands at negotiation time.

Wise communication planning includes the following measures:

- The superintendent should anticipate major demands of employee groups and keep the board of education and the district administrators informed.
- The chief school administrator, with the help of the communication specialist, should meet with board members and the chief negotiator to plan communication strategies. The specialist should constantly advise school officials on the public relations implications of certain decisions made by them.

- A workshop should be conducted on the role of board members in negotiations and during a strike. Individual board members are under an enormous amount of pressure from citizens either to get the students back in school or not to give away everything to the employees. Many times they are under personal attack with threatening phone calls and letters. Also, board members can often be drawn into a communication war in the media. Board members should be cautioned to refrain from this type of action and to realize that anything they say publicly may be taken as the feeling of the entire board. By law the position of a board can be formalized only at a legal meeting. Boards should act as a unit rather than with many voices during negotiations or a strike.
- A major part of a communication plan is the section that determines the publics with whom the school district must communicate, the information that should be passed along, when the communication should take place, how the information will be passed along, and who will communicate with various publics.
- An evaluation of the plan should be conducted to determine what should be retained in future plans, what should be dropped, what could be improved, and what could be added.

One Expert's Point of View: Understanding External Audiences

Sandy Cokeley, APR, is CEO of SCoPE School Surveys (www.scopeschoolsurveys.com) and an experienced school public relations practitioner, counselor, and planner with a background in both private- and public-sector communications programming. As Director of Quality and Community Relations for the Pearl River (NY) School District, she worked with the district's leadership team on communication and continuous improvement efforts that led the district to be named one of the first Malcolm Baldrige National Quality

Award recipients. Cokeley is co-author of the book "Malcolm and Me: How to Use the Baldrige Process to Improve Your School" and a contributor to the book "School Public Relations: Building Confidence in Education." She is past president of both the New York School Public Relations Association and the National School Public Relations Associations (NSPRA).

You are an advocate of research-based communication planning. Clearly research can help to

identify exactly who a district's key external audiences are. But what other things can research help us understand about these audiences?

Without communication research, you have no meaningful baselines or benchmarks against which to measure communication effectiveness and improvement. You have no real understanding of the specific informational and emotional needs your audiences possess. And you have no insights on how to best design your communication efforts to be both effective and efficient as you invest communication resources. Through research, you can determine critical knowledge such as how your audiences are currently getting their information, if they are getting the information they need, and whether they perceive the district to be open, transparent, and trustworthy. You can uncover important differences across your audiences and segments of your audiences; for example, parents of elementary school students versus parents of high school students. No two school districts or communities have the same school and communication needs, as our research with school districts at SCoPE has shown again and again. On-going research is key to driving the informed planning and programming that will work in each individual school system and community.

We often hear that working relationships with parents and other community members are essential to student and school success. How does communication factor into the dynamics of school-and-community relationship building?

It's critical. Relationships are built on a foundation of trust and credibility. And that means trust and credibility in the institution as well as the individuals that lead it and work for it. Communication will build the understanding essential to eventual support by all audiences in the community. These include both audiences with direct connections to students and the schools, such as parents, as well as those with more indirect connections, such as business or faith leaders. People are less likely to support an organization that they do not trust, that they do not perceive as credible. Ultimately, successful communication is about much more than creating nice brochures and state-of-the-art online media. We want people to enroll their children in our schools. To vote to support our budgets and bond issues. To stand behind schools and school leaders in times of controversy and crisis. These are the behavioral results that mark successful school-and-community relations efforts.

What role does internal communication and relationship building play in the quest to build understanding and support among external audiences?

Internal communication and relationship building are absolutely essential to a school district's external communications program. Keeping staff informed about district programs, events, and issues and ensuring they have the tools and knowledge to communicate effectively directly impacts the quality of their interactions, often on a daily basis, with parents and community members. Focusing a school communications program solely on external audiences does both the district and those same external audiences a serious disservice. People will believe what a front-line staff person tells them more than what they read in a glossy brochure or hear the superintendent say on the evening news. Everyone in the organization speaking with one voice will strengthen the messaging to external audiences as well as engender a collective.[9] ■

Questions

1. The relationship between parents and teachers obviously is key to fostering strong working relationships between schools and this key external audience. List the ways in which a school communications program helps to prepare and support teachers in their communication roles with parents.

2. Key communicator programs obviously play a key role in fostering two-way communication between the school and community. Explain how your school system could benefit from a key communicator program. What are the initial steps you would take to establish such a system?

3. Senior-citizen taxpayers are growing as an audience and they play key roles in school district issues and elections. What are the essential steps school leaders should take to communicate effectively with older citizens to keep them informed and supportive of local schools? What programs might you consider to effectively get seniors directly involved in schools?

4. Explain why it is important for all school employees to understand how to best deal with complaints and criticism from the community. What are the most important issues for a school leader to consider when meeting with critics to address issues or concerns?

Readings

Fuller, Mary Lou, and Glenn Olsen, *Home–School Relations*, 4th ed. Boston, MA: Pearson, 2011.

Gestwicki, Carol, *Home, School, and Community Relations*, 9th ed. Belmont, CA: Cengage Wadsworth, 2015.

Michaelson, David and Don W. Stacks, *A Professional and Practitioner's Guide to Public Relations Research, Measurement, and Evaluation,* 3rd ed. New York: Business Experts Press, 2017.

Moore, Edward H., *School Public Relations for Student Success*. Thousand Oaks, CA: Corwin Press, 2009.

National School Public Relations Association, *Diversity Communications Toolkit*. Rockville, MD: Author, 2013.

National School Public Relations Association, *Communication Planning and Strategic Tactics for Releasing High-Stakes Test Scores.* Rockville, MD: Author, 2017.

Samover, Larry, and Richard Porter, *Intercultural Communication: A Reader*, 14th ed. Belmont, CA: Cengage Wadsworth, 2014.

Stacks, Don W., *Primer of Public Relations Research*, 3rd ed. New York, NY: Guilford Press, 2016.

Videos

Tacoma (WA) Public Schools: What My Mentor Means to Me
https://youtu.be/_8sM_vF_e3Y

Nixa (MO) Public Schools: Students Go to Court
https://youtu.be/UZMj_dR1PzE

Nixa (MO) Public Schools: Grandparent Research Project

https://youtu.be/OUXAcs_gbQw

Parkland (PA) School District: Thank You School Foundation
https://youtu.be/_wGusA6Qjo8

Capital Region (NY) BOCES: Tips on Scholarships
https://youtu.be/QVr99NsCONc

Endnotes

1. National School Public Relations Association, *Rubrics of Practice and Suggested Measures* (Rockville, MD: National School Public Relations Association, 2013), p. 7.

2. http://scopeschoolsurveys.com/about/ Retrieved on internet October 17, 2017.

3. It's All About That Base: Setting Realistic Targets In Your Communications Plan, http://scopeschoolsurveys.com/about-us/articles/article112015/ retrieved from the internet October 17, 2017, Reprinted with Permission.

4. https://www.nspra.org/cap. Retrieved on the internet October 17, 2017.

5. https://www.census.gov/prod/2013pubs/p20-570.pdf. Retrieved on the internet October 17, 2017.

6. Goyer, Amy, "More Grandparents Raising Grandkids," *AARP* Online. December 20, 2014. Retrieved October 16, 2017, at http://www.aarp.org/relationships/grandparenting/info-12-2010/more_grandparents_raising_grandchildren.html

7. Reprinted with Permission from Ellen T. Morgan in "Communicating with Diverse Populations," *School Public Relations, Building Confidence in Education* (Rockville, MD: National School Public Relations Association, 1999), p. 225.

8. Compiled by Richard D. Bagin, Executive Director, National School Public Relations Association, Rockville, MD.

9. Interview with Sandra Cokeley, Taken from correspondence October 26, 2017 with Sandy Cokeley, CEO, SCoPE School surveys (www.scopeschoolsurveys.com).

9

Crisis Communication

This chapter reviews issues ...

■ For central administrators: The role of comprehensive crisis communication policies, plans, and training to serve the organization and community overall before, during, and after disasters and other emergency events.

■ For building and program administrators: How crisis communication preparedness supports buildings and programs—and their staff members—when the need to communicate quickly and accurately to key audiences during crisis events is essential.

■ For teachers, counselors and staff: The ways in which individuals need to train and prepare for roles as essential frontline communicators during crises affecting their schools.

After completing this chapter, you should be able to ...

■ Identify the components of a crisis communication plan.

■ Demonstrate the importance of crisis identification and avoidance in school–community relations.

■ Identify initial and long-term tactics for school crisis-communication management.

■ Describe the role of news and social media when communicating during a crisis.

No amount of planning can foresee every possible threat that schools today may face. However, rapid communication by school leaders who are prepared to act in a time of crisis can reduce the harm caused by such events and the related issues and concerns they often create. Quick response also can move a bad situation toward a faster resolution. Clearly, crisis communication planning and training must address key issues and make critical decisions before a crisis strikes, and prepare all school employees to respond effectively when it does.

Perceptions of how school leaders act and communicate during a crisis often become the focus of national and even international scrutiny. During any crisis, personal and organizational competence, character, credibility, and goodwill are challenged. Therefore, school administrators need to be prepared to respond to crises, even when the events have no direct connection to their school systems.

In its book *School Public Relations: Building Confidence in Education*, the National School Public Relations Association cautions:

> Communication planning is the foundation of any crisis planning, implementation, management and recovery effort....
>
> Effective communication will instill confidence that the district is doing everything possible to address the situation and prevent a similar tragedy from happening again. Leaders often lose the confidence of their communities—not because of the crisis—but because of how they responded to it. One misspoken phrase or one uncorroborated piece of information about a crisis often is replayed over and over again by local and national media.[1]

Instant news coverage—supported by cable and online news TV programming, online news sites, bloggers, social media, and so on—has allowed national and international issues to more quickly become issues for those responsible for managing communication in local school systems. School systems miles away from a news-making crisis can find themselves the subject of news coverage as local reporters and commentators, reacting to national news, develop their own stories on how local schools are prepared for potential disasters.

Increasingly, school communication administrators must stay plugged into breaking national news. Doing so helps them to develop an understanding of the national school issues that might prompt local news directors—and parents—to ask "Could this happen in our school system?" and "How are my local schools prepared to handle such an event?" National news events, announcements, and reports on school safety, terrorism, violence, health issues, and sexual misconduct are some of the issues likely to cause local media to seek comments from school administrators in their coverage areas.

To keep up with emerging crisis-related trends and news, school communications professionals increasingly are making regular use of local and national online news search sites, including the sites of the major networks and large daily newspapers, to study media reports as they are issued and updated. Many also consider it important to develop a network of peers—consisting of both communications professionals in the local community and school officials in neighboring districts—to quickly consult with before responding to crisis-related events or rumors.

Some crises are *emerging*. We can see them coming and prepare for them. Some are *ongoing*. Still others are *immediate*. When an immediate crisis hits, an organization must be ready to respond immediately.

By definition, a crisis is "an unstable or crucial time or state of affairs in which a decisive change is pending." A crisis can involve anything from fiscal and personal impropriety to outright violence. According to the U.S. Department of Education's 2004 publication *Practical Information on Crisis Planning: A Guide for Schools and Communities*, "a crisis is a situation where schools could be faced with inadequate information, not enough time or sufficient resources, but in which leaders must make one or many crucial decisions" (p. 10). Since the shootings at Columbine High School in Colorado in April 1999 and the terrorist attacks on September 11, 2001, even greater attention has been focused on crisis planning for schools.

Not all crises result from acts of violence. Many types of events can suddenly place local school systems in the eye of a media storm, including the following, for example:

- Health issues, from major items such as the potential for an influenza pandemic to minor events such as an outbreak of undefined skin rashes or head lice
- Misconduct by school personnel, from sexual abuse issues and related law-enforcement investigations to acts involving alcohol or drug use
- Safety concerns, from air-quality issues related to mold in school buildings or lead in drinking fountains to the need for seatbelts on school buses
- Weather-related events, from major disasters such as hurricanes and tornadoes to more localized issues such as snow-related closings or delayed openings.

A CRISIS PLAN IS ESSENTIAL

Without a plan, any crisis can prompt panic-like reactions. With the community and perhaps even the world watching, people expected to be in command of a situation are relegated to wringing their hands and asking "What do we do now?" A written crisis plan is essential, therefore, to avoid this kind of response.

This chapter focuses primarily on dealing with violence, and a similar framework will guide any organization through most types of crises. Although the specifics might change from one incident to another, the approaches will be similar.

What's Included in a Crisis Plan?

The format of crisis plans varies, depending on the nature of the community and the creativity of the people who develop the plan. A school system should not simply adopt another district's plan, since the development process leads to ownership and understanding. However, most plans include the following:

- *Reasons for the plan*—In a few words, the document should state why the plan is needed.
- *The types of crises covered in the plan, accompanied by checklists for responding to each one*—These crises might range from a chemical spill to an armed attack.
- *Procedures common to all crises*—Some procedures are basic in dealing with any crisis, such as making sure students and staff are safe; contacting law enforcement, fire, rescue, and other appropriate agencies; informing the superintendent and central office staff and referring them to the crisis plan; establishing the chief spokesperson; asking all office personnel to direct calls about the crisis to the office of the chief spokesperson; setting up news media operations; demonstrating concern while telling the full story; alerting the crisis counseling team; and getting and reporting the facts.
- *Emergency contact information*—Included in the plan should be phone numbers, e-mail addresses, and other contact information for key people and organizations that may need to be contacted in each of several types of crises.

The lists should also include alternate locations where people might be reached, such as home phone numbers, cell phone numbers, and personal e-mail addresses.

- *Detailed maps of each school facility*—These maps or line drawings of the school, school grounds, and vicinity will be essential if bomb squads, SWAT teams, firefighters, or other groups responding to an emergency arrive on the scene. In advance, the plan should also detail locations, generally outside the involved facility, where a command center might be established and where regular briefings might be held for the media.
- *Procedural information*—The plan should include guidelines for closing schools and lockdown or evacuation procedures. Some school systems also use codes as shorthand for various types of situations. For example, a *Code 1* crisis can be handled at the local school level. A *Code 2* crisis will require additional help but can be handled by the school district. A *Code 3* crisis, such as a fire, natural disaster, or act of violence, requires a broader community response.
- *Guidelines for effective communication with the media, staff, and community*—Systems for quickly communicating with staff, parents, nearby residents, and the news media all must be carefully outlined. The various communication problems that often accompany school disasters, such as the loss of telephone and electrical service, or the added online capacity needed to handle surges in traffic to the school website due to those seeking information and updates, also merit special consideration. Sample messages and "backpack letters" can be drafted in advance to be ready to be tailored to a specific crisis once the need arises.

SPECIAL CONSIDERATIONS

Planning should provide access to adequate cell phones and charged batteries; two-way radios; online communication tools; staff and student directories; fact sheets about the school and facilities; student and staff attendance records, including any substitutes who may be in the building; locations for the evacuation of students and staff; a transportation plan for evacuation; a list of staff who will be at the evacuation site; lodging and food for staff and volunteers; staff, departmental, and parent–community organization phone trees; a list of sources of outside support; a location for news media; and the specifics regarding who will handle related special events and activities.

Who Should Develop the Crisis Plan?

Generally, a board-adopted policy supports development of a crisis plan. This means the superintendent is ultimately responsible for having a plan in place. In practical terms, leadership for development of the plan is often handled by the school system's communications executive, working with a planning team. The Minnesota School Public Relations Association notes the school communication director should devise a plan "cooperatively with your superintendent and other key administrators," and notes that such a plan is "an agreement in advance on how communication will work in a crisis."[2] This type of planning is a prime example of school–community relations at work. At the school district level, members of the planning team will likely include the following:

- Superintendent
- School district communications, business, human resources, and professional development executives
- Representative teachers; secretaries; administrative assistants; counselors; school psychologists; school health professionals; information technology and other technical services staff; transportation, custodial, and cafeteria staff; and other personnel
- Students
- Representatives of law enforcement agencies (sheriff, police, state patrol), fire, rescue, poison control, phone company, electric and gas utilities, weather service, transportation, others
- Representatives of the media (newspapers, wire services, television, radio, other appropriate media)
- PTA and/or other parent–community representatives.

Planning and Preparedness

Any plan worth developing should never gather dust. Having a crisis plan that's not clearly communicated and readily accessible is tantamount to having no plan at all. Therefore, any organization, including a school system, should consider the following:

- *Central and area offices*—Training sessions should be held with all staff in these offices. How these meetings are organized will depend on numbers of staff and schedules. One meeting might involve the cabinet, another meeting might involve the entire management team, still another meeting might include support staff. If there are separate transportation, warehousing, professional development, and other facilities, each should host a training session. Whenever possible, all staff should meet together rather than separately, to promote teamwork.
- *School board*—The plan should be thoroughly reviewed with the board.
- *Individual schools*—Training sessions should involve the entire staff at each school.
- *Parents and community*—Although some parents and representatives of the community will be involved in developing the crisis plan, all need to know that the plan is in place.
- *Simulations*—To bring life to the plan and to demonstrate the community-wide nature of some crises, school systems and even individual schools might carry out simulations that involve not only school staff but other community agencies as well.
- *Copies of the plan*—Copies of the comprehensive plan should be distributed to each school and office in the district.
- *An abbreviated plan*—Since a crisis plan can be quite lengthy, many schools and school systems develop abbreviated checklists, spelling out what must be done immediately if a crisis strikes. A relatively small document that easily fits into pocket or purse might summarize the crisis plan, while providing specific bulleted lists of what each of several groups should do immediately, ranging from the school nurse and secretary to the superintendent and principal. Nothing should be left to chance. In some

A SAFE HAVEN VERSUS THE REALITY OF VIOLENCE

Schools are among the safest havens in any society. Yet over the last decade some of these sanctuaries for learning were hit with devastating, high-profile, armed attacks. Many students and educators died, and others were wounded. Those who staged the attacks ranged in age from 11 to 18. Most were 14- to 17-year-old boys.

Immediately, these incidents became worldwide news stories. Within minutes, live television turned the names of the schools, perhaps little known outside their immediate communities, into household names in the most distant reaches of the globe.

Those school systems best able to deal with these attacks had a crisis plan ready to go.

FACTS ON YOUTH VIOLENCE

Although high-profile incidents of school shootings and other violence tend to garner intense media coverage, data reported by the U.S. Centers for Disease Control and Prevention suggest that youth violence is in fact prevalent in school systems of all types in all regions of the United States.[3] For example, the following were determined in a 2011 national sample of youth in grades 9 to 12:

- Sixteen percent of male students and 7.8 percent of female students reported being in a physical fight on school property in the 12 months preceding the survey. The impact of violence can also have an impact on academic performance, as 5.9 percent of those surveyed reported that they did not go to school on one or more days in the 30 days preceding the survey because they felt unsafe at school or on their way to or from school.
- Weapons in schools present an issue as well, despite increased security efforts by many schools. Some 5.4 percent of those surveyed reported carrying a weapon (gun, knife, or club) on school property on one or more days in the 30 days preceding the survey.

Data reported by the U.S. Department of Education in 2012 revealed that in school year 2009–2010, 85 percent of public schools recorded that one or more crime incidents had taken place at school.[4]

The data also show that schools increasingly have taken steps to make their facilities more secure. In the decade between school years 1999–2000 and 2009–2010, more schools reported using safety precautions, including controlled access to the building during school hours (from 75 to 92 percent), controlled access to school grounds during school hours (from 34 to 46 percent), and the use of one or more security cameras to monitor the school (from 19 to 61 percent).

WHERE DO ACTS OF VIOLENCE TAKE PLACE?

A study conducted by researchers at the University of Michigan and the College of New Jersey concludes that acts of violence in schools generally take place outside the classroom in common areas without a great deal of direct supervision. Those areas include hallways, cafeterias, bathrooms, locker rooms, libraries, and school grounds.[5]

cases, emergency numbers are placed beside each office or classroom phone.

- *Flash drives and intranet*—Certain portions of the plan, such as prototype "backpack letters," might be distributed to those who need them on flash drives or might become a regular feature of the school system's internal online resources.
- *In case of emergency*—Because a building might be sealed in an emergency, administrators and crisis management team members might wish to carry copies of essential plans, including calling lists, in a special container in the trunks of their cars.

CRISIS MANAGEMENT TEAMS ARE VITAL

Crisis management teams should be established at the district level and within each school. These teams might vary in size from five to a dozen people. Each will have clearly understood responsibilities in the event of various types of crises. They will also ensure that the staff is regularly updated and simulations are held, if needed.

Although there are many types of crises, the most traumatic—those that cause the highest levels of stress—are human-caused and life-threatening.

However, each crisis demands appropriate attention. The types of crises requiring a crisis-management-team approach might include these:

- Accidents and injuries
- Armed attack or an armed intruder
- Bomb threat
- Child abuse, neglect, sexual assault
- Communicable diseases
- Criminal indictment
- Death of a student or staff member
- Demonstrations
- Fire
- Gas or chemical leak or spill
- Terrorist attacks that might involve chemical, biological, radiological, or nuclear agents or devices
- Tornado, hurricane, other extreme weather conditions
- Vandalism, property loss, theft.

WHEN A CRISIS STRIKES: WHAT TO DO

Communication is the essence of dealing with a crisis. The relationships and communications systems developed in the crisis plan must immediately spring into action. Lives are at stake. Therefore, people need to know what to do.

Demands are intense during a crisis, especially when it involves an armed attack or other life-threatening incident. This means a school system must be ready, on a minute's notice, to put first things first. Early action can save lives and lessen confusion that immediately surrounds any act of violence.

Immediate steps in dealing with an act of violence include the following:

- *Report the incident to law enforcement.* At the same time, don't be surprised if your first call comes from a reporter who has picked up the information from the police radio. *Avoid the temptation not to report an incident for fear that the school's reputation will be damaged. Not reporting it at once will cause the real damage.*
- *Get as many facts as possible.* Despite the demand for information, never report rumor.

- *If possible, verify that the school has initiated its emergency action plan.* Confirm that students and staff are being moved away from immediate danger, and determine the level of emergency that has been declared.
- *Be sure the superintendent or designee has been informed.*
- *Clear your schedule.*
- *Go to the scene.* Meet immediately with the principal or other person in charge of the control center, as well as with representatives of other agencies, such as public safety officials. Determine what decisions have been made and the dimensions of the crisis.
- *Support law enforcement in establishing controlled access to the site by the public and the media.* It is likely that the facility or area involved will be declared a crime scene, off limits to anyone other than law enforcement.
- *Be sure crisis intervention team leaders have been alerted.* These teams should immediately be deployed to work with students, staff, and parents.
- *Determine decisions yet to be made and make them.* An example might be letting parents know where they can pick up their children without tying up traffic to the detriment of emergency medical vehicles.
- *Dispatch people to help at emergency sites and student evacuation centers and to be present at hospitals and the morgue.*
- *Establish regular communication with hospitals.*
- *Determine and/or announce the location for a media camp.* During the 1999 incident at Columbine High School in Colorado, it was estimated that more than 750 media outlets were on the scene, with a large number of trucks and other vehicles.
- *Inform the media where and when an initial briefing session will be held.* Appropriate agencies on the scene, such as law enforcement, might be included in the initial briefing session.
- *Be clear about who will serve as the primary spokesperson.* Generally, the chief spokesperson will be the person in charge of districtwide communications.

- *Prepare and deliver an initial statement.*
- *Hold briefing sessions at appropriate intervals.* In the beginning, the briefings might take place hourly, then twice daily, and then daily.
- *Set up a phone bank where people can call for information.*
- *Place the contents of each briefing on the school district website.*
- *Determine when the superintendent, principal, and other key school leaders need to make statements.*
- *Call for outside help, if needed.* If assistance is needed in communications, contact the National School Public Relations Association (NSPRA) (nspra.org) or the state NSPRA chapter. If help is needed with crisis counseling, contact the National Association of School Psychologists (nasponline.org). In advance, if at all possible, arrange for low-cost or complimentary hotel rooms for volunteers who are invited to come to your community. Also consider how and when food and refreshments might be delivered to school district and volunteer staff working directly on the crisis.
- *Develop fact sheets.* Generally, fact sheets about the school already exist.
- *Be sure board members, central office staff, principals, and other staff in the school system are briefed.*
- *Prepare letters for distribution to parents.* These letters will explain the nature of the crisis and what is being done. Depending on the magnitude of the crisis, these "backpack letters" might be distributed by every school in the district.
- *Be prepared to deal consistently with copycat incidents.*
- *Establish a command center as a headquarters for communications personnel from all agencies working on the emergency.* Those agencies might range from the school system to law enforcement and human service organizations.
- *Schedule regular multiagency meetings at the command center.* At these brief meetings, information can be shared, efforts coordinated, rumors squelched, and plans made.

- *Consider holding a multiagency news conference.* The news conference might summarize what has happened during the first and second days of the crisis and provide additional time for questions.
- *Establish a central computer file for all statements and other documents produced in dealing with the incident.*
- *Hold regular debriefings.* Crisis management teams should hold regular debriefings to review what has been done and to consider strategic next steps.
- *Remember to eat and sleep.* In addition, those working directly on the crisis may need to delay their own personal grieving process.

Activate Your Communications Command Center

A command center is essential in dealing with any emergency. Whatever you call it, communications and coordinated decisions must come together at some point. Otherwise, the approach to dealing with a crisis may seem fragmented.

The following are characteristics of a command center:

- The site has been predetermined in developing the crisis plan.
- The site is near but not inside the school building or other facility that is the scene of the problem.
- All agencies substantively dealing with the crisis establish their communications operations at the center. Those agencies might include the school system, law enforcement, district attorney, Federal Emergency Management Agency (FEMA), and human service organizations.
- At least daily meetings are held involving at least one person from each agency who has strategic responsibility for dealing with the crisis. This communication promotes cooperation. Misunderstandings and misinformation are corrected. Coordinated efforts are planned. Observations, statements, and requests are shared.
- Adequate numbers of telephone lines are installed.

INITIAL COMMUNICATION IN A CRISIS

Crisis communication planners have long advised that the school's initial response to a crisis situation is important to effective communication during and after any crisis. This fact underscores the need for careful crisis communication planning. And the increasing use of social media, as well as changes in the way the news media operate, make this traditional advice even more important today. Some trends:

- Prompt communication can help to establish school officials as credible sources of information on breaking events. It can also help the school to position itself as prepared and organized to deal with the crisis.
- Students, parents, and others in the community generally will take to social media during an unfolding crisis to both post and gather information about the event. It's important that the school offer official commentary for people seeking information through social media.
- In the early stages of any breaking news event, traditional news media will often turn to social media postings to supplement their coverage. This can be an important extension for official social media postings by the school, provided they are available. In the absence of any school information the news media will often turn to other social media commentators for information and images.
- Many traditional news media now essentially operate around the clock as breaking news is posted on their websites and social media accounts when important news develops. While regular news briefings and news conferences are still important activities when handling crisis communication, ongoing communication may be more critical in the early stages of any events. Communication plans should accommodate both quick ways to disseminate information as well as prompt ways to monitor information being disseminated by others throughout the community.

Websites and other online information can be extremely valuable for disseminating information in a crisis. Use your district or school website to:

- Provide current, accurate information about the crisis and what actions the district is taking to protect students and staff.
- Post news releases and fact sheets.
- Provide tips on warning signs to watch for in children and suggestions for helping children cope with trauma.
- Provide links to other quality sites with resources and advice for parents.
- Provide a forum or chat room for parents, students, and community members to share feelings, concerns, and suggestions about the crisis and related issues.
- Post a message board for get-well wishes or condolences.
- Post safety and discipline policies and behavior codes and the consequences for violation.

Source: National School Public Relations Associations, *NSPRA's Complete Crisis Communication Management Manual for Schools* (15948 Derwood Road, Rockville, MD 20855, www.nspra.org, 2001), p. 67.

- Banks of cell phones, batteries, and battery chargers are made available.
- Banks of television monitors are set up to watch coverage from local stations and networks. A person is assigned to scan reports for new information, errors, questions that may need to be answered, and reactions to what has been said or done.
- Numerous computers are installed, all with the capacity to go online.

- All statements, memos, letters, and other written materials are stored in a common computer file as well as in daily paper files.
- News media requests are recorded on special forms. Each receives an appropriate response.
- Questions that require a specific response or action are relayed to those who can handle them.
- The school system communications staff, including qualified professional volunteers,

is organized around internal communication, external communication, news media relations, and volunteer coordination. One person is assigned to the role of strategist, observing everything that is happening, holding at least daily meetings, making strategic suggestions, and preparing crucial statements. Support staff will also be needed.

- Security is established at the command center.

WORKING WITH THE MEDIA

The news media play a critical role in times of crises as school officials seek to get information to a concerned public quickly and accurately. Being prepared to support the media in their reporting of news and information about a crisis is essential. The following suggestions can help when working with the media during a crisis.

Initial Statements Are Critical

As soon as possible after an incident, the school system and perhaps other agencies should be prepared to make an initial statement to the news media. Parents, others in the community, and often people around the world are waiting to hear what you have to say.

The following are guidelines for developing and delivering your first statements to the media:

- Try to deliver the statement in the place where later briefings will be held. The area was likely predetermined in your crisis plan.
- Plan for what you want to say and practice, keeping sentences short and words and ideas clear.
- Keep in mind that the media may already have reported some of what you have to say. However, don't allow that to deter you from reporting what people need to know. Make no assumptions.
- Remember that microphones may pick up whatever you say while walking toward or away from the briefing area.
- Keep the statement relatively brief.
- Ask yourself what you would want to know if you had a child involved.

- Objectively describe what has happened, what actions have been taken, and the present situation.
- Report that the immediate concern is the health and safety of students and staff, and perhaps others if they are involved. Share what you have done to secure their health and safety.
- Appeal to parents and other citizens. These appeals might include keeping streets and driveways open for emergency vehicles.
- Provide factual information about the school, such as enrollment, general location, name of the principal, spellings of certain personal and place names, and so on.
- Actively listen to your audience. Reflect their concerns and what they might be thinking. Help them feel confident that you share their concern and that the situation is being well managed.
- At an appropriate time, state that the education and safety of the students are driving decisions and that the school system will try to return to a sense of normalcy as soon as possible.
- Remind reporters of the school and district crisis plan and how it has been communicated.
- Provide operational information for the media, such as the time of the next briefing. You might even wish to say to the media, "Here is how you can help us…."
- Avoid taking on the role of law enforcement or health officials. Ask their spokespersons to provide relevant information, and make clear when an incident is under police investigation.
- Take questions. Use the questions as a lead for additional information that might be needed.
- Have an exit line in mind to wrap up the briefing, such as "I look forward to sharing any further information we have with you at 3:00 P.M."
- Thank everyone for coming.
- Leave the briefing immediately so that you can move on to other responsibilities.

Working with the News Media as a Crisis Continues

In a free and democratic society, the media report the news as they see it. Because of advances in technology, television and other media can, with some ease, have live pictures on the air before some key school district officials arrive on the scene. With satellites and the Web, those images may reach every part of the world within minutes of the incident.

Competition among the media has increased dramatically. Therefore, television, radio, wire services, magazines, websites, and other media will want to be on the scene early, if not first, and will constantly press for new information. The coverage of several school shootings, for example, has been wall to wall.

The general rules for working with the media still apply, such as always telling the truth. However, a crisis such as an episode of violence will require skills and actions that go far beyond the day to day.

The following are guidelines for working with the media throughout a crisis:

- The safety, security, and education of students, staff, and community are your first consideration.
- Report facts, not rumor.
- Provide regular briefings at a consistent location.
- Have the superintendent, principal, and/or other key official deliver a statement during one of the first few briefing sessions to express heartfelt concern and to give reason for confidence in how the incident is being handled.
- Set up media operations in your command center with all calls directed to the person(s) handling media requests.
- Develop a form for taking media requests. Respond appropriately to each one.
- While serving all media, set priorities, since time and the demands of the situation will make it impossible for you to handle all requests. Priorities might include local media, national and international media that serve as a source for others (e.g., CNN, Associated Press), other national media, and media from other countries.
- Accommodate as many media requests as you can. Reporters and producers will generally understand that your primary responsibility remains managing the crisis.
- Prepare talking points, brief statements that embody what the community needs to know.

Among them might be a statement that the school system's primary focus is the safety, security, and education of students and returning the schools and community to a sense of normalcy.

- Always keep in mind that if you don't provide certain information, reporters may find what they need from someone else, and it may be inaccurate.
- Investigative teams will want all questions answered by the day's deadline, despite the fact that the official investigation has only begun and may take weeks or months. Report only what you know.
- Listen to suggestions from reporters who have ideas about how to improve coverage. For example, a reporter at one briefing following a school shooting stepped from behind the camera and said, "Please, give us some new images so we don't have to keep airing that tape of kids running out of the school with their hands up."
- Remember that the site of the incident will likely be a crime scene, inaccessible to the media. First, law enforcement, and, eventually, the school system will decide when and how reporters will have access.
- Be ready for reports that certain types of media are offering substantial amounts of money for a picture from a surveillance camera or access to the crime scene.
- When needed, set up media pools (see the next section).

MEDIA POOL COVERAGE

The news media are usually helpful when the school system insists on pool coverage. Space limitations, the need to respect the sanctity of a remembrance service, or the establishment of a safe zone for students as they go back to school may call for the establishment of a media pool or, at the very least, special arrangements.

In a pool operation, one or two television networks or stations, a radio network or station, one or two photographers, and perhaps an online service might be asked to provide coverage and make it available to all other media.

Only those providing pool coverage are allowed into certain events. A special area is generally designated where they may sit. Consideration is given to where any media trucks might be stationed, sometimes at a distance or behind a barrier to lessen the appearance of a media circus. Special, highly visible badges are provided for members of the pool. Entrances are guarded, and only those with tickets or special badges may enter. Guidelines are set for the types of pictures that may or may not be acceptable—for example, no tight shots of grieving students or parents.

Most reporters are highly respectful of the need for pool coverage of certain events, such as memorial services, since they also want to respect the true meaning of the occasion. A few reporters will have just flown in and not heard of the pool arrangements. Some may try to break the pool and work their way in through other means. They should not be admitted. A cardinal rule is to never allow anyone to break the pool—doing so would send the wrong message to those who respect it.

In some cases, such as students returning to school, a special parking area might be set aside at some distance from but still in view of the school building. That arrangement will make it possible for students to return to classes without confronting reporters, while the media are still able to cover the event.

Media pools and restricted coverage are only for very special occasions or circumstances. They do not apply to day-to-day coverage.

Providing Media Access to Students and Staff

The health and safety of students and staff come first. However, immediately following an incident, reporters will very likely speak to people who were there when it happened. Reporters might also call the homes of students to get their reactions or to arrange interviews. These types of encounters are generally outside the control of the school system.

Students and staff might be involved in developing crisis plans. Through counselors, training sessions, or a student newspaper or newsletter, students might be informed about the short- and long-term effects of their comments. For example, in a crisis students will sometimes say things that they later deeply regret or will talk with reporters from publications or programs with which they may not want to be associated. In a crisis, they are vulnerable.

However, the school system, with parental consent, might make the student council president available at a media briefing or on the day students return to class. Some students may want to talk about what they have been through. Others may not.

The same is true of certain school system staff. For example, a teacher who came in direct contact with an attacker but was uninjured may be so upset by the situation that he or she is unwilling or unable to meet with reporters.

SPEAK WITH ONE CLEAR VOICE

When an incident occurs, everyone is tempted to express a point of view. However, yielding to that temptation can cause communication to break down and can even result in confusion. Reputations, and in some cases even lives, may be at stake.

All media calls should be referred to the communications office or to those assigned to handle that function. The assigned spokesperson should provide regular briefings and respond to most media requests.

The principal and superintendent will need to make statements, generally at a briefing, as soon as possible after the incident and at other appropriate times. They have other functions to perform in helping steer the system through the crisis. The superintendent and principal may also wish to call the families of those who were killed or injured, make hospital visits, and provide encouragement to the legions of staff, volunteers, community agencies, and media who are working day and night to deal with the aftermath of tragedy.

The board's primary role in a crisis is its advance consideration and adoption of a policy that supports a crisis management plan. Although board members should be briefed immediately after an incident and regularly during its aftermath, and their wise counsel should be sought, they should not speak individually with reporters about the incident. Others will have more immediate information. However, when appropriate, the board president might be asked to make statements at briefing sessions and at various events. Board members might also play key roles in comforting those who are suffering, providing support and encouragement for those on the frontline, and working with the community to remember those who were injured or whose lives might have been lost.

PREVENTION: YOUR FIRST AND BEST STRATEGY

The best way to deal with acts of violence is to stop them before they happen. One way is to pay attention to warning signs. In some cases, school systems have installed high-tech security devices. Although that type of hardware might be helpful, it is only part of the equation.

A growing body of evidence indicates that young people too often feel unaccepted, bullied, or left out. Cliques form, with names ranging from jocks and nerds to cowboys and the Trenchcoat Mafia. When certain groups gain unofficially sanctioned advantage, perhaps because they are stars of the football team, trust for the system breaks down, intolerance grows, and conflict is not far behind.

Effective communication is at the heart of a sound school climate and a culture of tolerance. Students need to be treated fairly.

According to the U.S. Department of Education, characteristics of safe schools include a focus on academic achievement, the meaningful involvement of families, solid links with the community, an emphasis on relationships among students and staff, open discussions of safety issues, students who are treated with equal respect, ways for students to share their concerns and to feel safe expressing their feelings, a system for referring children who are abused or neglected, extended day programs for students who would benefit from them, promotion of good citizenship and character, a willingness to identify problems and to assess progress toward solutions, and support for students who must make the transition from school to adult life and the workplace.

See Chapter 8 to learn how to apply the key communicator concept to identify sparks before they become fires.

RECOGNIZING THE WARNING SIGNS

In *Early Warning, Timely Response: A Guide to Safe Schools*,[6] the U.S. Department of Education, working with representatives of education leadership organizations, pinpointed a number of key warning signs to help schools identify students who might be at risk of committing an act of violence. Those warning signs include the following:

- Social withdrawal
- Excessive feelings of isolation and being alone
- Excessive feelings of rejection
- Being a victim of violence
- Feelings of being picked on or persecuted
- Low school interest and poor academic performance
- Expressions of violence in writing and drawings
- Uncontrolled anger
- Patterns of impulsive and chronic hitting, intimidating, and bullying behaviors
- History of discipline problems
- Past history of violent and aggressive behavior
- Intolerance for differences and prejudicial attitudes
- Drug use and alcohol use
- Affiliation with gangs
- Inappropriate access to, possession of, and use of firearms
- Serious threats of violence.

Immediate Warning Signs

If students exhibit certain immediate warning signs, schools should make safety a primary consideration and take immediate action. School security personnel and possibly law enforcement authorities should intervene. Parents and appropriate community organizations should be notified. Immediate warning signs include the following:

- Serious physical fighting with peers or family members
- Severe destruction of property
- Severe rage for seemingly minor reasons
- Detailed threats of lethal violence
- Possession and/or use of firearms and other weapons
- Other self-injurious behaviors or threats of suicide
- A detailed plan (time, place, method) to harm or kill others
- Carrying a weapon, particularly a firearm, and having threatened to use it.

HANDLING THE AFTERMATH OF A CRISIS

Following an act of violence, depending on the magnitude, a community and its schools should return, as soon as possible, to a sense of normalcy. Returning to "normal" and "bringing full closure" may not be realistic, since it is likely that life will never be the same.

Nonetheless, any organization or community that has gone through a period of crisis, especially when it involves an act of violence, must deal with the aftermath, while at the same time moving forward. For a school system, that means learning from what has happened, healing the wounds, and looking after the long-term health, safety, and education of students.

The following are steps to consider in dealing with the aftermath:

- *Hold debriefings.* Determine what went well and what didn't. Modify policies, plans, and procedures as needed.
- *Continue crisis counseling.* Psychological wounds may take time to heal. Many students, staff, parents, and others in the community may suffer from posttraumatic stress disorder and may have difficulty getting through the grieving process as they struggle with denial, anger, sorrow, and acceptance.
- *Be prepared for lawsuits.* When the immediate crisis subsides, people will often try to place blame. During the crisis, the school system should consult with its legal counsel and keep records of what it has done and said. A general policy of openness and a well-organized, thoughtful approach to dealing with an incident may lessen the likelihood of lawsuits.

- *Establish appropriate memorials.* Consider memorials ranging from sculptures to living memorials, such as a conference devoted to working together as a community to end violence. Preserve what people have left at memorial sites, from poems to stuffed animals.
- *Account for donations and gifts.* A school system may even want to seek further donations to fund ongoing activities in memory of those whose lives have been lost or significantly changed because of the incident.
- *Recognize those who have contributed, volunteered, or helped.* During the crisis, try to keep lists of people who have been a part of the team or who have made contributions.
- *Pay bills.* A crisis can also be costly in dollar terms. Many individuals and organizations will have incurred reimbursable expenses. Pay these bills as quickly as possible.
- *Examine school culture.* Each school should take a microscopic look at its culture and make needed changes. Exclusive versus inclusive cliques are a symptom of an even greater problem. Do some individuals and groups have advantage at the expense of others? What does the school do to make sure *all* students feel included and not excluded?
- *Be ready for long-term attention.* For years, perhaps even for decades, the news media may want to do follow-up stories; focus on certain regular events, such as back-to-school or graduation; or do flashbacks and status reports on the anniversaries of the incident. The community might also hold periodic remembrance ceremonies.

One Expert's Point of View: Crisis Communication Planning

Rick Kaufman, APR, is the Executive Director of Community Relations and Emergency Management Coordinator for Bloomington (Minnesota) Public Schools. He served in this same role for Colorado's largest public school system, where he led the Crisis Response Team for the Columbine High School tragedy in April 1999.

Kaufman is a nationally respected expert and consultant on crisis management and communications, media relations, community engagement, and communication planning.

He has provided media relations and crisis management counsel and training

(continued)

to numerous organizations, universities, and schools nationally, including the U.S. Bureau of Prisons for the Timothy McVeigh execution; the New York Education Commission and New York City Schools following the terrorist attacks in September 2001; the U.S. Department of Education; the Federal Emergency Management Agency (FEMA); the Los Angeles Office of the Federal Bureau of Investigation; and the Wisconsin Health and Hospital Association.

Kaufman stresses: "School safety must reflect the community, its capabilities, and the unique needs of local residents and students. Parents and community residents expect their schools to be a safe haven for learning and growing. As such, schools and school systems are best served when they engage parents, staff, and other stakeholders in determining what is best for their schools."

What are the most significant new, emerging trends school leaders should be paying attention to?

It is a fact that school shootings are rare and that children are safer in schools than they are outside of them. Despite these facts, it is more crucial today that schools remain vigilant in efforts to prepare for, protect against, and respond to any school emergency. No place is fail-safe.

Keeping students safe today requires better preparation, planning, and training, and adding structural elements to schools to improve security. It's a balanced approach to implementing strong security measures while maintaining a welcoming environment.

Preparation is more than saying one is prepared. It's actually having an all-hazards response plan that clearly articulates what school personnel will do in the event of a crisis. Today, more schools are embracing and implementing response plans aligned with the Incident Command System (ICS), a standardized incident management approach that allows for a coordinated response among various public and private jurisdictions and agencies.

It is one thing to have a plan; it is quite another to bring that plan to life. Merely publishing a "how-to" manual will not prepare a school system for a crisis. Being prepared is achieved through training, practice, and safety drills, because in a crisis situation, one will react as they are organized and trained.

Schools have stepped up crisis response training, from table-top scenario discussions to active shooter drills with local law enforcement and fire-safety partners. More states are mandating safety drills, including enhanced lockdown, shelter-in-place, and evacuation drills. The latter consists of unannounced or staged drills at the most inopportune times, such as passing periods or during lunch. After all, an incident can occur at any time. Crises know no time or structure limits. As educators, we can't predict when or how a situation will unfold. It is critical, therefore, to teach flexibility with the pre-established procedures for responding to an incident.

Emerging security measures designed to prevent or reduce incidents and exposure to harm and damage include access and visitor management systems, video surveillance, panic or duress alarm activation buttons, universal classroom doors with keysets that lock from the inside, and color-coded strobes in high-traffic areas such as gyms, auditoriums, and cafeterias, where public address announcements in emergency situations are ineffective due to noise levels.

Traditional news media remain important, but social and online media have become major players in crisis communication. What are the steps school leaders need to take now to be prepared to engage effectively online and in social media during a crisis?

In this age of social media, no school system should rely on any one source for sharing information about an incident. Emergency preparedness plans must account for multiple approaches to disseminating information throughout the crisis via traditional and, let's call it, "new age" communication.

When it comes to crisis communication today, here is a simple approach to being prepared:

Before the Crisis: Engage/Anticipate

Social media is a tool to engage parents and stakeholders in conversations. By doing so early (read, before a crisis), schools establish a community of participants (for example "friends" on Facebook, "followers" on Twitter, and so on), and a familiarity as the "go to" source for information about an incident (and how schools are responding). In an emergency, people will seek information wherever they can find it.

Huge dividends are afforded schools successful in creating a relationship with a community of participants. These "key communicators" become online influencers who have the ability to get to a wide range of audiences in times of a crisis to manage rumors and correct misinformation.

Social media also provides an alternate or redundant mode of communication when other systems are down.

During the Crisis: Communicate

While social media provides a whole new set of challenges and opportunities, the fundamentals of crisis communication don't change. Managing any crisis successfully is less about saying the right things and more about doing the right things.

Communication is the foundation of any crisis planning, response, and recovery. Therefore, keeping two-way lines of communication open will express better transparency and help re-establish the organization's reputation when a crisis hits. One-way messaging doesn't work anymore in a world where people crave dialogue.

After the Crisis: Communicate

Re-engaging on social media platforms may be the best opportunity to regain the trust of stakeholders, and to lead the way in connecting the community after a crisis to help in the recovery effort.

The more schools engage in social media from the beginning, the better positioned they will be to anticipate, communicate and regain trust in order to help manage and reduce the severity of a crisis.

Why are early identification of potential crises and early intervention in these areas becoming important steps in crisis communication management? And how can school leaders develop a system or procedures for the quick identification of potential problems?

The tragic events of Columbine, Virginia Tech, Sandy Hook, and others have made us painfully aware that our schools will continue to be targets of violence. Schools are an integral part of their neighborhoods—a microcosm of the environment in which they reside—and therefore are vulnerable to the influences and factors present in the larger community.

And, while schools are well suited to provide support and assistance during the crisis and in its aftermath, they must be equally adept at providing systems for mitigating or preventing incidents through early identification and/or intervention.

The most important steps a school can initiate in preventing violence involve the affective rather than physical environment. (Though physical changes to improve safety and security should not be discounted, but rather incorporated into a comprehensive security plan.) These include promoting a positive school climate and culture, teaching and modeling pro-social behaviors, and providing effective intervention when anti-social behaviors occur. Of critical importance are procedures for detecting early warning signs of violence, and school-wide screening procedures and mentoring or counseling programs that enable schools to identify and provide support to alienated or at-risk youth.

Students' access to and use of high-tech devices and social media platforms—what some dub as "Generation Text"—have resulted in a wave of school closures and other disruptions. Students texting messages or posting information on social media sites fuel rumors and misinformation that often create more anxiety than any actual threat or incident. School leaders must have a comprehensive crisis communications plan for managing rapidly escalating rumors around school safety incidents.

Finally, students are often the first to be privy to a leak of intentions or rumors about planned or real incidents—even those where suspected perpetrators, when caught, brush their intentions off as play—and therefore need to know they can come forward with information that may save their life. Getting that information to an adult or school official is a critically important mitigation measure.

When talking with communication directors and superintendents who have a crisis plan that hasn't been updated or tested in some time, what do you tell them? What concerns should they have? And how should they go about keeping plans ready for action in today's environment?

Two key points: 1) In a crisis situation, one will react as he or she is organized and trained; and 2) Knowing what to do can be the difference between chaos and calm, or even life and death. Therefore, a crisis plan is a necessity. Putting it into practice is an absolute.

An emergency operations or all hazards plan is only as good as the ability of students and staff to execute it. School drills save lives and property. Training prepares staff and emergency response teams to effectively manage emergency situations that cannot be prevented.

Drills and crisis response training creates a cultural condition that practice is important. It also demonstrates the necessary teamwork needed during a crisis. School personnel are more confident in making decisions to manage an emergency when they have proper training aligned with the school or district's plan.

School leaders need to know that when confronted with a crisis, the best they can hope for is to stay abreast of the evolving incident and its impacts. Crisis, by its nature, is reactive, and no two crises are alike.

Thus, school leaders are wise to periodically re-evaluate their security measures, response protocols, and procedures that may be missing or need to be improved to ensure students and staff are better prepared in the event of an incident. Crisis response plans are living documents, not meant to gather dust on a shelf, and certainly not meant to be pulled off the shelf for the first time when an incident occurs.

It should be noted that each crisis provides an opportunity for organizational (and staff) learning and a review of response plans. A post-crisis review—whether the incident was local or is one that plays out on the national stage—should be conducted. The guiding questions to be asked in this review: What worked well and what didn't work? What are the key lessons learned? What changes do we need to make to our school, procedures, and other steps?

How do school leaders handle fallout from crises elsewhere?

Think of it this way ... for a minute, our world is a calm pond. Toss a rock into the pond. The point of impact is the epicenter of a school crisis. The concentric

(*continued*)

circles ripple outwardly, violent at first, then eventually dissipating the farther out from the point of impact. This is the image I use to describe how a tragedy impacts school communities across the country.

The closer the school and community is to an incident, the more profound the impact and, subsequently, the longer the "return to normalcy" takes. The farther from the school and community, the less of an impact, both in the immediacy and over time. Yet we are all touched by school tragedies. Nothing is more tragic than a child's life cut short. Superintendents and principals nationwide are thrust into action when incidents of school violence garner intense media coverage. School leaders must be prepared to offer parents assurances that their child's school is safe, and measures are in place to respond to similar events. They must guide staff members about what to say to children, and make crisis counselors available should students need to talk.

Communication to parents and guardians is critical to reduce anxiety and fear, as are efforts to meet the emotional needs of students, many of whom are often steeped in the nonstop news coverage of the incident. Expect children refusing to go to school, new or copycat threats, and a whole host of controversial ideas from politicians and profiteers on how best to protect children.

Local media become a bit rabid in the wake of school violence, aiming to "localize" the tragedy that may be hundreds or thousands of miles away. While some school leaders opt out of responding to these types of media inquiries, others that choose to participate will do best to focus on a few key messages that reinforce XYZ school district's crisis response plans and safety measures.

There are pros and cons to each approach. Determining whether to participate in this very public discourse, and in some cases scrutiny, must be measured carefully and with one goal in mind ... how does this help our schools, our students and their families, and our staff?[7] ■

Questions

1. Beyond planning, what is the importance of rehearsing or conducting drills on crisis preparedness to ensure effective crisis communication?

2. How might a crisis in one school district cause another school district to become the focus of media attention—even when it isn't directly involved in the crisis? How can school communicators prepare for such media interest?

3. Explain the importance of using online and social media in crisis communication and the roles they can play in crisis communication.

4. What are the major steps to undertake in dealing with the aftermath of a crisis?

5. What characteristics and skills should be considered when choosing a spokesperson for a crisis? What's the most important ability needed?

Readings

Fearn-Banks, Kathleen, *Crisis Communication: A Casebook Approach*, 5th ed. New York, NY: Routledge 2016.

Lukaszewski, James E., and Kristen Noakes-Fry, *Lukaszewski on Crisis Communication*. Brookfield, CT: Rothstein, 2013.

National School Public Relations Association, *The Complete Crisis Communication Management Manual*, 2nd ed. Rockville, MD: Author, 2008.

National School Public Relations Association, "The Role of Communication in Crisis Management," *School Public Relations*, 2nd ed. Rockville, MD: Author, 2008.

Thomas, R. Murray, *Violence in America's Schools: Understanding, Prevention, and Responses*. Lanham, MD: Rowman and Littlefield Education, 2009.

Videos

Prince William County (VA) Schools: Crisis Management: What Parents Should Know https://youtu.be/mO9y-xFOfzU

Lamar (TX) CISD: CISD Family Springs into Action during Hurricane Harvey https://youtu.be/azwUxCn62vc

Nixa (Mo.) Public Schools: Community Update on Mold Issue https://youtu.be/mfxl5R4Pwp4

Montgomery County (MD) Public Schools: Emergency Preparedness Video https://youtu.be/vJFlUR5iKSg

Montgomery County (MD) Public Schools: Emergency Preparedness Video (elementary grades) https://youtu.be/7dBdbcnV0Bk

News coverage: lead testing https://youtu.be/X959LY30UXs

News coverage: preparedness drills https://youtu.be/SmsZ4T825PE

News coverage: safety inspections https://youtu.be/lHdvF0InpCY

News coverage: school violence event https://youtu.be/-QbbDrnxzoc

News coverage: health event https://youtu.be/KPft86n0aAY

News coverage: lockdown event https://youtu.be/ZAsQ-E7jPbc

News coverage: lockdown event https://youtu.be/sY3mn_7K9KI

News coverage: weather event https://youtu.be/1IPz7CkM67c

News coverage: environmental event https://youtu.be/6Yk6rwsn7E0

News coverage: transportation event https://youtu.be/Vqgv1cKGsp4

Other Resources

Some organizations providing research and resources on crisis communication planning issues for schools include:

The National School Public Relations Association, http://www.nspra.org.

The National Association of School Psychologists, http://www.nasponline.org/resources-and-publications/resources/school-safety-and-crisis.

The Readiness and Emergency Management for Schools Technical Assistance Center, http://rems.ed.gov>/.

U.S. Department of Education, https://www2.ed.gov/admins/lead/safety/crisisplanning.html.

Endnotes

1. National School Public Relations Association, *School Public Relations: Building Confidence in Education* (Rockville, MD: Author, 2007), p. 155.

2. Minnesota School Public Relations Association, *Crisis Communication 101*. Retrieved October 19, 2017, at https://minnspra.org/wp-content/uploads/2015/09/Crisis-Communication-Tip-Sheet.pdf.

3. Centers for Disease Control and Prevention, "Youth Violence: Facts at a Glance—2012." Retrieved September 14, 2014, at http://www.cdc.gov/violenceprevention/pdf/yv-datasheet-a.pdf.

4. National Center for Education Statistics, "Indicators of School Crime and Safety: 2012." Retrieved September 14, 2014, at http://nces.ed.gov/pubs2013/2013036.pdf.

5. University of Michigan, "Schools Can Help Stem Violence by Taking Charge of Public Areas," *Michigan News*, May 16, 1999. Retrieved at http://ns.umich.edu/new/releases/2741-schools-can-help-stem-violence-by-taking-charge-of-public-areas.

6. U.S. Department of Education, "Early Warning, Timely Response: A Guide to Safe School," August 1998. Retrieved September 15, 2014, at http://cecp.air.org/guide/guide.pdf.

7. Taken from correspondence in January 2014 with Rick Kaufman, APR, Executive Director of Community Relations and Emergency Management Coordinator, Bloomington Public Schools, Bloomington, MN.

Chapter

10

Communication about School Services, Activities, and Events

This chapter reviews issues . . .

- For central administrators: How contacts between the school and community should be assessed and supported in a sound school–community relations program.
- For building and program administrators: The roles that building and program leaders can fulfill to expand community visibility for and understanding of school services while building constructive working relationships.
- For teachers, counselors, and staff: The ways in which frontline employees can prepare for successful communication in community contacts and improve their personal communication effectiveness.

After completing this chapter you should be able to . . .

- Identify key school services and their relationships to school–community relations planning and practices.
- Distinguish the role of events in school–community relations programs.
- Outline the ways in which public interaction in the delivery of school services, and participation in school events, can influence public understanding, perception, and support.

Many sections of this text consider the importance of mediated communication and how schools use traditional and digital media to reach key audiences. But the ability to build strong working relationships with the community also depends on effective face-to-face communication in the many ways in which schools and community members typically interact. Interpersonal communication between school employees and those in the community creates the foundation of trust and respect essential to success.

Clearly, school leaders see the need for excellence in interpersonal communication in school staff. Consider the sample requirements called for in these three job descriptions for school public relations staff members:

- "Excellent oral and written communication skills. Outstanding interpersonal skills."
- "Excellent interpersonal skills and the ability to communicate effectively, orally, and in writing; excellent public speaking skills."
- "This position requires someone with excellent interpersonal and written communication, organizational and analytical skills."

Interpersonal communication might be viewed as the verbal and non-verbal communication, as well as the listening and language skills, used in direct communication with others—individually and in groups. The ways in which an individual or group communicates with others can in fact influence both the effectiveness of the communication as well as the health of the relationship between those engaged with one another. Some examples of how interpersonal communication can influence school–community relations include:

- Active, effective listening can, for example, communicate empathy for a point of view, while failing to hear or appearing unresponsive to someone speaking can communicate indifference or a lack of caring.
- Non-verbal actions while communicating, such as maintaining eye contact or using appropriate facial expressions, can reinforce spoken communication and display an interest in what others are saying. Looking annoyed or angry can weaken the ability to communicate.
- Tone, in both written and spoken communication, can influence communication effectiveness. Starting an e-mail with "Dear Mr. Smith" perhaps will communicate a more respectful and welcoming tone than just a curt "Mr. Smith." When speaking, a tone of anger, annoyance, or incredulousness also can influence communication.
- Even signage can influence face-to-face interactions. Prominent welcome signs can set a

hospitable mood facilitating effective communication. Something as simple as wearing a name tag when meeting school visitors also can offer an appearance of a willingness to communicate. Similarly, well-kept facilities can project an image of caring and pride while unkept facilities can appear unwelcoming or suggest a lack of concern for quality.

School leaders seeking strong, working school–community relationships need to assess the many ways in which the school system interacts with those in the community and the need to prepare all school representatives and school facilities to make those interactions as successful as possible.

This chapter considers many of the typical forms of school–community contacts that can influence understanding, support, and relationships.

CONTACTS WITH THE BOARD OF EDUCATION OR TRUSTEES

School board members and trustees can play a significant role in helping the school district build strong relationships with audiences throughout the community. What people think and how they feel about a school system are influenced by the board of education. Because of the board's central position, the behavior of members and the nature of their decisions are watched carefully by citizens and school employees.

Board Meetings

School board meetings offer the school district many opportunities to project a positive image supported by inclusive leadership and open communication. By law board meetings are required to be public meetings, specifically to keep the local citizens informed about their schools. A school board that conducts an informative meeting goes far in carrying out the spirit of the right-to-know statutes. Those boards that acknowledge the presence of local citizens at a public meeting by affording them an opportunity to address the board will build much trust and public faith in the community. On the other hand, boards that conduct public meetings in a vacuum, by not explaining certain actions to citizens in attendance, serve to build a climate of mistrust with the very folks who can help the schools. Helpful suggestions on what a board should and should not do at a public meeting are contained in the following list.

Some Do's and Don'ts for School Board Meetings

School communicators should:

- Make certain that any communication complies with local and state laws and regulations that govern such meetings.

DO

- Distribute agendas containing all the nonconfidential material the board members have.
- Start on time. Some attendees may turn into critics if a meeting is delayed for an unreasonable length of time without appropriate explanation.
- Provide adequate seating for guests.
- Have legible nameplates in front of every board member.
- Provide a special place for the press, preferably near the board members. Also assign a school representative to sit with the reporters to answer any immediate questions. A press table near the board will enable the reporters to cover all details of the meeting. This proximity to board action will minimize inaccurate reporting.
- Give citizens an opportunity to address the board.
- Explain to the public any action or discussion by the board that may need clarification.
- Be careful with off-the-cuff remarks and other commentary. Inappropriate, impromptu comments can easily offend others; with the press present, these remarks may appear verbatim in news coverage of the meeting.
- Take the opportunity to have some function of the school district highlighted. It is an ideal occasion to have students talk about studies, teachers explain a new course or program, or a noninstructional person discuss or present on transportation, food-service, or maintenance issues.

DON'T

- Do not permit nonresidents to address the board unless the content of their remarks is known ahead of time. It is not uncommon for organized groups to send representatives to board meetings to promote a cause and unwittingly spread unnecessary alarm and concern.
- Do not permit citizens to speak out at just any point in a meeting. A specific time should be set aside for them to address the board. If this policy is not adhered to, a school board will have no control over its own meetings.
- Do not interrupt a regular meeting with an executive session. Instead, when possible schedule such sessions before or after the regular meeting.
- Do not become involved in an argument with a citizen at a public meeting. A number of people who address school boards will attempt to use the meeting as a public forum, hoping that they will stir the anger of a school board. A polite "Thank you" after a citizen's remarks can often eliminate further problems.
- Do not become involved in spending an inordinate amount of time discussing minor items.

Many boards have made great efforts in recognizing citizens at board meetings and in keeping them informed about procedures and about board members. Many boards distribute a brochure and offer online information to help citizens understand how school board meetings work. Material should include the names of the school board members, information on how to address the board, the time and place of monthly meetings, and the names of the administrators. Such a publication is helpful to the people attending the meeting and shows them that the school district is sincerely interested in communicating with its citizens.

Politics and Boards

The political nature of both elected and appointed school boards is a fact of life for public school systems. Unfortunately, politically dominated school boards—which receive their orders from the local political machine and therefore make decisions that benefit the party in power—can present special problems for school–community relations efforts. Board decisions serve the community and the school system best when the input and concerns of school leadership, the community, teachers, students, and others—in addition to political concerns—are considered.

When politics appear to dominate board actions, however, the school system can be viewed as a haven for political patronage appointments, Local citizens also may place less trust in school districts with politically dominated boards. The news media can be less trusting of such school boards and may constantly question their decisions. No matter what the board does, even when its moves are educationally sound, the media may be more apt to see an ulterior political motive. Community groups can be reluctant to become actively involved in such school districts because of knowledge of the political control in the district. Even a structured community relations program can be harmed because the taxpayers may place little confidence in what a politically oriented school district says.

Boards that balance political priorities with school and community concerns are better able to project a dedication to sound decision-making focused on school and student success. Not enough stress can be placed on the importance of keeping the public informed of board business and decisions. In communities where good schools are steadily undergoing improvement, the board of education generally engages its community by sharing its problems with the people and educating them about the needs and policies of the system. This often is done by publishing complete and accurate reports of official meetings in school media and through local news coverage, by letting the public know what questions must be decided at future meetings, by inviting citizen expression of opinion before policy adoption, by authorizing the superintendent to prepare materials for the information of taxpayers, by having citizens involved in setting goals and evaluating them for a school system, and by fostering transparency by doing business in the open. Every board should develop a plan for informing the people about what it stands for and what it does in the interest of children and the community.

RECEIVING SCHOOL VISITORS

Board of education relations with the public are supplemented by face-to-face contacts between school employees and businesspeople, salespeople, job applicants, parents, social workers, and others who have occasion to visit schools and school system offices. These contacts are crucial in the formation of impressions that create public opinion. School employees should be trained to handle these contacts successfully, and the appearance of offices should be considered in terms of the effect these have on school visitors.

Staff Training

All school employees should know how to meet visitors. They should understand the importance of common courtesy and realize the importance of performing services willingly and efficiently. Periodic community relations workshops should be conducted for all noninstructional staff members.

FRONTLINE WORKERS

A thorough and specialized program should be developed for office workers. These individuals are in the front line of community relations. For a visitor to the schools or to a telephone caller they *are* the school. Often what they say or do creates a lasting impression on the public. The following suggestions are offered by the National School Public Relations Association:[1]

In order to build a positive image—good public relations—a school must have a warm climate and caring staff and must constantly encourage students to be the best they can be. In addition, the school must work hard at communicating its good image to others. The goal is to build support for the students, the school, and the school district.

The frontline army of communicators in most schools is the support staff. They are, more often than not, the first people to greet children and parents each day. Bus drivers are the first and last school employees many children see daily, school secretaries are the key office contact for parents and teachers, and the groundskeeper may be the only employee some homeowners (without children) near the campus ever see.

As frontline communicators, support staff have tremendous credibility with the public, and along with that a tremendous responsibility to deliver a good first impression of the school or district.

The following are some tips to help everyone in your school, not just support staff, to become better communicators:

- Know important facts about your school and district.
- Get to know the people who deal regularly with your school and its employees. They are often community opinion leaders, so help them get the answers to their questions.
- Treat every patron who comes to or calls the school like a board member. Treat every staff member like the superintendent.
- Acknowledge people immediately. Greet the parent *and* child. Learn names whenever possible.
- Don't appear to protect or cover for an administrator, but don't speak for him or her.
- Never act or appear superior to others.
- Use positive body language.
- Be empathetic. Deal with people from the heart.
- Don't give opinions. Listen to all sides of a story. Don't jump to conclusions.
- Let people know you care and have pride in your job and your school.
- Avoid gossip. Be mindful of confidentiality.
- Maintain a positive office/campus atmosphere.
- Know the process your school or district takes when handling inquiries. Share that information when parents and others ask you for assistance.
- If you hear rumors about your school or district, report what you hear to your immediate supervisor. Also, seek clarification on the rumor.[2]

As a follow-up to a workshop, a manual for good community relations can be developed for continual review by secretaries and clerical personnel. It should outline exact expressions and procedures to use in answering telephone or e-mail inquiries. Such topics as being friendly with people, the need for prompt and efficient service, situations calling for patience and tact, meeting requests for information, where to make referrals, and how to be a good listener should be included.

CUSTODIANS, MAINTENANCE WORKERS, AND BUS DRIVERS

Often forgotten in any community relations workshop are the custodians, maintenance workers, and bus drivers. Yet these individuals can be very instrumental in creating a positive image with the public. Often, they are the initial contact with the school system for many citizens.

In a community relations workshop, custodians and maintenance workers should be reminded of the importance of being helpful and friendly to visitors to a school. They should have a thorough knowledge of the school and the school system in order to give visitors proper directions and to refer them to the person most likely to be helpful. If there is an evening public event, the custodians on duty should be aware of the importance of their own appearance and that of the areas to be used by the visitors.

Bus drivers, in a sense, take the school physically onto the highways as they move along streets and roads in their conspicuous yellow vehicles. Their manner of driving, hopefully courteous and safe, goes a long way in advancing a school system's community relations program. Occasionally, they will meet parents at bus stops. They should be friendly and answer questions as best they can, avoid arguments, and be sensitive to the parents' innate concern for the safety of their children. Periodically, bus drivers should have the opportunity to attend workshops highlighting their community relations responsibilities as members of the school district family. Some school systems issue community relations guidelines for transportation workers. Districts that outsource transportation should provide written information about schools to the applicable bus drivers and work with vendors to assure that appropriate school–community relations training is offered.

FOOD-SERVICE WORKERS

Much of the community relations responsibility of school food-service workers occurs within the school itself during contact with students, other employees, and administrators. There are occasions, however, when food-service workers come in contact with the community, such as during meals served to the public at special events. Personal appearance, efficient service, and courtesy are paramount at such an event:

The impression made goes a long way in conveying a good image of the school.

Moreover, in their contacts with citizens away from the school, food-service workers should know where citizens can get the correct answers to questions about the school system. It is the responsibility of the administrators to schedule community relations workshops for these workers to help them carry out their public relations role.

Appearance of Offices

The appearance of school offices contributes to the impressions visitors take back into the community. As much as possible, offices should reflect the spirit and educational ideals of the system. All rooms where visitors contact office personnel and wait for appointments should be furnished in good taste, painted in attractive colors with pictures on the walls. Businesses have recognized the contribution of properly equipped offices and waiting rooms in winning the goodwill of customers, and they have employed receptionists or greeters who are trained to meet and welcome visitors. The same technique could be used by school systems at little or no additional cost by placing qualified secretaries or clerks in this position and scheduling other work for them to do at the reception desks.

HANDLING TELEPHONE CALLS, E-MAIL, AND CORRESPONDENCE

The number of direct personal contacts with school visitors is small compared with the number of contacts made through telephone calls, e-mails, and other forms of correspondence. Too often the use of these tools is taken as a matter of fact, and their part in a community relations program is not considered. Nevertheless, telephone calls and correspondence do determine the nature of the impressions people get of a school system.

Telephone Calls

Each time an employee of a school picks up the telephone to answer a call from a parent, to talk with someone in the community, or to inquire about the price of instructional materials, he or she is playing a vital role in the community relations program of the school. The telephone, which is taken so much for granted, is a powerful influence on school-community relations, for better or for worse.

Parents are naturally interested in their children and should feel that it is proper to pick up the telephone and inquire of a teacher when a question arises about a child's reading, writing, or mathematics or about something that occurred at school.

The handling of telephone calls to or from the home, involving children at school, also requires tact and good judgment. Messages from parents usually can be delivered to the child rather than the child being called to the telephone. Knowing that the child can be contacted if necessary leaves parents satisfied that the school is doing its part and that the child is in good hands.

The telephone is the most personal contact some citizens have with the superintendent and central office staff. Impressions of the type of people in the office begin with the receptionist handling incoming calls. It is easy to conclude that a school system is well run or poorly run by the greeting "Hello, City Schools" and the conversation during the next few seconds. In a business, this voice can mean a satisfied customer or the loss of a sale. In a school system, it can mean a vote for the schools at the polls or the loss of a friend of education. The telephone manners of the receptionist and other personnel answering calls should receive careful consideration at all times. Frequently transferred calls, long hold times, unanswered voice mails, and other abuses can play havoc with a school system's community relations.

Surprising improvement can be made in telephone manners and techniques when special instruction is given to employees. Simple demonstrations and periodic discussions of the problem are enough to bring about good results. The secret of continued success, however, lies in delegating responsibility to a staff member for supervising telephone service whether within a single building or for the entire school system.

Schools also can jeopardize good community relations by misusing voice-mail regardless of how much emphasis is placed on the economics of it. When concerned parents or citizens calling the school have to work their way through a menu of numbers and names they can quickly become irritated or worse. Inefficient or complex voice-mail menus communicate a "we don't care about you" message to callers. School communication planners should assess how voice mail and other telephone technology accommodates callers.

School Correspondence

E-mail messages and letters offer some advantages over face-to-face relations and over telephone conversations as a form of personal contact. Personal correspondence, whether online, through notes sent home, or through the mail, enables the writer to communicate directly and economically with the other person and to exercise more control over the expression of ideas. These advantages make correspondence an effective instrument in community relations, especially if the tone is warm and friendly and if mechanical details are correct.

No contact should be allowed to remain unanswered for several days. In fact, e-mail inquiries should be acknowledged promptly—ideally on the same day in which they are received. Common courtesy demands a prompt reply. Where facts must be gathered and opinions sought that will cause a delay, an interim e-mail message or letter should be written explaining the situation and promising complete information in the near future. In general, all correspondence should be concise and to the point, with thought given to an outline of the contents before they are written. If it appears that an inquiry or request requires a lengthy message, a telephone call may make it possible to handle the matter through a personal interview instead.

To tell an effective story, educators must consider the person with whom they are corresponding. When writing any correspondence, the following factors should be considered.

STEREOTYPED PHRASES
The quality of content in any correspondence may be lowered through the use of stereotyped business phrases, which tend to make replies stiff and formal. Antiquated expressions, such as the following, should be scrupulously avoided: *beg to advise, happy to inform you, please be advised, permit me to state, replying to yours, due to the fact that, may I call your* *attention to, wish to acknowledge, kindly advise, beg to assure, regret to inform.*

JARGON
As in every profession, there is a tendency among educators to employ jargon or a technical vocabulary in discussing their problems and to use phrases that are foreign to the thinking of other people. Words and phrases should convey ideas easily and understandably; they should not be barriers to communication. Jargon words and phrases, such as *cooperative learning, experience unit, heterogeneous grouping, integrated curricular progression, linguistic construction level, quantified standardization,* and *instructional media,* appear to exclude others from the conversation and weaken communication in correspondence.

POSITIVE AND NEGATIVE WORDS
It is always important to state ideas in a way that evokes positive rather than negative responses. Of the two lists given in Table 10.1, one contains words and phrases that are considered to provoke negative responses, and the other suggests ways of expressing the same ideas to elicit positive reactions. Both lists may prove helpful as a start in checking school correspondence and improving future writing.

TONE
The tone of an e-mail message or letter plays a prominent part in influencing the reaction of its reader. It should be warm, friendly, conversational, and, above all, written as though it were spoken directly to the person who reads it.

Getting the right tone also means finding the right words to express positive rather than negative images. Rich Bagin, writing in *Making Parent Communication Effective and Easy,* notes:

> The terse nature of e-mail means it has the potential to sound curt and impersonal. Be sure your copy sets the right tone—especially when you respond to an e-mail from an angry or defensive parent.[3]

SIMPLICITY
Words and ideas used in letters to the public should be simple and mean essentially the same thing to most

TABLE 10.1	Examples of Negative and Positive Phrasing

Use positive examples to convey information and details. Negatives often create a distrustful tone that is not conducive to prompting action. On the other hand, positive statements help create a positive tone. Add examples from your own experience.

Instead of . . .	Consider . . .
I can't send the grades until you sign a request form.	I'll send the grades as soon as we receive your signed request form.
I leave the school at 3:30.	I'll be in the school until 3:30.
The program is closed to all students with failing GPAs.	The program is open to all students with passing GPAs.

Source: Reprinted with permission from Rich Bagin, *Making Parent Communication Effective and Easy.* Copyright 2005 by the National School Public Relations Association, Rockville, MD, www.nspra.org.

people. A sentence intended for one of President Roosevelt's famous fireside chats in its original form was "We are planning an all-inclusive society." In the talk, the sentence had been rewritten to be "We are building a society in which no one will be left out." Simple words transformed this sentence into one that practically everyone could understand.

FORM LETTERS AND MASS E-MAILS

Form letters and mass e-mails, disseminated in large numbers, are economical and at times functional. Too often these communications are reproduced on poor-quality paper, designed badly, and easily overlooked if they appear too much like junk mail or spam. The number of form letters and mass e-mails should be kept to the barest minimum unless they can be given the appearance of personal correspondence. Otherwise, they may not be read.

HANDLING COMPLAINTS

Complaints are made about almost every phase of school operation and the educational program. In some respects, such complaints are the inevitable and normal outcome of institutional functioning. Coming from private citizens and organized groups, complaints are made to all personnel in a school system, including board members, administrative officials, teachers, and noninstructional staff members. Whether the complaints are justified or not, good community relations require that they be handled systematically and efficiently.

Importance of Complaints

The proper handling of complaints is important for several reasons. Parents and others who complain do so because they have grievances, real or imagined. They want them addressed and resolved. Unless the school welcomes their complaints, extends courteous treatment, and takes positive action within reasonable limits, goodwill will be destroyed and resentment increased.

Large business firms look upon complaints as one of their best sources of public relations information. Some keep careful records of all complaints, no matter how trivial they may seem, and review them periodically. This material enables them to get a picture of prevailing attitudes toward company policies and of shifts taking place in public reactions. Of somewhat greater importance, however, is the knowledge these firms acquire of weak spots in their organization and of services that are failing to meet the criteria of good public relations. Research indicates that when complaints are handled well, people tell others about the treatment they received and buy more of the product. When complaints are not handled well, people tell others and buy less of that product.

Schools too should look at complaints as an opportunity to improve relationships with the community and strengthen their image and reputation in the community.

Procedures for Servicing Complaints

School personnel who are called upon to handle complaints must learn the gentle art of listening while people purge themselves of the problems that weigh on them. For example, anger, fear, or resentment growing out of a feeling that a child has been mistreated builds up within the individual until finally release must be obtained. An understanding of the effectiveness of a sympathetic and attentive listener under these circumstances is important.

Complaints and criticisms usually should be allowed to flow freely. Experience has taught many superintendents and principals the effectiveness of listening without comment. When the relaxation that follows severe tension under such circumstances is achieved, it is often advisable to say that the matter will be investigated and that the person making the complaint will be called on for assistance at a later date.

When handled in this manner, most complaints seem to lose their intensity. Quite frequently the parent, citizen, or teacher who has demanded to see that justice be done will request that an investigation not be made if it will embarrass the wrong person. The complainant's reason for bringing the matter to the attention of the school official, it is pointed out, has not been to get the person in trouble, but rather to be sure that the official has all the facts. Chapter 8 gives further details on meeting criticism and attacks.

School personnel, especially those in administrative positions, must learn to analyze criticisms and complaints objectively. Unjustified complaints should be handled in a dignified and professional manner. A sincere belief that the schools belong to the people leaves no other course of action.

MEETING EVERYDAY CONTACTS

Every person who is connected with a public school system enjoys innumerable contacts with people in the community after regular working hours and over weekends, holidays, and vacations. Although little attention is paid to the import of these informal contacts for community relations, people get many of their ideas and impressions about a school system from them.

Boards of education and administrators must recognize that the everyday contacts of employees outside of the school are part of the community relations program. Ideally, they should see that teachers and nonteachers understand important facts about the system, feel responsible for representing the school in the best manner possible, and keep their disappointments and troubles within the institutional family.

REQUESTS FOR INFORMATION

Expressions such as "Do they think we should know everything?" have been used by school employees following telephone calls requesting information. Instead of being critical, school personnel should consider such a request a challenge and an opportunity. For those school systems that accept the supplying of information as a normal service function, certain techniques of community relations are to be observed and implemented. Since many requests will be made by telephone or e-mail, the basic principles of telephone and e-mail courtesy discussed previously must be observed.

Important printed documents that can assist school employees in answering requests for information are a handbook, directory, and school calendar. Citizens do not expect school staff members to be walking encyclopedias, but they do have a right to expect that these employees will have readily available certain basic information about the school system. If an employee is unable to supply the information requested, he or she should give the name and contact information of the person who can supply it.

According to the National School Public Relations Association, the majority of school superintendents surveyed reported "handling information requests" is one way in which effective communication adds value to the management and operation of the school district.[4]

All school records and documents, except those pertaining to individuals covered by privacy laws, are open and available to the public. Included, for example, are e-mails, computer files, financial records, databases, and videos.

It's imperative that school districts have a written policy covering requests for recorded information and support appropriate employees with training on managing requests for such information. Putting as much information as possible on the district's website can help reduce the number of such requests while creating a greater sense of openness or transparency for the school system.

Working with the school district's attorney, the public relations director and other administrators should become familiar with the Freedom of Information Act (FOIA), the Family Educational Rights and Privacy Act (FERPA), and the state's public record laws. These will provide the backdrop for answering requests for information.

PARTICIPATION IN COMMUNITY LIFE

The number of contacts increases and the school and its professional personnel take on new importance when staff members become identified with the social and civic life of the community. Thought must be given to staff preparation and opportunities for participation.

The Importance of Community Participation

Four significant gains are made in community relations when staff members become active in the life of the community. First, the attitudes of citizens change when they know the men and women who are responsible for their schools. Second, participation opens opportunities for social and civic leadership and, consequently, higher status in the community. Third, participation enables staff members to discuss the schools with many people. Fourth, evidence supports the hypothesis that citizen concern for education increases as staff personnel become more actively identified with the social and civic life of the community.

Staff Preparation

School personnel who take part in community life should have insight into and understanding of people and institutions if they are to function successfully in their capacity either as professional employees or as private citizens. They should be familiar with local history, ethnic and religious groups, customs, prejudices, and social restrictions. They ought to know something of the cultural and economic life of the community, its social agencies, form of government, and channels of communication. Awareness of social organization and community leaders is important.

The bulk of this information should be available from the findings of the sociological survey described in Chapter 3. With this knowledge, staff members are more likely to be tolerant of local customs, to avoid pitfalls and conflict situations, and to follow an intelligent course of action in their relations with the public.

Participation in Community Activities

Teachers and students have many opportunities to participate in community life. Neighborhoods and districts can present real problems for study and social action. There are hundreds of problems—including, for example, traffic hazards, proper methods of handling trash and recyclables, youth recreational needs, fire protection, clean streets, and so on. Public contacts growing out of successful study projects by students and teachers develop respect for the school and lay the groundwork for future cooperation.

Similar results have been achieved in districts where administrators, teachers, and students responded to requests for assistance from agencies and service organizations interested in the education and welfare of children. Some of the activities in which the school can participate are surveying community recreational needs, locating students who would benefit from special school or community services, organizing athletic events for after-school and vacation periods, participating in forums and public discussions on local issues, increasing public library or computer facilities, and developing summer study camps for young children.

Participation Identifies Local Talent

Another aspect of participation is that of using community resources for instructional purposes. Any number of competent men and women are available to talk with students about their special vocational and avocational interests, to lend objects and materials high in instructional value, and to share their knowledge and experience with teachers in curriculum study programs. Classes may be taken on field trips to worthwhile places and interviews scheduled with people in positions of leadership. Cooperative work experience and tours of business and industry are means for understanding the economic life of the community and appreciating employment demands. Each time such resources are used, they enrich instruction and create friendship between citizens and representatives of the school.

Participation Through Group Membership

Instructional and non-instructional employees should be encouraged to join community groups and organizations. Their own lives become richer by associating with people of different occupational backgrounds and interests and by engaging in activities of a challenging and enjoyable nature. At the same time, they are in an excellent position to interpret the school and to acquire a knowledge of how people react toward its programs.

APPEARANCE OF SCHOOL FACILITIES

The appearance of all school facilities, both outside and inside, has a continuing and cumulative effect on public attitudes toward a school system. An attractive facility—even though a building might be old and located on a site that falls below modern standards—is generally regarded as an asset to the community and an expression of educational accomplishment. People have a feeling for and a sense of pride in a system that maintains well-kept grounds and buildings. The appearance of school facilities is an important factor to be weighed in planning a community relations program.

In its publication *Principal Communicator*, the National School Public Relations Association encourages schools to perform a "Curb Appeal Check-Up" by considering questions such as these:

- Do your school building and grounds send a message that effective learning is taking place?
- Any litter and trash in the entrance area?
- Any old weeds? Any old leaves?
- Have shrubs been trimmed to an attractive size?
- Any there any dangerous cracks in the sidewalk or steps?
- Any graffiti near the front entrance or surrounding area?
- Is there evidence of "old litter" around doors and corners?

- Are windows clean and sparkling?
- Are parking lot and exterior lights in working order?
- Are signs up-to-date, welcoming, and friendly?
- Is there any work that requires the help of central facilities staff?
- Does your front office project a positive image?
- Is it bright and cheerful for visitors and students?
- Is there a sitting area for adults and children?
- Are materials about the school (PTA/PTO newsletter, community event flyers, Principal's News, handbook, etc.) within easy reach? Small touches, such as a bowl of candy on the counter or plants and posters, say a lot about your school's personality.
- Do your hallways look attractive?
- Are they brightly lit, and are all lighting fixtures working properly?
- Are the walls clean or freshly painted?
- Are there organized displays of posters and announcements, or do they look dingy and cluttered?
- Are the entrance halls clear of cartons and unused furniture?
- Are the drinking fountains clean and inviting?
- Does your cafeteria or lunchroom spark your appetite or quash it? Like the hallways, this room says a lot about your school's attitude towards its students. Is it clean, set up in a good grouping for students with lots of trash cans?
- How about your bathrooms? Nothing says more about a school—especially to parents and students—than an orderly and clean bathroom. Nor could a job be tougher and less rewarding for the custodial staff than keeping them that way.[5]

SPECIAL PROGRAMS FOR OLDER PEOPLE

Administrators who are sensitive to the importance of community relations cannot overlook the need for establishing special programs catering to the hobbies and interests of senior citizens.

Programs should not be restricted to the evening as many senior citizens prefer to pursue their hobbies or more formal educational activities during the day. Such programs have the added advantage of placing the adult in close contact with the regular school programs, particularly if carried out in the same or an adjoining building. Alarm over what modern schools are doing to children often changes to public statements of support as these older citizens become personally involved in special programs. Such programs are valuable also because they provide opportunities for these citizens to know teachers and administrators as people and to see firsthand that they are devoted to the education of all youth.

Programs for older adults can be initiated on the proverbial shoestring. The school system furnishes the buildings, facilities, and coordinating personnel, and the program is underway. Instructors are available in the ranks of the adults. School buildings become an investment that produces increased dividends when they serve all age groups. Bond issues are also more meaningful and better supported.

As the miracles of modern medicine continue, the senior citizen will become an increasingly important political and economic force in the community. The voting potential of the increasing number of older adults takes on an added significance when the support of schools is considered.

Gold Card Club

Quite popular with a number of school districts are the Gold Card Clubs for senior citizens. Usually, the member must be a resident of the school district and be 65 years of age or older. Each member who registers with the school district is issued a card annually, which entitles him or her to free admission to all athletic events, the adult school, concerts, plays, and other public school activities.

Often school districts will call on this group to become involved in the schools as speakers, as advisory committee members, and as feedback agents in the community. These fixed-income citizens often desire a feeling of belonging with a school system that they have helped to support long after their children have attended school. A Gold Card Club serves to satisfy this need among those over age 65 and in a small way expresses thanks for their support of the schools over the years.

Some districts have invited these citizens to participate in Thanksgiving and holiday luncheons held in the schools of the district. Usually, at these luncheons, the superintendent, a board member, and other staff members welcome the retirees and discuss the schools. A number of topics are discussed informally, from the cost of food and educational programs to budget preparation and even taxation.

Opportunities to recognize senior citizens and to provide school experiences for them are limitless, as are the community relations values that result.

OPEN HOUSE

Often held in the fall of the year, an open house is conducted by many schools to invite the community to visit the schools. Although some schools choose to operate in a constant fishbowl atmosphere by allowing visitors to attend classes at any time, many school officials prefer to invite parents and other interested residents to attend a special program once or twice a year. The purposes of an open house are to acquaint citizens with the nature of the school building and its teachers and staff and to help parents understand more fully the work of the school. Such events also provide opportunities for parents to see evidence of student accomplishment and lend themselves to building goodwill for the school system.

Open-House Programs

The programs presented by the majority of schools during an open house are fairly simple in design. A common type is that of an escorted tour, with students and teachers serving as guides. Visitors are taken through the building and shown its facilities, introduced to members of the administration and instructional staffs, told about objects on exhibit and instructional supplies and equipment used in classwork, entertained in various ways, and served light refreshments. Another form of open house may start with a meeting in the auditorium during which school officials talk about the educational practices of the institution and students furnish musical and other forms of entertainment. This part of the program is followed by visits with teachers in classrooms where students' work is on display and explanations are made of the curriculum in particular grades and sub-jects. The program is often rounded out with a social period for further visitation and refreshments. It is typical in secondary schools to have parents follow the class schedule of their children on a shortened-period basis. By going from class to class, parents meet teachers, see the physical setup of classrooms, receive information on what is taught and what is expected of students, and ask questions on points of interest.

Variations from these program designs include a day during the week for observing classes in action; afternoon socials for parents and teachers; discussion forums on school policies, challenges, and achieve-ments; clinics for parents on problems of child development; student assemblies open to the public; parent–teacher conferences; and faculty meetings open to students and the public.

Preparing Teachers

Open-house programs are most effective when teach-ers are adequately prepared to meet their responsi-bilities by attending to the many details that make a favorable impression on the public. Most teachers have little, if any, background to help them deal with the public in an open-house or back-to-school-night situation. Since many teacher preparation institutions do not prepare teachers for dealing with parents, it is the responsibility of the principal and other school officials to prepare them in this area.

Teachers should convey a feeling that implies that they welcome the opportunity to establish a cooperative relationship that will continue through-out the school year. They should be told of the inter-ests parents have regarding what is being done in the classroom.

An effective learning technique is to have expe-rienced teachers conduct back-to-school-night prac-tice sessions using role playing. This kind of approach will give new teachers the opportunity to get a feel for the kinds of questions and situations to anticipate. Such assistance is appreciated and pays dividends for the entire school family. At such programs, teach-ers should be refreshed on school policy regarding the controversial topics that might be introduced by visitors. If all employees are familiar with policies,

inconsistencies that breed problems can be avoided. School officials should not assume that giving new teachers a copy of the policy manual suffices in this regard. Emphasizing the controversial policies and providing specific suggestions to handle particularly challenging questions can be of great help. Teachers should be told which facts most parents are usually interested in so that they can include these in their presentation. In fact, teachers might be encouraged to seek feedback from parents to determine which top-ics to cover in the limited time available. Parents will appreciate the time taken to determine their interests, and teachers will be assured of an interested audience if the topics have been requested.

Teachers should realize that the way they pres-ent facts and material at the open house might very well be the single factor determining the image that parents have of them. They should present facts clearly to leave no room for ambiguity. They should be encouraged to use simple language that includes no educational jargon. Open house is an opportune time for teachers to communicate a warm concern for students, when they can convey that they want to work closely with parents for the same goal: the best education possible for children. Simply stated, this is a time when teachers and parents can develop a mutual respect that will serve the child well.

Attending to Details

Good public relations require school officials to spend an appreciable amount of time in planning efforts to guarantee a smooth-running open house. More and more school administrators are realizing that involving parents, teachers, and students in plan-ning open-house and other special programs means better programs. Parents, teachers, and students con-tribute sound ideas and suggestions for such events and support them more when they are involved in their operation. The planning committee for open-house programs should be established in plenty of time to ensure that no unrealistic deadlines cause frustration.

The date for the open house should be selected so that it does not conflict with other important com-munity events. It should also be chosen with televi-sion interests in mind. For example, if a sports event of national interest is scheduled for Monday night, it might be better to schedule the open house for another night. A good night to offer such events is the fifth "anything" of the month. Many organizations to which active parents belong hold meetings on the first Tuesday or the third Wednesday of the month. Because no day of the week occurs a fifth time every month, organizations do not meet then. Thus, the school is virtually guaranteed a no-conflict date by choosing such a night for the open house. The time should also be carefully determined. Too often school officials check to see what time the event has been held in previous years and reschedule it for that time. Did it work at that hour? Are new circumstances present that would suggest a change? For example, a split shift might necessitate a later start if custodians need time to prepare the building.

Other key considerations must include the following.

- *Effective invitations.* Too often parents and other visitors receive invitations that are written in a cold, almost officious, manner. Such writing is hardly conducive to enthusiastic attendance. Some schools, especially in the lower grades, have children prepare the invitation for their parents. The personal touch helps. Teachers can also call parents to invite them to the open house. Many school officials report that such calls result in appreciably larger attendance. The calls also serve to show that teachers do care about students and their parents and that school officials can call about something positive. (Many calls from the school are based on negative incidents.) Another effective technique is for individual departments to issue invitations to parents. Parents and other visitors should be given three weeks' notice of the event in an invitation from the school.
- *Adequate staff.* An important ingredient for a smoothly functioning open house is the availability of staff to meet any unexpected problems. This means that the administrator must anticipate possible problem areas and assign staff members to handle them. For example, some teachers may face unexpected emergencies, necessitating their missing the open

house. Extra professional personnel and a game plan for this possibility must be ready before the problem occurs. Any time a large crowd is expected, some special arrangement should be made to cope with a medical emergency. A nurse should be on duty to handle any such problem. Custodians should be present to handle sudden cleanup problems and to make sure that the building is in presentable condition for the visitors. Maintenance workers should also be available to overcome heating or lighting problems. Audiovisual specialists should be close by to cope with microphone, video, and projector problems.

- *Information areas.* Parents and other visitors are often frustrated when they don't understand the procedure to follow. They are often reluctant to ask questions of teachers and student guides because they don't want to appear uninformed. Information areas in the halls, staffed by students and teachers, enable people to ask all kinds of questions. For instance, parents who have forgotten their children's schedules should be made to feel comfortable about asking for another copy at an information center.
- *Comfort considerations.* From the time visitors enter the parking lot until the time they leave it, they are forming an impression of the way the schools are run. By having an organized parking effort and clearly marked signs directing people to the proper entrance, school officials can get visitors off to a good start. Alerting area police to the size of the crowd expected can be helpful in overall traffic control. If visitors will be wearing coats, provisions should be made for checking them or hanging them as easily as possible. Remember that many of the people will arrive at about the same time and that security is an important consideration. Routes to classrooms should be easily seen and restroom areas should be designated throughout the building. Displays of student work should be placed in key locations in the halls and lobby. However, traffic flow should not be impeded by poorly located displays that attract the attention of crowds and make it difficult for visitors to get from one classroom to another in the allotted time.

• *Feedback opportunities.* Administrators can learn much from people visiting the schools. All they have to do is ask for information. By providing visitors with easy-to-understand cards that ask for reactions to the open house as well as for comments about other key school questions, school officials can gain opinions that will help them know what some taxpayers are thinking. Ideas to improve the open-house program can also be solicited.

BUILDING DEDICATIONS

The dedication of a new school building (or re-dedication or re-naming of an existing building) can provide opportunities for good school–community relations. Frequently, however, many such opportunities are overlooked. To help prepare an effective dedication, many of the ideas advanced previously in this chapter regarding the open house can be applied. Yet it must be recognized that undertaking a dedication requires other specific plans. Overall, the dedication of a new building can be a source of community pride and achievement. School officials should make every effort to demonstrate how the building will benefit many people in many ways. For example, if a new gym is to be used by a large number of community groups, representatives of those groups should be invited to the dedication. Newsletters and news releases should point out how many people are expected to benefit from the facility.

Preparing Publications

Underlying the planning should be the thought that, whatever it is, the building will benefit children and others in the community in some way. This means that materials prepared for and about the official dedication ceremony should focus on the people the building will serve rather than on the building itself. The publication should applaud the efforts of the people who made the building possible. This includes all taxpayers, who should be shown how the building will contribute to the overall well-being of the community.

Key community figures should be invited to the ceremony. Area media representatives should be given sufficient notice to assign personnel to attend.

Often forgotten are board members who played important roles in the initial efforts to make the building possible. Frequently, these men and women are no longer board members when the building is dedicated; a good practice is to invite them and recognize them at the dedication ceremony.

Planning for the dedication must be thorough. To forget someone who contributed in a major way is one way to lose a friend for the schools. Checking and double-checking with people involved at various stages of the building program are necessary to ensure that no one is slighted.

AMERICAN EDUCATION WEEK

American Education Week is a national observance in support of schools. It was proclaimed in 1921 under the sponsorship of the American Legion and the National Education Association. Later the U.S. Office of Education and the National Congress of Parents and Teachers became sponsors along with the other two organizations. A number of education groups now also are co-sponsors of the event, including the National PTA, the American Legion, the American Legion Auxiliary, the American Association of School Administrators, the National School Boards Association, the American Federation of Teachers, the American School Counselor Association, the Council of Chief State School Officers, the National School Public Relations Association, the National Association of State Boards of Education, the National Association of Elementary School Principals, and the National Association of Secondary School Principals.

The most successful observances of American Education Week, which occurs in November, are planned and carried out cooperatively by the school and community. The leadership is usually taken by the board of education and the superintendent of schools. Parents and representatives of civic groups and organizations are invited to cooperate in planning this celebration. After a year or two, the entire project may be turned over to the community. The school then takes its place on committees in the same way as any other organization. It is expected, however, to furnish ideas, materials, and clerical assistance and to prepare a substantial portion of the week's program. This is logical in view of the nature of the celebration.

The school can meet these requests without dominating the situation or in any way destroying the feeling that the project belongs to the whole community.

Each year the national sponsoring organizations adopt a theme for American Education Week. An example is *Great Public Schools: A Basic Right and Our Responsibility*. Local groups are urged to foster store window exhibits, posters, social media programming, newspaper stories, open houses, museum displays, special printed materials, a proclamation by the mayor, pageants, and similar activities that illustrate the theme. These approaches can deepen public understanding and appreciation of what education has meant to this nation and what it means today.

BUSINESS–INDUSTRY–EDUCATION COOPERATION

More and more, business leaders are recognizing the importance of quality schools. Some school officials call on chief executives to provide financial support for specific school needs. Company executives, on the other hand, look to schools to help prepare solid workers. Some school administrators work closely with company managers to provide adult school classes that meet the training and literacy needs of workers.

Adopt-a-School is a form of business–school partnership. The Adopt-a-School commitment can take a number of directions, but it primarily focuses on ways a company or organization can help a school do a better job of educating students. Some companies participating in Adopt-a-School programs donate used and new equipment. Others provide executives as speakers and paper readers. All contribute a caring kind of encouragement that communicates a recognition of the school's importance.

Many schools report that a successful community relations venture is Business–Industry–Education Day. Worked out cooperatively, a day is set aside annually or biennially for teachers to visit different business and industrial firms in the community. Either the same or the next year, the school systems return the invitation to business, industry, and, in some instances, labor representatives. The purpose of this plan is to have each become better acquainted with the work of the other through firsthand observation and on-the-spot discussion.

COMMUNITY USE OF SCHOOL FACILITIES

The public schools belong to the public. One effective way to demonstrate this is to make school facilities available to individuals, groups, and organizations when regular classroom demands are over. Community use of the school at night or during vacations goes a long way toward showing some community members what their tax dollars are buying. People who have been in a school building during the year preceding a school finance election tend to support the needs of schools appreciably more than do those residents who have not been in a school building during that time. Allowing people to use the buildings is consistent with the function of the school as a social institution and is clearly a service in the public interest.

Use of Facilities

In an age of more and more leisure time when public education is no longer considered as something limited to people between the ages of 5 and 18, facilities are used by many people in a variety of ways. A senior citizen group may meet in a classroom or a special meeting room. A community youth group may use the basketball courts one night a week, and a local service organization may choose to conduct business in the school library once a month.

The cafeteria may be used for special community banquets and dinners; the gymnasium may be tapped by many groups for dances, athletic events, exhibits, and community recreational programs; the auditorium may be used hundreds of times a year for forums, conferences, movies, dramatic productions of community groups, and other entertainment; the industrial arts areas may be used for automobile and furniture repair so that valuable equipment does not stand idle.

The instructional materials center (or library, as most community members will call it) should also be made available to residents on a controlled basis. For recreational reading and for information about business and personal concerns, the school library can serve many people. Office and technology equipment might be called into service for classes to assist those who want to learn keyboarding skills or to use equipment in the evening or on weekends. Music rooms can bring satisfaction to those in the community who belong to choral or other music groups. The athletic fields can serve thousands of residents who would otherwise never consider the public school as being of any service.

Regulations

Community use of school facilities is a major ingredient in a solid school–community relations program. Yet too often plans are incompletely formed to cover the various requests that will be made of a board of education regarding such use. The board, to be thorough, should anticipate all kinds of requests and should establish written policies to cover those requests. The policies should be adequately publicized to prevent friction and to ensure all groups equal treatment. If the board does not have such policies, whatever decision is made regarding specific requests is likely to be interpreted by some segment of the community as unfair. The board runs the risk of giving the appearance of reacting to personalities and groups on an individual basis if fair policies are not established that can be applied to all requests. Such policies ease the administrative pressures of making facilities available.

The rules should specify when school facilities are available and the purposes for which they may be used. Also spelled out should be the procedure for applying and for securing approval. The fees should be stipulated, and the priority of school functions over other events should be clearly outlined.

Also imperative is the responsibility factor; those using the facilities must recognize their legal and other responsibilities. If insurance is required for those conducting a large meeting, this stipulation must be in the rules governing facilities use. What will the school district do regarding the facility? What must the organization do? These distinctions must be made in writing to avoid disagreements that could more than negate the goodwill fostered by the use of the facilities.

In establishing the regulations, school officials must consider the overall benefits accruing to the community. Special pressure groups and internal empire builders must not have the final say about use of facilities. The decision must be based on educational facts and the school's philosophy regarding the community's right to tap the school district's

resources. For example, an athletic director who feels that a football field shouldn't be used by the local midget team because the extra use will mar the turf should, of course, be heard by school administrators. However, the administrators must weigh the overall community good against the problems caused by such use. School facilities belong to the community, but guidelines for their use must be established.

ADULT AND COMMUNITY EDUCATION

The extension of educational opportunities into adult life is another service the school can perform for the community. Programs can be established—both formal and informal, cultural and practical—that are built around the personal and social desires of nontraditional students for learning and self-improvement. Courses can be offered to meet the needs of a wide spectrum of the community served by the school. Basic reading and writing courses will be needed in some communities to help overcome illiteracy. Others in that community may be interested in learning a skill or keeping up with the approaches to mathematics being learned by their children.

Determination of Need

An adult education program, to be sufficiently broad and vital, should consist of more than the offerings that school officials believe adults want or should take for their own betterment. It should represent the needs and interests of the adult population as closely as they can be determined. They may be determined with a fair degree of reliability by dividing the adult population in different ways—by age, educational achievement, socioeconomic background, family status, and group affiliation—and then analyzing the needs in each of the divisions. Or a council on adult education may be formed, consisting of men and women drawn from a cross-section of the community. This council can be asked to study the problem and to make recommendations for a suitable program of activities. However, better results are possible when both methods, or others equally beneficial, are employed.

An effective way to determine if a course will be popular and attract enough people to be feasible is to survey those attending adult school. Effective adult education programs are conducted by administrators who work closely on an ongoing basis with the people being served.

Program Possibilities

Numerous possibilities exist for developing interesting, worthwhile programs suited to the personal and social needs of adults. As examples, creative experiences may be offered in art, music, drama, crafts, and writing. Discussion groups can be held to consider local political challenges, intercultural relations, civic improvements, world affairs, and so forth. Special workshops can be offered to prepare leaders for community service clubs, the school board, and other organizations. Forums and debates on pertinent issues can be held, with the school supplying moderators and speakers. Industrial education offerings can attract large numbers of men and women interested in learning to use equipment to make and repair items. Hobbies and crafts are also commonly attractive subject areas that adult schools can offer. Foreign languages and recreational skills, such as golf and tennis, are being offered by more and more adult education programs as the amount of leisure time increases for some age groups. Some adult schools, located in communities in which a large segment of the population is college-educated, offer programs aimed at improving competency in jobs. Courses in public speaking, making effective presentations, leadership training, and other professional development topics are common in these instances. Some school districts cooperate with area colleges to offer undergraduate and graduate programs. The program possibilities are limited only by the desires of the people being served.

Community Relations Outcomes

Community adult education programs that meet the needs of large numbers of people are bound to have a favorable influence on public opinion regarding the schools. Those who take part in the programs almost always appreciate the opportunity provided for continuing their education and satisfying other interests. They become acquainted with regular employees, who teach many of the classes, and, through these relationships, have more confidence in the school system. Moreover, every class taught by a regular employee serves

to demonstrate the advancement made in instructional methods and materials over the years. Many are awakened to a deeper realization of the contribution education makes to their own lives and the lives of others, and they become stronger supporters of the school. The public goodwill and understanding thus created are worth much more than the cost of this service alone.

Publicizing Adult School Offerings

For an adult school to be successful, people must know about it and what it has to offer. This means that the administrator responsible for the adult school must be aware of publicity and communications techniques that will attract students. Many of the ideas explained in other chapters can be easily applied to this undertaking. Some specific publicity ideas follow:

- Work with an advisory committee to set up courses and to determine a calendar.
- Publicize the adult and community school offerings on a dedicated website or on the school district's website and in other school publications. Use social media messaging to extend online and other publicity efforts.
- Use local television and radio outlets in a variety of ways. Public service announcements, interview shows, and call-ins to talk shows can bring attention to adult school offerings. Brief news items explaining new courses and registration can be written for radio.
- Get the most out of area newspapers and online news outlets. News stories can be written about registration, the courses offered, and the number of people attending. Feature stories can be prepared about people and unusual results of a class. Classified ads designed for specific audiences can attract some students. Display advertising can be effectively used to list all courses. A tear-out coupon for registration can be used in the ads. Some school districts share the cost of a large ad in an area daily newspaper to provide general information about adult schools.
- Work with the various community groups. Prepare video to show the groups what adult school has to offer. Ask those attending the presentation to complete forms you distribute asking for course suggestions.

- Distribute evaluation forms at the last class. Ask people to suggest other courses and to candidly react to the course completed. Ask permission to quote them in advertising for the next session.

- Distribute a brochure that provides complete information about courses, registration, and so forth to residents at all homes served by the school district. If necessary, get professional help to do an effective job.

One Expert's Point of View: Face-to-Face Communication about Services, Activities, and Events

Asi Nia-Schoenstein, APR, is an instructor in the Department of Public Relations and Advertising at Rowan University in Glassboro, NJ. With more than 30 years of experience in international, corporate, and agency public relations, Professor Nia-Schoenstein has focused on cross-cultural communication in her work in the U.S. and in European and Middle Eastern countries.

School activities and events would seem to be an ideal place to reinforce communication by having community members and school employees meet face-to-face. Are there potential pitfalls?

Absolutely. Although we live in the age of advanced digital technology and social media, the value of face-to-face communication is more important than ever. So, no matter what your industry, you should get your audiences involved in in-person activities. First, the school district needs to think of its services, activities, and events as products. As such, their communication research should consider events and activities in terms of existing community, or customer, concerns and interests. These insights can help to craft effective messages employees can use when talking with community members about school services.Research on employees' communication concerns can also help to identify areas for training and support to help employees be as effective and

credible as possible when talking with community members.But perhaps the most important item to remember is to ensure proper preparation for these interactions. It's important to keep in mind that frontline employees in schools are like frontline employees in any business or organization—they are the ones dealing directly with customers every single day. As such, how they answer phone calls and e-mails, how they greet visitors, and the enthusiasm they express for their schools and programs directly influence what outsiders will think about the school system. Thus, each customer's first impression remains so important to any organization.

Why does the appearance of facilities and grounds have such a profound impact on what people think about an organization and its programs?

Let's be clear: People and their interactions with outsiders will have the biggest impact on your image and reputation with outsiders. But buildings, grounds, and even things such as furnishings and decorations play a role, too. Think of your facility as the moment of truth since it makes the first impression. In fact, your building will influence people upon their arrival even before your employees have a chance to make an impression. Clear signage and groomed

grounds make people feel welcomed and communicate that the organization cares. Confusing signage and scruffy facilities will put people in a negative frame of mind before they even meet your staff. These items may seem like little things, but the fact is they have a big impact on the ability to communicate effectively and persuasively with your organization's audiences.

Why should special events be considered communication opportunities?

As previously mentioned, people like it and remember better when they feel personally involved. So, whether it's an anniversary, a dedication, or some other milestone, special events really are celebrations of traditions and achievement. Special events provide an opportunity for people to gather and celebrate the good things the organization and the community have achieved. Events are great opportunities to deploy traditional public relations tactics, such as generating publicity or special online or published materials. But they also give the organization a unique chance to engage in memorable community relations activities as well, by helping people express themselves in regard to an organization, commemorate shared progress, and strengthen the working relationships so important to continued progress and success.[6]

Questions

1. Call your school district and see what kind of reaction you get. Don't identify yourself if a person answers the phone. If a person does not answer the phone, determine how long it takes to figure out the menu and how much time elapses before you can get to your party. Is this the kind of response that an angry caller will be calmed by?
2. Conduct a "curb appeal" analysis of some of the facilities in a local school system. What is appealing about the facilities as you drive by? What could be improved?

What is the overall first impression that you believe these facilities make on first-time visitors?

3. Review a local school district's policy on community use of school facilities. Do you find the policy to be clear? How might it be improved?
4. Why is it important that phone calls, e-mail, and written inquiries to schools be acknowledged and addressed promptly? What would you consider to be reasonable timelines for school employees handling inquiries?

Readings

Bagin, Don, and Anthony Fulginiti, *Practical Public Relations Theories and Practices That Make a Difference.* Dubuque, IA: Kendall Hunt, 2006.

Bagin, Rich, *Making Parent Communication Effective and Easy.* Rockville, MD: National School Public Relations Association, 2005.

Groom, Glen M., and Bey Ling Sha, *Effective Public Relations*, 11th ed. Upper Saddle River, NJ: Pearson Prentice Hall, 2012.

Hughes, Larry W., *Public Relations for School Leaders.* Boston, MA: Allyn & Bacon, 2000.

Kowalski, Theodore J., *Public Relations in Schools*, 5th ed. Upper Saddle River, NJ: Pearson, 2010.

Newsom, Doug, Judy VanSlyke Turk, and Dean Kruckeberg, *This Is PR: The Realities of Public Relations*, 11th ed. Belmont, CA: Cengage Wadsworth, 2012.

Seitel, Fraser P., *The Practice of Public Relations*, 13th ed. Boston, MA: Pearson, 2016.

Wilcox, Dennis L., and Glen T. Cameron, *Public Relations Strategies and Tactics*, 11th ed. Boston, MA: Pearson, 2014.

Videos

Clarksville-Montgomery County (TN) School System: First day of school https://youtu.be/bTH6XLTjCDE

Texas Association of School Boards: The Role of a School Board Member https://youtu.be/lTz4_itIiOw

Montgomery County (MD) Public Schools: Meet New Board Members https://youtu.be/5k3xRJr_f5A

Kenosha (WI) Unified School District: What Happens in 4K https://youtu.be/y02IJM7v5x0

Cleveland Heights-University Heights City School District (OH): Early Childhood Center Video https://youtu.be/w95fVFFgdj4

Rockford Public Schools 205 (IL): Special Programs @ RPS 205 https://youtu.be/qr0-u5sswq0

Bethel School District (WA): Where Does My School Lunch Come From? https://youtu.be/S1JG57Zzxi0

Nixa (MO) Public Schools: Magnet School Information Video https://youtu.be/JbyqoycUTGY

Riverside (CA) Unified School District: School Anniversary Celebration https://youtu.be/4dvqd44T2FE

Spring Lake Park (MN) Schools: Personalized Learning Program https://youtu.be/zmk4Lkux21w

Endnotes

1. National School Public Relations Association, "Best PRactices: Frontline Communication Tips for Support Staff," *PRincipal Communicator* (Rockville, MD: Author, February 2002), p. 1. Reprinted with permission.
2. Ibid.
3. Rich Bagin, *Making Parent Communication Effective and Easy* (Rockville, MD: National School Public Relations Association, 2005), pp. 79–80.
4. National School Public Relations Association 2009 Member Survey, retrieved Oct. 24, 2017, from https://www.nspra.org/node/3562.
5. Reprinted with permission from National School Public Relations Association, "First Impressions—Begin with a Curb Appeal Checkup," *PRincipal Communicator*, April 2007, p. 1.
6. Reprinted with permission from personal correspondence with Asi Nia-Schoenstein, College of Communication, Rowan University, Glassboro, N.J., November 8, 2017.

Working with the News Media

This chapter reviews issues . . .

- For central administrators: The roles emerging and traditional news programming can play in reinforcing a school district's communication to build public understanding and add credibility to school messages.
- For building and program administrators: How school and program administrators can use news media coverage to promote their activities, build better appreciation for their activities, and encourage public participation.
- For teachers, counselors and staff: The ways in which the activities and achievements of school personnel can contribute to public understanding through news and publicity programming.

After completing this chapter you should be able to . . .

- Distinguish the roles of controlled and uncontrolled media in school–community relations practices.
- Document the distinct roles new media coverage plays in developing public understanding of and support for educational activities and initiatives.
- Identify how media convergence has influenced the ways in which schools interact with the news media in print, broadcast, and online.
- Distinguish the key characteristics of effective media-relations management for schools and the media-relations roles played by various school personnel.

Dramatic shifts have taken place in recent years in the ways in which school–community relations programs deliver news and information to key audiences. Technological shifts in the ways in which traditional media can be produced and distributed have decreased production times as well as costs. More profound perhaps has been the emergence of digital media, offering both news organizations and schools new options for rapid, even instant, two-way communication with their audiences.

In Part 3: Communication Tools this and the following chapters will take a look at current tactical approaches being used by schools in their school–community relations programs.

This chapter will also look specifically at the traditional and emerging ways in which the news media are used and how school leaders can effectively work with and meet the needs of the news media.

UNDERSTANDING MEDIA TYPES

To help understand how emerging communication technologies and the new trends they have launched are affecting schools, it's important to consider the types of media through which school information can be delivered and, in some cases, through which feedback can be collected. Schools—like any other organization—have traditionally relied on advertising (sometimes called *paid media*); news and editorial coverage generated by news organizations and other commentators (sometimes referred to as *earned media*); publications, websites, audio, and video productions; and other tactics produced and disseminated by schools (often referred to as *owned media*).

Both so-called paid media and owned media sometimes are classified primarily as controlled media—meaning that the organization controls most aspects of the media, including content and the timing of distribution. Earned media, however, generally are classified as uncontrolled in that someone outside of the organization (a publisher, reporter, or blogger, for example) has control over the final message content and the timing of distribution.

Both controlled and uncontrolled media are perceived to carry certain advantages for communication programs. Controlled media obviously offer a higher level of authority over the precise message to be delivered and when it will be delivered. Uncontrolled media, however, offer a higher level of credibility or endorsement since the message may be perceived by audiences as having been vetted through an external source.

UNDERSTANDING MEDIA CONVERGENCE

It's also important to keep in mind the many ways in which various media deployed today can be integrated with one another. Such integration can both reinforce key messages and extend the reach or delivery of key messages to all audiences. Consider the following.

Controlled media: Publications that once were simply printed and mailed may still be produced and disseminated this way, but digital versions of the publication may now also be e-mailed to readers and may be made available online through school websites. Announcements concerning the availability of the publication can be made through social media outlets such as Twitter or Facebook, with links to take users directly to the publication. Also, the online versions may now be considered living documents, which schools can update or revise in real time when old information changes or new information develops.

Uncontrolled media: Schools might also use social media to alert parents or others to an important article appearing in a local newspaper—again with a link taking users directly to the article. They may also use their own media to comment on the article or add more information that might be helpful in giving audiences a better understanding of the issue the article covers. Readers themselves can also contribute to discussions about the article in traditional ways (with a letter to the editor, for example) or in newer ways (such as commenting in the newspaper's own online comments section or adding a comment to the affected school system's Facebook page).

Comprehensive school communication programs generally include a mix of controlled and uncontrolled media activities in their tactical delivery of messages in all phases of a communication campaign. It is important that the convergence of traditional and emerging media fueled by new technology appears to have supplemented traditional media tactics rather than supplanting them.

News Media Convergence

Although media options for school–community relations programs have both expanded and converged, these same trends for school communications also now apply in many ways to the methods by which news organizations now cover schools. Traditionally, school–community relations programs might have segmented their programs for dealing with the news media to print (primarily daily and weekly newspapers) and broadcast or electronic (primarily radio and television broadcasters). Those segments still exist. However, news organizations too have adapted new and emerging media in ways that have dramatically affected how school news is covered and have blurred the lines between print and broadcast media.

Many newspapers now operate websites to deliver news to readers. Some supplement their print coverage with video, audio, or other illustrations online. More in-depth coverage or supporting documents also may be made available online, supplementing both print and online coverage of a story.

Many newspapers also still operate with daily or weekly deadlines for their print editions, while their online news delivery may be updated continually day and night. *One result:* Traditional print media now enjoy an immediacy to their news delivery that was once associated more with broadcast media— meaning that schools now also need to be prepared to deal with ongoing news deadlines and instant news coverage.

Similarly, broadcast media still operate with set deadlines for regularly scheduled news and public affairs programs. TV and radio websites also now offer rapid coverage of breaking news in advance of scheduled newscasts.

Both print and broadcast news media also have adapted social media to alert followers to breaking news and steer them to online content. Many also use other online communication tactics, such as e-mail alerts, to notify subscribers of news and events.

Staffing and organizational changes at news media organizations also have affected the ways in which school officials interact with reporters and editors. More and more news is collected online as e-mail and websites have become the accepted communication methods by those collecting news and information. (See the case at the end of this chapter for more insights on how this trend has affected school officials who deal with the news media.) Staff

reductions and other efficiencies at news organizations also mean fewer face-to-face encounters with reporters who at one time may have been assigned to cover a specific school district, and more online interactions with reporters who may be covering multiple school districts in a region.

Media interviews have always been conducted by telephone with the results being used primarily in print news coverage or recorded audio used by radio broadcasters, but video interviews now are easily done remotely with the resulting video being used in various ways by print and broadcast media.

Emerging media have also created a new segment of news outlets covering schools that supplement traditional print and electronic news organizations. In many communities news organizations have evolved that operate exclusively online. From commercial news organizations with staffs of traditionally trained journalists to one-person news and commentary services operating with no more than a well-read blog or website, these news outlets also need to be accommodated by officials from the schools they cover.

One result of this new media and media convergence for school communicators might be, as Basso, Hines, and FitzGerald suggest, a need for "cross-trained" communicators capable of working in a variety of formats and skilled in the construction and delivery of information in ways that both inform and persuade.[1]

SCHOOLS AND THE NEWS MEDIA

Traditionally, news media have played significant roles in school–community relations programs—and they continue to do so. Studies show that the news media continue to be a prime source of information about schools, and local newspapers continue to play key roles as information sources. Along with newspapers, television and radio also remain important sources of information, news, and commentary about schools.

This trend might be better understood when considering the associated demographics. As the number of taxpayers with school-age children decreases, media tactics produced and controlled by schools have less of a built-in audience and external media

THE DYNAMICS OF MEDIA CONVERGENCE ON SCHOOL NEWS COVERAGE

The Allen Independent School District opened a $60 million stadium in 2012. The event understandably generated local and national news coverage, but incorrect reporting created major problems for the district.

An upstate New York newspaper incorrectly reported that the stadium in Texas was built for $120 million. That story was picked up by a blog in Washington, D.C., and reported as fact. Calls then came in from major national newspapers about the $120 million stadium.

The information was easy to correct from that point forward, but there was no way to find the source of the bad information at that time. The widely read blog had indignant readers reposting all over the country, and other news outlets ran the $120 million stadium story without verification. To their credit, the *New York Times* and *Wall Street Journal* both picked up the story, gathered the proper facts, and ran factual stories. Many other nontraditional news sources simply ran it or reposted it crediting the Washington blog.

It took research to find the contact information and phone number for the sources of bad information and a correction was eventually run. However, the erroneous information is still "out there" online and occasionally got reposted even a year later.[2]

channels, such as newspapers, radio, and television, will continue as important sources of information about schools. The online extensions of traditional newspapers and other news media also seem to guarantee a key role for such earned media outlets in the future.

Clearly the traditional advice that the astute school administrator should not underestimate the "power of the press" remains important. Appreciating the power of the news media, the administrator then must understand the role news media play in their dealings with the public schools. Educators are often suspicious of the news media, fearing that they will hurt the cause of the schools. But reporters and editors have a responsibility to report on all public institutions, including public schools.

In the book *Building Bridges with the Press: A Guide for Educators*, author Julie Blair expresses the situation this way:

Obviously, there are reasons to be wary of the press. Many administrators worry aloud about the exploitation of children in their care, the disruption of classes or testing schedules, or the possibility of liability issues. Others fret about being misquoted, having their words taken out of context, or being unfairly maligned. Many, functioning in a never-ending time crunch, wonder how they could possibly carve out time to work with reporters on a regular basis.

From the media's perspective, however, it seems that school officials don't trust us or that they have something to hide. We wonder: Are these administrators simply worried about children, or are they concerned that we'll unearth a problem they didn't know about or don't want the public to find out about?

Two perspectives—dangerously out of sync. The fears and distrust are the tangible result of a deep disconnect between the education press and those who manage, work and learn in K–12 school communities.[3]

The news media, of course, often have a legal right to most school data and information. School districts spend public funds. Thus, the news media have just as much right to report about the schools as they do about other government agencies. School officials should know their state law on the public's right to know. School administrators who are aware of the reporter's right to information can save themselves and their schools severe embarrassment. Too frequently school officials refuse reporters information that is eventually made public when a court intervenes. More damaging than the harm done to the relationship with the reporter is the mistrust generated if even the appearance of hiding facts is created.

If one of the objectives of the community relations program is to generate news coverage to build public understanding of and support for school needs, it is necessary to determine which topics taxpayers perceive as important. Thus, if the people are concerned with guidance and discipline, news releases about educational trips of administrators will do little to generate the desired coverage. Determining what people want to know about the schools is vital before other phases of the news relations program can be developed. Chapter 3 explained a number of methods for obtaining feedback on school issues, and these can be implemented to find out possible news topics that should be considered.

Interest in what parents and other taxpayers want to know about the schools began as early as 1929. Farley, studying 5,600 people in 13 cities, determined that parents are primarily concerned with pupil progress, achievement, instructional methods, and courses of study.[4] Since then, many studies have been reported showing that parents are primarily interested in curriculum and that other taxpayers care most about discipline and costs.

It is more important to know what taxpayers in your community want to know than to know what other taxpayers in other locations in another era cared about, however. Once school officials have determined the interests of the community, a planned program to provide information on those topics can be undertaken.

The good news is that schools commonly have several areas where community interest intersects with stories that schools have to tell. These include success stories that can be found in individual and group student achievements, success stories that can be found in faculty activities, progress being made in traditional and new academic programs, and opportunities being developed through extracurricular activities. Publicizing such stories can meet the public demand for information on key school programming while showcasing student, faculty, and school accomplishment.

GUIDELINES FOR WORKING WITH NEWS MEDIA

To help education department employees know what reporters have a right to know, one state superintendent of schools issued guidelines. An elaboration of these guidelines, as well as other suggestions, follows.

ANSWER QUESTIONS HONESTLY

Any responsible employee of the school is expected to answer questions about those topics concerning his or her position. The educator who appears to be hiding something by attempting to dodge or circumvent an issue only prompts additional investigation by the reporter.

Every school system needs an operating procedure for dealing with the news media. If this procedure fails to give reporters information when they need it, the procedure will undoubtedly come under fire in the news media. More than one school district has felt the wrath of both the news media and taxpayers when the superintendent was out of town and reporters were informed by all other administrators that "only the superintendent may speak to the news media." Such a situation will provoke three reactions: disgust by reporters, concern for their own competence by other administrators, and puzzlement on the part of citizens who wonder why people running the schools aren't allowed to talk to the news media.

All employees should know who can speak for the schools when the superintendent isn't available. The next person in line should be designated in case the number two person is unavailable. In fact, all employees should understand their roles in working with the news media. This includes administrators, teachers, and clerical employees. It may be necessary to conduct an in-service program for employees so that all will be comfortable when speaking to reporters. Local reporters will usually cooperate in such a program because it helps them do their job better and more easily.

RESPOND PROMPTLY

This guideline means knowing and respecting news media deadlines. The reporter who is told that an administrator "is busy and will call back" will understandably be irate when the return call comes too late to meet a deadline. Getting information on time is a reporter's job; if the administrator recognizes this pressure and assists the reporter, the reporter will appreciate it and will respond favorably.

Deadlines vary for different news media—and the emergence of online news reporting in some cases has created an even greater demand of immediacy in responding to media requests.

ALL REPORTS AND SURVEYS ARE PUBLIC PROPERTY

You may *not* withhold such data when they are requested, even though you believe the reporter is going to use the material to hurt a program. You generally may not have to release rough drafts, working papers, preliminary figures, or notes, but you may choose to do so.

DON'T PICK YOUR OWN TIME FOR PUBLICITY AND REFUSE TO PROVIDE INFORMATION UNTIL THAT TIME

Some administrators fall into the routine of sending out news releases every Friday because that's the day allocated to that phase of running the school. However, news is often timely, and waiting a few days to release it might jeopardize its chance of being printed. Reporters sometimes seek information about a project or innovation before the program coordinator or principal is ready to wrap up the final report. The educator should answer the reporter's questions when the questions are asked. This does not preclude the possibility of preparing a news release when the project is completed and all the information is available.

For example, much attention might be sought at the start of an innovative program. Yet few districts do much to report progress as the innovation is implemented. Frequently, school officials want to wait until the end of the year to chart and report measurable progress. Yet it's natural for the public and for reporters to ask for information before the year is over.

AVOID JARGON

The educator must constantly guard against using words that are unfamiliar to noneducators. This applies to talking with reporters. Few news media employ reporters with extensive backgrounds in education to cover educational issues exclusively. Thus, school officials should define educational terms when they use them or should substitute words that everyone will understand. A criticism sometimes leveled at educators is that they confuse the public with "educationese" and don't speak the language of the layperson. This contributes to a credibility gap between the school official and the public—a gap that breeds distrust.

DON'T BE AFRAID TO SAY "I DON'T KNOW, I'LL CALL YOU BACK IN TEN MINUTES"

Reporters looking for answers don't expect school officials to have every response every time. It is appreciably better to admit not knowing than to give

FREEDOM OF INFORMATION: COMMUNICATING IS THE LAW

Online communication options have made information sharing easier for citizens as well as the news media. As a result, school administrators need to be prepared to handle the increased requests for information that result from both informal requests and formal requests under freedom of information (FOI) laws and regulations. Specific FOI requirements vary by state and other jurisdictions, so local school administrators need to stay current on the specific rules that may govern their responses to such information requests. In addition, new communication technology, such as the increasing use of e-mail, e-newsletters, discussion boards, and other online information exchanges, is adding to the challenge of storing information and determining what is and is not covered under various FOI requirements.

The National Freedom of Information Coalition, a reference and research library located within the University of Missouri School of Journalism on the campus of the University of Missouri–Columbia, maintains an extensive website offering information on federal and state FOI laws and issues, sample Freedom of Information Act (FOIA) request letters, issues and background research, and so on. Its website can be found at nfoic.org.

Another organization, the Reporters Committee for Freedom of the Press, also maintains FOI information and resources on its website at rcfp.org.

Many state governments maintain Web resources dedicated to helping citizens and organizations comply with local FOI rules. The federal government, through its various departments, uses the Web to offer guidance on the federal FOIA. *Example:* The Department of Education (ed.gov) maintains an FOIA page with numerous reports and guidelines.

an inaccurate answer. Remember to get back to a reporter quickly if he or she is fighting a deadline. Don't allow other problems to intervene if information was promised by a certain time.

NEVER ASK TO REVIEW A STORY BEFORE IT IS PRODUCED

Just as a reporter is expected to respect expertise in educators, his or her reporting ability must be respected. Asking to see a story before it's released implies to most reporters that they are not trusted to write a sound story. If certain points should be emphasized in the story, emphasize them in the interview. Always remember that the reporter's idea of what's important and the educator's concept of what should be played up may differ. The reporter's responsibility is to the public and to his or her news organization, not to making the school and a program look good.

Don't ask reporters to send a copy of the story after it appears. They have other responsibilities to think about; besides, educators should be reading and watching news reports regularly.

A SCHOOL OFFICIAL WHO HAS TALKED TO A REPORTER ABOUT A SUBSTANTIVE ITEM SHOULD NOTIFY HIS OR HER IMMEDIATE SUPERIOR

The superintendent of schools should be informed immediately if the topic has districtwide implications or is the kind of topic that lends itself to comment from other school officials. If other key personnel don't know about this matter, the story might wind up being a series of statements from various administrators, each one contradicting the other.

BE A KEY MEMBER OF THE MANAGEMENT TEAM

School representatives responsible for media relations must enjoy the confidence of key school officials. Otherwise they will be ineffective. The school's media relations person must also have access to all information. This means attending all key administrative cabinet meetings, executive sessions of the board, and all major meetings. If this is not the case, the news media will consistently bypass the media relations representative, who will be relegated to writing news releases about PTA meetings and class trips.

BE ACCURATE

Reporters' reputations ride on the accuracy of their stories. If people read or hear something that is incorrect, they will have less confidence in the rest of that reporter's work. Thus, it's imperative that all information provided to reporters be checked for precision. This is especially important in the spelling of names and the placement of decimal points. People dislike seeing their names misspelled and will usually blame the reporter even if the fault lies elsewhere. Providing incorrect information that makes its way into news reporting will not enhance the school's relationship with the reporter.

KNOW ALL REPORTERS ON A FIRST-NAME BASIS

Probably the most important step that an educator can take to improve relationships with the news media is to get to know reporters on a first-name basis. When an administrator is just a title and a name, it's fairly easy for reporters to choose letters on the keyboard that can form critical words. Establishing solid rapport with reporters cannot be considered a guarantee that prevents criticism; however, it can be thought of as a way to ensure a fair chance to tell the school's side of the story.

Reporters will respect educators who make an effort to understand them and their job. This might mean leaving the office to meet with reporters at their office, or getting together for lunch informally. It's always better to meet a reporter when no pressure exists for information on a negative story. Once reporters know an educator, it will encourage them to call the school for facts rather than looking elsewhere for them. This ensures the opportunity to present the school's side of a story, an important ingredient when a controversial topic is in the headlines.

Make it a point to discuss what types of stories reporters are interested in and how the news should be handled. This responsibility should be assumed either by the superintendent or by the person in charge of media relations for the school system.

KNOW WHAT "OFF THE RECORD" MEANS

Talking to reporters "off the record" means you are offering information for their knowledge but that it is not to be reported. This can be extremely risky and can cause all sorts of problems if not properly understood by all parties concerned. Two schools of thought exist in regard to providing off-the-record information to reporters.

One school believes that reporters are always reporters and that any information given to them will eventually find its way into news coverage. Advocates of this position therefore remind school officials that reporters are reporters all the time, not just when carrying a clipboard at a school board meeting.

Others feel that off-the-record information enables reporters to bring a fuller understanding of complex and controversial issues to their reporting, even though such information is not used in their reporting.

BE AVAILABLE WHEN NEGATIVE NEWS OCCURS

One of the most consistent criticisms leveled against school officials is their inaccessibility when something that appears to be negative happens in a school. As one reporter put it, "Why are the same administrators who are always available when a student wins some academic recognition suddenly in hiding when a problem occurs?"

The day when board members and taxpayers expect schools to be perfect is over. However, the day of accountability and administrative responsibility has not passed. School administrators who are expected to provide leadership for a school district cannot abrogate that responsibility when the going gets rough.

No one expects educators to boast about problems that occur. However, attempting to cover up problems that affect an integral part of the school's operations can lead to much larger difficulties. The wise administrator will recognize the problems, propose alternative solutions, and explain why the solution selected is the most appropriate one. By ignoring problems, the administrator projects an image that will not build the confidence needed to gain public support.

KNOW WHAT NEWS IS

A major complaint of editors and reporters is that most school officials fail to recognize what news is. This has two results: (1) Important school news is not sent to the news media, and (2) news releases with no news value demand the time of editors. Educators can improve their understanding of what constitutes news by talking with reporters and editors. It's surprising to many school officials how helpful newspeople can be when asked. Also reading the area newspapers can be extremely helpful in determining what news is.

One of the most common errors made by educators is to assume that something is newsworthy just because it is of interest to them. The editor has a different yardstick: How many readers or viewers will the item interest? Answering this one question will encourage many stories to be written and will cause others to be rejected.

Furthermore, different news outlets have different standards. Local or community news organizations, for instance, might use a story about a class trip to a local factory because many in their audience would have an interest in the activity. However, a larger or regional news organization will usually reject such a story unless there's an unusual twist to it. Why? Because many classes visit local businesses and other sites and not many of their readers or viewers would be interested in this specific event.

School officials complain that reporters don't know enough about the schools. Yet few school people understand the workings and needs of a news organization. To improve the working relationship, school administrators must gain information about how a news organization operates and what its specific needs for information and content are.

COMPILE A DIRECTORY OF KEY NEWS CONTACTS

Keep a directory of key individuals involved with covering the school system and issues related to education. This directory should include office and home phone numbers and information about their working schedules and special interests. This will allow the school official to contact the proper people as soon as a news story is available.

GIVE PERSONAL CONTACT INFO TO MEDIA REPRESENTATIVES

Few situations bother a reporter more than having part of a story and not being able to get in touch with the knowledgeable person for other integral pieces of the story. School officials, especially the person in charge of community relations, should give the news media the home and cell phone numbers of school representatives as well as their e-mail addresses. News releases should also list home and cell phone numbers of the community-relations person and key people mentioned in the releases. Then, when reporters rework their story, they can easily contact people for additional information.

Know How the News Media Work

The people most school officials will want to know best are the reporters from the local news organizations who cover the school. Understanding the roles and responsibilities of these reporters will assist educators in their relations with the news media. Furthermore, good person-to-person relationships with reporters and editors can overcome fear of the news media. A few specifics that should help school officials better understand the role of reporters follow:

- Reporters seldom write headlines or promotions for upcoming news coverage. This is important to remember. More than one district has marred its relationship with a reporter by assuming that he or she was responsible for a headline or promotion that school officials considered negative.
- Reporters aren't always responsible for the errors that appear in news coverage. Proofreaders, editors, and others often deal with the content before it is released. This problem may be compounded when news is reported in multiple venues—in print and online, for example.

Changes are made for a number of reasons. Editors may want to shorten the story to make room for other stories. Changes may be made to accommodate the various formats in which the story is being produced. In so doing, they may delete part of the story you and the reporter thought was important. Editors also may want a different beginning or angle for a story because of some other related news event, or simply because they feel that something other than what the reporter wrote first should be the focus.

Help the Reporter

Reporters, like all of us, enjoy doing their jobs well. To help reporters do a better job, try these techniques:

- Distribute a list of key school personnel, their responsibilities, and contact information to all reporters. Give basic data about the school, including enrollment, growth, calendar, and other information that reporters might be able to use.
- If time does not permit preparation of as many stories as desired, periodically distribute a list of story ideas to all reporters. This list should contain ideas for stories, the people to contact, and their contact information. Of course, the staff listed as contact people should be notified of this so they will be prepared.
- If a good news story that is not school-related is detected, offer it to reporters. They will appreciate the tip. This helps build the necessary rapport.
- Alert reporters to an announcement that will be made soon. If possible, prepare background material that will enable them to do a more thorough job of reporting. For example, if at the board meeting the superintendent is going to announce a large grant to improve the teaching of reading, reporters will appreciate receiving as much information as possible about who presented the grant, how it was obtained, who will implement it, how pupils will benefit from it, where such an approach was tried before, and so forth.
- Remember the local reporters when news of statewide or national importance occurs. It's easy to forget the local reporters when major news organizations or national television personalities seek information from a school system. The schools may have a once-in-a-lifetime opportunity to gain national recognition. Quite naturally, cooperation is required with those who request information about your schools, but remember that the local news media must be taken care of. It's the local reporters who will cover the schools tomorrow and the day after tomorrow, and they should expect to receive special consideration when an extremely important story is available.
- Be selective in suggesting stories to reporters. Reporters often don't have time to pursue all possible stories. Just as editors dislike receiving news releases that contain little or no news, reporters resent spending time

FIVE SUGGESTIONS FOR WORKING WITH AGGRESSIVE REPORTERS

Tim Carroll, APR, deals with the media frequently in his role as director of public information for the Allen (Texas) Independent School District. He offered the following suggestions for handling difficult media inquiries:

- Never feel pressured to respond immediately—call back when ready.
- Anticipate the tough questions and draft answers with assistance from the superintendent and others on the leadership team.
- Only speak to topics that the school district is qualified to speak about.

- Legal consequences, condition of buildings, and so on, should be left to appropriate agencies.
- Sometimes ask for questions in writing or via e-mail and respond in writing instead of in a phone conversation.
- Learn and understand Freedom of Information regulations in your state.

Source: Adapted from "Sixty PR Ideas in Sixty Minutes," a presentation by Tim Carroll, APR, at the 2011 National School Public Relations Annual Seminar, San Antonio, TX. Used with permission.

on possible stories that are little more than attempts to publicize personalities. Point out why a possible story merits a reporter's attention.

- Issue a glossary of educational terms to reporters. Although this does not excuse school staff members from using understandable language, a reporter, armed with the glossary, might frequently avoid errors when reporting education news.
- Send all reporters a copy of the school district newsletter or other significant publications before they are distributed to the community. Also, consider writing a news release on one or two key newsletter stories and include the newsletter with the releases. Taxpayers who see the newsletter mentioned in the newspaper might look for it and read the articles referred to in news coverage.
- If reporters err in reporting a story, give them a chance to correct the mistake, if indeed it's worth correcting. School officials who immediately go over the reporter's head to an editor will hardly improve their relationship with the reporter. No one likes to be told he or she was wrong by a boss. Thus, bringing the error to the editor will only alienate the reporter. School officials may overreact to errors in news coverage. A demanded retraction might win the

battle, but it could very well lessen chances for winning the war.

- Perhaps the reporter and school officials can correct an error without a retraction. For example, a story which implied that a better background check should have been made on a teacher who was just dismissed might be followed a week later with a feature story detailing the many personnel procedures used before a candidate is hired.
- If a controversial story is breaking and reporters will be calling, prepare a statement that can be quickly given to them. This will do two things: First, it will enable comments to be consistent, and second, it will please reporters because a statement is ready. In fact, one of the most effective contributions to good working relationships with the news media is anticipation of what news is. By anticipating, educators can prepare positions and statements, clearly giving the impression that school officials are organized and know what they are doing.

Good Etiquette

Educators constantly admit their respect for the news media, and yet they can often treat the news media with suspicion or disrespect with some behavior or reactions.

Good media relations suffer when such common errors as the following are made by school people:

- *Threatening, denouncing, and bringing pressure on the editor to print or withhold a story.* Nothing produces friction faster and is resented more deeply by the editor.
- *Complaining when the facts of a story are reported incorrectly, when headlines give the wrong impression, or when individuals are misquoted.* The remedy lies rather in friendly discussion, accurate copy, and in some occasional cases an objective response in the letters-to-the-editor section.
- *Refusing to release timely information or pretending to be unacquainted with the details of a story.* Such action creates suspicion and reflects unfavorably on the institution. The story will be published anyway, without the cooperation of the school and the benefit of complete background material.
- *Complaining if stories do not get published.* It must be remembered that all news organizations work under space limitations and cover whatever they believe will appeal most to their audiences.
- *Becoming emotional with reporters and editors over unfavorable news stories.* School people must learn to accept the good and the bad in the normal flow of publicity.
- *Being drawn into controversies on a personal basis when the school is criticized or attacked in a news story.* No board member or school official has the right to speak for the system unless authorized to do so.
- *Creating the impression that educators know more about reader interests than either the reporter or the editor.* The persistence of this attitude is certain to antagonize the reporter and the editor.
- *Failing to invite the reporters to special school events that should be reported in the paper; or, having invited the reporters, failing to show the courtesy and hospitality that are expected.*
- *Causing reporters to sit in the waiting room for a long time for an interview with a school official.* If an interview must be delayed, word should be sent at once to the reporters. They have deadlines to meet and cannot afford to lose time under these circumstances.

THE NEWS MEDIA AND SCHOOL BOARD MEETINGS

School boards and school administrators must be accountable for the way public funds are being spent. One of the ways to be accountable is through the news media, and the relationships between school officials and reporters often determine the kind of news coverage provided.

All board members and key school administrators should be made aware of the importance of what goes into the creation of good working relationships with the news media. If these points are not learned from orientation meetings or from educational preparation, someone in the district should assume the responsibility for providing media training for board members and school leaders in a school district.

Before the Board Meeting

The superintendent should prepare for board members a succinct summary of each important item on the agenda. This summary should be delivered to board members long enough before the public meeting to allow them to familiarize themselves with the main topics to be discussed. It should include a statement of the problem, possible solutions to the problem, and the superintendent's recommended solution. Inasmuch as board members are usually busy people, succinctness is appreciated. A more thorough, in-depth presentation of facts and background material should also be included in the materials presented to the board.

Before the board meeting, reporters will appreciate the chance to meet with the superintendent, the board president, or the school communications specialist. If the board meeting is held at night, the meeting with reporters might be held in the afternoon. At this meeting, the agenda could be discussed and resolutions given to reporters. Prepared statements and background materials could be distributed.

For example, if a grant is to be announced at the meeting, provide reporters with plenty of background information, such as the following: Where is the money coming from? Who will be responsible for implementing the program? Has it been tried elsewhere? When will it start? Who can provide additional information? All of this information will permit reporters to write thorough stories instead of hurried, incomplete stories pressured by deadlines and the unavailability of key personnel at midnight following the meeting.

At the Meeting

Make reporters feel comfortable. Provide a work area or table somewhere near the action. Give reporters a copy of the agenda, and share with them photocopies of just about all materials that board members have. Only a few items might be considered confidential. With a copy of the agenda, reporters will be able to follow the actions of the board intelligently instead of groping for facts in a frustrated fashion.

Few actions alienate the news media and the public more than executive sessions of the board. Reporters' adrenaline flows at the mention of an executive session. If they think the board is trying to block the public's right to know about public business, they will move into high gear to ferret out the behind-the-scenes undertakings. Secret meetings (and that's what the public considers executive sessions) will guarantee negative commentary. Avoid them as much as possible, especially on the same night as the regular public meeting. Be sure you respect public meeting laws.

Schedule something of educational interest at each meeting. Focusing on students and learning can help to promote interesting and positive news coverage. Too many meetings have required the reporters' presence for four or five long hours, and the only story has been about a dull subject, such as who received the fuel bid, or flooring for a new building.

Every meeting should include a brief report on some phase of the school curriculum. The educator making the presentation should be concise and should have copies of pertinent materials for the news media. Reporters will often write a story on the innovation or progress taking place in the schools because the story has news merit.

During the meeting, the communications specialist or someone appointed as the board's media representative should be available to provide needed materials and to answer questions. Each board member should be clearly identified. This will eliminate the possibility of a quote being attributed to the wrong person.

Recording (audio or video) board meetings sometimes helps school officials and audience members choose their words more carefully. It also reminds everyone that everything said at a public meeting is public information. Nothing is off the record at a public meeting. After the meeting, school officials should be available to reporters to respond to questions. Radio stations may want to record a brief news spot early in the morning. Someone from the schools should work with the stations on this.

THE NEWS CONFERENCE

The most obvious consideration when deciding to hold a news conference is whether the reason is sufficiently newsworthy to justify taking reporters' valuable time. A news conference that results in little or no solid news for reporters prompts justifiable criticism and ensures sparse attendance at the next conference.

Planning the Conference

Once it's decided to call a news conference, notify all news media. The conference should be scheduled for a time that is convenient and accommodates the deadlines of the various news organizations invited.

An often overlooked phase of preparation is anticipating the kinds of questions that will be posed by alert reporters. Someone in the school district, preferably the person responsible for media relations, should play devil's advocate. This necessitates asking the kinds of controversial questions that reporters will pose. School officials must be prepared to respond to tough questions. An invitation to a news conference is an invitation to probe all areas related to the topic of the conference.

At the Conference

Distribute a kit of information and materials to all reporters who attend. This ensures that key statements are received accurately. For example, if a new superintendent is being appointed, the kit should include a photo plus a biography and some of the person's statements on key educational issues in the community.

At the conference, the key person should be surrounded by knowledgeable assistants who will be able to provide specifics as needed. For example, the superintendent should be able to call on an assistant superintendent to explain an important curricular change if the news conference will include discussion of curriculum in a new school.

Someone should be responsible for obtaining additional facts requested by reporters. This person should be known by the reporters, who should have no reluctance about calling him or her at a later date.

FOREIGN-LANGUAGE NEWS MEDIA

In addition to preparing materials for English-speaking audiences, school officials in some schools must be cognizant of groups that do not speak and understand English. To serve these groups, some school districts take advantage of foreign-language newspapers. Working closely with editors of these newspapers, school officials prepare articles in time for translation. In some cases, they use a staff member to provide the translation for the newspapers. This might mean extra effort for school administrators, but the effort extended should reap the reward of better overall support for the schools.

NEWS TOPICS IN YOUR SCHOOLS

Since school news must compete daily with material from hundreds of other sources for news coverage space, it must be newsworthy. Newsworthiness means that the information contains elements that make it readable—news that the news media will accept and the public will read.

Timeliness Is Important

Be sure the average reader won't have a "So what?" reaction to any story submitted. To avoid such a reaction, you should analyze why particular articles in the newspaper seem to interest readers.

First, to be of news value, the story should be timely. Most news media want stories as they happen. Something that happened yesterday might not be news tomorrow. Thus, it's imperative that someone in the schools know how to alert the news media when the stories are fresh.

If It's Unusual, It Could Be News

Frequently, a news story is news simply because it is unusual. Readers want to know about stories that occur for the first time or that have an angle or circumstance that makes them something out of the ordinary. For example, a class of students giving their teacher a report card and evaluating the kind of teaching done would be an unusual enough twist for an effective story. If done on the same day that students received their own report cards, the feature could lend itself to all kinds of interesting quotes. After attracting the editor's attention (and the readers' attention, too) with the unusualness of the story, the educator could explain how the report is part of an overall program to encourage teachers to determine how students perceive their teaching. It might be explained that feedback from students in specific areas will encourage teachers to continue certain practices and to modify others.

If It's Local, It Could Be News

Finding ways to suggest a local angle to a national story can help produce timely, positive news coverage. For instance, high school students studying political parties and elections might be of interest around election time. A story about the study of a particular foreign language might be especially timely if the U.S. president is currently visiting a country that speaks that language. If a national association of teachers passes a resolution advocating a certain approach to teaching writing, the school district can release a statement from the English department chairperson giving the district's views on the resolution. Because the statement is coming from someone in the community, it possesses the local flavor editors often are seeking.

Innovation Is News

Anything being initiated in the schools could be newsworthy. If it's being done in a way that differs from the way it was done when most of the readers attended school, the topic could rate newspaper consideration. When preparing a news release about an innovation, the educator should look for those bits of information that will appeal to the largest number of readers. This guideline, of course, should be applied to all newswriting.

A new approach to teaching science, a new way to correct tests, a novel approach to a particular class, or the use of a common teaching device in a different way can all be considered innovations, and as such they merit news consideration. Obvious questions will be posed by readers when an innovation is announced. The educator must keep these in mind when explaining the introduction of an innovation. *Example:* How much does it cost? Has it been used elsewhere, and if so, was it effective? How will it help students learn better? Who decided to adopt the innovation? How will it be evaluated? This last question is one that has gained prominence since accountability became a vital part of education.

Evaluation Is News

As accountability continues to gain importance in education, evaluation claims appreciably more attention in overall communications and public relations efforts. Evaluation means tests or some other measures that can be applied to determine if certain approaches or materials are working. Some schools have been making results of standardized tests known to the public for years. Other school administrators cringe at the suggestion of such score sharing with the public. Despite the numerous arguments of those opposed to making evaluations known to the public, the trend is toward disclosure.

The releasing of evaluation information requires a large amount of homework by the school administrator who is inexperienced in this area. Releasing such data without sufficient explanation can severely harm the school's relationship with the community and with the press. Most reporters and most laypersons simply do not understand the terminology used by educators in the field of testing. However, those same reporters and readers are intently interested in what the tests or other evaluations show about their schools. The help of a guidance counselor or testing expert can ensure a fuller explanation. Yet, this is not enough. Just as important is the involvement of someone who understands the kinds of questions that reporters and laypersons will ask. By anticipating these questions, the educator can prepare a news release or an in-depth series that provides information that people want to read.

Most readers will not enjoy statistic after statistic. More important would be an explanation of what the statistics mean or what the options are. For example, when evaluations are being published, school officials can use the opportunity to focus on programs and materials that are needed to improve a certain phase of instruction. If the educator doesn't offer possible solutions to obvious problems, laypersons will conclude that the educator lacks the answer. It is better to take the offensive in this situation rather than to react defensively later to the inevitable criticisms.

Controversy Is News

Educators generally overreact to school news that is controversial or negative. Yet people enjoy reading about controversy, and if readers want it, reporters will cover it. School officials can use this knowledge to their benefit by preparing news articles about the schools that show both sides of a story. This kind of news release is quickly accepted by editors and is well read by taxpayers. It shows that educators do consider more than one approach to solving a problem. A good example of showing alternatives that could be controversial would be the possible ways to close schools in response to falling enrollment. By explaining the various strengths and weaknesses of each possibility in some detail, school officials can demonstrate that various solutions have been considered.

Money Is News

An increase in school taxes is always news because it involves the money of many taxpayers. Thus, reporters will always seek information about school undertakings that seem to cost more money than others. Educators who give the impression of trying to dodge legitimate questions from reporters in these areas will suffer a credibility problem. Thus, it's imperative that school officials prepare concise but complete explanations of budget requests and other financial issues for reporters.

If possible, translate large figures into specific service results. For example, if two new speech therapists are being requested in a budget, explain in a news release that the two therapists will serve X number of children. Explain specifically what two new people, if approved, will do to improve the overall educational offerings of the school system.

Every time a new position is established, a lengthy explanation of the rationale for establishing it should be provided in a news release. How will this position help students? Why couldn't the responsibility be assumed by someone currently on the staff? What kinds of specific responsibilities will the person have? Do similar positions exist in comparable school systems? How will the position improve education in the school system?

When every tax dollar counts, school officials must be ready to justify the creation of a new position. The most effective way is to show, before the person is appointed to the position, how the job will enable the schools to do certain things better. This should be done before it appears as if the administration is on the defensive.

PUBLICITY OPPORTUNITIES

A variety of types of news coverage offer schools opportunities for publicity. Some of these coverage types include the news story, the special column or commentary, editorials, letters to the editor, and online commentary, radio programming, and TV programming.

The News Story

News stories are usually divided into two types: the hard (or straight) news story and the feature story.

The hard news story is a straightforward account of a happening. It presents the facts in an objective way, and the style is impersonal, direct, and uncolored. It answers the standard questions of *who*, *what*, *why*, *when*, and *where* about an event or happening. Some stories require inclusion of the *how* to complete the story. Details of the story are arranged in decreasing order of importance. This is done because editors seldom have enough space to run the entire story as presented. Frequently, stories must be shortened, and the easiest way is to omit the last paragraph or the last two or three. This points out the necessity of placing the most important facts early in the story.

The straight news story can be of different types. It can be an advance story, which tells as much as possible about an upcoming event. It can be a cover story, which relates in detail what took place at the event. This usually is reported the same day the event took place or on the day after. The follow-up story could report reactions of those attending the event and ideas they have implemented as a result of having attended the event.

The feature story presents factual information but does so in an interesting and lively way, frequently with a human interest touch. Although the feature story is considered more difficult to write than the hard news story, the feature does allow the writer to be more creative. It also permits emotional content and perspective to be included in the story. Built around some unique aspect of an event or a personality, it is designed to evoke a smile or laugh, to appeal to the imagination, or to stir the emotions of the reader. The supply of feature stories in any school is limited only by the number of people and ideas available. Some topics for feature stories might be a day in the life of a teacher, the first day of school for a kindergarten child, the role of a school volunteer, and so on.

The Special Column or Commentary

The newspaper column or broadcaster commentary is an often overlooked vehicle for communicating school news. The column can be used in two ways: either by providing information to columnists or commentators or by school personnel writing a regular column or blog. Local newspapers will often welcome a column written by the superintendent. Such a column allows opinion and provides a constant opportunity to inform readers about topics of the superintendent's choosing. Columnists and commentators are often looking for suggestions.

Editorials

The editorial is a type of story in which opinions are expressed on public issues. On most large daily newspapers, editorials often are written without the direct input of local educators. However, reporters' opinions are sometimes sought, and if the reporters have good rapport with educators, solid, helpful information can be provided to the editorial writers. In some instances, editorial writers will contact local education leaders for information before writing education editorials. The public's right to know about school issues, bond issues, career education, reading methods, accountability, test scores, student militancy, and teacher rights makes all these good subjects for editorials. Like all writers who face daily deadlines, editorial writers occasionally experience days when ideas come slowly. An occasional suggestion from an educator, with accompanying accurate information, would usually be accepted and used.

Consider preparing a column or article for the page opposite the editorial page. This allows an opportunity to offer opinions.

Letters to the Editor and Online Commentary

Letters to the editor and online commentary are views expressed by readers on questions of current interest, published by newspapers under such titles as "Voices of the People," "What People Think," and "Letters to the Editor." These letters and comments often rank high in reader interest. Letters to the editor have several possible uses in the school's publicity campaign. One use is to review and analyze them to evaluate the school interests of some people in the community. Although not necessarily representative of the community's thinking overall, letters to the editor and other commentary can indicate how some audience segments feel about certain school issues.

Letters to the editor also provide an excellent opportunity for expressing appreciation for services rendered to the school. Municipal officials who speak to classes on government, parents who help in a study of school building needs, or civic groups who cooperate in a scholarship program can be publicly thanked in this fashion. The general public can be thanked by school officials for attendance at school functions or for participation in some special school undertaking. The administrator will find that it pays to write a letter now and then commending the newspaper for fine coverage of significant school events and happenings.

Occasionally, a school official may wish to correct an error in the newspaper or respond to criticism with a letter to the editor or commenting online. This decision, however, must be made on the individual merits of each case. Most school public relations practitioners agree that a verbal battle in the letters-to-the-editor or comments section seldom increases public understanding of an issue or enhances public confidence in educators. If the chief school administrator, for example, challenges a critic, the general public often will side with the underdog against the public official. There generally are better ways to address such challenges.

Radio Programming

Radio stations offer a wide range of opportunities for schools, including the following:

Spot announcements. Short 10-, 20-, 30-, and 60-second announcements can be information-giving or can be appeals for support for special school undertakings. They can be succinct interviews with various staff members, or they can be a series of quick comments from students and staff members about a topic of general concern. The shorter the show (or spot), the better the chance of its being used.

Sports programs. Local stations will sometimes broadcast school football, basketball, or other games.

Music programs. There is public interest in school bands, choruses, and other musical groups. Special shows are sometimes taped, especially during the holiday season. If properly informed, local stations might consider taping a brief segment of a musical presentation to use in their regular programming.

Discussion programs. A good panel show on a topic of general interest can be attractive to stations. Roundtables and debates, if properly planned, can be fast paced and interesting. Topics and participants must be carefully selected.

Dramatic programs and documentaries. Student-produced dramatic productions and special in-depth programs that probe strengths and weaknesses of a specific school topic can serve the community and show that the schools are providing service to a public other than those actually attending the schools.

Talk and interview shows. The expertise of administrators, teachers, and students can be showcased on appropriate talk and interview programs. *Example:* Teachers and their new approaches in classrooms are often overlooked for interview shows. Yet they can be extremely informative and stimulating guests, especially inasmuch as many listeners are concerned with what's new or different in the classroom.

TV Programming

As in radio, commercial TV stations devote a percentage of their broadcasting schedule to public affairs programs. School-sponsored programs usually fall into this category. Such programs can establish a more direct and almost personal relationship with residents. Local viewers can be shown what a new school building is like and how it functions. Or viewers can be shown why a district needs more money to build, expand, or remodel current facilities.

A TV program dealing with problems of the schools is almost as effective in stimulating thought, discussion, and action as a forceful speaker, panel, or roundtable held in a school auditorium before a live audience.

For the most part, the same kinds of programs that are aired on radio may be aired on TV. In fact, a number of programs are interchangeable. Spot announcements, sports and music programs, discussion and panel shows, and interviews and news releases can serve double duty. Once these spots are produced for TV, the voice tracks can often be extracted from videotape or film and dubbed onto audiotape for use on radio.

NEWS SOURCES

News is found everywhere in the school system. There is never a scarcity of it. For every story published, a dozen more could be written containing important information. A checklist, like the following, indicates sources from which stories may be drawn. If the checklist is developed with the aid of professional reporters, it will be richer in ideas and practical suggestions, in addition to having the further value of familiarizing the reporters with the makeup and operation of the school system. Referring to the checklist leads to better copy and broader coverage.

Checklist of News Sources

Administrative Activities

Board meetings

Board actions

Board members

Board elections

Board officers

Speaking engagements

Programs under consideration

Speeches made

Recognitions received

New administrators

Surveys conducted

Changes in organization

Cost of education

Record systems

School budget

Decline in number of employees

Interviews with board members

Interviews with administrators

School calendar

Website enhancements

Social media campaigns

Research studies

Educational needs

Long-range challenges

Attendance at conferences

Participation in community projects

Classroom Activities

Field trips

Methods of teaching

Online learning activities

Curriculum changes

Testing programs

Results of testing

Special study projects

Exhibits

Demonstrations

New instructional materials

Textbook selection

Library references

New equipment

Trends in teaching practices

New classroom technology

Homework policies

Parent participation

Guidance and counseling suggestions

Course offerings

Educational objectives

Service programs

Community Activities

Services to community

Use of community resources

Citizen participation in school program

School–community projects

Staff participation in community affairs

Cooperation with community groups

Community surveys and opinion polls

Graduate Activities

Business success

Special awards and honors

Reunions

Success in college

Contributions to school

Alumni programs

Opinions on educational issues

Civic work

Career outlooks

Employment after graduation

Staff Activities

Scholarships, awards, and special honors

New faculty and staff

Exchange teachers

Summer learning activities

Professional interests

Avocational interests

Professional development

Attendance at conferences

Work in the community

Retirement

Visiting educators

Rewards of teaching

Special talents

Offices in professional organizations

Books and articles written

Promotions

Biographical material

Speeches

Fund-raising projects

Parent Activities

Parent–teacher association programs

Services to the school

Conferences with parents

Participation in school

Special parent projects

Parent publications

New online material or initiatives

Officers of parent–teacher association

Attendance at educational conferences

Facilities

New building construction

New building financing

New building locations

Sale of a building

Features of new buildings

Community use of buildings

Special recreation programs for adults

Building maintenance

New installations

Building openings/dedications

Safety measures

Renovations and expansions

Student Activities

Academic achievement

Career education

Scholarships, awards, and special honors

Hobby interests

Success in special fields

Outstanding talent

School clubs

Musical programs

Athletic events

Various competitions

Assembly programs

Student government

Pageants and festivals

Attendance

Graduation exercises

Special projects

Opening of school year

Donations to charity

Speeches

Special Activities

Open-house programs

Observances—birthdays, holidays, special weeks

Operation of cafeteria

History of school

Demonstrations and exhibits

School bus service

Visits by celebrities

Guidance facilities

Drives and campaigns

Outstanding graduate selects teacher who influenced life

Research projects

Health measures

ORGANIZING SCHOOL NEWS EFFORTS

No matter whether a school system is large or small, some form of organization is necessary to provide news. In larger systems, news responsibility is usually divided between a communications director and the individual principals. The person responsible for communications or community relations may be known by a variety of titles. Among them are assistant superintendent in charge of communications, and coordinator (or director) of community relations, public information, or public relations. The person responsible for handling communications is generally charged with news originating from the board of education or central administration. In addition, this person provides leadership for other departments and personnel, helping them understand what news is and how to get it to the media.

The communications person also arranges interviews with key school personnel and builds rapport with reporters and editors. To help identify news stories, he or she usually develops a news-collecting network. To do this, each principal appoints someone in the building to work with the communications person. Frequently this person is a teacher. In some school systems, the principal sends the information or news release directly to local media with a copy to the public relations director. In other systems, all news first is sent to the public relations director, who then filters it or refines it before sending it to the news media. This process is commonly used in many school districts. To encourage teachers and other employees to suggest news, easy-to-use forms are placed near staff mailboxes (see Figure 11.1) and

```
┌─────────────────────────────────────────────┐
│            NEWS REPORTING FORM                │
│                                               │
│   Name of school _____ Date _____   │
│   Who _____ │
│   What _____ │
│   Why _____ │
│   When _____ │
│   Where _____ │
│   How _____ │
│   Picture possibilities _____ │
│   Remarks _____ │
│   Reporter _____ Phone _____  │
└─────────────────────────────────────────────┘
```

FIGURE 11.1   Form for News Reporting.

the "It's just as easy as a phone call" approach is used. This approach ensures coverage of all schools in the system, immediate reports of stories that break, and the professional treatment of releases.

If the director of community relations is employed on a part-time basis, then he or she may find it expedient to turn the material from building representatives over to a high school English or journalism class, especially in cases where news is compiled weekly for a school page in the local newspaper. Members of the class edit the material and write releases under the guidance of the teacher, who is often the person in charge of community relations. Copy is checked for news content and style of presentation, and the better stories are selected for publication. Important news from administrative offices is taken care of by the director of community relations.

It is common in small districts for the superintendent or supervising principal to serve as the news representative for the school system. Success in publicizing and interpreting the educational program depends on a sense for news, the ability to write interesting copy, and the time invested in the work.

GETTING THE NEWS TO THE MEDIA

Various ways exist to get news stories to the media. Included are the news release, the fact sheet, the news memo, and the news conference. The last method, the news conference, has already been considered. Of the other methods, the news release is the most common approach to disseminating news items.

News Release

News releases traditionally have been mailed, faxed, or hand-delivered to the news media. Increasingly, many reporters and editors prefer to receive news materials by e-mail.

Schools operating in larger cities and regionally may want to consider using a variety of commercial news release distribution services. Two such services are BusinessWire (businesswire.com) and PR Newswire (prnewswire.com).

Preparing News Releases

Editors assign more space to school news when releases conform to media standards. The standards take into consideration style of writing, quality of writing, and the mechanical makeup of the copy. Many editors will confess that they use some stories that are not as good in content as some they reject. Why? Simply because those accepted were received in a style that enabled them to be used with a minimum of editing. This is especially true with small news organizations, where rewrite time is a scarce commodity. Editors are busy people who receive a large number of news releases daily. Seldom do they have time to read every release from start to finish. Thus, the first rule for writing an effective news release is to put the key news in the first paragraph. This will attract readers and will also gain the attention of the editor.

Most newspaper articles, especially hard news stories, are written in what is called the inverted pyramid style (see Figure 11.2). The most important elements of the story are told in the first or lead paragraph, with each succeeding paragraph being somewhat less important than the one before it. The story has no climax or conclusion. Stories are written in this style because many readers read only the headline and the lead. Also, as noted, this style allows the editor to cut the story at any point and know that the least important paragraphs are being lost.

The lead paragraph usually addresses some of the following: who, what, where, when, why, and how. However, not all of these questions can always be covered in a lead. A common error of the novice is to try to cram all of this information into one sentence, which becomes a marathon challenge to any reader. Most good leads are written in fewer than 30 words;

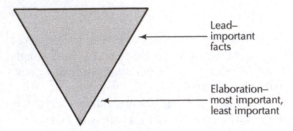

Lead–
important
facts

Elaboration–
most important,
least important

FIGURE 11.2   The Inverted Pyramid Style.

in fact, most readers prefer leads of 20 words or fewer. In writing a hard-news lead, emphasis is usually placed on the single fact or aspect of the story that is likely to have the strongest reader appeal. In feature stories, the lead varies with the writer and the nature of the material. In either type, the lead can make or break a story, no matter what information follows it. The writing of a concise, forceful lead is an art that requires a sound sense of news and much practice. One way to sharpen lead-writing ability is to read good newspapers and focus on their leads. Here are two leads that present facts concisely:

A new reading program designed to upgrade reading achievement of Blankville's students was announced last night by Superintendent of Schools Harvey Jones.

Enough spaghetti to stretch from Blankville to Green Bay was served in Blankville's school cafeterias yesterday.

The second example could be an unusual lead for a story about the school lunch program. Students might have been involved in determining how much spaghetti was served and how far the spaghetti would stretch if laid end to end. Having attracted the editor's (and reader's) attention, the educator could continue the story to elaborate on the school lunch offerings and the nutritional aspects of the program. Contrast this lead with those routinely submitted by most schools, such as this one:

During the first fiscal quarter of this school year, a large number of Type A lunches were served to students in both the elementary and secondary schools of Blankville, according to Superintendent of Schools Harvey Jones and Food Services Director William Smith.

The reaction of most readers would justifiably be "Who cares?" It might be fine to explain how many such lunches were served, what the Type A lunch is, and why it is nutritionally sound to provide such lunches. This information should come later in the story, and it should be written in an interesting way.

Following are additional examples of effective leads:

Local high-school students will meet with the mayor at 11:00 a.m., Monday, in the Council chambers to plan a workshop on city government.

This is considered a *conventional lead*, giving the basic who, what, when, where, and why information. Although traditionally this lead has been acceptable, the newspaper would make for monotonous reading if every lead were presented in the same style. Variety is necessary for the newspaper; it's also vital for the success of the person writing news releases.

What do high-school students know about their government?

The *question lead* can be effective, especially when it involves the reader. Some readers will find themselves answering the question. This entices them to read more to see if their answers agree with those presented in the story. Other readers will continue reading after the lead to learn the answer to the problem.

"We want to know where our tax money will be going so we're meeting with the mayor," said James Buren, president of Blankville High School's Student Council.

The *quote lead* makes the story come alive from the beginning. It seems to add a dimension to the story. In fact, using quotes throughout news releases, when appropriate, provides a certain liveliness that encourages readers to continue reading.

Whether the lead features one news element or another depends on the nature of the story. For example, if the governor has declared that school building costs must be cut, the who element would be emphasized because of the governor's prominence. If a similar statement came from a school board member, the stress might well be placed on the effects of the proposed cuts for local taxpayers.

The lead is followed by the *body of the story*. The body consists of one or more paragraphs explaining the facts. The details are arranged in order of importance, thus making chronological treatment seldom feasible. Paragraphs should not be too long because they become cumbersome for the reader's eye when put in one column in the newspaper. One typewritten line could well become as many as three lines of type in the newspaper column. Thus, the typewritten paragraph of 10 lines necessitates the editor getting the pencil out simply to save the appearance of the paper. Too many long paragraphs make the paper appear too gray.

It is not necessary to worry about smooth transitions when writing hard news. It is more important to limit the paragraphs to five or six typewritten lines. For a change of pace, there is nothing wrong with a one-sentence paragraph. Many effective leads are just that—a one-sentence paragraph.

Quality of Writing

News organizations want copy in clear, concise, simple language. Editors do not want to sift through the pompous writing of the educator who is trying to impress rather than trying to communicate. Here are some tips to help school officials who are preparing news releases. Much of this information can be applied to writing for school publications and online content as well.

- *Use familiar words that are easily understood.* Using comfortable words indicates that educators understand their audience members and are writing for them. The use of short words for long ones tends to make news material easier to read. For example, use *total* instead of *aggregate*. When *use* fits, use it instead of *utilize*. One of the enemies of clear writing is the persistent use of words with more than three syllables. Educators often also use too much jargon that is not in common use by external audiences. Be alert to educational terminology and explain it if it's used. Although educators will quickly relate to *block scheduling*, *accountability*, *team teaching*, and *percentile*,

the average news reader or viewer often will not relate easily to such unfamiliar terms.

- *Use short, simple sentences for the most part.* Although sentences should vary in length and kind, most sentences should be of the subject–verb–object kind. This allows the main thought to be communicated without phrases and clauses getting in the way. Most journalists say it another way: Limit each sentence to one idea. A key roadblock to easy reading is the long sentence. A series of long sentences makes the reader work too hard to get the writer's message. In an era with so many competing messages, the writer who wants to be read must communicate as effectively as possible.

- *Use action verbs as much as possible.* Check releases for the overuse of the verb *is* and other forms of *to be*. Substitute stronger verbs that communicate action and a sense of movement when possible. Too many educators insist on writing in the passive voice. When overdone, this communicates a stodgy stiffness and encourages readers to look elsewhere for interesting reading. Editors will change passive voice writing to active in most cases. For example, don't write "The bill was received by the superintendent, and payment on it was made by the board." Instead, write "The superintendent received the bill, and the board paid it."

- *Identify people when their names are used.* Give full names and titles, not just last names. If a staff member has a certain responsibility that relates to the story, give the title and responsibility. Too many educators take this a step further and insist on giving credit early in a story to all who worked on an undertaking. Readers are seldom as concerned with the names and titles of the people who helped develop a program as they are about what the program offers, how it will be implemented, and how much it will cost. Give credit, certainly, but later in the story.

- *Don't make judgments.* Avoid adjectives that are someone's judgment or opinion unless, of course, they appear in a quote that is attributed to that someone. A statement in a release that lauds the school's "excellent" science program should only be made if the person calling it excellent is identified. Using such adjectives marks the school official as a novice in news release writing; the good editor will cross them out.

MECHANICS OF THE NEWS RELEASE

Newspaper editors use a style sheet or style book to prepare their copy. This guideline allows reporters to be consistent in writing certain words. For example, some newspapers spell out the word *street* when it appears as part of an address; other newspapers prefer to abbreviate the word. Knowing the style of the newspapers can enable school officials to prepare copy the way editors want it—a definite advantage in the overall news release program. Although newspapers may differ somewhat on technical requirements for abbreviation, capitalization, punctuation, and spelling, most generally adhere to guidelines in publications such as *The Associated Press Stylebook* (apstylebook.com).

For news releases that will be printed and mailed or faxed, most professionals agree on the following standards:

- The story should be prepared on white or light paper.
- The releases should be typed, double-spaced, on one side of the paper only.
- The date that the story is being sent and the date it is to be released should appear at the top of the page.
- The name of the person sending the release, the person to contact for more information, and the school name, address, and telephone numbers should appear at the top of the first page. The e-mail address and cell phone number of the media contact person should be included.
- Copy should begin about one-third of the way down the page so that enough space is available for the editor to write in a headline. The editor might also use this space to write comments for the staff to follow up on the story.
- Limit the release to one or two pages unless unusual circumstances are present.

WRITING FOR BROADCAST

Generally, it's advisable to write separate copy for the broadcast media. The following are some guidelines for broadcast copy. It should be remembered that broadcast news is geared more toward the ear than the eye—as it accommodates listeners instead of readers.

- Write simple, spoken English.
- Try to keep one thought to a sentence.
- Try to use the present or present perfect tense.
- Use strong action verbs to help the listener visualize the story.
- Avoid using the word *today*. This will permit news editors to date the story to meet their individual needs.
- Do not use synonyms. Synonyms can confuse the listener.
- Do not use pronouns. Repeat proper names.
- Avoid direct quotes. Paraphrasing is safer.
- Keep adjectives to a minimum. Adjectives tend to clutter speech and obscure the main line of the story.
- Use verbs—do not drop verbs. Listeners need verbs.
- Avoid using appositions. Many appositions are not natural to speech and may be confusing to listeners because they don't see the necessary punctuation. For example, instead of writing "Mary Smith, a Central High School student, won the scholarship," consider writing "Central High School student Mary Smith won the scholarship."
- Do not start sentences with a prepositional phrase or a participial phrase.
- Give attribution at the beginning of a sentence, not at the end, so the listener knows who is speaking before a quote is given. *Example:* "Mayville High School Principal Mary Jones explained XXX" rather than "XXX, explained Mayville High School Principal Mary Jones."
- Pinpoint the location. If a release is written to be aired in the same town as the subject of the release, precede the location with "Here in Blanksville" (*Example:* "The principal of Wilson High School, here in Blanksville.")

- Always find a way of repeating a location. Repeating the location toward the end of a story is important for the listener.
- Avoid the first person. Use first person only if you, the writer, really mean *you*. For instance, when speaking of the school district, do not use *we* or *our*. Simply say "The Blanksville School District."
- Be conversational. Do not try to be too formal. Choose words that are concise, precise, and grammatically correct.
- Be specific. Do not use vague language or imagery.
- Every release should focus on only one topic or subject. Additional topics should be covered in later releases.

PREPARING FOR TELEVISION INTERVIEWS

As broadcast opportunities present themselves, school officials should be ready. Schools should invest time preparing staff for television appearances.

In its text *School Public Relations: Building Confidence in Education*, the National School Public Relations Association suggests these basic communication strategies:

- Always prepare for any interview or media appearance. Find out what the interview will cover and gather as much relevant information on the topic as possible.
- Develop key message points. Write key points so you can refer to them during the interview. Be brief and use language that will be memorable. Try to keep points in sound bites of only a few seconds.
- Practice bridge answers to make key points. *Example:* "I can't address this specific personnel issue, but what I can tell you is. . . ." "But what I can tell you" helps to build a bridge from the question to the answer you can offer.
- Build credibility by answering clearly and factually.
- Get some media training. Practice working in front of a camera or microphone. Review your replies and work on perfecting your delivery.[5]

One Expert's Point of View: Schools and the News Media

Tim Carroll, APR, has served as Director of Public Information for the Allen Independent School District in suburban Dallas since 1995. Prior to that, he held a similar position for 14 years with the Penn-Harris-Madison Schools, located near South Bend, Indiana. He has over 20 years of experience managing community education and outreach programs for school districts. He also teaches as adjunct faculty in the communications department at Texas A&M University at Commerce.

We have seen some major shifts in the way news is gathered and reported. Online news outlets have become a major source of information for people. Staffing at many traditional media outlets has been reduced. How have these trends affected the ways in which media report on schools—and what should school leaders be doing to respond to these trends?

A major difference in online news gathering is that most of the news is gathered, well, online. What was once a local news story about religious freedom in the public schools can become a national cause if it is picked up by a well-read blog or news outlet. The editors of online publications may have no knowledge or background on your school district, so it is more important than ever to monitor your online communications. It is also prudent to monitor your district's image on the Web to avoid surprises. Because of the shift away from traditional beat reporters, local news gathering organizations also rely more on content provided by schools and organizations. School communicators are less likely to receive a clarifying phone call. In fact, they may not even know the names of the people handling the news at the other end.

Because news generated by the school district can be read by the public and the media simultaneously, the reliance on newspapers and electronic media to "get the word out" has greatly diminished. This puts more power in the hands of the PR person to get immediate and unfiltered information out to the public.

Despite all the new trends in reporting, do some of the traditional rules of media relations still apply when it comes to getting fair and accurate coverage of your schools?

Trust and accuracy are as important as ever. Reporters today are often editors, photographers, and designers as well. Their time is limited, so providing accurate and efficient communications can help them and benefit the organization as well. Styles and mediums have changed, but the inverted pyramid is still the best way to present information to the media. Loading the most important information at the top of a story with a strong lead still allows the editor to cut from the bottom up with few changes. Posting news releases is a good practice, but a good PR person follows up those postings with e-mails and calls to media contacts. The volume of information pouring into a news operation is greater than ever, and pitching a story is still a good practice. It also helps build a more personal relationship with the reporter/editor.

Social media and other forms of communication have made it easier for the news media to reach all employees in a school system. What is the proper role for employees when it comes to dealing with the media—and how can school communicators support employees in succeeding in these roles?

The school communications director's role has expanded with social media, but a bigger responsibility comes with that role. The school district's policy regarding communicating with the media must be publicized to employees and reinforced as needed. That same policy should be communicated to the news outlets covering your schools. There should be an expectation that requests go through the proper channels. That being said, it is more common for employees to post negative information on social media or send anonymously to news outlets. This cannot be entirely avoided, but it is a good practice for the school district's regulations on this issue to be clearly outlined in the employee handbook. Monitoring what employees are posting through school channels on blogs, Twitter, and campus websites is important. Some districts require that employees file passwords and logins for campus Twitter and Facebook accounts so that the communications office can correct or delete information if necessary.

The news media still offer a strong outlet for getting out news and information about our schools. What should school communicators be doing in today's media environment to make sure their good stories get told?

A large segment of the population still looks to newspapers and television news for objective coverage of local schools. A positive relationship with media representatives throughout the year can only help when bad news strikes. Know reporters by name, customize news releases and statements for their use, and provide background photos or data when possible to build that relationship. When bad things happen (and they will happen at some time) your reputation among reporters will make a big difference. Making yourself available to reporters and responding quickly and honestly to information requests is critical if you want to build your reputation and get your story told.[6]

Questions

1. Explain the primary advantages controlled media offer school–community relations efforts.
2. Since schools do not control the messages or timing of uncontrolled media, explain why schools use them. List the benefits uncontrolled media offer to school–community relations programming.
3. Explain the importance of avoiding educational jargon when preparing messages for outside audiences. List the other characteristics of good copy prepared for the news media.
4. List the pros and cons of providing information or comments off the record with a reporter.
5. Discuss the implications for school administrators and communicators in the observation that new media emerging in recent years have supplemented—rather than replaced—media traditionally used by schools.

Readings

Basso, Joseph, Randy Hines, and Suzanne FitzGerald, *PR Writer's Toolbox: Blueprints for Success,* 2nd ed. Dubuque, IA: Kendall Hunt, 2013.

Blair, Julie, *Building Bridges with the Press: A Guide for Educators.* Bethesda, MD: Education Week Press, 2004.

Collins, Ross F., *Editing Across Media: Content and Process for Print and Online Publication.* Jefferson, NC: McFarland, 2013.

Hilliard, Robert L., *Writing for Television, Radio, and New Media,* 11th ed. Belmont, CA: Cengage, 2014.

Howard, Carole M., and Wilma K. Mathews, *On Deadline: Managing Media Relations,* 5th ed. Prospect Heights, IL: Waveland Press, 2013.

Newsom, Doug, Judy VanSlyke Turk, and Dean Kruckeberg, *This Is PR: The Realities of Public Relations,* 11th ed. Belmont, CA: Wadsworth, 2012.

Smith, Ronald D., *Becoming a Public Relations Writer: Strategic Writing for Emerging and Established Media,* 5th ed. New York, NY: Routledge, 2016.

Wilcox, Dennis, *Public Relations Writing and Media Techniques,* 8th ed. Boston, MA: Pearson, 2015.

Endnotes

1. Joseph Basso, Randy Hines, and Suzanne FitzGerald, *PR Writer's Toolbox: Blueprints for Success*, 2nd ed. (Dubuque, IA: Kendall Hunt, 2013), pp. 4, 13.

2. Adapted from correspondence in January 2014 with Tim Carroll, APR, Director of Public Information for the Allen Independent School District, Allen, TX. Used with permission.

3. Julie Blair, *Building Bridges with the Press: A Guide for Educators* (Bethesda, MD: Education Week Press, 2004), p. 7.

4. Belmont Mercer Farley, "What to Tell People about the Public Schools" (New York, NY: Bureau of Publications, Teachers College, Columbia University, 1929), p. 1.

5. National School Public Relations Association, *School Public Relations: Building Confidence in Education,* 2nd ed. (Rockville: MD: Author, 2007), pp. 100–102.

6. Adapted from correspondence in January 2014 with Tim Carroll, APR, Director of Public Information for the Allen Independent School District, Allen, TX. Used with permission.

12

Creating and Delivering Online and Print Communications

This chapter reviews issues . . .

- For central administrators: The key communication tactics to be considered when planning districtwide communications programming and disseminating information and messages to internal and external audiences.
- For building and program administrators: The various options in developing communication materials that school and program administrators can use to deliver information in line with overall district messages and images.
- For teachers, counselors, and staff: The communication methods school personnel can use to communicate directly with parents and other community audiences.

After completing this chapter you should be able to . . .

- Document the ways in which communication tactics are developed and deployed to deliver information and messages in school communication programs.
- Distinguish the various tactics and the possible roles for each in communication efforts supporting school and community relationships.
- Define the two-way nature of digital communication tactics and describe the opportunities they offer in effective public engagement.
- Recognize the ongoing evolution of communication technology and the various opportunities and challenges it poses to school leaders.

Published materials traditionally have been important communication tactics used by school–community relations programs.

As "owned media" (see Chapter 11 for a discussion of paid, owned and earned media), school-published materials of many types are used to deliver official news and information to school audiences on behalf of the school system. The controlled nature of these tactics—that is, the organization manages the content, design, and delivery of them—allows schools to deliver specific messages to specific audiences according to a specific timeline.

Traditionally, printed materials have been—and continue to be—one efficient means of getting information to audiences. Production, printing, and distribution costs can be relatively low, considering the large numbers of people that can be reached through publications.

But the emergence of new technology and new media has created a number of new communication tactics for school systems and their communication planners. Driving this media convergence has been the expansion of Internet access in communities and the increasing familiarity with and use of new communication technologies by parents and others in the community.

Importantly, however, these new tactics, in many organizations, often are supplementing traditional communication tactics and not supplanting them.

Both the pace of change and the breadth of new communication tactics present an ongoing challenge for school leaders. Emerging practices offer new channels for disseminating information as well as new options for integrating and expanding traditional communication activities. Since new tactics generally are being integrated with traditional programs, the complexity of communication programs has increased. In addition, Internet-savvy consumers increasingly expect rapid availability of school information, and they expect to be able to access information through a variety of channels.

EMERGING TRENDS

Consider a few recent trends observed in school–community relations practices resulting from new online communication options:

- Use of printed publications and other materials has declined while the use of online communication tactics has increased. Online production and dissemination of documents, however, has not replaced printed publications or other communication tactics (such as meetings and presentations). Online and print efforts reinforce or supplement one another.

- Greater access to online services in many communities combined with both the cost and time savings offered by the distribution of information online offer opportunities to enhance both the effectiveness and efficiency of school–community relations communication efforts.

- New publishing options, also driven by technology, have helped print to remain viable by cutting both time and costs associated with producing printed materials.

- Online options have supported a merger of what once were distinct tactics. Video and audio, for example, can be embedded in online publications. In addition, online material can be used to supplement print efforts. Links to more in-depth information, or audio and video material, can offer print readers easy-to-access options if they want or need more detail.

- Social media have created new options for creating communities and connecting audiences to key points and additional information on emerging and ongoing school–community relations issues.

- Rapid evolution of software to create and manage online communication tactics has put the ability to communicate into the hands of nearly all school employees. The on-demand aspect of information online also has increased audience expectations for thorough and timely school communication.

The expansion of online communication activity has emerged in two phases over the past 20 years. In the initial phase, growing access to high-speed Internet made online communication an option for schools. According to a report from the National Center for Education Statistics, only 35 percent of schools had Internet access in 1994. By 2002, nearly all schools (99 percent) had Internet access, with 94 percent of those schools using broadband, or high-speed, Internet connections.[1] Five years later nearly all school systems reported using a district website to provide information to the community, and the National School Public Relations Association (NSPRA) reported that more than 70 percent of its member districts also had developed websites for individual schools.

In the next phase, growth of online communication began moving rapidly to basic websites. The continued support for and growth of online communication activities—as well as the ongoing use of traditional communication activities—was observed in a 2013 survey of members for the Wisconsin School Public Relations Association. Among some of its findings, the survey found school districts in that state reported using district websites (97 percent), parent online access to student information (89 percent), teacher websites (75 percent), school websites (70 percent), Facebook (49 percent), and Twitter (28 percent). Districts, however, also reported still using traditional communication methods, such as annual reports (71 percent), news releases (69 percent), district newsletters (56 percent), and school newsletters (49 percent).[2]

While online communication tactics have allowed schools to disseminate information in new ways, the two-way communication features of these latest tactics also have enhanced inexpensive and effective ways to collect feedback and insights online as well (see Figure 12.1).

Schools are analyzing posts and comments on social media and websites as well as actively soliciting feedback through websites and online publications—for example, to collect secondary research and data relevant to school planning and communication issues; to identify and track emerging and trending issues and concerns and to detect rumors or circulating misinformation; to encourage participation in online surveys; and to facilitate online forums, panels, and focus groups. Online monitoring services that use keywords to collect and report new postings about an organization or an issue (such as Google Alerts, google.com/alerts) can be used to track new online postings about specific issues or schools by traditional news sources as well as websites and blogs.

The adoption of online communication tactics by schools mirrors a shift in reported audience preferences for news and information sources. A 2012 survey on news consumption conducted by the Pew Research Center for the People and the Press found (when asked "Where did you get news yesterday?") that the number of people who reported getting news online jumped from 24 percent in 2004 to 39 percent

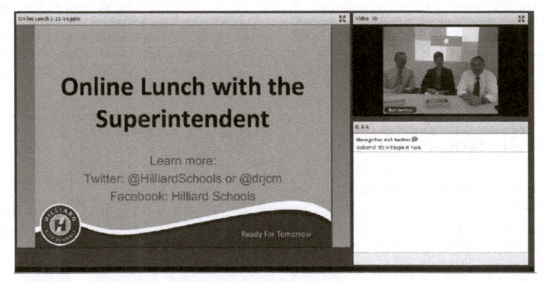

FIGURE 12.1 Creative Use of Online Media, Hilliard City Schools, Ohio: Online Lunch with the Superintendent.
An increasing use of online media by schools does not mean less direct communication with school leaders. In fact, because of its convenience and ease of use, online media can be used to enhance direct communication and relationship building between schools and their communities.

Source: Reprinted with permission from Hilliard City Schools.

in 2012. Meanwhile, those reporting getting news from television dropped from 68 percent in 1991 to 55 percent in 2012, and those reporting getting news from newspapers fell from 56 percent on 1991 to 33 percent in 2012.[3]

A DISTRICT CASE STUDY

Tim Carroll, APR, has served as a school public relations director for more than 30 years.[4] Since 1995 he has been Director of Public Information for the Allen Independent School District in Allen, Texas. The Allen Independent School District serves about 40,000 households in a rapidly growing suburban community located 23 miles north of Dallas. Student enrollment has more than tripled over the last 20 years. The district currently serves about 20,000 students in 17 elementary schools, three middle schools, one freshman center, and one high school.

The school system's communications efforts have been repeatedly recognized for excellence by NSPRA and the Texas School Public Relations Association. According to Carroll, the development of online communication efforts and the resulting changes and benefits are typical of those that can be found in many formal school public relations efforts.

Declines in Print Tactics

"We have significantly reduced our use of print materials over the past ten years," Carroll said. The district recently sought to cut expenses across the board and the majority of cuts in public relations came from reducing or eliminating some print publications, such as annual reports, calendars, and handbooks. Because new online communication efforts were developed to fill the void, Carroll said the cuts created little impact on programming and little public concern. "One big surprise was that we had no reaction to these cuts, and the big reason is that more and more the expectations of our public is that 'If I want it, I can get it online.' As a result of this, we make sure our online presence is robust—and that includes the availability of publications online. Everything you could possibly want to know about our schools is available at the click of a mouse."

Printed publications continue to have a place in school public relations efforts. However, that role has changed to one that targets smaller or segmented audiences. Publications are used less to reach mass audiences, which now can access information and publications online. "We still print publications, though," Carroll said. "For example, we still print an annual report and corporate brochure. But we once printed 35,000 copies and mailed it to every household in the community. Now we print only 3,000 copies and mail it to key communicators throughout the community, and we make the annual report available online. Print newsletters mailed throughout the community used to be a mainstay of the communications program. We have completely eliminated the print newsletter in favor of e-newsletters delivered online.

"What we have found is that readership has not gone down—people have just changed preferences in the way they get information and we are just repackaging it in different ways to accommodate different delivery modes."

Some Shifts in Preferences

A new shift toward Facebook and other social media outlets has required the school district to provide links that point to online data and publications (see Figures 12.2, 12.3, and 12.4). Often, younger patrons feel that the webpages are information-heavy and they prefer digesting school news in small bites.

Some audience segments served by the Allen Independent School District still have a preference for print. The school public relations program accommodates these readers with magazine racks in all schools for displaying key publications. Carroll stressed that the need for some publications generally is not an issue of residents lacking Internet access or skill. The need is based more on specific needs of some audience segments. Carroll explained: "The degree to which you still need to offer a mix of online and traditional information documents is more a matter of knowing and accommodating the various segments in your community. Typically, ESL (English as a Second Language) programs, calendars, school bus routes and other publications such as these—publications that people may

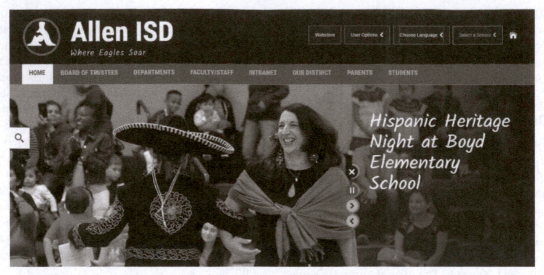

FIGURE 12.2   Web Portal Page for the Allen (Texas) Independent School District.
School websites have become information-rich resources linking schools with their communities using text, images, audio, video, and access to database-driven services.

Source: Reprinted with permission from Allen Independent School District.

FIGURE 12.3   Facebook Page of the Allen (Texas) Independent School District.
Social media have become key components of online media programs in schools.

Source: Reprinted with permission from Allen Independent School District.

have more of a need to hold in their hands and look at—are best disseminated in both online and print formats.

"One way to measure is to consider that publications that are more technical and less editorial in nature tend to perform better when offered online and in print. Those publications that focus more on editorial issues—covering strategies, issues, and goals—do well when distributed online."

Planning for Change

The convergence of media has also changed the way communications are planned and implemented.

What's New

National Merit Semifinalists

North Texas Giving Day

North Texas Giving Day

Coach Gregoriew 700

Preston Elementary Dedication

Homecoming 2017

Allen ISD Is Hiring

Community Pep Rally

College Night

Welcome To Fast Track

Welcome to Fast Track, Allen ISD's Email News Service. Thank you for subscribing.

Twenty Named National Merit Semifinalists For 2017

FIGURE 12.4   Online Newsletter Produced by the Allen (Texas) Independent School District. E-newsletters and other online publications now supplement the more traditional use of print publications in school–community relations programming.

Source: Reprinted with permission from Allen Independent School District.

Communication efforts to provide information during bond issue campaigns are one example, according to Carroll. Face-to-face communication remains key to such efforts. However, the initial communication planning focus has shifted from print efforts to online efforts supported by print.

"In our most recent campaign, rather than plan publications as we once did, the first step was to gather and create as much information and content on the issue as possible," Carroll explained. "With the content assembled, we then developed a content-rich website in advance, covering the issues related to the bond issue (referred to as a dark website). In this way, as soon as the bond program got underway the website was ready to go and people in the community could begin using it to learn more about the election. Next came a brochure with key facts and figures, which was printed and was made available through the schools. We printed about ten thousand of those inexpensive pieces. Next came a kind of prospectus brochure—an eight-and-a-half-by-eleven-inch document with photos and more information in the plans for the bond funding. About a thousand of these were printed for distribution to key communicators and others who requested it.

"So the new emphasis now is first on electronic or digital distribution—meaning online distribution. These communication efforts then are reinforced with targeted printed publications in a way that is much more efficient and cost-effective than older print campaigns, using community-wide mailings, might have been."

New Technology for Traditional Tools

On-demand publishing, using high-quality laser printing, has also contributed to options open to school communicators. Such in-house printing has made short-run printing cost-effective and has given schools the ability to customize content—meaning different versions of a basic brochure can include different information customized for different audiences. On top of this, the basic print versions can also be made available online—either in the exact same format or formatted in a slightly different way to better accommodate online readers—further supplementing the distribution of actual printed copies.

Here's how this might work in a typical project, according to Carroll: "Suppose a bond issue is designed to support 10 new building projects throughout a community. A brochure might list and describe all of those 10 projects. Each time a school official goes out to make a presentation to the community, the project listings in the brochure might be reordered to highlight the one or two projects that the audience might be more interested in. Using the same strategy, when a publication is placed online, the 10 projects might be listed by name with links to more information on each particular project. In this way, online readers can click through to get information only for those projects in which they have an interest."

Added Flexibility

Digital and online production and distribution have given school communicators a new level of flexibility and immediacy to their communications that enhances the potential for better serving the information needs and interests of key audiences.

"You cannot do this if you are printing everything," Carroll explained. "In the old days—before digital and online options were available—someone would have written and designed a brochure, paid to have thousands of them printed, paid more to get them distributed, and that would have been that. Changes or customizations to update information or meet the needs of specific segments of an audience would not have been possible because of cost and time issues. Today, digital production coupled with online distributions offers an almost unlimited potential to update and customize products to better serve the interests and information needs of every audience segment."

Incorporating Video and Visuals

Beyond print, video and other presentation support materials (such as PowerPoint presentations) can effectively be distributed online to supplement their use in face-to-face meetings in schools and throughout the community.

PowerPoint-type presentations are especially effective in small to medium-size audiences where more costly video productions might be too expensive, according to Carroll. "Despite the growing use of video, PowerPoint presentation materials when produced well can be extremely effective with audiences both in person and online," he said.

One benefit of online distribution of print, video, and presentation material is that school officials making public presentations and running community meetings can direct audience members to a school website for copies of materials used in a meeting or to get additional information on topics discussed.

"It's a tremendous benefit when a school official can tell an audience that 'all of this material and more can be found on our website,'" Carroll said. "So in a meeting, for example, a school official can talk about a new tax rate resulting from a planned bond issue, and he or she might review tax rates for the past five or ten years. But if someone wants even more historical information on tax rates they can easily get it if you make that kind of supplemental information available on a website. Detailed Web-based information, supplemented by the specific information made available in presentations and print publications, can bring a level of total transparency to school decision making and communications."

Access Is Key

In a survey of its community, Carroll's school district found that 94 percent of households reported now having Internet access. "This trend has allowed us to make tremendous changes in the way we distribute information—and made that process more effective and efficient in the process," he noted.

One example: The district published a student handbook annually that ran more than a hundred pages. With more than 20,000 students—and every student getting a copy—this was an enormous print-and-distribution effort. Today, the district still produces that handbook, but it is distributed mainly online. It still prints about 1,000 copies of it and makes it available in all of the schools. Any parent or student who wants a printed copy can get it, but the school district now distributes only about 700 printed copies, saving $30,000 per year. The rest of the copies are distributed online.

PLANNING COMMUNICATIONS TACTICS

The strategic mission of all communication tactics must be carefully evaluated when planning the development and execution of tactics supporting school–community relations. As with traditional print communications, websites and other online communication methods now are part of systemwide communication programs. But as the technology driving these tactics became easier to use, individual schools and programs often began developing their own content and materials—sometimes independently from systemwide programs. Increasingly, however, school-communication planners are recognizing the important role of both systemwide and school and program communications in the establishment of the system's brand and reputation, as well as the repetition and reinforcement of key messages.

In essence, all communication supporting school–community relations efforts seeks to establish strong working relationships between the school district and its key constituencies. In fact, school-communication planning (see Chapter 4) often focuses on the desired behavioral outcomes that can result from the understanding and support these relationships can foster.

Some aspects of online communication—its capacity to facilitate two-way conversations, its ability to support online communities, and its immediacy, for example—offer school communicators many new tactical options that can, when appropriately managed, be supportive of both traditional print tactics and other relationship-building strategies. Data showing that audiences are relying increasingly on online information sources for news and information also underscore the growing need to carefully assess online-communication strategies.

Another aspect of online communication is its ability to allow more and more people to engage in the development of communication tactics. Newer technologies, such as desktop design software for publications and content-management systems for websites, allow almost anyone to create a publication or contribute material to a webpage or website. As a result, teachers, principals, program directors, and others—with little technical or design skill—have the potential to develop or contribute to a variety of communication tactics in their areas of responsibility. School-communication planners, however, must carefully assess the amount of control and direction they wish to establish over such communication activities. Such planning should not be viewed as restrictive.

Rather, strategic communication planning should seek to provide the guidance and support necessary to help all appropriate communication activities be as effective as possible at meeting the district's identified communication goals and objectives.

This guidance generally is addressed at both the policy and planning levels. Most school systems now have formal policies or guidelines governing social media and other online communication activities, sometimes addressing online communication by both employees and students. Such guidelines often address online decorum for both official and personal online communication activities. Policies and guidelines need to be carefully developed to make sure they are consistent with federal and state and local laws and regulations that can apply to online communication activities. (See the "Social Media, Schools, and the Law" sidebar.)

Although guidelines and policies help to guide individuals in their responsibilities related to the use of social media–related online communication, communication planners also should focus on the use of online tools to support the school district's relationship-building objectives.

All communication tactics should be developed to support the desired outcomes of the district's overall communication programming. This generally means that communication tactics at all levels need some level of coordination to ensure consistency in both design and messages. When not coordinated, content-management systems can result in disorganized online offerings where visitors to school websites, for example, feel little or no connection to district websites. The same lack of connection can be seen in social media when Facebook pages or Twitter accounts operated by schools are not guided by global planning from the district overall. Even print publications, produced in ways that do display constancy in design and messages, create a disjointed look for the district's communication and, more importantly, fail to take advantage of the potential to reinforce key school district messages and themes.

Working together, however, communication tactics produced at various locations throughout the school system can provide readers and viewers a consistent experience that better supports relationship and image building as well as a better understanding of overarching messages and missions.

SOCIAL MEDIA, SCHOOLS, AND THE LAW
By Joseph N. Basso, J.D., Ph.D.

The widespread use of social media as catalyst in creating a marketplace of ideas has transformed education. However, this ever-changing communication landscape also brings with it a myriad of legal issues. Used effectively, social media can provide an opportunity for children to access information tailored to meet their own learning styles. However, social media, used impulsively, can muddle the learning environment and create social and legal challenges for school districts.

School districts must be aware of two major federal policies when using social media in schools—the Children's Online Privacy Protection Act (COPPA) of 1998 and the Children's Internet Protection Act (CIPA) of 2000.

The Federal Trade Commission administers COPPA to give parents control over what information websites can collect from children. In essence, COPPA protects students under the age of 13 from having their personal information collected without the consent of a parent or guardian. COPPA requires

social media sites targeting users under age 13 to bolster their privacy measures and restricts marketing to these users. The expanding use of social media among pre-teens and the growing number of users has caused controversy among those lawmakers who want COPPA updated and expanded to cover mobile Internet sites.

CIPA requires schools to provide Internet filtering to prevent student access to offensive content. The federal E-rate program, designed to make certain communications technology more affordable for eligible schools and libraries, requires these institutions to craft Acceptable Use Policies for their school-based network.

SCHOOL STAFF

Hurtful and disruptive speech existed in school districts long before social media changed the communication landscape. However, electronic communication presents its own unique challenges. In order to address the challenges, districts must begin with the body of case law concerning speech by public employees generally.

In *Garcetti v. Ceballos* (2006) the Supreme Court of the United States clearly articulated that school district employees have no First Amendment protection for statements made in the performance of their assigned job duties even when the statements relate to matters of general public importance. In the alternative, statements made by school district employees acting as private citizens fall under the governance of *Pickering v. Board of Education* (1968), which prescribes a balancing test allowing broad discretion in criticizing the district and its officials as long as the criticism does not undermine the close working relationships. *Pickering* does not, however, offer First Amendment protection for speech addressing purely personal concerns.

At the state level, several cases have applied the holdings in *Garcetti* and *Pickering*. A Connecticut federal court considered a First Amendment retaliation claim brought by a high school English teacher after the district refused to renew his contract. In *Spanierman v. Hughes* (2008) the holding in *Garcetti* was applied and found that the teacher did not enjoy First Amendment protection. The English teacher claimed he used MySpace to communicate with students about homework, foster a better relationship among the students, and discuss non-school related subjects. The evidence showed that much of the communication went beyond the teacher's assertion and it was deemed inappropriate to address subjects like whether a student was "getting any" and included a facetious threat about detention. When the school district learned about the teacher's actions it demanded that he shut down the account. He later opened a new account under an assumed name and continued the communication. The Connecticut court found that since the teacher conducted the communication outside of his official duties and the communication failed to deal with matters of general public concern, then First Amendment protection did not apply.

In 2009 the Ninth Circuit rejected a First Amendment defense by a female coach who used her personal blog to lambaste a male instructor hired to take over some of her job responsibilities and a union negotiator involved in the hiring process. She included in her blog post this statement about the union negotiator: "What I wouldn't give to draw a little Hitler Mustache on him." The court, using the analysis set in *Pickering*, stated the administration had a legitimate interest in avoiding speech that "disrupted co-worker relations, eroded a close working relationship."

A Pennsylvania federal court dismissed a First Amendment claim by a student teacher who posted on her MySpace a photograph showing her wearing a pirate hat and holding a plastic cup with the caption "Drunken Pirate." The court in *Snyder v. Millersville University* (2008) failed to find a violation of her First Amendment right because of the denial of the opportunity to obtain her teaching certificate after being released from her student teaching position. The court reasoned that her online postings did not implicate matters of public concern.

School districts should also be quick to adopt formal, written policies concerning teacher and student communication on social media sites outside of school. These policies should be augmented with training programs. Often what begins as innocent online banter between a student and a teacher may escalate into personal matters. The lightning speed, permanency, and impulse of online communication may blur the boundary line of the student–teacher relationship. The written policies must be tailored to meet the individual needs of the community. In many small districts, teachers may live in the community and play a vital role in a host of community activities. In more urban areas, student and teacher communication may be necessary only for school purposes.

STUDENTS

The 1969 Supreme Court decision in *Tinker v. Des Moines School District* generally governs with respect to student speech. The Court in *Tinker* held that the students did not lose their First Amendment rights to freedom of speech when they stepped onto school property. In order to justify the suppression of speech, the school officials must be able to prove that the conduct in question would "materially and substantially interfere" with the operation of the school. In 2013 the Third Circuit in *B. H. v. Easton Area School District* adopted a complex three-part test for assessing First Amendment protection for public school students concerning lewd or profane speech. The case involved a public school district's punishment of students for wearing wrist bands reading "I ♥ boobies! (Keep a Breast)" in school in order to advocate for breast cancer awareness. The Court reasoned:

(continued)

(1) Plainly lewd speech, which offends for the same reasons obscenity offends, may be categorically restricted regardless of whether it comments on political or social issues, (2) speech that does not rise to the level of plainly lewd but that a reasonable observer could interpret as lewd may be categorically restricted as long as it cannot plausibly be interpreted as commenting on political or social issues, and (3) speech that does not rise to the level of plainly lewd and that could plausibly be interpreted as commenting on political or social issues may not be categorically restricted. Because the bracelets here are not plainly lewd and because they comment on a social issue, they may not be categorically banned.

Source: United States Court of Appeals for the Third Circuit

The decision in *B. H.* will make it more difficult for school administrators to punish students for engaging in political or social speech that deals with health and/or sex and sexuality. This decision, coupled with early decisions concerning time, place, and manner restrictions, will have a far-reaching impact on school

districts as they develop their social media policies. School districts should also monitor the progress of districts like Glendale, California, which, in 2013, hired a firm to monitor and report on 14,000 middle and high school students' posts on Twitter, Facebook, and other social media for one year. The district reported success early on, claiming that information obtained helped the district save the life of a student who posted online about ending his life. Opponents, of course, claim that the social media monitoring invades the private life of the students.

As social media continues to grow in importance, school districts can expect more legal challenges to their attempts to regulate inappropriate online behavior. Districts would be well advised if they adopted clear, smart policies for online behavior. Furthermore, state legislatures across the country must be diligent in engaging in deliberative policy making that balances traditional First Amendment rights against the need to safeguard students, teachers, and staff in the online environment.

Source: Reprinted with permission from Dr. Basso is an attorney and professor of public relations and advertising at Rowan University.

PRINT AND ONLINE TACTICS

Websites

Websites remain a core online tool for nearly all school systems. Many districts now manage complex websites operating at a variety of levels and seeking to serve the specific needs of many different audience segments.

Research conducted during the communication planning phase of a website's development should take into account overall items or subject areas to be included among the site's design and content. Surveys should be conducted among users or potential users (including, for example, parents, teachers, taxpayers, prospective residents, area businesses, and so on) to assess each group's Web behaviors and specific information needs.

Audits or reviews of school-district websites serving nearby communities or similarly sized school populations might also provide ideas on key content areas to include—as well as suggestions on design and technological aspects that might be considered.

Generally, school district websites include the following at a minimum:

- A home or entry page, including a brief description or statement about the district, often accompanied by a brief welcoming statement and easy-to-follow links to all major content areas
- Names and contact information for key district and program administrative leaders, schools, principals, and school board members
- Current news or happenings around the district
- Web versions of recent district print and electronic publications, including key policies, student handbooks, and so on
- Information on academic programs, student achievement, notable accomplishments, accreditations, and so on

- Information on extracurricular and athletic programs
- School and district key dates and calendars
- Basic district information, such as operating hours for various facilities, key phone numbers, and so on
- Employment opportunities and human resources information
- Registration information and other data for new parents or residents new to the district
- Basic information, policies, and contacts for support services, such as transportation, nutrition, facilities, and so on
- Links to the websites of outside organizations or partners working closely with the district, such as a school foundation, parent organizations, alumni groups, business partners, social service agencies, and so on
- A site map offering a quick navigational guide to key content areas.

Often, website home or entry pages also offer quick access to audience-based Web content to help users guide themselves through a site. For example, the initial entry page might offer links to content with titles such as these:

- Information for Students
- Information for Parents
- Information for Residents
- Information for Staff and Teachers
- Information for News Media.

School district websites also often play host to special services, such as database-driven programs to aid visitors in searching and finding specific information. Web-based, online databases can help community members and school employees find information they're seeking without having to ask school officials to track it down for them. Such databases may offer school attendance information when searched by street address. Budget information may be selectable by topic or expenditure amounts. Some schools offer maps and driving directions to school facilities and events. Many school districts also offer online grade books and assignment portals to help both students and parents access up-to-date information on instruction plans, activities, and outcomes.

Social Media

A rapidly expanding area of online communication for school–community programs includes the many commercial services now available among so-called social media. Facebook (facebook.com) has become a common component of many school-communication programs. Twitter (twitter.com) also is playing a bigger role in many efforts (see Figure 12.5). Some schools also use special-focus social media, such as LinkedIn (linkedin.com) for professional networking and human-resource communication activities.

However, many other existing and emerging social media tools—such as Pinterest (pinterest.com), and Instagram (instagram.com)—also are being tested and used by school communicators to meet specific communication and audience needs.

Case studies show that school systems using social media tools are finding ways to use them to successfully meet various school–community relations needs. Facebook has become a popular way for school systems to build and communicate with online communities. The interactive nature of Facebook allows schools to engage in two-way communication and to respond directly to specific information needs of and questions posed by users. In reviewing the growing use of social media tools in school–community relations programs, NSPRA has reported:

- LinkedIn is a way school leaders can connect with thousands of educators, including other superintendents, public relations professionals, and principals, from around the country. Through LinkedIn groups, school leaders can participate in discussions and share links. NSPRA's LinkedIn group provides a way for members to get to know each other through their professional profiles. Users can also find members with expertise in areas they need.
- Twitter enables the exchange of quick, frequent postings of a limited number of characters between individuals and/or organizations. While schools use Twitter to promote events and highlight available material on their websites and other sources, Twitter also is used

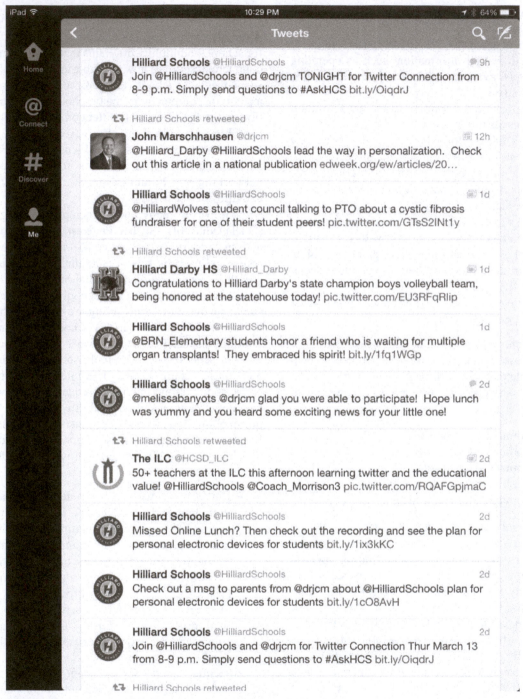

FIGURE 12.5 A Series of Twitter Messages from Hilliard City Schools in Ohio.
Schools are finding new ways to use social media tools such as Twitter to quickly announce news and share information with their communities.

Source: Reprinted with permission from Hilliard City Schools.

for major announcements and to release news. *Example:* One school district broke a news story about the school board's decision to appoint a new superintendent directly from its board meeting using Twitter.

- Superintendents, principals, and other school leaders can use social media such as Facebook and Twitter, as well as blogs, to connect with stakeholders.[5]

Mobile Apps

Mobile applications for smartphones and tablets are another option for increasing online communication by schools. These applications offer users direct access to specific district and program information (see Figure 12.6). They also are used to incorporate access to school online services by registered users, such as calendars, online grade books, and other student information.

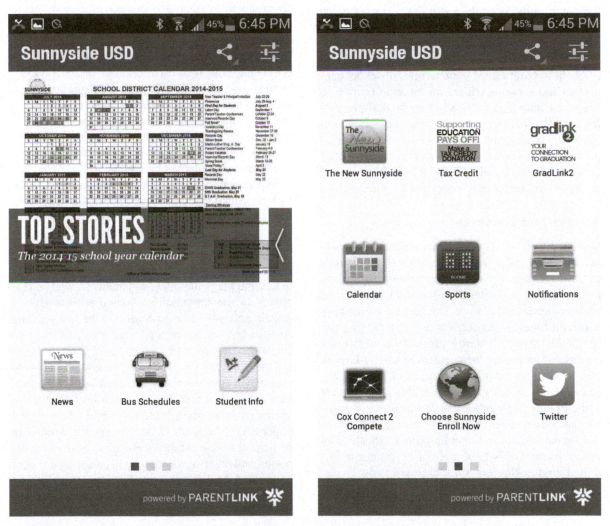

FIGURES 12.6A AND 12.6B Smartphone Application, or App, Used by the Sunnyside Unified School District. School districts with comprehensive communication and engagement programs, such as Sunnyside Unified School District in Tucson, Arizona, are using many new tools to allow communities to access school information online.

Source: Reprinted with permission from Sunnyside Unified School District.

E-newsletters

The use by both school districts and individual schools of electronic newsletters, or e-newsletters, has been growing rapidly in recent years. E-newsletter growth is being fueled both by the development of software that makes it easier for organizations to develop and distribute online publications and by the wide acceptance of e-mail as a communication medium by both educators and the general public.

Web-based publications offer school districts the opportunity to easily and quickly stay in touch with important communicators in schools and the district, including parents, community groups, business partner groups, and others. E-newsletters in particular can help to build linked communities of school supporters and serve as critical information sources to keep these individuals active and involved. E-newsletters can also provide options for immediate communications by sending messages and information in times of crises or disasters. In such situations, the ability to communicate rapidly is crucial to maintaining the credibility of the school district and its officials.

E-mails and Listservs

Despite the growing use of social media and e-newsletters, traditional e-mail lists and listservs continue to be used in many school communication plans to offer quick news items and announcements that must be disseminated to parents and the community at certain times. Many schools use such programs to communicate quickly during times of school closings because of inclement weather, for example. They're also used to communicate in times of crisis, when news events involving a school or even an event near a school may cause panic and confusion among parents and others. These e-mail devices also are used in less urgent situations, reminding parents to attend an upcoming back-to-school night or to participate in a school fund-raising event, for example.

Audio and Video

Many types of school events—from monthly school board meetings to class events, from school plays to football games to graduation ceremonies—are finding their way onto school websites in video format. These videos can be offered as "streaming video" or audio "podcasts" in which Web viewers watch the video on their personal computers as it is sent directly from the school's Web server or commercial online video hosts such as YouTube (youtube.com) and Vimeo (vimeo.com). The video or audio files also may be offered as downloads so users can keep the files for later use.

Print Newsletters

Regular newsletters covering school and district issues are produced by many school systems. Newsletters—distributed in print, e-mail, and online and produced at the district, school, and program levels—provide a regular means for reaching key audiences throughout the community with the latest information on school developments and plans. Newsletters for internal audiences, such as employees, also are produced to keep these audiences up to date with important school and district news and information. With the ever-increasing demand for transparency, accountability, and public engagement in education, regularly published newsletters can play an important role in helping school administrators fulfill their obligation to regularly communicate to the school district's internal and external audiences.

Annual Reports

Annual reports produce an overall report on achievements and plans important to parents as well as taxpayers in the community. Annual reports should contain not only accomplishments of the past year and comparisons and contrasts with previous years but also challenges and problems yet to be solved by schools and their communities. Including these topics will help to establish more relevancy and credibility for the publication. Some school districts also effectively use the annual report to provide information on the role and importance of schools in the community, which can be helpful to real estate agents, new residents, businesses, and others involved with helping people better understand the community and its offerings.

Calendars

Traditional print calendars provide important planning information on school and community events and promote parental and community involvement (see Figure 12.7). The calendar should be attractive

Their Future, Our Vision

Glenellen Elementary students practice their digital literacy skills while researching history's complex lessons for a class presentation.

February 2018

SUNDAY	MONDAY	TUESDAY	WEDNESDAY	THURSDAY	FRIDAY	SATURDAY
January S M T W T F S 1 2 3 4 5 6 7 8 9 10 11 12 13 14 15 16 17 18 19 20 21 22 23 24 25 26 27 28 29 30 31				1	2	3
4	5	6	7	8	9	10
11	12	13	14	15	16	17
18	19 Presidents Day No School	20 School Board Meets 6 p.m.	21 Progress Reports	22	23	24
25	26	27	28			March S M T W T F S 1 2 3 4 5 6 7 8 9 10 11 12 13 14 15 16 17 18 19 20 21 22 23 24 25 26 27 28 29 30 31

  At Jostens, our story is told by your stories. Our personalized class rings, school yearbooks, and more help you celebrate your moments. www.jostens.com **www.cmcss.net**

FIGURE 12.7 School Calendar.

Annual calendars are used by school districts to disseminate key dates, policies, and other information to the community.

Source: Reprinted with Permission from a calendar produced by the Clarksville Montgomery County, Tennessee, School System.

enough to grace a kitchen wall for the year. It should feature students throughout. Part of the space for each day might be filled with scheduled school activities; another part can be left blank for family messages. The calendar might also combine student and parent guide information to serve as a ready reference, offering information about the schools and key policies and procedures, such as absentee procedures, inclement weather announcements, online and social media addresses, contact information for key personnel, and so on. Most school districts supplement printed calendars with online calendars listing key dates for school operations and activities

Finance and Budget Publications

Finance and budget publications help to build an understanding of and support for school funding needs and focus on regular budget issues as well as special information needs tied to special bond or budget elections.

Handbooks and Program Guides

Handbooks and guides provide access to school policies and procedures and can play a role in helping schools to welcome students, parents, and others in the community as informed partners in the school enterprise.

Magazines and Special Reports

Magazines and other in-depth publications use both words and visuals to bring a special focus to specific programs and initiatives.

Marketing Publications

Marketing or branding publications help schools compete for enrollment and funding support in the increasingly competitive environments in which they operate today.

Special Purpose Publications

Special-purpose publications (including brochures, fliers, posters, information kits, pamphlets, and more) directly target the special information needs of distinct target audiences. *Examples:* A "Welcome to the School Board Meeting" publication can be used to identify board members and school leaders and provide biographical information for community members attending board meetings. It also can explain procedures to be used by those who wish to address the board and help to dispel any misunderstandings about how meetings are run. Many schools also provide a wrap-up of board of education meetings to employees and to the community. If it is distributed the morning after the board meeting and if the information is accurately and fairly presented, this publication can help improve employee morale and community understanding. Staff and teacher recruitment publications also can be used to help districts attract talent to a school system by outlining the benefits of serving in the school system and living in the community it serves, as well as outlining career opportunities and application procedures. Such publications also might be helpful in recruiting teachers in certain subject areas where shortages of qualified applicants may exist.

DESIGN AND CONTENT ISSUES

Good design and copywriting help users grasp the key messages that are being presented by creating a focus on the main points and ideas. Design and copy also work together to help users quickly make judgments about what content to read or skim, based on their personal information needs. Successful design and copy also combine to help users develop trust in any communication tactic—from websites and social media to printed brochures and newsletters—as a dependable information source.

In a sense, design and copy are partners in this process. Neither can perform these jobs alone. Good copy presented in a bad design or a good design with poorly written copy will hurt the effectiveness of any tactic. Design and copy also work together to signal a clear starting or entry point for viewers and readers so users naturally know where to begin scanning or reading. The way in which the design presents its copy and illustrations helps to create a logical "flow" for users.

Those trained in the design of print publications might be tempted to apply print design devices and standards to online or digital communication tactics. However, although many design devices, such as headlines, subheads, photographs, and colors, are employed in both print and online design, the rules for using such devices are not always the same for the two venues. The smaller "page" space offered by many computer screens usually means online designs must be shorter in length than their counterpart print designs might be. The quality of images, including type, can vary onscreen as well. The act of scrolling on some online communications such as websites—users essentially moving a page up and down and at times from side to side—presents a different set of placement needs than those faced by designers of a static print page.

Websites, however, do offer writers and designers the ability to better segment information and articles into appropriate, easy-to-read "bits" of information that can be linked to a main page or article. This gives readers the option to access the information only if they feel they need to, and to do it when they want to. Links can be created to open new pages on the screen, retrieving information stored on other pages.

Helping users navigate their way through these mazes of pages is an important design element, too. It's important that all types of communication tactics include components to make sure that readers and users never get the feeling that they've become lost in a jumble of information.

Content for Special Issues and Audiences

Sections of school communication tactics can be developed to offer content serving the special information needs of certain audiences. Such informational efforts can provide schools with cost-effective ways in which to reach audiences that may be too small to reach with more expensive print communications.

Many school districts, for example, now offer special online communication and print communication tactics to deliver information or key district publications in languages other than English.

Special online and print communication tactics might be devoted to delivering details on specific programs or campaigns, such as budget planning,

pending bond or finance elections, new school construction progress, public engagement activities, new curriculum, and so on.

Posting communications online also can be an efficient way for school districts to reach wide audiences in times of special need. In a major crisis that receives coverage from the news media, for example, individuals around the world may turn to school district social media and websites for more specific information and details. School administrators should therefore include procedures for quickly using online communication tools to offer statements with current information about a crisis situation, as well as steps being taken to ensure the safety of students and others. The district website and social media also can be used to relay basic facts about any incident and to offer links to more information related to other organizations or agencies that may be of assistance to those affected by the event.

Policies on Content

Although they vary among school districts, most school programs have guidelines or policies in place to govern the use of information to protect student safety and privacy. In general, such policies often prevent the use of any student names or images in communication tactics unless the district has a signed release from a parent or guardian for students, or from a staff member or other individual for adults. Personal information, such as addresses, telephone numbers, and personal e-mail addresses, are rarely if ever used.

Many districts do list employee e-mail addresses so parents and others can contact teachers and staff directly. Other districts, however, choose to list only general district or school e-mail addresses to protect staff from unwanted e-mail. As one way of restricting access, some schools choose to privately offer teacher e-mail addresses only to the parents of students enrolled in a teacher's class; others list a teacher e-mail address or private messaging forms behind the secure areas of online grade books on webpage that only registered parents can access. Whatever the individual policy, school district communication planners must strive to find a balance between protecting staff e-mail addresses and not appearing to be overly restrictive in allowing access to teachers and others by those with genuine needs and concerns.

Photographs and video pose another challenge to communication planners. Some policies suggest not using any images in which individual students can be identified. Some districts prevent the use of images showing elementary-school students but are less restrictive in the use of photographs showing older children. Generally, however, most policies call for a signed release to be on file for any image displaying individuals.

One option used by some school systems to avoid identification issues is to use images of students in school settings purchased from suppliers of stock photography. Still, some school communicators argue that incorporating local photos and video plays an important role in communicating accurately about local schools and personalizing their online communication efforts.

Aligning Tactics with Communication Objectives

It's important for communication planners to assess what specific communication tactics will most efficiently and effectively move audience understanding and action toward specific desired outcomes.

Strategically, school-communication planners must assess the best publication options for effectively engaging with audiences and establishing credibility for the school system and its messages. Tactically, the cost in time and finances also must be assessed to ensure the efficient use of communication and publication investments.

A communication plan drives efforts toward meeting specific, stated objectives. Communication tactics, therefore, need to be linked to these specific objectives. To help, the first step in developing a publication should be a written statement of purpose. Such a statement determines how the tactic will be developed, what audiences it is designed for, and how its effectiveness will be evaluated.

Generally, online and print communication tactics are used to deliver information to identified audiences when that information cannot efficiently be delivered through face-to-face methods (meetings, workshops, or personal conversations, for example).

Consider communication tactics being used with internal audiences such as employees: Employees want to know what is going on where they work. Knowing key information and the rationale behind decisions and initiatives helps employees better understand their role in the educational enterprise and feel more valued by it and engaged with it. An internal publication, therefore, would deliver messages that work toward meeting objectives related to enhancing employee engagement and bolstering employee productivity and morale.

Tactics designed to serve external audiences, such as specific community groups or taxpayers in general, might work toward meeting communication objectives that seek to keep citizens informed of the policies, practices, and needs of the school system and create a sense of partnership in advancing the cause of public education. Before community members can be expected to support schools and school programs, they must understand the underlying issues and priorities their schools are confronting. Various communication tactics can be used to deliver and reinforce messages and information, building the kind of understanding that is needed to lead to increased participation in the school system and support for it. Online and print communications created for the community can build a better appreciation for how school tax dollars are being spent, report on educational achievements, correct misconceptions, address misinformation, and recognize contributions by individuals and groups to the schools as well contributions by schools to the community. They also can explain problems and possible solutions and can pave the way for important changes in education practice, as well as help inform government officials, sometimes leading to gaining their support.

Understanding the Audience

One of the first considerations when assessing potential print and online tactics: Know the audience. School planners should avoid the temptation to prepare content and publications that will appeal to other school administrators. Readership of any publication is optional, so the publication and its content must be prepared in ways that will attract readers by appealing to and meeting their information needs.

In other words, publications should determine and address what readers want to know and not simply address what school officials want to tell them.

A good place to start in aiming at a specific audience is to determine, from a content standpoint, what the audience already knows about the schools. A common error is to assume that readers know almost as much as the school officials. This assumption, especially when coupled with a writing style that features educational jargon, frustrates and discourages readers. Educators frequently use terminology or abbreviations that only they understand, forgetting that most people are not responsive to educational jargon.

- *Use familiar language.* In addition to using educational terminology, educators can be guilty of using words and terms that may not be readily or comfortably understood by typical readers. Before preparing a publication aimed at the public, school officials should determine the reading level of that public and write at that level. An easy way to determine the reading level is to apply a readability formula. One such formula commonly used is the Gunning–Mueller Fog Index, which considers average sentence length and the number of words with three or more syllables. For ease of reading, sentence length should seldom be more than 17 to 20 words, and the two-syllable word is clearly preferred to the five-syllable word. One mark of any successful communication is the ability to convey messages at a level that a specific audience will understand and be comfortable reading.

- *Determine audience interest.* Before starting a new print or online tactic, an attempt should be made to determine the interests of those who will be expected to read or view it. For instance, a teacher-recruitment brochure should apply research findings in this area and include such information as the proximity of graduate schools, cost-of-living data, and the specific opportunities and challenges that make the district what it is. A newsletter targeting audiences in the local community should meet the interests of that community. Particular interests should be determined before the newsletter is started

and rechecked periodically. Again, this guarantees that the publication will present issues and information in ways that will capture and hold audience interest and improve readership.

Choosing Content

Online and print communication tactics that are properly designed, produced and well written will gain the attention of potential readers and viewers, but the content must appeal to reader interest as well. Too often school publications can focus on awards and recognition received by the schools while not focusing enough on issues and exploring solutions confronting schools and the community.

If content is constantly about the achievements of the district with no mention of problems, people will dismiss the communication and see it as an unbalanced "puff piece" or propaganda promoting schools and school officials. Such a view could cause taxpayers to question the wisdom of using tax money to support school communications.

To appeal to audience interest, content should focus on issues and individuals as well as buildings and programs. Students learning, teachers teaching, and people involved in the education process—in schools and in the community—can bring balance and meaning to content.

For example, instead of content focusing only on the mechanics or cost of a new program, consider profiling how a staff member or student is benefiting from the new program. Of course, money is important and people want to know how their tax dollars are being used. Use content to help readers better understand and appreciate those investments by going beyond figures and expressing the implications in terms of students, staff, and the community.

Content always must be balanced. To be successful, readers must see school communication tactics as credible information sources, and presenting information that is timely, complete, and balanced is important to establishing credibility for the message.

Writing Copy and Content

Perhaps no single decision is more important in the development of successful online and print tactics than deciding who should write and edit them.

This decision may be particularly challenging for districts that lack a community relations or public relations staff with writers trained in journalistic writing styles. Enthusiastic teachers, administrators, and volunteers may be excellent sources for content ideas and information, but they may not be best suited to write sound and readable copy appropriate for use in school communications. In districts without professional communications staff, hiring a part-time or freelance writer to prepare final copy often is a wise investment to ensure final copy will appeal to reader interest and enhance readership and use.

With convergence of media, it's important to keep in mind that the same or similar copy will be deployed over multiple publishing formats: print publications, online publications, and social media. Thus, preparing copy that can appeal to and accommodate readers and users in multiple venues is essential. Poorly written copy can result in failure of multiple readership opportunities. Well-written copy will ensure high levels of readership and the efficient delivery and reinforcement of key school messages.

In general, copy for school publications should follow the basic rules and styles essential to writing good news copy (see Chapter 11). As Basso, Hines, and FitzGerald suggest in *PR Writer's Toolbox: Blueprints for Success*, writing effective copy "involves more than a grasp of English grammar."[6] When describing successful publication copy, they note that readers assess copy by asking, "What's in it for me?" Characteristics of successful copy cover a wide range of issues:

- Content matters. If you include a variety of topics and sections, you'll appeal to a wider group of readers. Try using sections like newspapers do: opinion, letters to the editor, features, and so on. Break up the layout with brief tips or reviews.
- Answer questions. Use the "five W" questions (who, what, when, where, why) to establish a news tone.
- Make it readable. Use short, concise, clear language. Use a style guide for consistency.
- Use interesting headlines. Use action verbs to evoke curiosity. Use subheads to break up the text.

- Proofread. Read for typos but also for consistency of tone and voice. Don't leave proofreading to spelling and grammar check tools.[7]

Setting Standards for Communication

As technology has changed and the convergence of media has placed the ability to write, produce, and disseminate school communications into the hands of many school employees, school systems have found it helpful to produce style and use guides to advise employees on style for publications as well as other communication activities.

Communication Guidelines published by the Prince William County Public Schools (PWCS) in Manassas, Virginia (see Figure 12.8), for example, provides school employees guidance with sections covering "The Basics (What Every PWCS Communicator Should Know)"; "Critical Communication"; "Media Relations"; "Visual Identity"; "Web Site Guidelines"; "Style Guide"; and "Special Events."

Options for Printed Tactics

New printing and digital publishing technologies continue to evolve and offer new options and decisions for producing printed school publications.

Increasingly, publication planners think of their products as school "documents" instead of school "publications"—reflecting the varied ways in which these items may be stored and distributed. Today's school publication—or document—planners should make sure first to review options in three main areas:

- *Digital publishing* can be used to produce publications that can be accessed by readers through e-mail, through downloaded files, directly online, or on DVDs and CD-ROMs.
- *On-demand printing*, using high-speed laser or other printers, can be used to quickly print limited quantities of documents when needed. This technology has also improved the cost-effectiveness of producing color publications as well as printed materials for very small audiences—two options previously too costly for many school publication programs.

Introduction

Effective communication—both internal and external—is vital to the success of the School Division. It enables us to positively influence attitudes and behaviors that lead to a wide range of desired outcomes, from enhanced student safety and performance, to securing support for school programs, improving staff recruitment and retention, and achieving higher overall customer satisfaction.

Appropriate communication allows you to avoid mistrust and misunderstandings while building support. It is well worth the time, effort, and investment needed to reach out frequently and fully to every target audience.

This handbook offers valuable guidelines for developing communications and supporting materials that reach your audience at the right time and in the right ways to effectively deliver your message and reinforce the positive image of PWCS.

That image, and what it stands for, constitutes our brand-image in the same way that specific brand elements shape your perception of Disney or Coca-Cola. We must live up to our responsibility to communicate openly and honestly with all stakeholders while remaining every bit as protective of our brand as the international consumer companies are of theirs.

Please familiarize yourself with each of the brief sections of this handbook. Then, use them, as needed, along with supporting materials in the Communications section of the PWCS Intranet. Together, they will help you to fully and effectively share information with our many audiences, while staying true to our brand and the ongoing story of PWCS.

FIGURE 12.8   Sample Guidelines.

School districts should publish guidelines for employees involved with communication activities to support the effectiveness of communication activities districtwide and ensure that all communications adhere to the district's standards. Such guidance also supports the district's overall image and brand.

Source: Reprinted with permission from guidelines produced by the Prince William County Public Schools in Manassas, Va. Copyright © by Prince William County Public Schools.

- *Traditional printing*, using traditional press and finishing machinery (either in the school print shop or by hiring an outside print shop), is still used to produce large quantities of newsletters, brochures, handbooks, and other publications.

New printing options and the convergence of new and old media means school publication planners now must consider a variety of potential distribution channels. In some cases, certain publications (e-newsletters, for example) may only be disseminated online. Traditional newsletters (carrying the same content) may still be produced and mailed to some audiences or made available in school lobbies or other community gathering places.

School calendars, too, might be printed and disseminated at the beginning of the school year. An online calendar, hosted on a school's or district's website, can be maintained and updated throughout the year to supplement the print calendar.

Social media (Twitter and Facebook, for example), video streaming (through the district's website or commercial services such as YouTube), and audio podcasts also must be planned in conjunction with publication efforts to make sure messages delivered through each of these channels are properly coordinated to reinforce key points and build the synergistic effectiveness that results when all communication tactics work together.

PRIORITIES FOR EFFICIENCY

The best guarantee for using the most efficient method for creating communication tactics is to have someone on the staff who knows the communication and publishing technologies involved and understands how traditional and digital communication techniques can effectively work together.

Maximize Technology Investments

Many large school systems spend significant amounts of money on sophisticated technologies, many of which can serve both administrative and communication needs. Other smaller school systems manage to create effective communication tactics using little more than a single personal computer, commercially available social media website hosting services, some publishing software, and a laser printer.

Many communication technologies are constantly undergoing rapid changes, dramatically reducing some costs but making it challenging for schools to stay current and to know how to best invest in the new, emerging options. School systems' technology leaders and communication leaders both need to constantly evaluate emerging technologies, with a focus on how new technologies can be used efficiently and effectively to interact with school district audiences.

As school budgets tighten, communication planners will face increasing demands to document that the school system's use of and investments in communication technology are appropriate.

Edit for Efficiency

Schools can boost efficiency by preparing content copy with an eye toward using it across various platforms. Brochure copy, for example, might be written to also be useful on a website. Schools also can trim printing costs simply by tightening copy to reduce a publication's size and make it communicate efficiently. Shorter publications might also work better when placed online.

Avoid Rush Jobs

Communication planners will always face urgent requests of one type or another, but planning that anticipates communication needs is another way to save resources. Urgent requests for copy or production can increase the need for short-term temporary help, and rush jobs by printers and other vendors will generally cost more.

Design for Efficiency

Elaborate designs for online content as well as printed materials (such as special folds or binding requirements) may also entail costs that outweigh benefits. Be sure that the design in some way enhances the message and is not merely design for the sake of design.

Odd page sizes can also cause cost issues; odd or oversized paper sizes may increase purchase prices as well as mailing or other distribution costs.

Odd page sizes also can create problems when documents are placed online; users may not be able to print them or view them easily.

Money might also be saved by avoiding the placement of unnecessary dates on publications, thereby avoiding the obsolescence common to dated publications. Regular publications, such as community newsletters, of course must be dated. Other publications, such as a teacher-recruitment brochure, might not. If only some material in publications must be updated over time, then inserts might be a cost-efficient way to keep publications up to date without completely reprinting them.

Maximize Design Investments

Along with copy written for use in multiple products, art, illustrations, and photographs also should be created in ways by which they can serve multiple purposes. In addition to reducing costs, multiple use of these materials can also work toward reinforcing the school district's messages and image.

For example, a school district's logo should be used in consistent ways in all online content, publications, and stationery. An effective logo can communicate the spirit of the school district and serve to identify the publication as coming from the schools (see Figure 12.9).

FIGURE 12.9 Trademarked Logo.

This trademarked logo developed by Prince William County Public Schools in Manassas, Virginia, supports the district's overall image and is important to building consistency in communications districtwide.

Source: Reprinted with Permission from Trademark of Prince William County Public Schools.

It's important, therefore, to design a logo that can be used across a variety of publications both in print and online. Often, a logo conceived for an annual report cover looks fine when displayed full size. If it is also to be reduced to letterhead or business-card size, the type may become illegible or the lines on the artwork may be too close together.

Once chosen, design items such as a logo may be used to support branding for the school system by creating and reinforcing a consistent image throughout all school publications over a period of time.

Protect Design Assets

Schools also should consider legally protecting their designed material, such as logos or mascot images. Such protection for these assets can prevent the unauthorized use of these materials and protect the value they have created for the school system.

School communications staff should work with the school attorney on the need to trademark items (words, phrases, designs, symbols, names, and so on) and the need, if any, to copyright other items (original works of authorship). Basic information on trademarks is available through the United States Patent and Trademark Office (www.uspto.gov). Basic information on copyright issues can be found at the U.S. Copyright Office (www.copyright.gov).

PRIORITIES FOR EFFECTIVENESS

Good design, like well-written copy, should support the readability of any communication tactic and thus increase its use and readership. Content will fail to be effective when its copy and design do not work together to attract readers.

It's important to consider why readers click on one link and not another, or why they might pick up and read one publication and toss another in the wastebasket. Reasons differ from one to another, but one of the most common initial reasons is the design of the content—something about the design grabs the user's attention and communicates a promise of useful information. To not consider the impact of design on readership is in essence a failure to make the most out of the investments in school publishing. After all, the cost of creating and distributing a well-designed document is generally the same as creating and distributing a poorly designed one. The real value is created when the publication is read and used.

One way to increase the chance of a publication being read is to make it attractive to the reader's eye in the first quick glance. Remember that all school publications compete with other publications for the reader's time and attention. People are not required to read any school publication. The decision to read is entirely voluntary. Since most school publications have not been specifically requested by the users for whom they are prepared, there is an even greater need to prepare them in ways that will quickly attract attention and communicate benefits to potential readers.

Another good technique is to collect materials that are appealing. By analyzing them, most editors can come up with ideas that have worked for other people and apply them to their own work. One good source for communication samples is those that have been recognized by the National School Public Relations Association (nspra.org) in its annual Publications and Electronic Media Awards competition. The names of winning school systems are posted on the organization's website, and many of the winning materials can be found on the winning school districts' websites. The competition recognizes excellence in a number of categories, including Annual Reports, Blogs, Branding/Image Packages, Calendars, E-Newsletters, Finance Publications, Handbooks, Internet Websites, Magazines, Marketing Materials, Podcasts/Audio, Print Newsletters, Social Media, Special Purpose Publications, and Videocasting/Videostreaming.

The following ideas offer some general suggestions for preparing communication tactics that will be visually appealing and enhance attractiveness to readers:

Prepare Every Publication for Three Kinds of Readers

If school district officials conducted a study of the way readers look at school materials, they would probably be able to group them into three categories: the 30-second readers, who casually glance at the material; those who spend two or three minutes looking at the material; and those who read most or all of the content presented. The educator who prepares materials with specific elements to serve all three kinds of readers gets the most out of every communication dollar invested.

Accommodating Those Who Skim

The 30-second reader, the one who flips or scrolls through pages not really looking for anything, should have messages especially designed to catch the eye as it quickly skims across the page. One of the most eye-catching methods also serves as a copy-breaking device: the bold one-sentence or one-phrase statement that "teases" the reader to read the article from which it is taken. Called a *blurb*, this device also provides an opportunity for school officials to communicate a few key points to just about everyone who picks up a publication or glances at online content. Subheads also can work to break up copy and accommodate skimming readers by offering small bits of facts and information. Inasmuch as the segment of the audience that spends less than a minute on a school publication is relatively large in most districts, it makes sense to include items such as blurbs and subheads.

Accommodating Those Who Scan

For the audience segment that spends about three minutes scanning, for example, a school newsletter, headlines are vital to both inform and work to pull these scanners deeper into the content. So, too, are photo captions that provide basic information. These should be written with the assumption that the accompanying story will not be read—so they provide basic information. For these readers, too, it is important that the first sentence of every story contain vital elements of the news that the editor deems readers should have. This first sentence should also entice readers to continue reading.

Accommodating Those Who Read

The final segment of the readership audience is the group that will read most of the stories most of the time. However, in most school districts, this segment is the smallest of the three groups. Few people should be counted on to read every word in every publication. Still, certain design elements can work to support those who are committed to careful reading. Type size and column widths should be comfortable to the reader's eye while short sentences and brief paragraphs keep the content from looking too dense or requiring significant effort to read. Links in online content can be placed in ways that effectively guide the user to and through additional supporting information.

Use Space Effectively

School officials are justifiably concerned about getting as much as possible for every tax dollar spent, but the desire to get value from every dollar spent should not be misapplied by thinking that every page of every publication should be crammed with as much information as possible. Remember with publications that efficient use of investments is better measured by high rates of readership and use. The publication that has no or very little open, or white, space is read less than a publication that uses white space effectively. Open space helps to highlight important content, provides contrast, and offers a resting point for a reader's eyes.

In printed materials, the "dollar-bill test" is used to determine if a publication is violating one of the basic rules of layout and design. *How it works:* Place a dollar bill anywhere on a page of the publication at any angle. It should always be touching something other than text. This means that the dollar bill should touch a subhead, headline, photo, other type of graphic, or blurb at all times. If this is not the case, the page should be redesigned to avoid the long blocks of type that will undoubtedly cause some readers to reject the page because it looks like too much to read. In addition to the use of blurbs and subheads, editors can apply other copy-breaking devices, such as an occasional box around an article, or tint, or boldface type over tint blocks for easy legibility. Bullets or numbers can also be used to break up a long list. A head-and-shoulders shot of a speaker or some other appropriate graphic or image can be inserted in a story to break up a solid stream of text.

Maintain Page Balance

Theories abound regarding the best approach to maintaining balance on a page of a publication, especially newsletters. The trained editor understands this vital aspect of layout and design, and the beginner should realize primarily that each page must seem pleasing to the audience. It must not be top- or bottom-heavy. This means that not too much visual weight should be located on any one section of the page. For example, the logo and nameplate and two photos should not all be at the top of the page with all copy on the bottom two-thirds.

Consider Standard Designs

Communication materials issued periodically may lend themselves to a standard design that can be used time after time with minor variations. Design templates can save time and money, while reinforcing the school district's branding, in both online and print products. Design templates from the school district's website or social media accounts should be used by schools when developing their own websites or social media offerings. A community newsletter, internal newsletter, or school newsletter should use the same basic format each time. This, of course, saves time, but it also helps to build familiarity among readers. Such a standard design immediately identifies the source of the material and guarantees that just about any editor with basic layout knowledge can implement the design concept effectively. Basic design templates adopted by various schools throughout the system offer a consistency in look and bolster the effectiveness of design systemwide.

Know What to Emphasize

A common error is to give all stories or content equal emphasis. Perhaps for internal morale or ego purposes, school officials sometimes demand that each story be of approximately the same length. However, such a decision will not support readership. People expect communication materials to point them to the more important information and not to do so can confuse readers. Emphasizing some stories helps readers get a feel for what the school district considers important. The editor must decide, after consultation with the superintendent, what the most important news is for emphasis. Then the design and layout must be determined to communicate the appropriate importance of the presented information.

Work Wisely with Color

The judicious use of color can enhance communication materials and attract additional readers. The misuse of color in an ostentatious and gaudy fashion can turn off readers and add expense to printed publications. When competing with top commercial magazines for attention, school publications can easily spend a lot of money. Perhaps it is better to offer quality one-color publications than to sprinkle color throughout. If in doubt, consult an expert.

When choosing colors, have a specific rationale or basis for a color choice and don't rely only on personal preference. Color should support the material's identified purpose. *Example:* Consider the psychology of colors. A controversial topic might best be handled with a cooling green as a second color. A brochure explaining the school budget probably should not be printed in red ink.

People are accustomed to reading body type (the text) in black. Research indicates that black on yellow or white background supports legibility. A trained editor or designer who knows colors might effectively deviate from the standard combinations, but making such shifts without a specific rationale may communicate an amateurish appearance rather than an innovative one and drive down readability in the process. Designers should also be careful to avoid colors or color combinations in print and online materials that can create accessibility issues for readers dealing with color blindness. See some suggestions https://www.usability.gov/get-involved/blog/2010/02/color-blindness.html

When preparing printed materials, design colors and paper also must work together. Printers can be helpful when it comes to selecting design colors and appropriate paper. Schools usually should avoid the impression of spending too much money for expensive papers, so heavy and highly finished papers should be avoided in most cases. Choose paper with a dull or glossy finish, but avoid the high-gloss sheets. Contrast between ink color and paper is important, so do not use a color in design that is close to the color of the paper. An off-white or cream-color paper can give a rich look and still provide the desired contrast.

The opacity and weight of the paper are important, too. Will the reader see the ink showing through from the other side of the paper? If a publication is to be mailed, will the difference in weight between 60-pound and 70-pound paper necessitate adding postage for each mailing? Will the publication be read once and recycled, or will it be kept for future reference? The answers to these questions should help dictate the kind of paper used.

Don't Overprint Photos and Illustrations

Every once in a while, a designer or editor might decide it would be clever or creative to print copy over an illustration, photograph, or other artwork. Usually this backfires—although it may seem like a creative use of technology, overprinting usually makes the copy more difficult to read and thus will not support readership. Black or dark type over an illustration will usually be readable only if the illustration is screened very lightly in the background (5 to 15 percent, depending on the color) and not printed at 100 percent. So this is a graphic device that should be used sparingly and only with a specific intention.

Select a Body Typeface That Supports Readability

Communication technology and design programs offer a multitude of fonts, and inexperienced online and print publishers may be tempted to use a variety of them in a single publication. It is best, however, to stick to one basic font for body copy to avoid a disorganized or circuslike appearance that can result from mixing a number of fonts for text. Each typeface has its own characteristics. Some are traditional; others are more modern. Some are excellent for headlines but less effective as body type. One consideration should outweigh all others when picking a body type: Is it easy, or comfortable, to read?

Although designers producing online publications increasingly use sans serif fonts for body copy (typefaces such as Helvetica, with no finish strokes or feet on the letters), traditionally certain serif fonts (typefaces such as Times Roman, which do have strokes or feet on the letters) have been considered more legible for body copy in print publications. Most readers obviously will not consciously affix readability characteristics to fonts, but the school publication editor and designer should consider them when choosing fonts. Some serif typefaces generally accepted as being highly legible are Times (New) Roman, Baskerville, Bodoni, and Caslon. Sans serif typefaces frequently considered highly legible include Helvetica, Avant Garde, and Optima.

Avoid Overusing Script, Italic, and Bold Type

Highly stylized or special fonts might be useful for creating a specific emphasis or making a design statement, but they generally should not be overused for body copy, subheads, and headlines because of the problems their overuse will create with a document's readability.

Script type, which looks like handwriting, is difficult to read. It sometimes is chosen by school publication editors, who might argue that it seems more personalized. This may be true, but typeface decisions should be based on legibility, and script is one of the least legible types available.

Overuse of font styles can create readability problems as well, even when used with fonts traditionally considered more readable. Italic type, for example, is also among the less legible typestyles. Editors sometimes will put large blocks of copy in italics, thinking that will create an emphasis for the message that has been italicized. However, italics should be used sparingly, occasionally to emphasize a point or for a blurb. It should not be used for large blocks of copy. Boldface type also should be used sparingly, for emphasis or for headlines.

Use Upper- and Lowercase

The most legible type, in terms of capital and small letters, is what audience members are accustomed to reading. This means the kind of type in which this paragraph is set. Capital letters are used for the first letter of each sentence and for proper nouns, and lowercase letters are used for the remainder of the words. Research indicates that this is the most legible combination. It is also one that readers find comfortable. Occasionally educators use all capital letters for a publication, perhaps thinking this will create an emphasis for or draw attention to a section of content. Yet the use of all capital letters often slows the reader and uses more space than standard upper- and lowercase type.

Headlines (heads) also are more readable in upper- and lowercase letters. One popular style for heads is the first word and any proper nouns capitalized, with the other words lowercase. This is especially useful when the head is written in subject–verb format.

Use Sensible Column Widths

Font selection must work with column width to create an inviting look and comfortable reading environment for publication users. Many printed school newsletters and other school publications make a negative first impression on potential readers by using only one column of type across most of an 8 1/2-by-11-inch page. This is too wide a column for the eye to follow without a considerable amount of work. In addition, most people won't work that hard to get information about schools. The problem is easily solved. If the paper size is 8 1/2-by-11 inches, use two columns, or one column no wider than 5 inches. Use the remainder of the page width for miniheadlines, or use the white space functionally.

An easy rule to consider is to limit column width to twice the point size of the font in picas (6 picas = 1 inch). For example, for 11-point type, the width should be no more than 22 picas, or 3 2/3 inches. Designers producing publications that also will be distributed online should consider columns and page design based on the screen sizes. As more and more audiences rely on tablets and smartphones—with smaller screens—to access publications, designs intended for the standard-size printed page may not be usable. Print designs can sometimes convert easily to desktop and laptop computer screens, whereas alternative designs may be needed for users accessing materials with mobile devices.

Consider Type Size and Readability

Just as some people might insist on using no white space and cramming information on every available square inch of paper to appear to be getting the most from money spent on publications, some also believe that using a small type size boosts efficiency by fitting more words on a page. However, small font sizes are more difficult to read and will decrease readership—which actually will decrease the efficiency of investment in a publication. Generally, typography experts suggest that 10-point or 11-point type be used for body copy. (There are 72 points to the inch.) Leading, or line spacing, is the space between the lines of type. Allow at least 2 points of leading between lines. The greater the width of the column, the more leading needed.

Consider Horizontal and Vertical Layouts

A large number of school newsletters use the vertical layout concept. They employ a three-column format for text on the page, with each column running the full length of the page. A horizontal layout might be considered; it allows more typographic versatility without overpowering readers with overly long columns of type. (Samples of vertical and horizontal layouts are offered in Figures 12.10 and 12.11.)

USING PHOTOS TO ENHANCE COMMUNICATION

A photograph should be used to communicate a message, not merely to break up copy. The availability of high-quality digital cameras on smartphones and other devices has made it easier than ever for school communicators to get usable photos for their materials. Ease of availability has also increased the potential for bad or ineffective photos to find their way into school materials. Too many editors are guilty of using sterile, posed, unnatural photos of poor composition.

Photos can serve two important purposes: They provide a bit of information to the skimming or scanning readers. They also may help attract those skimming material to articles, thus improving readership of content. Also, more attitude changes occur with a story and an accompanying picture than with the story alone.

Basic head-and-shoulders shots, though not imaginative, can add to the overall layout and can identify people with whom citizens will be dealing. Action shots are best, and because children are what schools are all about, school publications should contain shots of students in learning situations. Too many publications use photos such as the superintendent sitting behind a desk, or the front of a new building (with no students), or a four-member teacher committee posing for the camera.

LINES
OF COMMUNICATION

From the Dean

Dear CCCA colleagues and friends: It's hard to believe that the year is coming to a close. I think having Thanksgiving happen so late this year has played havoc with all of our internal clocks. As is expected, there is quite a hustle and bustle right now in the halls of Bozorth, Hawthorn, and Westby, as classes wind down, and the end-of-semester grading moves into full swing.

With everything that has gone on in the last few months, we could have probably filled thirty pages of *Lines*, but we've confined ourselves to what you see here, and even that includes items as diverse as bronze casting, charity marathons, textbooks, media festivals, student organization successes, faculty accomplishments, and more.

As I was writing this column today, I spoke with the father of a junior student in the College. Often, parents call when they are upset about something. But this time, the father was calling to ask a question about career planning—and to tell me what a great experience his son was having at Rowan in our College and how happy they both were. It was wonderful to hear, and I know largely due to the efforts of members of this College. We are pretty great!

I hope you enjoy reading about what has been happening recently in the College, and how we continue to evolve, along with the University. I wish you all the best for a happy conclusion to 2013 and a wonderful new year.

Dr. Lorin Basden Arnold, Dean

Susan Bowman

Pouring Fire
Jan Conradi

Using foundry facilities in Westby Hall, the Department of Art is proving that bronze ingots melt at 2300 degrees. So do stereotypes of artists as solitary creatures quietly creating in isolation. Faculty, staff, and students in Westby have been working with Bradley Tucker, Technical Studio Assistant for North Carolina–based artist Mel Chin. Tucker came to Rowan to prepare pieces of a bronze sculpture, *The Shape of a Lie*, which will be featured in Chin's 2014 retrospective exhibition.

Above: Lifting the crucible of melted bronze from the furnace.

Lost-wax casting is an intricate multi-step process. Ideas are first brought to life in clay. Wax molds are made from the clay and then invested (enclosed) in plaster that is dried and kiln-baked until the wax melts away. The plaster casts are cooled enough to be moved; then they are buried in a sand pit so the void where the wax was can be filled with molten bronze. Sculpture instructor **Charles Tucker** (no relation to Bradley) said, "There are limited materials suitable for creating objects for public spaces and outdoor installations, so this tradition is still relevant. It is valuable for art students to understand the

FIGURE 12.10 Sample Vertical Design.

Regular newsletters published by educational organizations can help to keep audiences informed about events and progress. The newsletter uses a three-column vertical design.

Source: Reprinted with Permission from Lines of Communication, Newsletter published by the College of Communication and Creative Arts at Rowan University. Copyright © by Rowan University.

PRincipal Communicator

Concise, practical public relations help for your school

PR Tips for PRincipals

Creating easy-to-read copy relies on choosing the right words and putting them to work in an appropriate combination of short to medium-length sentences. In other words, it doesn't need to be complicated!

✓ **Smaller words in short sentences communicate better.** This doesn't mean that you should shy away from larger words or long sentences. But, word choice and sentence length must be monitored.

✓ **Keep sentences to 14 words or fewer.** Readership falls dramatically as the length of sentences increases above this number.

✓ **Editing is the key.** First-draft copy usually has all of the facts, but tends to be heavy with jargon and complex structure.

✓ **Provide a feedback loop.** Don't forget to provide an appropriate contact who can assist parents and answer questions. It might not always be the principal - sometimes it's a counselor, PTA president or department chair.

From NSPRA resource files.

December 2017

The building blocks of a successful school family

Johnita Readus is the kind of person who would rather greet you with a hug than a handshake. She welcomes you to Sumner Elementary with a warm smile and an invitation to her office. But a visit to this principal's office is far from intimidating.

The space is bright and cheerful, with family photos and student notes and art prominently displayed. She's known for having an open door policy and for being a good listener.

Readus was named the 2017 Elementary Principal of the Year for Guilford County Schools. She's so beloved at Sumner Elementary that students and staff planned a school-wide parade in her honor following the district's announcement.

When Readus first joined Sumner four years ago, she was one of 18 new people at the school. She wanted to boost staff morale and improve reading proficiency among African American males.

"It was imperative that I become the school cheerleader," Readus said.

Last year, reading proficiency among African American males increased 50 percent, which closed the achievement gap at her school. Discipline referrals have decreased 73 percent, and the suspension rate has dropped by 85 percent. Sumner is now a State and National School of Character.

She's created a school environment that invites parent and community involvement. For Readus, it comes down to her love for the children and the role she plays in educating them.

A Special Kind of Leadership

"Being a principal, you see and experience children soaring from year to year. As a lifelong learner I appreciate watching a teacher create magic in the classroom. That's one of the best parts of being a principal," Readus said. "Teachers give of themselves daily to educate our students. I am proud to be an educator."

Sumner is located in a rural area of eastern Guilford County, N.C., tucked away in a spot that could feel isolated. But the sense of community that students, parents and staff feel for their school is evident from the first step into the building.

The parade honoring Readus stretched from the main building to the edge of campus. Staff members said the students chanted, "We are proud of you," for so long they thought that surely the children would tire of repeating it. But they never did.

Continued on page 2

PRincipal Communicator is funded by the
National School Public Relations Association and its subscribers.
© 2017 National School Public Relations Association

FIGURE 12.11 Sample Horizontal Design.

This newsletter, published by the National School Public Relations Association in Rockville, Maryland, uses a double-column width in its right-hand column to produce a horizontal design.

Source: Reprinted with Permission from Principal communicator: Connect with the Influential 'Word-of-Mouth' Network among Your Parents and Community. Copyright © by National School Public Relations Association.

The following are some suggestions regarding photos for school publications:

- Use large photos whenever possible; small ones are noticed less and forgotten more quickly.
- Take a close-up shot if possible. If not, crop extraneous background material to focus on the action.
- Have the action in the picture point toward the story; if the action is going the wrong way and if no type appears in the photo, flip the image. (*Example:* If a photo runs on the right-hand side of the page, make sure that any subject in the photo is looking to his or her left—toward the copy that accompanies the photo.)

- Place a related photo near its story, preferably above it. Research says stories get higher readership with a related photo nearby as opposed to an unrelated photo placed nearby.
- Always include a caption, preferably below the photo. Write captions with care. Remember that those skimming through publications often are more likely to focus on photo captions, so they should convey important bits of information.
- Try to create photos that communicate something unique about your school. A teacher-recruitment brochure showing a teacher and a child sitting at a table tells nothing about the distinctiveness of your schools or programs.

SERVING ALL AUDIENCES

More and more school systems are developing publications and other communication activities to reach non-English-speaking audiences (see Figure 12.12).

In some school systems, all district publications and major documents are produced in different languages both in print and online. In other cases, only certain documents or materials are produced in additional languages or special translation services are used on an on-demand basis.

The publication editor should carefully research the language needs of various audience segments served by the school district and assess the best ways in which publications can address these needs. Editors also must consider the design issues that may result when producing translated documents—as copy

lengths may change and accompanying art and photographs may or may not be apt for use in all editions.

NSPRA offers publications and information for schools on how to create publications and activities to effectively communicate with diverse audiences.

DISTRIBUTING PRINTED PUBLICATIONS

A printed school publication, no matter how well written and designed, does little good unless it is properly distributed. Making the right publication available to the right audience requires planning and implementation.

The first group to receive any publication—even those aimed at the general public or at teachers to be recruited—should be the internal audience. Distribution should be made internally first so that employees will be able to discuss topics in the publication intelligently with friends and neighbors.

The obvious approach to distributing the publications is not always the best one. For example, many schools send newsletters home with students and assume that parents are receiving the publications. Studies have shown that after about fifth grade, very few students give the publications to their parents.

Newsletters from a school principal directed exclusively at parents serve a purpose. The information ordinarily concerns students, parents, and the school staff; therefore, it is imperative that it be received by parents. Some principals announce in a newsletter mailed home early in the school year that newsletters will be sent home with the students on certain dates. The

FIGURE 12.12 Communication Translations.

School districts often offer translated communications to serve diverse audiences. These online materials from the Allen (TX) ISD offer numerous language options.

Source: Reprinted with Permission from Meeting announcements, produced by the Wichita, Kansas, Public Schools. Copyright © by Wichita Public Schools.

distribution of newsletters and other material might also be announced on the school website and social media.

A traditionally effective vehicle for delivering printed publications is, of course, the mail. In an era when the public demands better communication from the school, the expense of a newsletter mailed to parents might be justified if the home and school are to work together effectively.

If mailed, districtwide newsletters should be made available to all residents. School officials might consider sending community newsletters only to parents of students and include nonparents only before a school finance election. School publications, however, should be connecting with all taxpayers on a regular basis to build the kind of effective credibility and long-term understanding essential to school–community relations success. Newsletters and other publications generally can be mailed to all households cost-effectively by taking advantage of the school's nonprofit status to use the lowest possible nonprofit postal rates. Local postal authorities will work with school publication planners to help them decide on the most efficient ways to use various postal options and to make sure publication designs will meet standards for the most cost-effective mailing. Information can be found online as well at usps.gov.

Schools use different ways to decide on a mailing list for their publications. Some hire mailing firms to send the publications to all people on their list in the geographic area served by the school district. Others prepare their own list, working from taxpayer rosters, voter registration lists, and public-utility customer lists. No approach is foolproof; each is time-consuming to keep up to date. The time and effort expended by school employees must be weighed against the cost of employing an outside firm to handle the mailing.

Another technique for community-wide distribution is to explore inserting your publication into a local newspaper or other publication. Depending on how well read the paper is, your newsletter may get wide distribution. It will also be read at the same time the recipient chooses to sit down and read the paper.

In addition to mailing the community newsletter, school officials should place copies in stores and other places commonly frequented by area residents. Placing copies in offices and shops where people must wait for services, such as hair salons and medical and dental offices, is a practical technique. Some publications might be made available through the cooperation of area groups. Real estate agents, for instance, often are pleased to have a general publication about the schools to distribute to potential or new residents. Members of the local chamber of commerce and other business or service groups could easily distribute the same kind of publication through their businesses. Copies should also be placed in all local libraries.

EVALUATING ONLINE COMMUNICATIONS

Schools should use a set of performance metrics to assess online communication effectiveness overall, along with evaluations of specific content. Virginia's Fairfax County Public Schools, for example, evaluated usefulness of content, clarity of design, frequency of updates, ease of navigation, and adherence to Fairfax County Public Schools' Web policies in a competition among websites throughout the district. Their evaluations also considered content items, such as links to other district information and Web services.

NSPRA evaluates and recognizes excellence among school district websites and social media in its annual Publications and Electronic Media Awards Program. Some school districts recognized for excellence include the following:

Websites

Allen Independent School District, Allen, TX

https://www.allenisd.org/

Cooperstown Central School District, Cooperstown, NY

http://www.cooperstowncs.org/

Dalton Public Schools, Dalton, GA

http://www.daltonpublicschools.com/

Fairfax County Public Schools, Fairfax, VA

https://www.fcps.edu/

Frederick County Public Schools, Winchester, VA

http://www.frederick.k12.va.us/

Granite School District, Salt Lake City, UT

http://gsdfuture.org/

Minnetonka Public Schools, Minnetonka, MN

http://www.minnetonkaschools.org/

Northwest ISD, Fort Worth, TX

http://www.nisdtx.org/

Prince William County Public Schools, Manassas, VA

http://www.pwcs.edu/

Questar III BOCES, Castleton, NY

http://www.troycsd.org/

Vancouver Public Schools, Vancouver, WA

http://welearn.vansd.org/

York County School Division, Yorktown, VA

http://yorkcountyschools.org/BacktoSchool

Social Media

Alexandria City Public Schools, Alexandria, VA

Baltimore County Public Schools, Towson, MD

Kennewick School District, Kennewick, WA

Highline Public Schools, Burien, WA

Reading School District, Reading, PA

St. Tammany Parish Public Schools, Covington, LA

E-Newsletters

Community Unit School District 308, Oswego, IL: Chapters Newsletter

Houston ISD, Houston, TX, HISD Bond: Building Excellence eNewsletter

Northwest ISD, Fort Worth, TX: Northwest News

Pine-Richland School District, Gibsonia, PA: Pine-Richland School District E-Newsletter

Plano ISD, Plano, TX: Plano ISD—eNews

EVALUATING PRINT COMMUNICATIONS

The school administrator who is responsible for publications should evaluate them regularly to determine how well they are being read and used. The evaluation can be important to assessing the performance of investments in publications in a school–community relations program. The evaluation also can provide insights on what's working and what's not working to further improve the performance of future publications.

Various ways exist to determine whether or not people are reading publications; among them are questionnaires, interviews, focus panels, online tracking and usage statistics, and ongoing online feedback. The questionnaire can be included as a readership study in the publication itself. To encourage readers to return the questionnaire, make it an easy tear-off form that takes no more than a few minutes to complete. Even with this approach, a very small percentage of readers will return the questionnaire, and it is not appropriate to conclude that the nonresponding public shares the views of those who responded. The telephone survey and the in-person interview can provide data on which to base publication decisions. These latter methods can be more representative than the tear-off survey. Instant polls in online publications also can provide quick user feedback.

An editor can learn much from inviting a number of people receiving the publication to discuss it in a small group, such as a focus group. Four groups of five or six people can help the editor see strengths and weaknesses as perceived by these groups.

Another way to improve publications is to have them evaluated by publication experts who have no vested interests to protect. Often school publications reflect the thinking and biases of a couple of school officials who control the content and the design. Outsiders who know the publication business can suggest improvements. If the intent of the school publications is to inform as many people as possible, investing in a small consultant fee to improve the publication will, in the long run, reduce the cost per article read. Another way to have school publications evaluated is to enlist the service of an association or company that offers a critique service. A source for evaluation information is the National School Public Relations Association (www.nspra.org).

Other Sources of Communication Support

A number of companies offer communication technology and research support for schools. Vendors also offer products and programs for supporting or developing integrated notification systems (telephone, text messages, e-mail, social media, and so on), social media programs, surveys and other online feedback tools, and message and content development. Some vendors offering services and information in these areas for school communicators include the following:

Blackboard

http://www.blackboard.com/k12

e-School News

https://www.eschoolnews.com/

K-12 Insight

http://www.k12insight.com/

Peachjar

https://www.peachjar.com/

SCoPE

http://www.scopeschoolsurveys.com/

Thoughtexchange

https://thoughtexchange.com/

West School Messenger

http://www.schoolmessenger.com/about/

Several associations and organizations, such as the following, offer online communication resources and publications that can be helpful to school-communication efforts:

Consortium for School Networking (CoSN), cosn.org

eSchool News, eschoolnews.com

International Association of Business Communicators, iabc.com

International Society for Technology in Education, iste.org

National School Public Relations Association, nspra.org

Pew Internet & American Life Project, pewinternet.org

Public Relations Society of America, prsa.org

Society for Technical Communication, stc.org

One Expert's Point of View: Creating Successful Online and Print Communications

John Moscatelli, APR, Fellow PRSA, is an experienced communications executive with more than 50 years of senior-level service and an extensive background in crisis communications, media relations, product publicity and promotion, community relations, internal communications, spokesperson training, and speech and script writing. He served 10 years as Senior Vice President and Chief Operating Officer for Anne Klein Communication Group and previously served as Senior Vice President and Associate General Manager of Earle Palmer Brown Public Relations. Moscatelli has been an adjunct faculty member at Rowan University for 25 years, teaching advanced PR writing, PR planning, and crisis communications.

Why is it essential to keep up- to -date on the rapid developments in new communication technologies?

Three reasons. The first has to do with communication effectiveness. As technologies change, audiences change, too. Suddenly audiences have new options for how they get news and information, and history has shown us people are not shy about changing their reading and viewing habits. A generation ago many school communication programs focused on a newsletter, a local newspaper, and maybe a couple of local TV and radio stations to get the word out. These media are still important, but a whole host of online news and social media options have been added to this arsenal. Communication planners need constant research to understand how people prefer to get their information and then they need to develop tactics to accommodate these preferences.

The second reason has to do with communication efficiency. No communication program has an unlimited budget— – especially true for schools. With new options in the mix, communication planners have new ways in which they can become more efficient in disseminating news and information, using multiple tactics to reinforce key messages.

The third reason is the profound effect new technologies have on communication during emergencies and crises. Given that virtually every student, faculty member, and staff have access to external communication— – smart phones with cameras, iPads, laptops— – means administrators must be prepared to respond in real time to maintain credibility with external audiences.

How important is it to consider audiences when assessing tactics?

Considering audience needs is critical. We must first understand who the audience is, what audience members already know about a topic, and how they prefer to receive information. The answers to these questions will help communication planners determine what tactics may work best— – perhaps some combination of a newsletter, a brochure, web content, social media messages, and more. But the answers also will help planners decide what communications to share via those tactics— – that is, what messages will work best. Let's say you want to change a bus schedule. Perhaps it's no big deal and people will have no problem with the new schedule. All you may need to communicate is the details— -- the new times in the schedule. But if the change could create controversy you may have to offer arguments as to why the change is needed when you announce the new times. In this case your messages may need to both inform and influence.

How can communication leaders best manage programs in such a changing environment?

The challenging news is that the communication toolbox is getting bigger and communication programming is growing more and more complex. In a sense, this is good news. Communicators have more and more ways to engage with audiences, to share information and insights, and to build understanding and support. But this proliferation of delivery channels underscores the need for ongoing research to drive communication planning. Research and planning efforts set benchmarks for ongoing evaluation of communication efforts. In any program, some tactics work and others don't. Among tactics that work, some will work better than others. Responsible communicators know they need to be accountable for producing communication outputs that produce meaningful outcomes. Communication research and evaluation supports such accountability.[8] ■

Questions

1. List the impacts the expansion of online communication options has had on school–community relations programs and outline the challenges that media convergence has posed to school communicators.

2. Describe the different types of readers that communications aimed at the community will attract and how content might be developed to accommodate each of these reader types.

3. How can online communications work effectively with traditional communication methods to reinforce key messages and information?

4. Outline the ways to formally and informally collect insights and data on how audiences are reading and using your school communications.

5. Review at least one school website recognized by the National School Public Relations Association. List the key components of the site that facilitate communication between the school district and its communities.

Readings

Anton, Kelly Cordes and John Cruise, *Adobe InDesign CC Classroom in a Book.* San Jose, CA: Adobe Press, 2017.

Bagin, Rich, *Making Parent Communication Effective and Easy.* Rockville, MD: National School Public Relations Association, 2010.

Basso, Joseph, Randy Hines, and Suzanne FitzGerald, *PR Writer's Toolbox: Blueprints for Success.* Dubuque, IA: Kendall Hunt, 2013.

Brooks, Brian S., and James L. Pinson, *The Art of Editing in the Age of Convergence,* 11th ed. New York, NY: Routledge, 2017.

Dixon, Brian, *Social Media for School Leaders: A Comprehensive Guide to Getting the Most Out of Facebook, Twitter, and Other Essential Web Tools.* Hoboken, NJ: Jossey-Bass/Wiley, 2012.

Essex, Nathan L., *School Law and the Public Schools: A Practical Guide for Educational Leaders,* 6th ed. Boston, MA: Pearson, 2015.

Moore, Edward H., *Mastering E-Newsletters: Helping You Get the Most from Your E-Communication Efforts.* Rockville, MD: National School Public Relations Association, 2005.

Moore, Edward H., "Web Pages and Electronic Communication," *School Public Relations,* 2nd ed. Rockville, MD: National School Public Relations Association, 2007.

National School Public Relations Association, *Principals in the Public: Engaging Community Support,* 2nd ed. Rockville, MD: Author, 2007.

Porterfield, Kitty, and Meg Carnes, *Why Social Media Matters: School Communication in the Digital Age.* Bloomington, IN: Solution Tree Press, 2012.

Poulin, Richard, *The Language of Graphic Design: An Illustrated Handbook for Understanding Fundamental Design Principles.* Minneapolis, MN: Rockport Publishers, 2012.

Strizver, Ilene, *Type Rules: The Designer's Guide to Professional Typography*, 4th ed. Indianapolis, IN: Wiley, 2013.

Williams, Robin, *The Non-Designer's Design Book,* 4th ed. San Francisco, CA: Peachpit Press, 2014.

Videos

Kearney (NE) Public Schools in 107 Seconds
https://youtu.be/nfUcJzogIX0

National School Boards Association: Stand Up for Public Schools
https://youtu.be/aRbIbXeIje0

National School Boards Association: Why We Do What We Do
https://youtu.be/fdZb2e-9vUs

Anoka-Hennepin (MN) Schools: Buddy Bench Program
https://youtu.be/w9ctWgTHYbM

Arlington (VA) Public Schools: How Arlington Public Schools makes the decision to delay or cancel school
https://youtu.be/8D2-nVfX-wA

NSPRA: Video Award Winners
https://youtu.be/Ir0qFUnFtr0

South Washington County (MN) Schools: Anti Bullying PSA
https://youtu.be/uODRKMy43eU

Elmhurst CUSD 205 (IL): Welcome to Elmhurst District 205
https://youtu.be/AaVM7M-tOfg

Spring Lake Park Schools (MN): Welcome to Westwood Intermediate School
https://youtu.be/77M2_E0qNl0

Oregon School Boards Association (OSBA), The Promise of Oregon
https://youtu.be/PeYg55Z0rMk

Fayetteville Public Schools (AR): Annual Report to Our Patrons
https://youtu.be/m8XA9XTmpPk

Williamson County Schools (TN): Distracted Driving Public Service Announcement
https://youtu.be/ZQbZMwOVM9s

Riverside (CA) Unified School District: State of the District
https://youtu.be/zUNL8Na0J6s

Putnam/Northern Westchester (NY) BOCES: Taking Communications into Our Districts
https://youtu.be/fBN18WXdEJU

WGAL-TV: Social Media and Schools: Does It Work?
https://youtu.be/9tLYGvE7w4g

Hardin County (KY) Schools: Social Media
https://youtu.be/t7zwZdWnoRk

Endnotes

1. Internet Access in U.S. Public Schools and Classrooms: 1994–2002 (Washington, DC: National Center of Education Statistics, 2003). Retrieved March 13, 2014, at http://nces.ed.gov/pubs2004/2004011.pdf.

2. *WSPRA Communication Practices Survey Results* (Wisconsin School Public Relations Association, 2013). Retrieved March 13, 2014, at http://www.nspra.org/files/docs/WSPRA%202013%20Communication%20Survey%20Report%20-%20Final.pdf.

3. "Trends in News Consumption: 1991–2012" (The Pew Research Center for the People and the Press, 2012). Retrieved March 13, 2014, at http://www.people-press.org/files/legacy-pdf/2012%20News%20Consumption%20Report.pdf.

4. Reprinted with Permission from correspondence in February 2010 and January 2014 with Tim Carroll, APR, Director of Public In-formation, Allen Independent School District, Allen, TX.

5. "Are You on Facebook? Do You 'Twitter'? How about a LinkedIn Account?" *Network*, National School Public Relations Association (www.nspra.org) (Rockville, MD: NSPRA, June 2009). Reprinted with permission.

6. Reprinted by permission from Joseph Basso, Randy Hines and Suzanne FitzGerald, PR Writer's Toolbox: Blueprints for Success. Copyright © 2014 Joseph Basso.

7. Ibid.

8. Taken from personal correspondence with John Moscatelli, Department of Public Relations and Advertising, College of Communication and Creative Arts, Rowan (NJ) University on November 24, 2017.

13

Conducting Special Issue Campaigns

This chapter reviews issues …

■ For central administrators: The need for and benefits of specific research and planning for communication to address special needs facing the school district and its communities.

■ For building and program administrators: The ways in which communication supporting special-issue campaigns can help to engage communities in the process and result in decisions benefiting schools and their communities.

■ For teachers, counselors, and staff: How working relationships and open communication among individuals in the schools and the community are essential when planning to address the needs presented by special issues.

After completing this chapter you should be able to …

■ Distinguish the roles of communication campaigns to support specific school–community relations initiatives.

■ Identify how new ideas and change can be influenced through appropriate communication programming.

■ Define the role of marketing communication in supporting schools and their relationships with key audiences.

■ Outline the significance of comprehensive communication planning to support successful campaign outcomes.

Building working relationships between the school and community depends on organized communication designed to produce results over time. School communication should not be a sporadic enterprise to be turned on and off as specific issues and situations come and go. Communication among constituencies occurs all the time, whether or not communication activities have been organized by the institution.

Too often educational leaders may see the development of community support as something that can be created through a short-term campaign designed to produce votes or some other specific expression of approval. However, building working relationships with informed, connected, and engaged parents and taxpayers demands carefully planned, comprehensive, on-going, two-way communication efforts.

Special communication initiatives focused on specific issues often need to be developed, of course. These initiatives must be built within a comprehensive, overall communication program that has developed the kind of trust and relationships that can only be fostered successfully over time.

Organized communication efforts that begin only when a school system is facing a crisis or some other sudden predicament can create understandable skepticism and criticism from parents and taxpayers. Sporadic communication can appear to be self-serving, and it can create the appearance of a school system that reaches out only when it needs something from the community. Sporadic and self-serving communication does not portray the school system as committed to building long-term, mutually beneficial relationships with the community it serves.

Gaining community acceptance for a new initiative or support for a potentially controversial decision—whether it is a new bond issue, redistricting plan, or curriculum change—requires an organized plan for continuing communication that nurtures meaningful engagement. *Reason:* Communication alone is not enough to ensure success. It has long been established that community support and acceptance are contingent on the development of trust and understanding—and trust and understanding are best developed over a period of time.

This chapter provides information about the ways in which a community typically accepts new ideas and decisions. It offers examples and guidelines for how communication efforts can best support innovation and change.

HOW A COMMUNITY ACCEPTS A NEW IDEA

Although every community possesses its individuality, research findings have long held that, in most cases, a new idea is accepted or rejected in basically the same fashion from community to community. Although researchers differ on the number of specific stages in the acceptance or rejection of a new idea, many agree that five stages exist. These are often referred to as the *awareness stage*, the *information stage*, the *evaluation stage*, the *trial stage*, and the *decision* (adoption or rejection) *stage*. Beal has conducted numerous studies in the areas of diffusion of information, communication of innovations, and acceptance of new ideas.[1] He points out that face-to-face communication is the key at the all-important evaluation stage.

It is generally recognized that one-way communications play an important role in the early stages of the adoption process. Newspapers, radio, television, newsletters, and other such communications efforts are vital during the awareness and information stages. Thus, school officials should capitalize on the availability of these media outlets in presenting information to the public. They should also prepare newsletters explaining how the particular innovation or finance issue will benefit the people to be affected by it. Yet these efforts, though important, must not be considered the end of the endeavor to gain acceptance of the idea.

As noted by Beal and others, it is the evaluation stage that presents the case for face-to-face communication.[2] When people are considering the merits of an innovation or a bond issue, they want the opportunity to ask questions or to determine how others feel about the issue. Rogers notes that adoption occurs in stages over time and depends on social networks or communication linkages between those in the community as information and opinions are shared and assessed.[3]

Hall and Hord note that this concept applies to organizations of all types, including schools, businesses, and communities, and that the number of people engaged in making and receiving communication are vital components to rates of adoption.[4]

The school administrator, appreciative of how communication best facilitates understanding and change, must prepare a campaign that incorporates a large number of opportunities for people to learn about an idea in face-to-face, two-way communication settings conducive to developing understanding and acceptance over time. This means utilizing ideas such as small-group meetings, presentations (with questions and answers) to community organizations, and advisory groups.

In *A Guidebook for Opinion Leader/Key Communicator Programs*,[5] the National School Public

Relations Association (NSPRA) seeks to align school communication initiatives with the long-held beliefs concerning the acceptance or rejection of a new idea by the community.

During an initial awareness stage, those in the community might become aware of a new school issue or idea generally through traditional news media or through media produced by the school district itself. As NSPRA notes, "However it happens a seed is planted."

Once awareness of an idea or issue has been created, interest is then generated as audiences seek to educate themselves and "satisfy the natural curiosity a new concept can bring." Media continue to play a role as audiences seek information, but people also turn to others in the community, including school officials, for information and opinions.

With interest generated, those in the community next react—positively or negatively—to each other's information and opinions in an evaluation phase. Opinion leaders throughout the community become crucial during this phase. Endorsement by opinion leaders "will go a long way toward influencing a new positive outlook toward schools."

Audiences next enter a trial phase. "Here we begin to adopt the idea and give it a 'trial run.'" Opinion leaders remain critical during the trial phase. "If enough of the people we trust agree with our new opinion we move on to the next phase."

"The adoption phase takes us on a journey to find reinforcement for our newly adopted view on public education." As an idea is adopted its acceptance by audiences is reinforced as people seek out others and information that reinforces their newly held point of view.

"So then the key to getting people to adopt a new idea or change their attitude about anything … relies on getting the concept in front of them and then having people they trust support it."[6]

THE CHANGE AGENT

To effect change in a community or to establish a climate conducive to community approval of an innovation, the schools must identify and use a *change agent*. This person must be given the responsibility for conducting the campaign. When schools neglect

to charge any one person with the leadership role in a campaign, floundering inaction, conflicts, and confusion result. Often it is assumed that the superintendent, by nature of the position, should be the change agent. This is not always the case. At times the change agent should be someone other than the superintendent, especially if the superintendent has recently suffered a loss in credibility because of some controversial issue. Public confidence in the person selected as the change agent is a necessary ingredient for any successful campaign.

It is vital that schools find spokespersons who are believable. This is especially important when the schools want the public to vote for a levy or accept an innovation. The selection of the right change agents as people work toward accepting or rejecting a new idea is critical for schools, according to NSPRA.

The following are among NSPRA's recommendations:

- Listen to different people on different subjects. "It is rare to find someone as the 'go-to' source on more than one topic."
- Rely on both formal and informal structures. "Some are no brainers: the mayor, the city council members, ministers, chamber of commerce director." Others may be individuals outside of the formal power structure but people whom others in the community seek out for information and commentary. "They may be the three B's: barbers, beauticians and bartenders." *Another example:* "How about the custodian at your school? He may be a deacon of a large church in the area. To people in the community he is the school system."[7]

HOW PEOPLE ACCEPT CHANGE

Not everyone accepts an innovation at the same time. People bring different backgrounds and attitudes to the introduction of an innovation. Therefore, they react differently to the efforts of a change agent or school system when information is presented. Educators who want to acquire community support for an idea should be cognizant of the different categories that people fall into as far as their rate of adoption is concerned. A person's innovativeness is generally recognized as the criterion by which one is categorized as an early or late adopter of a new idea. Many researchers use five categories to identify rates of adoption. The categories are innovators, early adopters, early majority, late majority, and laggards.

Innovators

Usually the first 2.5 percent of the people who adopt an innovation are eager to try new ideas. They communicate with other innovators who may live great distances from them. They usually possess more technical knowledge than later adopters and are often employed in high-risk occupations. Innovators frequently have a better financial base than others, allowing them to fail with an innovation and still remain comfortable. The innovator seeks new ventures; he or she is willing to take risks.

The school wishing to gain early support for a new idea should tap the innovators. Usually, almost immediate acceptance of the innovation will be forthcoming simply because it is a change from what has been done before. Educators must remember, though, that innovators do not provide the kind of communication leadership that will encourage large numbers of people to accept the idea.

Early Adopters

Usually considered the next 13.5 percent to adopt a new idea, the early adopters differ from the innovators in that they communicate more with other people in the community. In fact, this group could be considered the most important one to reach because it is looked to by others for opinions regarding a proposed change or finance issue. Early adopters are frequently active in community service groups or are part of the informal power structure of the community. Such people may not appear on the formal power-structure charts, but they are sought by many others in the community when decisions are to be made regarding the schools. Such people might be found among barbers, beauticians, bartenders, retired school employees—actually, in just about any occupation. These are the people who talk to many other people, the people others seek out for advice regarding new ideas. They are respected for their judgment and will seldom accept an innovation as rapidly as the 2.5 percent innovator group.

School officials who identify the early adopters in the community are one step ahead in their campaign. By knowing who these people are, the educator can be sure to provide them with sufficient information early enough to ensure that they will disseminate it to others in the community. Early adopters, because of their position of importance among peers, should be placed on a list of key communicators and should be given appreciable information about the schools during the year. This builds confidence in school officials—a confidence that will serve educators well when they present facts to the group before community acceptance is needed for a new proposal.

Early Majority

Representing about the next 34 percent to adopt a new idea, this group provides the necessary numbers for a majority. People in this group are usually joiners—people who belong to various organizations but seldom hold office. This group follows the lead of the early adopters but is reluctant to accept a new idea too quickly. Because this group often belongs to many of the same organizations as the early adopters, it is possible to communicate with them through these groups. Again, this points out the wisdom of working with the early adopters in the community, for they will in most cases communicate with the early majority.

Late Majority and Laggards

Making up 34 percent of the population, the late majority is skeptical and usually adopts an innovation only after social pressures are applied. Laggards, representing 16 percent of the population, are the last to adopt an innovation. Dependent on the past, they are not receptive to change or those who advocate change.

INTRODUCING AN INNOVATION

School officials planning to introduce innovations to the educational program should consider the communications and public relations phase of the undertaking with great care. The best innovation, if improperly introduced and implemented, can backfire. If people feel that school officials are not divulging all pertinent facts, they will develop a distrust that can breed all sorts of problems for administrators. Many parents and taxpayers are well educated and highly connected to many information sources. Therefore, they do bring knowledge and opinions to the education process. Despite this, a lack of knowledge can be a perilous thing when the necessary facts and accurate information about new programs are not properly presented. People fear the unknown, and if they realize they aren't being told enough about a new program, they will eventually criticize it, causing school officials to react defensively.

As with all communications efforts, the first question to be asked before introducing the innovation is "Who is the audience?" The first audience to be considered is the internal one—teachers and other employees. Community residents expect those who work in the school to know what's going on there. In addition, morale suffers if employees are not among the first to know about innovations. The next key audience to be considered must be parents of students involved in the change. These are the people who will challenge the change if they do not understand it. Some administrators precipitate problems by assuming that the time it takes to communicate could be better used for immediately pressing tasks. This kind of error leads to problems of time-consuming magnitude—problems that could have been easily avoided with solid communication attempts.

SCHOOLS AND MARKETING COMMUNICATION CAMPAIGNS

Changes in enrollment and funding policies have ushered in a variety of changes that schools must carefully articulate to their communities. To do this, more and more school systems increasingly are turning to marketing communication campaigns to supplement traditional public relations activities. School-choice initiatives, such as open-enrollment programs and charter schools, mean that more school systems must compete for new students and their families for their school systems. Securing funding from traditional sources is becoming more difficult—resulting in more schools turning to school foundations and other fund-raising activities to help fill funding gaps. Whether attracting new students or seeking new funding, marketing communications and marketing

campaigns are finding larger roles in overall school communication efforts.

School marketing expert Dr. William J. Banach[8] notes that marketing first requires that school districts ask the people in their communities to define the education that they need and want, and that they then provide this type of education—to the best of their abilities and resources—to the students in the community.

Banach uses a five-step marketing process based on a "commonsense model." According to Banach, "The model actually can be used for a variety of purposes, from passing a bond to school improvement to strategic planning and more. That's why I often call it 'the process for anything.' In reality, it is nothing more than common sense systematized." Here are Banach's five steps:

Step One: Analyzing the Environment

Analysis is the first—and most important—step in the process. It begins with a study of the environment in which a school functions, and includes projections of what—in that environment—leaders want their school to become.

A school's environment has two dimensions: internal and external. The internal environment relates to perceptions of a school and the people in it. All the people working in a school need to be aware that they are continually sending signals. Taken together, these signals—how people perform, how they dress, what they say, how they behave, the language they use, and the initiatives they champion—all send powerful messages to students, parents, and others. This is why schools that commit to marketing attend to things like continuous staff development, frequent communication with parents, greeting visitors warmly, responding promptly to calls, and so forth. These little things matter because they all contribute to shaping a school's image or identity.

The external environment is related to "the big story" unfolding every day. It has to do with change and its implications. For example, long-term shifts in demographics have potential for affecting student enrollment. That's why schools must monitor population trends, housing starts, and the number of building permits issued in their community.

Schools should consider beginning the development of a school marketing program by thinking about the internal and external environments—that is, by conducting a simple analysis. *Ask:* Do you really know what people need and want from your schools?

Step Two: Developing a Strategy

The development of a strategy is the second step in the marketing process. However, before a school can develop a strategy, school marketers must ask some questions about their schools and the way they operate.

How: Start by asking what you want to market, to whom, and why. Those questions lead to a strategic marketing concept called targeting, and the key question associated with targeting is *Who cares?*

When you identify what you want to market, you should ask *Who cares?* The answer to this question will indicate the odds of your communication being "on target."

Step Three: Writing a Marketing Plan

The planning step in the marketing process translates analysis and strategy considerations into a written plan that details what is going to be done, how it is going to be done, by whom it will be done, and by when it will be done.

It's easy for schools to shortchange themselves during the planning step. Instead of identifying goals, objectives, and related activities, they simply make a list of three or four "marketing things" they should do, and then they start work on their "to do" list.

It is important that schools have broad goals and related objectives to operationalize these goals. It also is important to identify specific activities, detailing who is going to do what by when. The planning step underlines a commitment to doing something, serves as a communication vehicle for those who will execute the plan, and establishes the baseline for evaluation of the marketing initiative.

Written plans are essential, according to Banach. Here are some typical questions he suggests addressing when developing a written school marketing plan:

1. Who are the primary target audiences for (your school)?

2. What do these target audiences think about when they think about (your school)?

3. What do you want these target audiences to think about when they think about (your school)?

4. What target audience perceptions do you have to change, and what behaviors do you have to influence?

5. What is the key message(s) you should deliver to these target audiences?

6. Who will deliver this message(s), and by when?

Note that items 4, 5, and 6 can be translated into goals, objectives, and activities, respectively.

Step Four: Execute the Plan

In step four of the marketing process, the tactics outlined in the marketing plan are implemented—that is, school marketers do what they said they were going to do in the plan.

Although this step usually takes more time than all the others combined, implementation is easy because everything—goals, objectives, activities, who is going to do what by when—is spelled out in the plan.

Step Five: Evaluate the Results

The marketing process comes full circle in step five. This is where school marketers determine what is working and what needs adjustment.

The marketing plan is the logical foundation for this evaluation. First, review the activities to see if they were completed on the timeline that was identified. Second, use this "activities assessment" to determine if the objectives were addressed and the goals were attained. Third, determine if any goal can be deleted from the plan, whether it should be continued, or whether it should be modified.

Although school leaders should be thinking about how things are going on a regular basis, it makes sense to formally assess the marketing plan twice each year. If a plan is on a 12-month schedule, consider evaluating it in November and again in May. This will position marketers to "recycle" the marketing process for the start of the next school year. That means they can update their analysis, check their strategy, and modify their plan during June, July, and August.

A CAMPAIGN EXAMPLE: THE UNITING OF TWO HISTORY-RICH SCHOOLS

Colorado Springs (CO) School District 11 responded to a common issue—the need to close a school—with a not-so-common approach: A comprehensive communication campaign seeking to engage community members and build unity among neighborhoods in the interest of student and school success.

Their effort earned a Gold Medallion Award from the National School Public Relations Association. Their description of the campaign's research and planning, delivery, and assessment follows.

Synopsis:

Colorado Springs School District 11 (D11) is home to approximately 28,000 students in 55 schools. Enrollment has been slowly declining over the past decade, and because of this, D11 has restructured, repurposed, and closed several schools. The north and east areas of our school district are experiencing the most growth, with newer housing and newer schools, while the southern portions of our region continue to age.

In 2009, D11 closed nine schools as part of an efficiency restructuring initiative. Three of the schools on the potential list of closures were John Adams, Helen Hunt, and Ivywild Elementary Schools. Helen Hunt Elementary was located between John Adams and Ivywild Elementary schools, so, due to the proximity of the schools, the Board of Education decided the best option for the students from both schools was to have them attend Helen Hunt. Ivywild and John Adams were closed. Shortly after Adams closed, a charter school moved into the property and occupied the building until May 2015. The charter school dissolved, and the Adams building sat vacant for a year while conversations were held about its future.

Since the 2009 closures, board membership turned over and a new superintendent was hired, leading to new ideas on how to use the Adams building. Meanwhile, discussions about the Hunt facility were happening, with the discussions centering on concerns regarding split campus safety and aging buildings and infrastructure. The original Hunt Elementary School was built in 1902, with several additions being made over the years. Another building was erected in 1962, and as the student population grew, both buildings were used to capacity.

With city growth primarily to the north, newer schools were built in north and east sections of the District. The current board did not feel it was right for more impoverished areas of town to have only older buildings and technology.

Issue: Helen Hunt Elementary School is a split campus, with the original building erected in 1902 and a second building built in 1962. To bring the building up to safety standards, it would cost District 11 approximately $14 million. The school, although old and housing aging infrastructure and systems, is a community fixture, and closing it caused concerns in the low-income neighborhood of blight, decreased property values, and limited childcare resources. Meanwhile, John Adams Elementary School, constructed in 1963, is sitting vacant and neighbors of this school have similar concerns.

Problem Statement: All children deserve equity and the best, safest facilities possible in which to learn. Balancing what is right for our students with being a good neighbor, and doing all of this with a conservative budget, District 11 is tasked with making the best decision for children, for the community, and for future generations.

Both the Hunt and Adams neighborhoods are rooted in history, with loyal citizens who care deeply about their communities, in which many were born and raised. Because of the history of the past board deciding to close Adams and leave Hunt as the designated school for that neighborhood, the challenge for the current board and administration was to acknowledge that Adams could be a viable option to remodel and, therefore, possibly close Hunt. It would take $14 million dollars just to bring Hunt Elementary School up to safety and ADA compliance codes.

It would cost an estimated $7 million to reopen John Adams as a newly renovated school, complete with modernized floor plans, technology, furnishings, energy saving enhancements, and landscaping.

School District 11 has a successful history of repurposing and integrating schools and buildings back into the community with a thriving culture. Ivywild Elementary School, which was closed in the 2009 efficiency restructuring, is now a thriving brewery, eatery, and community resource with meeting space, local artwork, and gardens (http://ivywildschool.com/#menu-item-104). Wasson High School was D11's second oldest high school. Due to declining enrollment, Wasson was closed as a traditional high school and repurposed as a campus with a collegiate feel, offering a menu of schools, programs, and opportunities to meet the needs of every student (http://rjwac.d11.org/Pages/default.aspx). These are only a couple nationally recognized examples of the District's repurposing efforts.

Regardless of our successful repurposing efforts, it is never easy to close a neighborhood school, even with a promise to provide students, and possibly the community, with a better offering.

Situation Analysis

- Colorado Springs School District 11 is the largest school district in the Pikes Peak region, serving approximately 28,000 students in 55 schools.
- The average age of D11's schools and buildings is 50 years old.
- D11 serves a diverse student population. More than 30 percent of students are Hispanic and over 7 percent are black. Sixty percent of students qualify for free or reduced lunch.
- Much of the growth of Colorado Springs is to the north and east, with newer schools accommodating this growth.
- Because of the demographics and growth in Colorado Springs, older school buildings are typically serving higher poverty student populations, while the newer schools are serving more affluent student populations.
- In 2009, the D11 Board of Education and superintendent at the time voted to close nine schools. The three schools on the southern border of the District were all considered for closure, but, due to the proximity of Helen Hunt (between John Adams and Ivywild), the Board decided the best thing to do, at the time, was to close John Adams and Ivywild Elementary Schools and leave Hunt open.
- Since 2009, many have discussed the decision by the previous board and superintendent, due to the age of Hunt's buildings and facilities, its failing infrastructure, and how to best serve the 400 students now attending the school.
- John Adams was closed as a D11 elementary school in 2009, but a charter occupied the school until May 2015, when the charter dissolved. The building sat vacant for one year.
- People in both the Hunt and Adams neighborhoods are rooted in history and have strong ties to their neighborhood schools. Many residents attended their neighborhood school and sent generations of their families through the two schools.
- D11 has had a successful history of repurposing schools, reintroducing them back into the community as a productive, functioning contributor to the community.
- Funds from the sale of another District 11 property, along with general fund reserves, could be enough to retrofit the Adams building into a "new" school, but would fall short of bringing the Hunt building up to ADA and legal compliance by about $7 million.
- Honoring both neighborhoods' history, being a good neighbor, and doing what is right for students are the major points to be considered.

Research

Goal 1: Provide a state-of-the-art school for students in the southeast portion of District 11.
Objective 1: By August 2016, open a school that has been remodeled and refurbished to provide students in the southeast portion of D11 with a "near new" state-of-the-art facility.
Objective 2: By August 2016, close the school that will no longer house students, communicating to families the plans for the new school year and retain enrollment at 100 percent of current numbers.

Goal 2: Regain the trust of both the Hunt and Adams neighborhood communities.
Objective 1: By December 2016, receive a majority of positive feedback from citizens in both neighborhoods, as measured through phone calls, e-mails, social media comments, and visits to the new school.

Informal Primary Research: Colorado Springs School District 11 closed nine schools in 2009, and closed two elementary schools and repurposed a traditional high school to a nontraditional campus in 2013 (http://gazette.com/d-11-board-votes-to-close-wasson-two-elementary-schools/article/150720). Looking back on the process of closing/repurposing these schools, researching archive information, and documenting staff and board experiences with these processes gave good insight on the things that went right, what to avoid, and what to consider as the District and board moved forward toward a final decision. Because of this research, it was determined that public forums were necessary to gather input from both communities. Four public input meetings were scheduled. Two meetings were held at Hunt and two at Adams (http://gazette.com/community-split-over-proposed-move-of-colorado-springs-elementary-school/article/1561139). D11 administrative staff determined an agenda for the meetings to present background information as to what led to the need for the public input. Included in the presentation were the current issues facing both Hunt and Adams.

At each meeting, attendees were asked to fill out comment cards with their thoughts, questions, concerns,

(*continued*)

and ideas. A total of 68 comment cards were collected. There were a couple of main themes that the neighbors of Hunt relayed through their comments. The first was that they didn't want the school to close and become a blight on their community, therefore negatively impacting their property and crime rates in the community. The second concern was that they wanted to be sure an affordable preschool option was available to them, since Hunt housed Head Start and District 11 preschools. They proposed that if Hunt closed, the building be repurposed to be a community asset, with possible health, educational, and community resources to support the neighborhood.

At the Adams public input meetings, community members were very excited about the possibility of the school reopening in their neighborhood. While the comments received were positive overall, there were some lingering trust issues the residents had with District 11. Some long-time residents were concerned that the District wouldn't carry through on providing a state-of-the-art school, given the history of the closing of the school in 2009, then the closing of the charter school that occupied the building for five years.

After all community input meetings were held, district administrative staff met to hold a TregoED Decision Analysis to determine recommendations to bring forward to the Board of Education. (http://tregoed.org/strategies/description-of-strategies.html). This process helps evaluate and identify considerations that most or all stakeholders would support, and helps makes difficult decision-making clearer. At the community input meetings and other district meetings, a total of nine possible considerations were presented in the decision analysis for the repurposing of Hunt:

- A community center;
- A preK-K school with potential after-school program;
- A lab school with higher education support;
- Relocate district security and volunteer and student services offices to Hunt;
- Relocate district SPED and Educational Data and Student Support Services offices to Hunt;
- Relocate district records department, with proposed community center;
- Move science kits from district warehouse to Hunt;
- Allow a charter school access to the property;
- Provide a day care facility.

The decision analysis provided district administrative staff the direction necessary to recommend to the Board of Education that Hunt be repurposed as a community center.

The District would actively engage with local foundations to pull together a group of sustainable 501c3 non-profit organizations that collectively would reside at the current Hunt site and provide community services to the neighborhood. At the time, there were no guarantees which non-profits would be included. The District could ask for specific themes of services or specify entities to be considered. The District considered such non-profits as: the YMCA, Peak Vista Health, a tutoring non-profit, and non-profits that have a focus on arts, perhaps even a community garden. Most likely any foundation would entertain some sort of cost-of-operation type fee to cover operating expenses, but not a high rent fee, in order to attract and sustain non-profits.

This option resulted in a real estate transaction whereby the District conveyed the property for $1 with the intent it be turned into a community center with sustainable non-profits. Selling it for $1 would allow for other funding to be put into the site for renovations to occur.

On February 4, 2016, the District 11 Board of Education voted to close Hunt, convey it to a local non-profit foundation to repurpose and reopen as a community center, and repurpose Adams to be a state-of-the-art, remodeled school for students in the southeast portion of the District. See: http://gazette.com/article/1569326.

Planning

On February 5, 2016, an executive steering team was assigned to ensure all aspects of the move from Hunt to Adams would run smoothly. Departments represented on the steering committee included: Superintendent, Communications, Procurement, Facilities and Planning, IT, Human Resources, School Administrators (principal and executive director for the school), and Business Services (financial and budgetary planning). The target audiences were identified as:

- Hunt students
- Hunt families
- Hunt staff
- Hunt neighbors
- Adams neighbors
- Prospective students and families
- Voters throughout School District 11
- Families and students living in the former Ivywild boundaries.

Planning dashboards were developed for each of the departments involved in the steering committee. Communications planning included letters and notifications for current Hunt families (including those living in the Adams neighborhood), letters to families living in the Ivywild neighborhood to notify them of busing/school choice options, planning the closing/honoring of Hunt and ribbon cutting at Adams celebrations, organizing and facilitating naming committee to possibly re-name the Adams facility, and how to market and brand the new school. There were additional planning elements for internal staff to determine the logistics of the move from Hunt to Adams, including how school staff was to ensure their property would get to the intended location.

Budget

Item	Cost
Printing letters, flyers, brochures, invitations	$400.00
Adams Ribbon and Farewell Celebrations	$650.00
Mailings	$94.00
Translation Services	$125.62
Communications Staff Time (engagement, videos, meetings, presentations, media, articles, website design, etc.)	Salary of communications staff—internal

Communication/Implementation

Letters to the Hunt families were drafted and sent to all enrolled families, available in both English and Spanish. The Hunt administrative staff and front office staff fielded questions about the renovations to Adams, busing logistics for students, and any other questions or concerns families had. The Board ultimately decided not to change the name of the school, after hearing from several community members who urged the Board to keep the name John Adams. Follow-up communication with families throughout the rest of the school year and in the summer of 2016 continued through e-mail, automated phone calls, letters, and website updates.

A joint press release between District 11 and the local non-profit foundation that now owned the Hunt building was released to local media. The press release generated several news pieces on what the building's future would entail. See: http://gazette.com/article/1591746.

Key Messages

- All students deserve a high-quality learning environment, regardless of where they live
- D11 is a good neighbor and cares about our communities

- D11 is fiscally responsible and looks for operational efficiencies to save taxpayer dollars
- D11 will provide excellent, distinctive educational experiences to equip all students for success today and in the future.

Tactics

- E-mail notifications to impacted families and staff
- Administrative staff meetings/steering committee meetings
- Printed/mailed invitations
- Printed/translated/mailed letters to impacted families
- Automated phone calls to impacted families
- Media articles (also see previous links)
- Videos
- Website of upcoming events (District homepage https://www.d11.org/ and Adams homepage https://www.d11.org/Domain/8)
- Board of Education meetings
- Community forums
- Social media posts (District Facebook https://www.facebook.com/cssd11/ and Twitter https://twitter.com/cssd11?lang=en) (Adams Facebook https://www.facebook.com/John-Adams-Elementary-School-1754594284798051/ and Twitter https://twitter.com/adams_d11?lang=en).

Evaluation

Helen Hunt Elementary School officially closed the doors to over 100 years of public school memories on May 23, 2016. John Adams Elementary re-opened on August 15, 2016, and the project was completed on time and within budget. Enrollment data shows Adams opened the doors to 45 more students in August 2016 than what Hunt showed in May 2016. Enrollment has continued to grow at Adams from 432 in September 2016 to 460 in December 2016. Verbal positive feedback about the school has been given to the Superintendent, the school staff, and the Board of Education. To address the community forum attendees' concerns about before- and after-school care, Adams has a Beyond the School Bell Program, as well as transportation to a nearby community center. After-school activities are also offered.

The Hunt building is anticipated to open between August and October 2017. So far, half the building is filled with non-profit organizations. The new owners have raised more than $2 million for construction efforts, which are slated to begin April 1, 2017.[9]

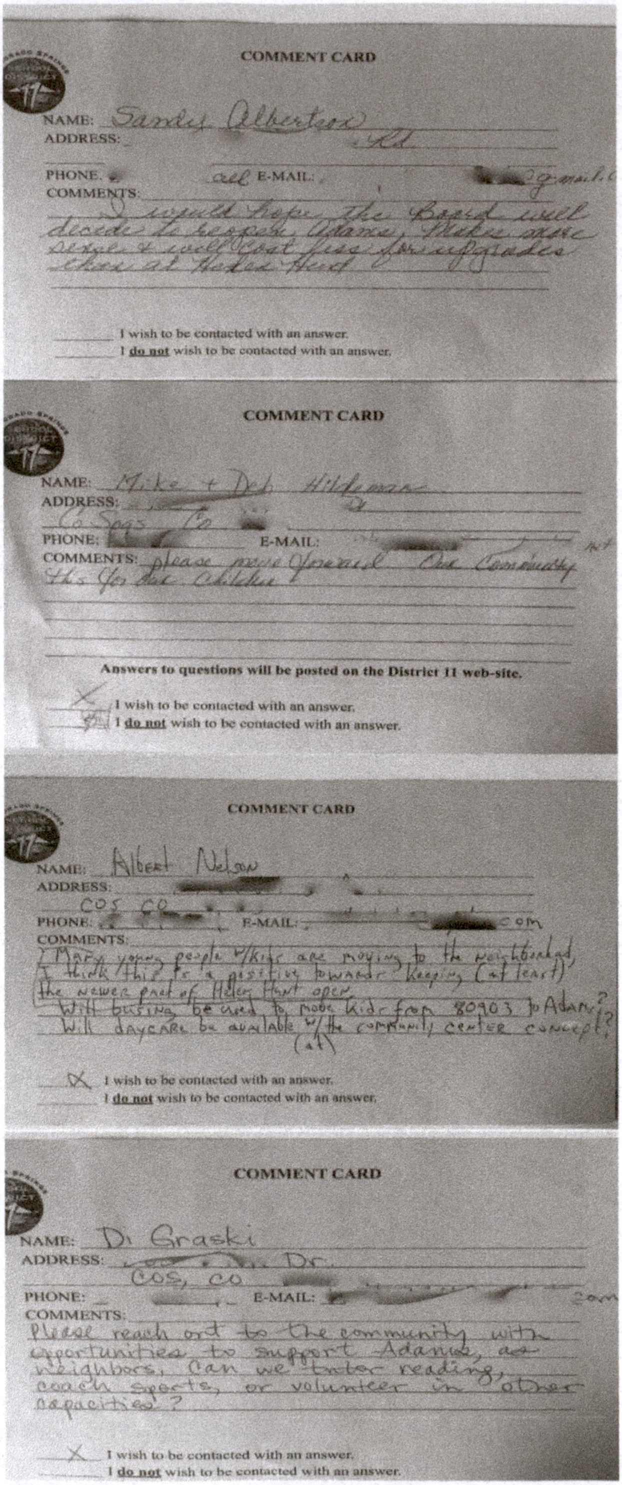

FIGURE 13.1 Sample comment cards.

Attachment One
Optimization of Utilization Plan for Hunt Elementary
Decision Analysis (What course of action do I take?)

Type of Situation →	Decisions
Typical Pitfall →	Jumping to considerations
Process →	*Decision Analysis*
Steps →	1. State the decision 2. Establish and classify the objectives 3. List considerations 4. Evaluate considerations 5. Consider the risks 6. Trust your work

	Objective	Questions that guide the process	Questions the client should ask
Decision Analysis	To make a decision or recommendation	- What are we trying to decide? - What is important to consider in selecting a consideration? - Are some objectives more important than others? - What choices or considerations do we have? - Does this consideration meet the more important objectives? - How well does this consideration meet each of the other objectives? - What are the risks with each consideration? - Which consideration should we choose?	- What is the compelling need this decision or recommendation is addressing? - Who was involved in making this decision or recommendation? - What criteria were used to make this decision or recommendation? - Which criteria were judged as more important than others? - What other options were considered? - What are the risks associated with implementing the recommended option? - What are the risks with implementing the other options?

Attachment One
Optimization of Utilization Plan for Hunt Elementary
Decision Analysis (What course of action do I take?)

Decision Statement: Which considerations or other ideas presented by the working committee and school community groups best respond to the effective and efficient use of the Hunt Facility?

Objectives • What results do we want or need? • What is important to consider in choosing a consideration?	Establish and Classify Objectives • Which objectives are mandatory? • Which wants are most important—give it a ten (10)?	Considerations: What Choices are available? • Against the Musts –Does this consideration meet this MUST? Yes or NO • Against the Wants – How well does this consideration meet this want? **Which consideration best meets the want?** (Give it a ten.) Compared to the top performer, how well do the others meet the want? (0-10)			
		Consideration	Consideration	Consideration	Consideration
		#1 Community Center	#2 PreK-K with potential After School Program	#3 Lab School with Higher Education Support	#4 Relocate Security, Volunteer Services, Student Services
1. Level of feasibility to implement (cost)	Mandatory (dollars available to perform required action)	LOW	HIGH	HIGH	HIGH
2. Stakeholder acceptance	Want 7	10	9	5	3
3. Level of operational feasibility	Want 5	8	9	8	4
4. Wise business decision (economy of scale)	Want 9	8	10	5	4
5. Value to K-12 Education, community and students (instructional economy of scale)	Want 10	4	10	8	4

FIGURE 13.2 Decision analysis chart.

Attachment One
Optimization of Utilization Plan for Hunt Elementary
Decision Analysis (What course of action do I take?)

Objectives: What results do we want or need? What is important to consider in choosing a consideration?	Establish and Classify Objectives: Which objectives are mandatory? Which wants are most important—give it a ten (10)?	Considerations: What Choices are available?			
		Consideration #1 Community Center	**Consideration** #2 PreK-K with potential After School Program	**Consideration** #3 Lab School with Higher Education Support	**Consideration** #4 Relocate Security, Volunteer Services, Student Services
6. Improves utilization of impacted school facility	Want 8	8	6	9	5
7. Adds to the District Portfolio of Innovation	Want 7	8	9	10	2
8. Level of Student Safety	Want 10	10	7	7	8
9. Level of staff safety	Want 10	10	7	7	7
10. Site location to proposed function	Want 8	10	9	7	2
TOTAL		622	621	538	337

Attachment One
Optimization of Utilization Plan for Hunt Elementary
Decision Analysis (What course of action do I take?)

Objectives: What results do we want or need? What resources are available?	Establish and Classify Objectives: Which objectives are mandatory? Which wants are most important—give it a ten (10)?	Considerations: What Choices are available?				
		Consideration #5 Relocate SPED and EDSS Services	**Consideration** #6 Relocate Records with Proposed Community Center	**Consideration** #7 Move Science Kit from Warehouse	**Consideration** #8 Charter Access	**Consideration** #9 Day Care Facility
7. Adds to the District Portfolio of Innovation	Want 7	3	7	3	5	6
8. Level of Student Safety	Want 10	9	9	9	7	7
9. Level of staff safety	Want 6	5	5	9	7	7
10. Site location to proposed function	Want 8	3	5	2	8	2
TOTAL		388	505	344	486	378

FIGURE 13.3 Decision analysis charts.

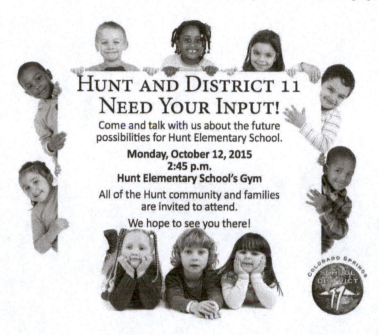

HUNT AND DISTRICT 11
NEED YOUR INPUT!

Come and talk with us about the future
possibilities for Hunt Elementary School.

Monday, October 12, 2015
2:45 p.m.
Hunt Elementary School's Gym

All of the Hunt community and families
are invited to attend.

We hope to see you there!

Add/Edit Notice

Notice

Save | Cancel | Copy Notice | Save As Template

Name   ADAMS COMMUNITY MEETING

Description   (Used in Archive and as Preview Text in HTML/Plain Text Email)

Monitor Email   Test

Text

Shared ☐   Archive ☐   Enable Comments ☐   Auto Translate ☐

HTML Email   Send ☆
Type your email message for this notice in the editor below. You can add links to your website or other EzCommunicator Functions.

Subject   ADAMS COMMUNITY MEETING

There will be a Community Meeting on Monday, November 16th at 5:30 p.m. in the gym at the Adams building, 2101 Manitoba Drive.

This meeting is open to all Hunt and Adams community members and parents who want to discuss the future of the Adams Elementary School site.

Plain Text Email   Send ■
Type your email message for this notice in the editor below.

FIGURE 13.4   Public meeting communication.

FIGURE 13.5 Remodel renderings.

Communications and Community Relations
1115 North El Paso Street, Room 204, Colorado Springs, Colorado 80903
(719) 520-2005
Fax: (719) 577-4546
www.d11.org

March 9, 2016

Dear Parents,

This letter is to inform you that on Wednesday February 10th, 2016, the Colorado Springs School District 11 (CSSD11) Board of Education approved the relocation of Hunt Elementary School. The new location will be at 2101 Manitoba Drive Colorado Springs, Colorado, 80910 (formerly Adams Elementary). The process for renovation and renaming has already begun.

Because your current address is within a specified boundary, your student/s have the option to continue to attend their current school, Midland International Elementary or the new school (formerly Hunt Elementary). CSSD11 is committed to providing your student/s the very best education, and is able to offer transportation to students who attend the new school (formerly Hunt Elementary) and to Midland International Elementary School.

If you would like your student/s to continue to attend their current school you do not need to do anything. If you would like your student/s to attend the new school (formerly Hunt Elementary) or Midland International Elementary School, you need to complete the attached Choice Enrollment Form and return it to Hunt or Midland on or before April 15, 2016.

If you are unsure of your decision and would like further information, please join us Wednesday, March 16th, 2016 at Hunt Elementary School at 6 p.m. for an informational meeting. The principals from Hunt and Midland as well as representatives from CSSD11, will be there to answer your questions.

Hunt Elementary at the Adams Campus	Midland International Baccalaureate Elementary
• Newly renovated building • Technology focus: Interactive Promethean Board in Every Classroom, 1:1 Chromebooks in 3rd – 5th Grade, Class sets of 6 ipads in K-2 • Next Gen learning spaces • New Playground System • After School Program • Additional After School Opportunities: Tutoring, Homework Club, Battle Of the Books, chess club, sports challenge, Dance Connection, Art Club, Coed Basketball Team • Highly qualified teaching staff • 12 minutes, 3.5 miles away	• Authorized International Baccalaureate school • Highly qualified teaching staff • Small class sizes • Wide range of After School Activity choices • Activity bus 4 days a week so all kids can participate in activities • Spanish language classes K-5 • Art every week for all students • 11 Minutes, 3.7 miles away

West Brookside St. & Woodburn St. to Adams Campus 2101 Manitoba Drive

West Brookside St. & Woodburn St. to Midland Elementary 2110 Broadway St

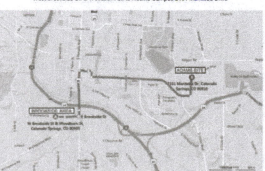

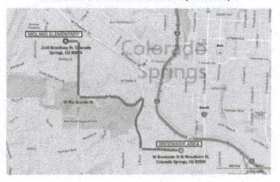

FIGURE 13.6   Option letter to families.

The staff and students of Hunt Elementary School would like to thank all of our generous sponsors.

John Poma III, Store Manager
Sandy Dolan, Personnel Office
Walmart #1200
3201 East Platte Avenue

Marie Woodworth, VPC Department
Walmart Super Center
707 South 8th Street

Samantha, Community Liaison
Walmart Super Center #3582
Space Center Drive

Desiree, HR Personnel Manager
Walmart Neighborhood Market
Union Blvd.

Brady's Rental Company, Owner Operator
3807 Palmer Park Blvd.

Dr. Nicolas Pruett
Broadmoor Dental

Akayla Gutteridge, Marketing Director
Chick-fil-A, The Citadel

A special thank you to the following people for their help in preparation of this event.

District 11 Catering Department

Lisa Martinez, Administrative Assistant
Wasson Academic Campus

Dr. Brien Hodges, Executive Director

Devra Ashby, Public Information Officer

Donna Hines, Communications Specialist

CELEBRATING *114* YEARS OF EDUCATING CHILDREN AT HUNT ELEMENTARY SCHOOL!

Friday, May 13, 2016
4:30-7 p.m.

Platform Guests: Dr. Brien Hodges, Executive Director
Dr. Mary Thurman, Deputy Superintendent/
Personnel Support Services
Devra Ashby, Public Information Officer

Honored Guests: Board Members
Mayor John Suthers and Janet Suthers

Program

Welcome: Nate Hansen, Principal
Christina Butcher, Assistant Principal

Pledge of Allegiance: Led by the Helen Hunt Choir

America: Sung by the Helen Hunt Choir

Message from the Superintendent: Dr. Nicholas Gledich

Musical Presentation: Helen Hunt Choir
Mary Ellen Zimmerman, Director
Victoria Darpino, Director

Reflection of Helen Hunt Elementary School

Musical Presentation: Stratton Elementary Deaf Choir
Sue Ann Gurwell, Director

Toast: Nate Hansen, Christina Butcher, and Elnora Lillard

Light Refreshments will served following the program, with music provided by Thomas Dawson from the Commodores.

Hunt students will be giving tours of the West building.

FIGURE 13.7   Farewell flyer and program.

Press Release for Hunt Building Transaction

May 6, 2016

FOR IMMEDIATE RELEASE

Contact: Devra Ashby, 520-2286
Kris Odom, 520-2462
Zachary McComsey, zmccomsey@lanefoundation.org, The John E.
and Margaret L. Lane Foundation

Helen Hunt Elementary School Building's Future will be Discussed at May 11 Board of Education Meeting

The Colorado Springs School District 11 Board of Education is excited to discuss and possibly approve a real estate contract to convey the Helen Hunt Elementary School building at 917 E. Moreno Ave. to the John E. and Margaret L. Lane Foundation. The D11 Board of Education voted in January to close the Helen Hunt Elementary School and move the students to the current Adams Elementary site, which was vacant at the time. The Hunt Elementary building will continue to serve as a D11 school until the end of the 2015-2016 school year.

Considering the community input about the future of the Hunt building, the D11 School Board and the Lane Foundation feel it is important to repurpose the building to be a community resource. The Lane Foundation is committed to spending a minimum of $2 million to renovate the Hunt property and anticipates selecting non-profit organizations and programs to be housed in the buildings. The desire from both parties is that the Hunt Elementary property will be a community resource that will compliment such services provided by the Hillside Community Center, and will be a sustainable community asset. Zachary McComsey, Executive Director of the Lane Foundation says, "The Lane Foundation considers it a privilege to partner with D-11 and local nonprofit organizations to ensure the Helen Hunt School and Campus remains a vital and protected community asset for a long time to come." District 11 Board of Education President, LuAnn Long, believes this potential property transaction will give the Helen Hunt community peace of mind and says, "the community's desire will be fulfilled with this action to keep the property as something that offers help to those who live in the area."

This real estate contract will go before the D11 Board of Education as an action item on the May 11, 2016 regular meeting agenda. If approved, the projected closing date will be August 24, 2016. To view the board agenda, please visit http://www.boarddocs.com/co/d11/Board.nsf/Public and click on meetings.

FIGURE 13.8   Press release for building transaction.

SAVE THE DATE!

The John Adams Elementary School
Ribbon Cutting and Grand Re-Opening
Ceremony will be held on
Monday, August 15, 2-3:30 p.m.

The John Adams Elementary School
Public Open House will be held on
Wednesday, August 17, 6-7:30 p.m.

The School District 11 Board of Education and
Administration formally invite you to attend
the Ribbon Cutting Ceremony for
Adams Elementary School
2101 Manitoba Dr.
on Monday, August 15, 2 p.m.

We hope you can join us for the celebration as we
open this newly remodeled school in the southeast
portion of School District 11. Refreshments will
be served, and tours of the building will be given.

Please call 719-520-2162 by August 5
to RSVP for this event.

FIGURE 13.9 Ribbon-cutting invitations.

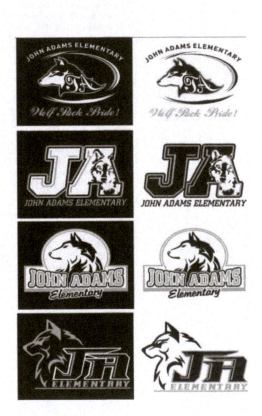

FIGURE 13.10 Logo prototypes.

John Adams Elementary Ribbon Cutting
Dr. Gledich Talking Points
August 15, 2016 2-3pm

- Thank you! This truly is a wonderful day! It is wonderful to have you all here to celebrate; it is wonderful to be able to open a state of the art school on the southeast portion of District 11; and it will be wonderful to see the expressions of the students who will walk through these doors on Thursday and experience a school they most likely have never been able to experience before.

- When the District 11 Board of Education faced the decision last school year to close Hunt and relocate the students to Adams Elementary, they did not take it lightly. It was a difficult decision, but one that afforded us the opportunity to give students a beautifully remodeled school with brand new technology and furnishings. When students are comfortable in their learning environment, they become better learners and that is why we do what we do!

- One of the founding fathers of our great country once said, "Let us tenderly and kindly cherish, therefore, the means of knowledge. Let us dare to read, think, speak and write." That man was John Adams, the second President of the United States for who this school is named, and that quote speaks to how School District 11 teachers and staff provide the means for our students to read, think, speak and write.

- Through the actions of the Board of Education, the work of our construction and architect partners, and dedication of our staff, the educators at Adams now have the best facility and tools with which to provide these means.

- As you step foot in this school today, know that so many people have worked—and continue to work—to create a magnificent place for children to learn. You may see people who are still working in the school today to prepare for our students.

- We are honored that you came here to celebrate this remarkable project and we hope you continue to partner with School District 11 so we may prepare every student for a world yet to be imagined!

FIGURE 13.11   Ribbon-cutting talking points.

One Expert's Point of View: Conducting Special Issue Campaigns

As the Public Information Officer for Colorado Springs School District 11, Devra Ashby, APR, directs a team of 10 people in the communications department for the largest school district in Southern Colorado. The National School Public Relations Association gave the district its Gold Medallion Award for its communication work (previously described) aimed at uniting school communities during a time of school closings.

Ashby previously served in public relations positions for the City of Colorado Springs and St. Mary's Hospital in Grand Junction, Colo. She also worked as a TV anchor and reporter for KKTV/KXRM in Colorado Springs.

We know that research and planning is important to an overall school communication effort. But what is the value in conducting research and developing specific plans for a special communication issue such as repurposing a school facility?

Overall plans serve a district's ongoing, over-arching communication needs but it's important to research and plan for individual situations when addressing many specific school issues. For example, many of our schools have been entrenched in the community for a very long time and with a school as old as Hunt there is a lot of history with the neighborhood. It's very important to understand what the neighborhood was

expecting in a case such as this. It was also important to understand the needs and interests of the Adams community. Obviously, we wanted to avoid doing anything that would be perceived as negative. Communication research and planning, and the engagement with the communities involved that follows, helps to make sure that the school district can be sensitive to existing values and make decisions that provide a benefit to all involved.

How important is understanding audiences—what people know, what they want, where they get information and opinions—to assembling information and creating messages that will encourage the kind of understanding and action a successful communication creates?

It's extremely important. In our case we were dealing with two different and diverse communities that had a number of audience segments, each with unique interests and messaging needs. One segment, for example, might be very family-oriented with a high priority of keeping children together in schools. Communication efforts have to accommodate all concerns such as this. But as in any communication campaign, audiences extended well beyond the families involved. We had to work with politicians, neighbors, neighborhood organizations, and many other groups

with an interest in the use of these schools. This is a process and it needs to make sure each of these audiences and segments receives information and messages crafted to address their concerns and interests.

Some would argue that a successful outcome such as generating community understanding for a project such as a new use for school facilities ultimately also supports student success. How do you see community engagement and student success linked?

Obviously, it is ultimately important for us to see student success—that is always a big consideration. But community understanding and support is equally important to the success of the overall organization. In this equation it becomes clear that working with the community is a vital part in ultimately assuring student and school success.

It is never easy to close a school. We've had previous experience with this that showed us it is very, very important for us to work with the community and engage them in the process. You don't want people to come back and say, "Well, you already had your minds made up." By making the community a part of the process, trust is strengthened, working relationships are created, and the school district and the community benefit.[10] ■

Questions

1. Explain the process by which any community typically evaluates a new idea. Why is it important for school administrators to understand and engage in this process?
2. List some key audiences that might be addressed in a typical communication campaign. What might be the best ways in which to reach each audience you listed?
3. Explain the critical roles opinion leaders play in the acceptance or rejection of new ideas. Why is it essential for school–community relations campaigns to engage opinion leaders?
4. List the ways in which schools now face new competition for students and resources. Explain why new choices in education are creating a need for marketing communication campaigns.
5. Discuss some of the challenges school leaders face as marketing efforts attempt to align realities with the various perceptions that may be held among key audiences.

Readings

Bagin, Rich, *Making Parent Communication Effective and Easy: Communication Guidebook for Teachers and Their Schools.* Rockville, MD: National School Public Relations Association, 2005.

Banach, William J., *The ABC Complete Book of School Marketing.* Lanham, MD: Rowman and Littlefield, 2001.

Banach, William J., *The ABC Complete Book of School Surveys.* Lanham, MD: Rowman and Littlefield, 2001.

Banach, William J., *The ABC Marketing Disk.* Ray, MI: Banach, Banach & Cassidy, http://www.banach.com, 2006.

Banach, William J., *The ABCs of Teacher–Parent Communication.* Ray, MI: Banach, Banach & Cassidy, http://www.banach.com, 2006.

Bobbitt, Randy, and Ruth Sullivan, *Developing the Public Relations Campaign: A Team-Based Approach,* 3rd ed. Boston, MA: Pearson, 2013.

Hall, Gene E., and Shirley M. Hord, *Implementing Change: Patterns, Principles, and Potholes*, 4th ed. Boston, MA: Pearson, 2014.

Hendrix, Jerry A., *Public Relations Cases,* 9th ed. Boston, MA: Wadsworth, 2013.

National School Public Relations Association, *A Guidebook for Opinion Leader/Key Communicator Programs.* Rockville, MD: Author, 2002.

National School Public Relations Association, "Without Ongoing Community Engagement, School Closures Can Devastate," *Counselor,* Rockville, MD: Author, August 16, 2013.

Singhal, Arvind, and James W. Dearing (Eds.), *Communication of Innovations: A Journey with Ev Rogers.* Thousand Oaks, CA: Sage Publications, 2006.

Endnotes

1. George M. Beal, "The Communication Process in the Purchase of New Products: An Application of Reference Group Theory," paper presented at the American Association of Public Opinion Researchers, Chicago, 1958.
2. George M. Beal, "Validity of the Concept Stages in the Adoption Process," *Rural Sociology* (1957), pp. 166–168.
3. Singhal, Arvind, and James W. Dearing (Eds.), *Communication of Innovations: A Journey with Ev Rogers* (Thousand Oaks, CA: Sage Publications, 2006), p. 63.
4. Hall, Gene E., and Shirley M. Hord, *Implementing Change: Patterns, Principles, and Potholes* (Boston, MA: Pearson, 2011), p. 224.
5. The quoted material that follows in this section is taken from National School Public Relations Association, *A Guidebook for Opinion Leader/Key Communicator Programs* (Rockville, MD: Author, 2002), pp. 7–8.
6. Ibid., pp. 7–8.
7. Ibid., p. 11.
8. Banach, Banach & Cassidy. www.banach.com. See www.banach.com/School_Resources.html for quoted material throughout this section.
9. Taken from correspondence October 25, 2017, with Devra Ashby, Public Information Officer, Colorado Springs (CO) School District 11.
10. Taken from correspondence November 1, 2017, with Devra Ashby, Public Information Officer, Colorado Springs (CO) School District 11.

14

Communicating School Finance Issues

This chapter reviews issues ...

■ For central administrators: How comprehensive communication planning can build public understanding and community support on vital school finance issues and related communication campaigns.

■ For building and program administrators: The ways school administrators contribute to public understanding of school finance issues in the schools, programs, and communities.

■ For teachers, counselors, and staff: The roles for school employees in building community understanding of key school functions and the related school finance issues essential to successful school programming.

After completing this chapter you should be able to ...

■ Distinguish the numerous financial communication issues that school communicators often face.

■ Identify the importance of understanding how laws can influence how schools can communicate on finance issues and distinguish the critical nature of following local laws and regulations.

■ Outline the importance of ongoing communication on financial issues to build public understanding of school financial needs and practices.

■ List the key components of financial communication campaigns.

The complex nature of school financing and the emotional characteristics of discussions about taxes and government spending combine to present significant communication challenges to school administrators. In addition, school districts are among the few providers of government services that—in many jurisdictions—must seek direct voter approval for spending in some areas. Practices vary from state to state, but many school districts must seek voter consent for financial issues, such as the following:

- Approval of annual operating budgets
- Bond issues for new construction or capital improvements
- Increases in tax or millage rates.

Keeping communities informed about finance issues is key to gaining voter approval when needed. If a school district does not maintain ongoing and clear communications with its parents and taxpayers on finance and budget issues, confusion and distrust can develop.

Brimley, Verstegen, and Garfield note that both critics and friends of public education are increasingly demanding that schools be held accountable for making output commensurate with input—seeking proof that educators are reaching their objectives while making efficient use of tax dollars.[1]

The National School Public Relations Association (NSPRA) notes that educators must use organized and ongoing communication to create advocates for specific needs, such as bond issue support, capital projects, or other financial issues.[2]

Communication by schools on finance issues, therefore, must be conducted on a continuing basis. Doing so can help to sustain an essential level of public understanding and engagement that can provide an important framework for communication when campaigns for specific financial initiatives, such as a new bond issue, are undertaken.

Many external issues, not always directly linked to local schools, can influence thinking on school finance topics and create communication dilemmas for school administrators. Some education critics focus on school finance issues when disparaging school policies or practices. Claims about spending on administrative support or other activities not directly linked to instruction can create confusion among taxpayers. Budget communications also must address the entire community served by the school district. Those without children in the local schools also pose challenges for school administrators when trying to communicate the benefits of spending on local schools and their programming. Competition for limited tax resources, ranging from the need for road and bridge repair to health care services, also can influence school finance issues.

It is recognized that many schools are faced with gaining support for annual budgets, an increasingly difficult task as teacher salaries increase and the cost of other services and materials continues to rise. Some school systems need poll support to increase taxes in order to maintain the level of educational efforts; others want to improve their programs. In either case, the requirement is the same—getting enough votes for approval. Although much of this chapter focuses on bond issues, many ideas offered are easily adaptable to budget elections as well as school-finance communication overall.

A look at the past can be helpful before planning campaigns. In fact, for some reason many school officials have been working with incorrect information regarding plans for bond issue campaigns. The following research findings should provide background for a campaign. Perhaps more important for the school official is a look at the history of similar elections in the school district. Because of the turnover of board members and administrators, those planning a campaign sometimes forget the importance of an advisory committee or the date of the election or some other specific issue that could affect the vote outcome.

WHAT THE RESEARCH SAYS

Studies have shown that voters' resistance to bond issues is based on many variables. These are not consistent from school system to school system or from state to state. Some factors in campaigns vary considerably. It is incumbent on school officials to consider local factors before making decisions on these items.

Most important for school officials working on a campaign are those factors that research indicates lead consistently to a favorable vote. They follow.

- *Support of the Municipal Government.* Too many school officials forget about the people responsible for governing the town—until they need them. Every educator should remember that elected or appointed town officials have a large following of people. A liaison that encourages an ongoing exchange of information and ideas between school officials and their government counterparts must be conducive to a better overall relationship. Such communication minimizes conflicts and ensures that both groups will not, for example, publicly announce their desire to use the same site for different purposes. Although some educators still adhere to a "politics and education don't mix" theory, most school officials recognize the need to work with municipal officials and certainly are cognizant of the basic requirement of keeping them informed. A sound idea is to encourage the board of education to appoint one member as liaison to the municipal governing body. The town council can reciprocate, thus making a commitment to better communication between the two groups. If the municipal government opposes a bond issue, either publicly or quietly, the school faces a severe challenge to winning the election.

- *Demonstrated Need for Additional Classroom Space.* People tend to vote for additional classrooms more than they vote for other building needs, such as administration centers or cafeterias. Thus, it is imperative that school officials clearly communicate the need for classroom space. This, of course, must be done honestly because any attempt to make the situation appear worse than it is could backfire and damage the district's credibility. If classrooms are crowded, show evidence to prove it and demonstrate the effects. Most people see schools when students are not there; hence, it is difficult for them to realize the problems caused by overcrowding. The educator must demonstrate how an additional building will overcome crowded classroom problems and how it will help students learn better. Statistics, if not overdone, can be helpful, especially if the capacity of the building has been exceeded. Student complaints about how learning is hindered could be useful in a campaign.

- *Promise of Additional Curriculum.* How does the new building fit into the overall educational plan of the school system? This question, asked by some sophisticated, well-educated parents, is sometimes answered less than adequately by school officials who develop a plan for numbers of students without giving sufficient thought to the educational program and how it would be facilitated by the proposed building. If the building will make new opportunities available in career education or will allow additional individualized instruction, people should be told so. If more students will have more chances to learn more things better, this should be said.

- *Increasing Student Population.* For too many years, it was fairly easy to explain the need for new buildings. As the number of school-age children increased, the need for more school buildings was accepted. As the demographics of the United States changed and declining enrollment became the norm, those communities with new developments and increasing enrollment faced a new challenge. For example, a formerly rural area might have become the latest suburb, with the rapid growth that such change brings. Voters will need to be convinced that their community is different from most others. Asking for the help of service organizations to conduct a school population projection might be a sound strategy in such a situation. The added credibility that such involvement gives a campaign is well worth the time invested.

- *Dissemination of Information Through All Media.* Using every available newspaper, radio station, television, and online news outlet, the campaign director will move one step toward building the kind of public understanding essential to success. Although the face-to-face phase of the communications effort has the greatest impact in changing attitudes, the media can be important at the information and awareness stages of accepting a new idea or voting for a bond issue. The best job can be done if a sound relationship has been established with representatives of the media before the bond issue need is imminent.

- *A Large Percentage of Parents in the Population.* Although parents of public school students are not to be counted automatically in the yes column, enough studies have been made to indicate that these parents vote for bond issues more than do the remainder of the population. Parents should be kept informed about the school's accomplishments and needs on a year-round basis. They should be encouraged to visit the schools and to participate in school activities when possible. Involvement of this nature is conducive to people feeling that the schools are indeed theirs. This can usually be translated into positive votes.

- *Citizens' Advisory Participation.* Research frequently shows that school systems that have involved a representative group of citizens on a committee to help gain support for a bond issue have met with more success than those that have failed to stress citizen involvement. The role played by citizens in the bond issue undertaking must be an active one if overall citizen support is to be expected. The advisory committee should function at the study-of-needs stage of the bond issue. In other words, the group should help determine the system's needs and study alternatives before working for any recommended solution to meet the needs. This kind of involvement builds citizen trust in the schools.

Consistent factors leading to an unfavorable vote are opposition from any organized group, controversial placement of buildings, a large percentage of parochial school students, lack of public use of school facilities, and a large percentage of people on fixed incomes.

- *Opposition from Any Organized Group.* When people organize to defeat a bond issue, school officials face an increased challenge. Thus, it is incumbent upon educators to find out why people oppose the bond issue. Does the group offer reasonable alternatives that school officials have failed to investigate? Have any members of this group been asked to participate on the advisory group investigating the district's building needs? Does the group have specific concerns that could be overcome with additional information provided by school officials?
- The well-planned campaign will consider the role of the opposition and take steps to minimize its impact. For instance, a group gaining publicity might imply that it represents a large number of taxpayers. An investigation might divulge that the group numbers six members—an important fact for reporters and other voters to know. The opposition thrives on public meetings. Such forums present an opportunity for publicity because public meetings are usually covered by the press, which seeks controversial statements. Thus, if public meetings must be held, school officials should be sure that proponents of the building make presentations to offset the thrusts of the opposition.
- *Controversial Placement of Buildings.* If voters feel that a building site has been improperly chosen in terms of location, cost, accessibility, or some other factor, the vote will suffer. People, especially those whose children will attend the school in question, want to feel that the site selected is the best possible one for their children. Accordingly, it is imperative that the rationale for the site selection be presented to voters with a full explanation of the positive considerations that might otherwise be overlooked.
- *Lack of Public Use of School Facilities.* The movement toward community education emphasizes the desire of many people to tap school resources more than is commonly done. Inasmuch as the public schools belong to the public, school officials should encourage community use of school facilities. As more people benefit directly from the buildings, they will undoubtedly feel more a part of the school system. Such a feeling should engender additional positive votes.

PLANNING A CAMPAIGN

As noted, the research done on bond issue support can be helpful. More helpful is the time that school officials invest in researching their own community before starting a bond issue campaign. For example, a study of past bond issues might show that three bond issues have passed with the help of advisory committees and that two bond issues without advisory committees have failed. In some systems with rapid turnover of school officials, this fact may not have been remembered. A good starting place for planning the campaign is a thorough look at facts from previous campaigns.

Surveying the building needs of a school district can require several months to a year. Some school officials undertake this responsibility themselves;

others choose to employ consultants for this purpose. It should be remembered that many taxpayers are concerned about buildings they consider monuments to school officials. One governor chastised educators for building palaces that are monuments to architects and engineers. If one elected official criticizes another in this manner, certainly taxpayers will have their doubts about some of the buildings proposed by school boards. One way to alleviate this concern is to include a cross-section of citizens in any group studying the building needs of the district. The use of a consultant sometimes helps obviate taxpayer doubts about school officials asking for more than is needed.

In addition to surveying building needs, the administration should assemble all data pertinent to the problem before any public announcement of an election is made. Included among the data will be the following:

- A complete report on how funds from the most recent bond issue have been or are being spent, including lists of completed projects, current projects, and proposed projects. (The report should also include such facts as square-foot costs and the number of children for whom the projects have provided schooling.)
- An analysis of enrollment trends over the past several years.
- An analysis of current enrollments by grades to determine future classroom requirements in the upper grades.
- A census of preschool children by attendance areas. (Members of advisory groups, parent–teacher associations, or other service groups are usually willing to conduct the necessary surveys to provide this information.)
- An enrollment projection for the next five years, including data about proposed housing and apartment developments.

Most of these facts are newsworthy, and the superintendent will want to take advantage of every opportunity to inform parents and the general public. The media are usually receptive to stories about enrollment, school building programs, and community surveys. A continuous program of information about these topics will prepare the public for announcements regarding additional building needs.

DETERMINING A PROPOSAL

As soon as these preliminary steps have been taken, the superintendent and staff should begin developing the specific proposal for meeting the building needs of the district. Every alternative should be examined, including community education, 12-month schools, additions to existing buildings, split sessions, and whatever else any member of the community might propose. By looking at all possible solutions in depth, school officials can anticipate the arguments of opponents of any proposed program. It is, of course, helpful in gaining community approval if members of all segments of the community are involved in the vital stages of studying the alternatives. Included in this committee should be parents, other taxpayers, students, teachers, and other staff members.

Once a proposal has been determined, a careful check should be made with state authorities to determine the proper procedures to follow to ensure that the bond proposal is presented in a legally correct way. Such thoroughness negates the possibility of embarrassment caused when a proposal must be postponed or changed because of the intercession of a state official.

ESTABLISHING A PHILOSOPHY

Some school officials adopt a "win at all costs" philosophy for their campaigns. Others select a "tell the people the facts and whatever they do will be the proper result" approach. Some educational leaders feel strongly that it is their responsibility to gain public support for bond issues if, indeed, buildings are required to maintain education at a predetermined level. Others feel that the schools should reflect the will of the community, and therefore little more than factual presentation should be used to woo community votes. Each superintendent and board must decide which approach is better for their needs. This decision will affect other decisions, such as the naming of the campaign director.

NAMING A DIRECTOR

Leadership is an extremely important ingredient often overlooked in a campaign. Too often the responsibility is delegated to administrators who face numerous other time-consuming responsibilities. Somehow they are supposed to find the time to exert the needed efforts to guide the campaign and still perform all their other duties. If administrators assume the leadership role for the campaign, they must receive assistance with other duties. If no such help is available, the superintendent must apprise the campaign director of priorities so the administrator will know how to budget time.

Campaign directors must possess the ability to feel comfortable as change agents. They must be able to get along with all kinds of people and possess organizational ability. It is helpful if they have had experience dealing with the mass media and if they know how to meet deadlines. Occasionally, a noneducator can serve as campaign director. If this person has served on a committee studying the district's building needs, commands the respect of the community, and has the time and ability to lead the campaign, he or she should be considered. Of course, this means that the person's relationship with school officials would have to be clearly communicated to all employees. If such a person were not given proper cooperation by the staff, enthusiasm would wane and leadership efforts could be minimized.

TIMING OF A CAMPAIGN

Well-planned campaigns usually have three distinct phases. The first, which can begin a year to a few months before the election, should include a careful survey of the building needs. It should include a detailed plan for the campaign itself and should identify community leaders who will assist in campaign efforts. This phase should also pinpoint the various audiences to be reached during the campaign. This phase can also include voter registration.

The second phase of the campaign should be a period of community education concerning the building needs of the schools. Newspaper articles, presentations to community organizations, public meetings, and distribution of materials to parents and other taxpayers are activities to be carried out during this phase. This informational program must be implemented far enough before the election to allow community discussion of the needs and to provide answers to the questions prompted by the information disseminated. During this period, much face-to-face communication should occur.

Phase three of the campaign usually takes place from a month to two weeks before the election. Informational materials are distributed throughout the community, house-to-house canvasses are conducted, brochures are mailed, and advertisements are placed in the media. A feeling of reaching the campaign climax must be experienced by campaign workers just before the vote takes place. A campaign hastily patched together with little organization and insufficient time to establish any momentum seldom succeeds. On the other hand, an overly long campaign in which campaign workers and the public lose interest before election day can backfire, especially if opponents mount an offensive during the last few days. Knowing the climate of a community can be helpful in planning the campaign length.

FINANCING ACTIVITIES

It is essential that administrators understand the laws governing the spending of tax dollars on financial or advocacy campaigns in their state before any campaign work gets underway. Investigations of—or even allegations of—the improper use of tax dollars on campaign activities during the course of an effort can create controversies that can detract from and even threaten the success of a campaign.

In many states, school districts are prohibited by law from spending public funds on campaigns that attempt to directly influence voter behavior. Although many states allow schools to provide information explaining the needs of the schools and the advantages of the proposed building, schools nevertheless are often prohibited from urging a yes vote by using school money.

Such laws often extend to issues beyond how money is spent on advocacy activities. School district employees, for example, may be prevented from working on advocacy projects during their workday. Other school resources, such as telephones and copiers, might be allowed if used for informational purposes but not allowed if used for advocacy purposes.

Often money is collected by businesspeople, service groups, PTAs, advisory groups, and other organizations that support the need for a new building to create an independent advocacy campaign that operates separately from a school system's informational campaign. Laws covering such outside advocacy campaigns generally differ from those governing activities by schools and public employees. A citizens' organization—if it is organized independently from the school system—often is free to work to convince voters to support the school system's proposal at the polls.

In such an effort, a separate budget should be determined to pay for advertising, brochures, billboards, consultant help if needed, and surveys. Such outside advocacy groups often also solicit volunteer help from talented members of the community to help to generate voter support. For example, a polling firm executive might donate his or her talent or facilities to feel the community's pulse a month before the election. A public relations firm president with children in the schools might offer his or her expertise to prepare election materials.

CITIZENS' ADVISORY COMMITTEE

As noted, the existence of an advisory committee enhances the chances of generating public support for a financial issue. The committee is most effective if it, or another similar committee, has studied the needs of the district and has been involved in the recommendation of the proposed building. People believe their friends and neighbors in most cases; thus, it is important to involve as many people as possible in the campaign. When people become involved, they feel more committed to the schools and will remember to vote and encourage others to join them at the polls.

An effort should be made to include members from as many interest groups as possible. Parent–teacher associations, the League of Women Voters, the American Association of University Women, labor unions, veterans' groups, service clubs, the Jaycees, the chamber of commerce, faith leaders, taxpayers' associations, businesspeople, realtors, media representatives, members of the school staff, and students

should be represented. Every effort should be made to include representation from all socioeconomic and racial groups in the community. If the group is handpicked by school board members and includes only friends, the committee could justifiably be considered a rubber stamp for the board.

The school superintendent or the board of education, independently or together, usually invites citizens to serve on the advisory committee. The group should be organized before final decisions are made concerning the amount of the bond issue and the date of the election. The organization should take place from three to six months before the election. Any proposal submitted to the citizens' committee should be tentative, subject to change on the recommendation of its members.

The following are suggested steps for organizing and working with a citizens' advisory committee. These suggestions represent a synthesis of the opinions expressed by many school administrators in literature dealing with this subject:

- As soon as a definite proposal for a school bond election is announced, preferably at a meeting of the board of education, an open invitation should be extended to all citizens who may be interested in serving on a citizens' advisory committee.
- The school administration should then prepare a letter, signed by the president of the board of education or the superintendent of schools, to be sent to every known organization in the district, inviting each one to send a representative to the organizational meeting of the citizens' advisory committee. It should be explained, however, that committee members are to serve as individuals, not as representatives of the groups.
- Letters of invitation should also be sent to other persons who may have influence in the community or who would be able to make worthwhile contributions to the work of the committee.
- At the first meeting, members of the board of education and the administrative staff should present the current and anticipated building needs of the district, the proposal for meeting these needs, and the estimated cost of such

projects. A detailed report covering these points should be distributed to everyone in attendance. This report should also be mailed to groups not represented at this first meeting.

- At least two subcommittees should be chosen at this meeting—the first to make an intensive study of the proposal and to prepare a report for presentation at the next meeting, and the second to prepare a report on committee organization. This second subcommittee could nominate a general chairperson and suggest other needed subcommittees and their chairpersons at the next meeting. The administration should offer all help necessary for these subcommittees to carry out their assignments.

- After allowing enough time for a thorough study of the proposal, a second meeting of the citizens' advisory committee should be called. In the interim, follow-up letters should be sent to all groups not represented at the first meeting. These organizations will be urged to be represented at the second meeting.

- The first order of business at the second meeting should be the presentation of the report from the first subcommittee. This should be in considerable detail, and any modifications in the original proposal should be thoroughly explained. Following discussion, the citizens' committee should vote on the proposal. If the vote is overwhelmingly favorable, the committee can proceed to organize as a working committee to assist in planning and conducting the campaign. If any appreciable number of people oppose the issue, the committee should be asked to continue its study of the problem. Anyone unwilling to accept the recommendation of the subcommittee should be asked to serve on this study group.

Other subcommittees usually formed to assist in carrying out specific tasks of a bond campaign are those on finance, endorsements, speakers, printed materials, newspaper publicity, and radio and television publicity. Ordinarily, a steering committee is also selected to coordinate campaign activities.

OTHER PARTICIPANTS

Certain individuals and groups play important roles in school bond elections. Among these are board members, school administrators, teachers, students, and parent–teacher associations.

Members of the Board of Education

The board of education, of course, is responsible for officially determining the amount of the school bond issue and for authorizing the holding of an election. Its responsibility does not end at this point, however. Board members are also responsible for doing everything in their power to ensure that a vigorous campaign is waged. They should be involved at every step. They should assist the superintendent, the school staff, and the citizens' advisory committee in planning the campaign and they should volunteer their services to the speakers' bureau and other committees that can benefit from their talents. The board should constantly strive to build a climate of confidence and trust by conducting most business at public meetings, with a minimum number of executive meetings. Board members should remember that their friends and neighbors can learn from them what the needs of the schools are. Some studies indicate that board members' neighbors fail to vote in school finance elections because they lack sufficient information about the finance issue; their board member friend never discussed the subject with them.

School Administrators

All school administrators have made friends in the community and have an even larger number of people who respect their opinions as educators. They should be totally aware of the bond issue facts before they are made public, and all employees should be extended this courtesy. This is good for morale, and it helps the campaign effort as this information is disseminated to other people who assume that the employees know what they are talking about. Principals enjoy a special position with the neighborhoods they serve. They should establish a communications network with parents and others in the immediate community. This network might include a weekly lunch with a different group of six or eight people. It might include an informal newsletter or an occasional principal's forum held to encourage feedback and discussion with parents and others. Whatever the communications channels are, they should be employed to inform people about the bond issue.

Teachers

The role to be played by teachers in school finance elections is still a topic for discussion among school officials. Yet many leaders of teachers' associations agree that teachers can play an integral role in gaining public support for the budget or bond issue. Teachers' salaries command a large portion of the school budget; therefore, many school officials feel that it makes sense for the teachers' association to campaign for the passage of the budget. Others argue that ostentatious efforts by teachers might backfire if taxpayers interpret such efforts as self-serving. A national teachers' group suggests that it is not a question of whether teachers should participate in a school tax campaign but, rather, in what way.

Understandably, teachers would like to be part of the planning group that determines what the building will be like. Frequently, they can suggest changes that will make the building more functional and also save taxpayers money. In any event, teachers who participate in planning the building can be expected to support its needs more than those who play a spectator role. Teachers' associations can be of appreciable assistance during the campaign. Some associations have members who possess expertise in bond issue campaigns and also have access to excellent bond issue materials prepared by state and national teacher associations. The school officials who minimize the role to be played by teachers do the campaign a major disservice.

Students

When most educators consider the role of students in finance campaigns, they think of the ways students can help sell the building needs to the community. This is a difficult area, at best. Using students to sell school needs—unless the students, themselves, organize—can provoke negative reactions from taxpayers. It is generally felt that students should not be used to distribute campaign literature or to make posters in art classes, for example. A contribution often made by students without any prodding takes place at public hearings. Often students will testify at public hearings about the need for more space, citing specifics that only they can fully realize.

Too many schools neglect an important educational responsibility with respect to students and their understanding of school finance elections. Somewhere, in every curriculum, an opportunity should be included for students to understand how public schools are supported. Every high school graduate should know how local schools are financed. High school students who are 18 years old should be encouraged to register to vote. Most young voters pay no property taxes and therefore do not feel the impacts of increased taxes mandated by a positive vote on election day. Election results indicate that most 18-year-olds vote for school finance needs.

Parent–Teacher Associations

Strong support for school bond proposals is likely to come from parent–teacher association members. For this reason, school administrators should engage them early and seek their aid at every stage of the campaign. Following is a list of suggested ways to use the aid of parent–teacher association members:

- Invite every parent–teacher association unit within the district to be represented on the citizens' advisory committee.
- Arrange through the district council to have meetings of all units. Administrators, board of education members, and district council officers should plan the programs for these meetings.
- Invite the parent–teacher association to assist in carrying on the registration campaign.
- Invite the parent–teacher association to make periodic surveys in all attendance areas of the school district to determine the number of preschool children in each area.
- Ask the parent–teacher association to help in preparing campaign materials and related online content, assembling speakers' kits, addressing postcards and letters, taking notes

at meetings, and duplicating and distributing minutes.

- Ask the parent–teacher association to organize and conduct the house-to-house canvass, if this technique is employed in the campaign.
- Ask the parent–teacher association to organize election day tasks, such as driving voters to the polls.

KNOW COMMUNITY THINKING BEFORE AN ELECTION

After determining which groups can help in the campaign and the roles they can play, an early step should be finding out the community's thoughts and opinions regarding the need for the building. Too often school officials conduct surveys after elections to discover why the referendum failed. It is wiser to survey well before the elections to determine the best kind of campaign to wage. Surveys can elicit useful information regarding how much people know about the building, specific objections to the referendum, unanswered questions, and misinformation. Given this information, school officials can plan a campaign that answers the community's questions and helps eliminate misinformation. If, for instance, the survey reveals that a large segment of the community feels that additions to existing buildings would be preferred to a new building, much of the campaign will have to be directed to demonstrating that additions were fully considered but rejected. Reasons for rejection must be clearly stated and the rationale for the new building shown. School officials, acting on information from a survey, might want to reconsider their proposal before making the commitment on a referendum.

A survey can be conducted by the advisory committee, by the PTA, by service groups, or by school officials. It can be sent to all homes or to a sample of the community. The survey can also be done in personal or phone interviews, both of which lead to a solid percentage of response. If a written questionnaire is distributed, most public relations practitioners agree that the results should be made public. Hiding the results arouses suspicion, and suspicions and doubts are to be avoided at all costs. (See Chapter 3 for information on surveys.)

ADOPTING A THEME OR SLOGAN

Many public relations experts claim that a slogan or theme that captures public attention can serve as a plus for the campaign. It must be remembered, however, that a poorly chosen slogan can be a disadvantage. What works in one community could miss completely in another because of the different makeup of the public being served. If a theme is used, it should honestly represent what the referendum is all about. It should ideally focus on students and should somehow imply benefit for the community and, if possible, for the voter. The slogan should help voters remember the issue and the way that the educators would like them to vote.

Many campaigns are based on instilling fear; slogans such as "Save Our Schools" imply that ruin or disaster is imminent if the building is not approved. Yet, following a defeat, the schools will continue to service children, perhaps in a less ideal way than if the building had been approved, but nevertheless in a way avoiding the ruin implied by the slogan. Slogans based on confidence and hope are usually more effective than those prompting fear. A campaign can effectively put across positive feelings in many ways—emphasizing a better curriculum, new kinds of learning resources, or more facilities for more people to use more frequently.

Certain statements lend themselves to positive impact, again depending on the public receiving the communications. Some worth considering for a building campaign follow:

- To parents, the public school represents their children's future; for all citizens, it represents the welfare of our country.
- Good schools produce taxpayers, not tax users.
- Poor schools are the most expensive tax burden.
- The schools belong to the people, and they must answer to the children.
- Inflation affects schools, too.

Remember that few people are antichildren, and most Americans believe in the value of education. Thus, educators have a solid ground on which to build a campaign. Parents, especially, find themselves caught between two of their prized possessions: their children and their money. If they believe that the referendum will help their children learn better, usually they will opt for their children over the money.

PERSONALIZING A CAMPAIGN

Too often administrators prepare a campaign aimed at a mass audience that doesn't exist. Although certain materials (online content, newsletters, brochures, etc.) sometimes have to be written for the general audience, much of the campaign should be developed for specific targeted audiences. The first rule of any effective communication is to *know your audience.* In the case of a campaign, this can be interpreted as meaning "Show voters how the referendum will help them in some way." Although many voters join the yes column because they are sold on the educational soundness of the proposal, many others are prompted to vote yes by one small phase of the building program. The following questions might be heard outside almost any polling place on referendum day: "Where do I vote on remodeling the middle school?" "Is this where I vote on building a new high school?" Many people are motivated by some personal need that will be met by having the building constructed.

"What's in it for me?" is the question many people ask themselves before committing themselves to a higher tax payment. School officials should make every effort to show how the new building will favorably affect different kinds of people. An early part of the campaign planning should be devoted to listing the various organizations and how they might benefit from the building. Similar lists should be developed for groups of people: the Golden Agers, the young voters, and so on.

KEEP IT SIMPLE

As in all communications from school to home, the message should be prepared in easy-to-understand language. This means eliminating educational gobbledygook and long polysyllabic sentences. Many taxpayers are befuddled by the conflicting tax increase information that is spread a few days before the election. To avoid this kind of confusion, educators should distribute simple fact sheets that clearly state the resulting tax increase if the referendum is approved. This means including an average house in the community, giving its market value, and the tax increase. Such specifics negate ill-founded rumors that invariably occur late in the campaign.

The basic facts are usually sufficient for most voters. The traditional pie charts, graphs, and in-depth statistics are noticed by few readers and understood by fewer. Some campaigns have effectively used a gimmick for visual impact to communicate costs. One community used a pound of coffee in all literature, and speakers carried a pound of coffee to all meetings. This communicated that the cost to the average homeowner would be a pound of coffee a week. It is also important to explain what the new building will mean to the community. Lower maintenance costs should be communicated as well as increased community use of facilities.

WORKING WITH THE NEWS MEDIA

As noted, rapport with media representatives should be established before the campaign. The daily and weekly newspapers are, in most communities, the main source of media news, both in print and online, about the referendum. Superintendents who enjoy a sound relationship with local editors enhance their chances of gaining favorable editorials for the building. Early in the campaign, the superintendent or campaign director should meet with all editors to talk informally about the building and what it can offer the community. Such a meeting can encourage editors to check with school officials before printing negative editorials.

A series of articles prepared for all area newspapers about the building needs would be welcomed by many newspapers. Although some daily newspapers won't find room for them, they nevertheless should receive them. Weekly newspapers usually thrive on such information. Stories concerning the needs of the school district should begin appearing many months before the election; in fact, they should appear before the election is even announced. A survey focused on preschool children that would indicate future increases in enrollment can be the subject for one or several stories. Reports by the superintendent of schools to the board of education on enrollment trends, overcrowded classrooms, and dangerous or outmoded physical conditions in the schools should be publicized. Planned, continual newspaper publicity will furnish voters with an adequate background regarding the school district's needs and will thus make the proposal to meet these needs more acceptable.

The appointment of the citizens' committee and its discussions and actions are newsworthy. If the newspapers have no representation on the committee, appoint someone capable of covering meetings of the committee and writing stories for the press. Develop a story on every talk made before service clubs and other community groups. Report each endorsement voted by an organization. Submit architects' sketches of proposed buildings, charts, graphs, and pictures for use by newspapers.

Capitalize on the community grapevine by working with key communicators to share information and dispel incorrect rumors during the campaign. Letters to the editor will be written by those opposed to the bond issue; school campaigners should have people writing letters of support for the bond issue throughout the campaign. Key communicators can play a major role here.

Radio and television stations should also be contacted early in the campaign with requests to help disseminate information. In most cases radio and television stations may be willing to assist school administrators in planning informational programs, public service announcements, and other types of informational content, such as podcasts or online video and audio. Radio call-in shows should be listened to in order to determine concerns of taxpayers regarding the referendum. In addition, school officials should appear, if possible, on community shows that allow questions to be called in. Cable television can be beneficial in many communities. As is the case with radio, materials must be prepared professionally because the reputation of the station, as well as the school, is involved. For help, check with the staff of the stations. If television is available, an effective program could be a brief video reviewing the school system's budget or referendum needs followed by a half hour or more of telephone calls from viewers with questions to be answered on the spot by school officials.

PUBLICATIONS CAN HELP

Online information and informational brochures are essential to informing voters about the campaign's key issues. Informational brochures should be distributed to all registered voters of the district by e-mail, mail, or house-to-house canvass. Brochures and online information should be attractive and easy to read but should not appear to be expensive. They should briefly explain the needs, the proposals for meeting these needs, and the cost to the average taxpayer. All materials should be prepared by someone who knows how to design effective publications and online content. Architects' renderings should be seriously considered before being used; often they contain embellishments that will not appear when the building is erected. And those embellishments (a lake or wooded surroundings) could lead readers to conclude that a palace instead of a school is being proposed.

In informational material for the campaign, children should be featured. Too many school materials exclude pictures of what schools are all about: children. Parents especially appreciate photographs of children in schools. Publications and other materials should present information honestly and provide voting information, including a sample ballot. Addresses should be given for new residents who won't know the locations of polling places. Phone numbers of school officials and advisory group members should be included to encourage people with questions to call them. In at least one publication, alternative plans considered to meet space needs should be shown and the reasons for their rejection given.

SPEAKERS' BUREAU

A speakers' bureau should be organized as soon as the school bond election has been announced. The person designated to coordinate the activities of campaign speakers should be certain that speakers are thoroughly familiar with all aspects of the proposal. Informational kits, therefore, should be carefully prepared. Briefing sessions should be scheduled. Visual materials such as PowerPoint presentations, slides, charts, videos, and pictures should be furnished. Don't ask for volunteers; instead select only those board members, administrators, and laypersons who speak effectively.

As noted, it is important to contact every local organization as early in the campaign as possible and endeavor to schedule a speaker for each one. Request each unit of the parent–teacher association to arrange for a meeting during the campaign when a speaker or a panel of speakers may discuss the school bond proposal. Arrange for talks broadcast online or over radio and television stations. Video or audio of such presentation might also be posted online for later viewing. Prepare special letters to all religious leaders of the community inviting their support as "speakers" for the referendum.

ENDORSEMENTS

Obtaining endorsements from community organizations can be an effective campaign technique. These endorsements, often received after a speakers' bureau representative has talked at a meeting of the organization, can help in three ways. First, they communicate to members who missed the meeting that their organization is behind the referendum. Second, publicizing each endorsement can cause a bandwagon effect on the part of the community. Third, toward the end of the campaign, a list of organizations supporting the building can be distributed, communicating to the community that a broad spectrum of the district is behind the proposal.

SMALL-GROUP MEETINGS

The small-group meeting has met with much success in many school districts. This kind of get-together allows 6 to 10 people to meet with a school official or a representative of the citizens' advisory committee to discuss the bond issue. Such meetings can be held in homes of parents and other concerned taxpayers. Questions asked at the first few meetings might provide material for an inexpensive question-and-answer sheet to be distributed later to all residents. Questions that cannot be answered by school representatives at the meetings should be answered the next day by phone. Parents who are working during the day, when most such meetings are usually held, might want to attend an evening meeting. Such meetings are conducive to attitude change and allow the all-important process of two-way communication to occur; when well organized, they reach large numbers of people and contribute much to the success of the campaign.

EXAMPLE OF A FINANCIAL COMMUNICATION CAMPAIGN

Although there often is great focus on communication when schools face the challenge of seeking voter approval on specific financial needs, ongoing communication to seek public understanding of and support on key school funding issues is essential.

One such campaign, recognized by a Gold Medallion Award from NSPRA, is a School Advocacy Campaign by the Queensbury (New York) Union Free School District. A summary of its campaign follows.

CAMPAIGN OVERVIEW

Even after a successful budget vote in May 2012, members of the Queensbury Board of Education knew the district faced an ongoing fiscal challenge: Costs would continue to rise for the foreseeable future while aid reductions and tax levy legislation restricted revenue growth. Since 2009, the district had cut 75 staff positions, classes at the middle and high schools, and services for students at all grade levels. Continued reductions were not a viable long-term solution to the problem, so school leaders turned to advocacy to seek relief from the mandates driving up the cost of education.

Under the direction of the school board and superintendent, the district's public information specialist developed a strategy to increase the strength, frequency, and effectiveness of local school advocacy efforts. A district-hosted summer advocacy workshop gave board members from throughout the region an opportunity to expand their knowledge of the issues and strengthen their advocacy skills. The local school board then adopted three advocacy priorities, which were shared during a fall advocacy workshop for community members. Workshop participants received tool kits, sample letters, and other resources designed to make advocacy less intimidating.

Advocacy messaging was later incorporated into two community forums held in conjunction with the winter budget development process. It was also included in letters to legislators and promoted on the district website and Facebook page throughout the year. Workshop exit polls, news coverage, and verbal feedback from legislators and community members indicate that these efforts were helping increase local school advocacy. The district also received significantly more aid in the adopted state budget than originally anticipated, a feat attributed in part to advocacy with local legislators.

RESEARCH

In May 2012, voters in Queensbury Union Free School District passed the proposed 2013–14 school budget by 75 percent.

Although members of the Queensbury Board of Education were happy the budget met with voter approval, they were concerned that for the fourth straight year the district had to reduce programs, services, and staff—down by 13.4 percent at that point. Many reductions took advantage of attrition and declining enrollment, but school board members knew they could no longer just "trim around the edges."

Long-range school budget projections showed the cost of educating local students would continue to rise for the foreseeable future. At the same time, state and federal budget projections indicated total school aid for Queensbury would remain relatively flat or decrease in the coming years. Combined with the new tax levy limit legislation, that meant the school board wouldn't likely encounter enough of a revenue increase to avoid future reductions.

That knowledge led the school board to look at the issue of mandate relief. A state survey of school districts found that of the 151 mandates that "represent the greatest challenges to districts in terms of financial burden and required time," 69 percent come with no funding. New York also has 227 distinct special education mandates above and beyond those required by federal law, one of the reasons it ranks first in the nation for per-pupil instructional expenses.

For decades, school and state leaders have discussed, researched, and reported on how to reduce mandates for school districts and subsequently reduce taxes. Very few proposals have actually been enacted; in fact, the governor, Board of Regents, and state and federal governments regularly enact new mandates that districts must follow. In Queensbury, the school board decided it must become a stronger advocate for mandate relief and inspire its community to do the same.

Most of the district's key stakeholders currently hold its academic, co-curricular and extracurricular programs in high esteem, as was evident in the comments received during a series of community forums in 2011 and 2012. It was also evident in the May 2012 budget vote exit survey results. With 72 percent of the 1,659 voters participating in the survey, 64 percent gave the district an A grade for the quality of education and 31 percent gave it a B grade.

So Queensbury schools already benefit from a great deal of community support. To help the district employ this support in seeking relief from state and federal mandates, the public information specialist laid out the following objectives:

- To increase local public awareness of the negative impact of the cost of mandates on the Queensbury school budget, and as a result, on programs and services for students
- To increase the number of individuals advocating for mandate relief on behalf of Queensbury schools
- To have local legislators introduce or support legislation that would provide significant mandate relief.

ANALYSIS/PLANNING

In May 2012, the public information specialist began developing a formal advocacy campaign for the school district. That campaign was outlined in an annual communications plan for the district and in mini-communications plans geared toward specific advocacy events. Those plans were developed in conjunction with the review of a variety of advocacy resources, tips, and materials (used by other school districts and state-level advocacy groups) that identified best practices that could be used to meet the Queensbury objectives. The public information specialist relied on peers within the education communications field to help vet and strengthen her plans and materials as well as to assist with various advocacy events.

The public information specialist also assisted the superintendent in his work with the school board to develop its advocacy priorities. After coming up with a lengthy list, the school board narrowed it down to three key advocacy issues that were important and feasible to address. The public information specialist researched the issues and developed materials to succinctly explain them to community members. Those materials helped guide future decisions about which issues to focus on during the advocacy campaign.

COMMUNICATION/IMPLEMENTATION

In August 2012, Queensbury hosted a school board advocacy workshop that was coordinated by the district public information specialist in conjunction with the public relations specialist from a bordering school district. A personalized invitation was extended via

(continued)

e-mail and mail to the school boards and administrators of all districts within the local Board of Cooperative Educational Services (BOCES).

Nearly 50 school board members and administrators from six different school districts took part in the event. Guest speakers from the Capital Region BOCES Communications Service and the New York State Council of School Superintendents delivered presentations on advocacy skills and working with state legislators. Participants then took part in an advocacy skills/mixer session where they could visit six different advocacy skills stations, each with a 30-inch-x-40-inch display board and a variety of relevant handouts. They also received an advocacy tool kit, a local legislator profiles packet, and a link to the Queensbury advocacy webpage, where they could find more advocacy information throughout the year.

In November 2012, Queensbury hosted an advocacy forum for the wider community. The district sent personal invitations to 143 people, including local business leaders, senior citizens, politicians, and concerned citizens who had attended previous community forums. The district also mailed a flier to all student households and promoted the event on its website, on its Facebook page, in a fall newsletter, via releases carried in local newspapers, and on the plasma monitors in school lobbies. More than 70 people attended the event, including district residents, residents from neighboring school districts, and a local legislator. The forum began with an opening presentation by the superintendent and concluded with an open discussion. Participants were able to view the advocacy display boards and received updated versions of the advocacy resources used at the summer workshop. In particular, they were asked to immediately contact their congressional representatives about the federal sequester, which threatened to take effect in January and cut school aid.

In late January 2013, the district held the first of two community forums as part of its annual budget development process. The district again extended personal invitations and spread the word via various print and online methods. About 30 people took part in the forum, which included discussions on the school board's advocacy priorities and participants' willingness to advocate on behalf of Queensbury schools. Participants also received signature-ready advocacy letters addressed to the governor as well as state and federal representatives. In March 2013, the district held a second community forum that again weaved advocacy messages into budget development information. A personalized invitation that addressed the topic

of advocacy went out to more than 1,200 Queensbury homes, and 50 people attended the forum.

Throughout the school year, the public information specialist assisted the superintendent with other advocacy activities, such as reaching out to local legislators via letters, e-mails, phone calls, and in-person visits.

EVALUATION

Exit polls conducted after each of the four major events have helped the school board, superintendent, and public information specialist evaluate the success of the advocacy campaign. The following are some of those exit poll findings:

- Prior to the school board advocacy workshop, the majority of the survey respondents were not confident in their ability to be effective advocates. After the workshop, 100 percent of respondents felt more confident in their ability to be effective advocates.
- The same finding held true at the advocacy forum in November. Only 58 percent of respondents were confident in their ability to be effective advocates prior to the forum, but 91 percent felt more confident afterward.
- At the March forum, 100 percent of respondents indicated they would participate in a similar meeting next year.
- Based on verbal feedback from legislators and legislative aides, the advocacy campaign, in conjunction with regional advocacy efforts, ultimately helped secure significantly more state aid for Queensbury schools than originally anticipated.
- These efforts are believed to have helped pave the way for improvements in the Gap Elimination Adjustment, the passage of fewer unfunded mandates (so far), and the provision of a modest pension stabilization option for schools.
- Aspects of the school board's advocacy priorities remain unaddressed, so the public information specialist will continue to explore new ways to mobilize the community around school advocacy. Though no one district can shift legislative will, the superintendent and school board believe that adding their voices and those of the greater Queensbury community to regional and statewide advocacy efforts will ultimately be effective.

Source: Reprinted with permission from Queensbury Union Free School district. ■

One Expert's Point of View: School Finance Communication

Kelly Avants, APR, is Chief Communications Officer for the Clovis (CA) Unified School District (http://www.cusd.com/). The district comprises 32 elementary schools, five intermediate schools, five high schools, one adult school, and six alternative education campuses serving nearly 43,000 students with a staff of about 5,000 full- and part-time certificated and classified employees. Avants has also served on the board of directors of the National School Public Relations Association (NSPRA) and the California School Public Relations Association (CalSPRA) and has contributed to a number of NSPRA publications.

What are some of the issues a communication planner should consider when a school district begins planning for financial communication programming?

Financial communication programming should be considered within the framework of ongoing, regular school communication programming. There are many issues to consider. For example, schools and their communities are always evolving. Media and the channels through which people exchange information are constantly changing. And the many forces that shape the ways in which people think about and act toward institutions such as schools are always developing.

All of these issues matter because they affect the level of trust—or skepticism—that audiences may have in their schools and the people who lead them. Schools need to develop strong community trust and support before they can begin to think about successfully taking financial initiatives, such as a bond issue or tax increase proposal, to the voters. Long-term, two-way communication is key to building the kind of working relationships between the school and community that result in understanding and trust. Therefore, it's important to consider financial communication planning in the overall context of comprehensive, school communication planning.

Where communities are already engaged, school districts will find greater support and understanding for the wide variety of issues, including financial issues, that can suddenly challenge schools and their leaders at any time.

In an era of social media and other online communication options, how important are traditional communication tactics in financial communication efforts?

They're essential. It is true that social media, websites, and other digital media have become very efficient ways in which to deliver large amounts of data and content to audiences. But you will need advocates and champions in the community who are willing to vocally support financial initiatives to be successful. Relationships like these are only built through more traditional forms of communication, face-to-face interactions, and time. This means meeting with people throughout the community remains critical. Talking with and listening to people is a vital part of the process.

Old-school, face-to-face communication continues as one of the most effective means of communication. Engaging with internal and external audiences also can help to identify areas of concern that must be addressed before, during, and after financial communication efforts are implemented. To find success at the polls, there is no substitute for on-going, authentic, and direct dialogues between schools and their communities.

How important is research focusing on financial issues to the planning and communication process?

There is no shortcut to doing the kind of research essential to communication planning, especially when considering financial issues.

Understanding where the community stands now is essential to building the kind of communication that will bring them to the place they need to be to support any financial initiative. A successful campaign needs to project a single, clear vision that the community can support and be enthusiastic about. Community insights and input, gathered as part of a transparent research and planning process, is an essential part of tapping into and fostering the kind of community trust and support that any financial communication effort needs to be successful.[3]

Questions

1. Explain the importance of understanding your state's laws on what school districts can and can't do when running campaigns for and communicating about financial elections.
2. List the benefits of ongoing communication on school finance issues as opposed to only communicating during times when a vote is near.
3. Why is it important to involve all taxpayers, not just parents, in the schools?
4. Why is it important to keep a focus on children and benefits when developing informational material for finance campaigns?
5. How can partnerships with businesses, civic groups, or other community organizations be helpful when trying to communicate various school budget and finance issues?

Readings

Brimley, Vern, Deborah A. Verstegen, and Ruland R. Garfield, *Financing Education in a Climate of Change*, 11th ed. Boston, MA: Pearson, 2012.

Campbell, Gay, "Bond Issue and Levy Elections," *School Public Relations*, 2nd ed. Rockville, MD: National School Public Relations Association, 2007.

National School Public Relations Association, "Campaign Planning for a Successful Bond Election," *NSPRA This Week*. Rockville, MD: Author, November 7, 2017, p. 1.

National School Public Relations Association, "Financial Support Depends on Ongoing Communication," *Network*. Rockville, MD: Author, November 2005.

National School Public Relations Association, *Election Success: Proven Strategies for Public Finance Campaigns*. Rockville, MD: Author, 2007.

National School Public Relations Association, *Grassroots Organizing Toolkit*. Rockville, MD: Author, 2012.

National School Public Relations Association, "Surviving Financial Tough Times: Good Communication Remains Key," *Network*. Rockville, MD: Author, February 2004.

Videos

Adams 12 Five Star Schools (CO): Bond Approval Thank You
https://youtu.be/eImaPHoVoCM
Adams 12 Five Star Schools (CO): Funding Challenges
https://youtu.be/6zM8QRzmOP0
Fairfax County (VA) Public Schools: An Explanation of the Budget
https://youtu.be/yiPyj62qKUY
Community Unit School District 200 (IL): Referendum Overview

https://youtu.be/xsrVN1P0sdM
Questar III BOCES (NY): Brunswick CSD Capital Project Video
https://youtu.be/FxYMpL2cyqg
Capital Region BOCES (NY): School Budgets 101 Video
https://youtu.be/BRdNgyG_jmM
Plano (TX) ISD: Bond Election Overview Video
https://youtu.be/kwMOd0qX8-s

Endnotes

1. Brimley, Vern, Deborah A. Verstegen, and Ruland R. Garfield, *Financing Education in a Climate of Change*, 11th ed. (Boston, MA: Pearson, 2012), pp. 45–46.
2. National School Public Relations Association, "Grassroots Organizing Toolkit." (Rockville, MD: Author, 2012), p. 7.
3. Reproduced with Permission from personal correspondence December 12, 2017 with Kelly Avants, Chief Communications Officer, Clovis (CA) Unified School District.

15

Communication Assessment and Accountability

This chapter reviews issues ...

■ For central administrators: Methods for comprehensive communication research, planning, and activities to align programming with accepted practices and to document accountability for meaningful outcomes.

■ For building and program administrators: The ways in which school administrators can develop and assess program communication in line with the district's mission and overall strategic and communication objectives.

■ For teachers, counselors, and staff: How school employees can contribute to communication about school functions in their areas of responsibility and the links between that communication and student success.

After completing this chapter you should be able to ...

■ Distinguish how accountability for school–community relations investments can be established by appropriate assessment of communication and engagement efforts.

■ Define the ways in which school–community relations results can be documented.

■ Describe how school–community relations outcomes can be linked to both school and student success.

■ Identify the research tactics that can be used to assess school–community relations programming.

Leaders and employees in organizations of all types—including school systems—face increasing demands to document accountability for institutional and personal performance and results. Also, as technology drives the ability to compile and assess data, simple observations of work output and descriptions of perceived accomplishments increasingly do not suffice as true measurements of accountability. Boards, elected officials, and school stakeholders increasingly are seeking hard evidence of returns on investments in the education enterprise.

Accountability, however, has long posed a dilemma for communication programming and practitioners. While research overwhelmingly shows support by practitioners for accountability in communication practice, there is no universal agreement on just how accountability should be tracked and assessed.

There are, however, several common areas that should be included when measuring communication accountability in schools:

– *Communication planning.* This increasing demand for accountability in education mandates ongoing research, comprehensive planning, and formal evaluation for school and community relations programming. These efforts should establish measurable, programmatic objectives, as well as the benchmarks against which progress toward meeting the objectives will be measured.

– *Tax investments.* School–community relations programs consume both financial and human resources. It's important to remember that in many communities the school district may be the largest consumer of local and state tax dollars. Accountability efforts, therefore, should align specific, measurable outcomes with communication activities to assess how efficiently these investments have performed, and to suggest ways in which ongoing efforts might be made more efficient.

– *Community engagement.* Given the link between student achievement and community engagement and support, accountability efforts should assess the types of parental and community engagement and support that the school–community relations program engenders. Program assessment should document the role communications have played in supporting this kind of relationship building and the resulting student and school achievements.

IDENTIFY ACCOUNTABILITY MARKERS

There are numerous characteristics to be identified and quantified when seeking to assess school-communication accountability. Among them:

– Effective community-relations planning generally is described as outlining research-based, objective-driven programming that includes ongoing, measurable activities supporting transparent, two-way communication between the school system and key audiences—internal and external. Communication plans also should be linked to a district's strategic plan and designed to help the school system reach its strategic mission and goals. Such coordination can enhance the efficiency and effectiveness of the communications effort by providing a framework for evaluating potential communication activities in terms of how well they will support the objectives of the strategic plan. This structure can also offer benchmarks for demonstrating accountability by aligning with evaluation criteria in the strategic plan. Increasingly, in efforts to enhance transparency and accountability, school systems are posting their communication planning and assessment documents online for community review.

– Planning, monitoring, and evaluative communication research should be used to aid communication planners in identifying audiences, their information needs, communication preferences, and aspirations for school and community success. And such research should then measure how well communication activities functioned to build understanding, support, and engagement between schools and the community.

– Communication programming should be reinforced by board policies supporting open communication efforts. In addition, it should be reinforced by school and program executives, managers, and employees who have been supported with communication training and who have specific communication roles outlined in their areas of expected job performance.

– Comprehensive communication programming should include a wide range of two-way communication tactics to deliver and reinforce key messages to audiences and receive feedback and insights from them. Such programming generally includes print and online communications; social media programming; news and publicity activities; and presentations, meetings, and other face-to-face communication activities. It also incorporates such planned programming at the school and program level in addition to district-wide programming.

– Comprehensive communication programming also accommodates the special programmatic needs beyond the many day-to-day communication demands of running schools and programs. Such programming, for example, considers the school district's and community's communication needs related to crisis communication, marketing and customer communication, financial communication, employee relations, and so on.

Some specific metrics, for example, that may be tied to targeted community relations activities could include:

– Graduation rates
– Remediation rates
– Student attendance rates
– Parent participation rates
– School violence, bullying, and other safety trends
– School volunteer, mentorship, and business co-op activities
– New student recruitment and retention trends
– New employee recruitment and retention trends
– School foundation and other fundraising results.

The National School Public Relations Association has developed *Rubrics of Practice and Suggested Measures*, which offers rubrics and sample measurements for what it calls "critical function areas." Included among the critical function areas are Comprehensive Professional Communication Program; Internal Communications; and Parent/Family Communications.[1] (For more information see https://www.nspra.org/e_network/2013-12_leading_off.)

In *Experiences of Texas Public School Communication Directors in the 21st Century: A Phenomenological Study*, Sonja Lopez notes that two sets of standards were prominent among school communication professionals interviewed for the study: The

Professional Standards for Educational Leaders (PSEL) (http://www.ccsso.org/Documents/2015/Professional StandardsforEducationalLeaders2015forNPBEAFI-NAL.pdf) adopted by the National Policy Board for Educational Administration, and criteria developed by the National School Public Relations Association (https://www.nspra.org/files/docs/StandardsBooklet.pdf).

Lopez reported, "The communication directors discussed the large amount of time they spent promoting alignment of the district vision and initiatives," in line with both PSEL and NSPRA standards.

Study participants also commented on the importance of using multiple methods of information dissemination and a variety of communication channels to promote the district, practices that also align with standards. "NSPRA's criteria specifically suggested school public relations professionals engage in multiple methods of communication with all stakeholders."[2]

School leaders also have a particular role in supporting communication accountability and helping to model communication practices and provide leadership for community relations success.

The use of communication and the technology that supports it are key traits considered by the National School Public Relations Association when assessing nominees for its "Superintendents to Watch" award program. The organization looks, for example, at how superintendents have implemented a district communication program that integrates new communication technology with "more standard communication tools"; have integrated district communication goals and strategies with the district's strategic plan; and have been personally and visibly engaged in the communication effort.[3]

Among the abilities evaluated by *eSchool News* in seeking leading superintendents for its "Tech-Savvy Superintendent Award" are the superintendents' ability to understand the role of technology in education and articulate that understanding to all school district stakeholders; ability to model the effective use of technology; and curiosity and open-mindedness in considering emerging technologies and weighing non-traditional solutions.[4]

In interviews conducted with 17 superintendents who had been named "Superintendent of the Year" by the American Association of School Administrators, a survey by the National School Public Relations Association found that the majority (16) of them reported that "effective communications has a 'significant' impact on the success of moving the district's vision forward." Among the study's conclusions was an observation that successful superintendents "clearly and consistently point to the critical contribution of communications to student success, realizing the district's vision, and successful leadership of a school district."[5]

RESEARCH TO DOCUMENT RESULTS

The role of research in school–community relations programming is perhaps too often viewed as a key part of the planning process. However, ongoing research is essential in all phases of school communication efforts.

Research does play a crucial role in initial planning activities. It is essential to document the current state of communication and understanding among key school constituencies. It also helps school leaders better understand how people receive and process information about schools. Initial planning research also provides clues to the types of communication strategies, tactics, and messages that will succeed in improving understanding of and support for schools and their programs.

Once a program is planned, however, the need for ongoing research remains essential to program assessment and performance. Tracking or monitoring research helps school communication administrators assess programs underway, document how well those efforts are working toward meeting the plan's objectives, and suggest possible adjustments to tactics and strategies to improve performance. In short, a communication plan is always a work in progress—with ongoing assessment and adjustment needed as it is implemented. Initial research in the planning phases may have missed essential insights that become evident as program implementation is monitored. New, emerging issues or unexpected changes in the communication environment also may create the need for midcourse corrections once a plan is underway.

Finally, once a program has been fully implemented, evaluative research is important to accountability for results: *How well did the program work in meeting its stated objectives?* Evaluative assessments also make an important contribution to future planning and communication programming: *What insights from this effort can make future communication efforts more effective and efficient?*

The ongoing role of research—and its importance to assessment and accountability—is circular in nature:

STANDARDS FOR EVALUATION OF SCHOOL PR PROGRAMS

In its publication *Raising the Bar for School PR: New Standards for the School Public Relations Profession*, the National School Public Relations Association (NSPRA) urges the following:

- Every major communication effort is evaluated to determine whether planned goals were met and objectives achieved.
- The organization and each of its units engages in both formal and informal evaluations of its communication practices and the levels of satisfaction with its performance.
- Overall personnel evaluations of district administrators and staff include a component addressing the need for effective internal and external communication practices and the levels of satisfaction with their performance. Job descriptions and regularly developed goals and objectives also include a focus on communication responsibilities.
- Whenever possible, evaluation methods are built into each element of the organization's annual communication plan. These evaluations are used to create, modify, or discontinue practices or projects.
- Each of the organization's regular communication channels and vehicles is evaluated at least every two years to determine its relevance, interest, and ability to communicate important information.

Source: Raising the Bar for School PR: New Standards for the School Public Relations Profession, National School Public Relations Association (www.nspra.org), 15948 Derwood Road, Rockville, MD 20855. Reprinted with permission.

School–community relations programs should be built on a solid foundation of communication research used to formulate specific measurable objectives and the communication efforts that have the best chance to reach them. Once underway, monitoring research helps school communicators assess progress toward those objectives and make changes—based on sound insights and data—that might be needed. When finished, evaluative research provides the data needed to help administrators document the success of communication outputs and the impact on students and schools. These final insights, then, provide a platform for understanding what's needed now and what will work best going forward, and a new communication planning phase begins.

The crucial nature of research in this process is explained in the *School PR Research Primer*:

> Without research, school public relations planners are like a semi-truck driver, careening down a busy highway in a dense fog at 80 miles per hour. As long as the road is straight and everybody else gets out of the way, that truck may reach its destination just fine. But chances are that won't happen. And the resulting wreck, which could have been avoided, will cost money and time that could have been saved. Even worse, the truck, its contents, and its driver, may never get to where they wanted to go.

Research is how school public relations planners can move their programs out of the fog. It is how they build efficiency and effectiveness that can be tracked and measured into their programs. It is how they build real accountability for communications into their programs.

Without the solid data and insights that good research offers, school officials are communicating with no sense of direction or mission. They have no guidance on what messages should be delivered and reinforced—or on what audiences are key targets for those messages.[6]

SUPPORTING COMMUNICATION ACCOUNTABILITY

Despite the commitment in education to research-driven programming in curricular areas, school communication administrators may find support for research efforts in community relations activities lacking. Communication research may be viewed as expensive and time-consuming—something that can't be afforded when there is urgency to act on issues related to school communications and when tight budgets might cause decision makers to think that limited resources might be better dedicated directly to communication rather than research.

In this kind of environment, it's important to stress the integral links between communication research and action. Investments in communication research are, in fact, investments in communication. Without commitments to research, accountability for communication activities cannot be achieved.

In addition, research supporting assessment and accountability need not be costly or time intensive. Appropriate combinations of primary and secondary research—both formal and informal—often can be designed to quickly and efficiently create the benchmarks needed to effectively plan and implement school communication programming.

Just as school leaders review reliable data before making decisions on new educational programs or capital initiatives, they also need to review sound data before making communication investments.

DOCUMENTING OUTCOMES

Accountability for results includes much more than measuring only dissemination issues. Accountability efforts need to go beyond measuring communication tactical outputs and seek to measure behavioral outcomes.

Output *examples:* How many newsletters were mailed? How many viewed the webpage?

Outcome *examples*: How many parents attended the meeting? How many students enrolled in the new program?

EXAMPLE

Suppose research turned up ongoing problems with new-student registration for a district's preschool programs. Parents are confused by deadlines, don't know how to get more information, and often miss opportunities to enroll their children in available programs.

Additional research into the issue suggests that an effective way to address these problems would be to develop a web-based information program for parents of prospective students—and to support it with an informational campaign delivered through traditional news media outlets. Once designed, monitoring assessments as the new effort unfolds might follow traffic at the new website, measure news coverage in local media outlets, review questions coming in from the website and over the telephone, and compare RSVPs for registration meetings with figures from past years.

Final accountability efforts once the program is completed, then, would not only document how many people visited the new website but also show how resulting enrollment figures compare to those of previous years. In other words, did the new communication effort result in increased awareness and understanding of the enrollment process *and* result in increased enrollment?

USING RESEARCH

The following techniques, reported in the *School PR Research Primer*, can be helpful in documenting and assessing the results of school communication activities:

> *Network and literature reviews.* Surveys of members of NSPRA consistently cite networking with other professionals as a key reason people join the group.

IN-DEPTH INTERVIEW OUTLINE: MANAGING ENROLLMENT GROWTH

Example: A school district is suddenly facing an unprecedented surge in enrollment due to rapid new development. It will be building schools and hiring staff faster than at any time in the district's history. In researching these issues to revise their communication plan, school officials come across a school district in a nearby state that has, over the past five years, navigated a similar growth surge. Fortunately, nearly the entire leadership team still is in place. Their experience could be invaluable, so in-depth interviews might be arranged to tap the brains of those who've accomplished what this district now faces.

Here's an example of what an interview outline for an in-depth interview might look like:

1. Tell me about your background. Where did you attend college? What jobs did you hold before this one? How long have you held this position?
2. What is a typical day on the job like?
3. Talk about this school district. Over the last decade it successfully navigated a 50 percent jump in enrollment. What about this district made it capable of managing that kind of challenge?
4. Think back to when you first saw the projections for enrollment growth. Did you believe them? Did you panic? When you walked out of that meeting, what was your number one priority?

5. Communication would seem to be key in this kind of situation. You have new employees to orient, new and veteran residents to keep updated, rumors to manage, change to implement. Walk me through where communication was in your list of priorities and how you planned to manage communication.
6. As the growth came and change unfolded, what areas were you least prepared to handle—and how did you regroup to address them?
7. What areas did you get right? What one or two things do you still think about and feel proud of?
8. How would you describe a typical resident of this community? What are they like? If I ask them about your schools, what would they tell me?
9. It is apparent that schools here enjoy a high level of community support. Why is that? What secrets can you share to help other schools build that kind of understanding and support?
10. How would you advise another district facing this kind of growth? What are the top three things you would want to make sure they understood about your own success with growth?

Source: Reprinted with Permission from Edward H. Moore, *School PR Research Primer* (Rockville, MD: National School Public Relations Association, 2008), p. 9.

The reason for this peer networking. To get a handle on how others have handled similar situations and what their experiences can teach us about what works and what doesn't.

Books, magazines, newsletters, newspapers, reports, and more also can offer insights and advice that may relate to communication issues being researched in any school district. A literature search might focus on general media for insights into how communication issues have been investigated or covered. Or the search might focus more on trade and professional documents that have investigated and reported on relevant communication issues.

Many state and local agencies produce and analyze a variety of reports and studies that can be a help to the school communication researcher. Business groups, such as local and regional chambers of commerce, as well as businesses themselves (major local employers, for example) also might offer data, insights, and trends from economic, development, and other commerce-related issues. Many might have ongoing research projects that a school system could get involved with or cooperate in.

Content analyses. Perhaps the most familiar form of the content analysis in school communication is a study of media coverage. In its simplest form, the content analysis may tally the number of times certain school issues were covered in the local news media. A more complex content analysis might go on to assign values to the coverage—using some qualitative judgments as to how many stories were positive, negative, or neutral. Beyond media coverage, content analyses can also be used when studying the effectiveness of school newsletters, brochures and flyers, websites, and so on.

Focus groups. The focus group has become a staple of much school communication research. Generally, focus groups consist of 5 to 10 individuals who participate in a guided conversation on an issue or set of issues over about an hour. There is no universally accepted number of focus group participants—groups can be as small as 2 or 3, or they can be as large as 20 or more. In general, many focus group facilitators consider a group of 5 to 10 as optimum, given the short period of time devoted to the discussion. There also is no hard-and-fast law on the length of a focus group session. An hour—give or take a few minutes—is preferred by many facilitators. An hour is seen by many as the maximum amount of time you can keep such a group clearly focused on a particular issue.

In-depth interviews. In-depth research interviews generally follow a set script and procedure and delve into significant detail. Although some in-depth interviews may take only a few hours, others may take even more time, depending on the situation—and willingness of participants to sit for them. In-depth interviews are useful when you have individuals whose knowledge and experience can be of extreme value to your communication efforts. (See the "In-Depth Interview Outline: Managing Enrollment Growth" sidebar.)

Informal feedback. Online polling has become common on many websites—including school websites. Although the results of such polls represent only the thinking of those who have participated in them, they can be useful in tracking interest in certain topics as well as the strength of some developing issues. Technology has made the ability to field such polls relatively easy and inexpensive, so school communication researchers, although aware of the limitations of such polls, might consider using them when appropriate. Online tools also offer many other feedback options. Click-to links that can open comment boxes and e-mail blanks offer ways for online visitors to quickly share thoughts and comments with school officials. Websites and e-publications should always take advantage of opportunities to solicit feedback and ideas from visitors on a regular basis.

Observation or contact reports. Formal reporting of observation or contacts tries to bring some order to the informal and formal information exchanges that take place throughout a school system every single day. They might document questions and comments made to those answering school phones—helping to assess the type of inquiries school staff members are faced with and suggesting new messages and tactics to handle them. The reports might also cover questions or other comments heard at various public meetings, such as back-to-school nights or other forums in which question-and-answer sessions can offer insights into areas of concern or information voids that exist among key audiences. These reports need not be complicated nor overly detailed. The objective is to get some basic information to school communication planners so it can serve as a type of early warning system on emerging issues, misinformation, rumors, and so on.

Key communicators. A network of key communicators can be a positive influence throughout an entire school communication program (see Chapter 8 for more on key communicators). *Example:* Rumors can grow and get out of hand and are usually inaccurate. An established system of key communicators helps to keep rumors under control—not only by rapidly communicating the real story behind a growing rumor but also by serving school communicators as a vital feedback link to the community. Key communicators are true two-way communicators. Although they often are thought of as a vehicle for getting information to the community, key communicators also function as research agents, reporting rumors, misinformation, and other important insights that they see and hear throughout the community.

Communication audits. Communication audits combine a number of research tactics to complete a thorough programmatic assessment of communication activities throughout a school system. Auditors, through literature reviews, interviews, and focus groups, analyze current communication efforts. They assess district policies, demographic analyses, communication or marketing plans, internal and external publications, e-newsletters and websites, budgets and expenditures, and other important aspects of the organization and its communication program. Audits often are conducted by independent, external researchers provided through groups such as NSPRA.[7]

Polls and surveys. Polls and surveys, using direct interviews with a sample of a population, are one of the best methods available to school systems for ascertaining whether or not the views and behaviors of citizens on selected problems and issues have changed as a result of communication efforts. The nature and amount of change can best be assessed, with reasonable accuracy, when polls are taken at regular intervals and the findings compared. Polls and surveys can be conducted online, in person, by mail, or over the telephone. (Chapter 3 discusses surveys and their related issues in more detail.)

One Expert's Opinion: School Communication Accountability

Rich Bagin is Executive Director of the National School Public Relations Association (NSPRA). Under his leadership NSPRA and its members have initiated several research and resource initiatives targeted at supporting school-communication accountability. Bagin has worked with hundreds of school districts throughout North America on school communication issues.

A former teacher and school administrator, he is a veteran of more than 30 years in school public relations. He has written and presented extensively on school PR topics. He is the author of the NSPRA book Making Parent Communication Effective and Easy: A Communication Guidebook for Teachers *and an author of and contributor to numerous other NSPRA publications.*

What recent trends has NSPRA been tracking and working to help make school communications more accountable?

Most recently the association and the practice of school public relations has been focused more than ever on finding meaningful ways in which we can collect insights and data to directly document the impact of school-communication investments.

For example, after considerable study and work, NSPRA produced its *Rubrics of Practice and Suggested Measures*. The resource offers school leaders a specific framework to classify various programming components in program planning, internal communication, and parent and family communication as emerging, established, or exemplary, and to create a blueprint for continuous program improvement aligned with best practices.

For many years NSPRA has conducted comprehensive communication audits for school systems. These research efforts continue to help school leaders identify strengths and weaknesses in current programs, through focus-group research, reviews of plans and research, assessments of online and traditional communications, and in-depth interviews with cabinet leaders and board members. Combined with new resources offered in the *Rubrics of Practice and Suggested Measures* these efforts can go even further over time in helping school-communication practitioners to both prove the value of their programming and define ways to make programming even more effective and efficient. These rubrics are also a part of new survey instruments developed by an NSPRA partnership with SCoPE, School Communications Performance Evaluation group, now being offered for NSPRA's Communication Review service.

Advancing education through responsible public relations and communication that support student success is at the core of our mission. Nothing is more important than developing the tools and insights that can help schools support their students as much as possible with proven communication programming that works.

Why has the communication accountability issue been so difficult for schools to manage?

It's not just schools. Historically, all kinds of organizations and the professional associations that represent them have wrestled with the best ways to document communication returns on investments in meaningful, bottom-line ways.

One problem has always been the intangible items that communication can influence, such as trust in the organization or its leaders, for example. There are many ways in which trustworthiness can be measured, but the measurement gets more difficult when you try to tie a current level of trust to specific communication initiatives. So, getting the profession and its practitioners to agree on common methods and rubrics has been a long process that continues.

More than 10 years ago, for example, NSPRA started its Communication Accountability Project to conduct and compile research on the links between school communication, community involvement, and school and student success. There was considerable research available but few places where all of the insights had been compiled in a way that school-communications practitioners could learn and benefit from. The Communication Accountability Program has helped to make that happen.

What have been some of the best insights for schools from these efforts?

The evidence in terms of student success emerged as overwhelming and powerful: Communication is more important than ever. As a result, educational leaders have an obligation to continually assess the effectiveness of their school communication efforts and hold all school staff accountable for communication results.

We found that parents and others in the community want to work with schools. They want to know how they can help children learn more. They want to know what the expectations are for children and how children are progressing. They eagerly seek guidance on helping their children achieve. Engaging with schools and school staff in meaningful ways that will help children become successful is the new top priority for many in the community, and school communication is essential to building effective working relationships between communities and schools.

Research underscored the important benefits of strong working relationships between schools and their communities. Just consider some of the conclusions in the reporting:

- "No longer can an educator get by just slipping a monthly newsletter into the backpack and ensuring that the local paper gets the sports schedule. In an age of instantaneous access and 24/7 demand, schools must be able to manage the flow of information not only from teacher to students sitting in a classroom, but also to parents at the workplace and home. Administrators must be able to handle the news media's asking about incidents texted from student cell phones or to respond to queries about school performance reports posted on the web. School staff must be creative and innovative as the means of communication and the expectations expand rapidly. At a time when school choice, vouchers, and charter schools provide more alternatives for parents, selling a school becomes more of a priority."

- "Communication is the foundation of effective partnerships. To build effective partnerships with families and the community that will enhance student achievement, schools must first talk to—and listen to—parents, community groups, business leaders, and others with a stake in student learning. Any strategy must accommodate the diverse language, cultural needs, lifestyles, and

(continued)

schedules of all parties. This means the school often must take the initiative in reaching out to its community and parents. Successful partnerships require sustained mutual collaboration and support—from school staffs and from families at home, at school, and in the community. It requires a school environment that welcomes its partners and encourages them to raise questions and voice their concerns, as well as to participate appropriately in decision-making."

Some of the research compiled is compelling. For example, research conducted by the founder of Family Friendly Schools, Steve Constantino, a former principal who tracked the trends over four years at one high school as it dealt with increased communication with parents, showed these results:

- Parent satisfaction rose from 34 percent to 59 percent.
- Teacher satisfaction rose from 39 percent to 76 percent.
- The average SAT score rose 61 points, with an 18 percent reduction in disparity between minority and non-minority scores.
- The dropout rate fell from 11 percent to 3 percent.

Is there a financial aspect to the communication accountability as well?

Absolutely. For one thing, as competition for students heats up and more and more school choice options emerge in communities everywhere, financial performance of communication and marketing efforts becomes critically important. Schools without successful programs to promote, without effective marketing communications, without trust in their schools and the employees that run them, will not survive.

NSPRA past president Nora Carr, chief of staff for the Guilford County (NC) Public Schools, advocates that schools calculate the return on their communication investments. For example, she wrote for us:

"It's time we stopped looking at school communications as a luxury that risks the ire of taxpayers and start viewing it as an investment in our children's futures.

"In most districts, if you spend $105,000 on better communications, you only need to recruit 15 kindergartners at $7,000 each in per pupil funding to recoup your investment. If those 15 students stay in your district for 11 more years, that initial investment in school marketing will yield more than $1 million.

"Effective public relations are purposeful, systematic, and measurable. Accountability for results doesn't stop at the school house door."

With the accountability movement affecting schools in many different areas, you've often advocated that the public relations functions in schools might be viewed as the Director of Public Accountability. What do you mean by this?

Effective school communication programs must constantly address public accountability issues for their schools. Accountability is the foundation of credibility and trust for the school system and accountability and trust must be achieved before meaningful working relationships with the community can be forged.

School communication programs and their leaders need to be the trusted resource that parents, taxpayers, employees, the news media, and others in the community go to to learn more about their school district. School communications must be designed to engage staff and community leaders to help them understand and appreciate the complexities of today's schools and to involve them in making their schools better and more accountable on all fronts.

We suggest seven simple steps for all school leaders to start making school communications accountable:

1. Hold yourself responsible for communicating with and engaging your community.
2. Recognize communication as an important management function and hold people accountable for results.
3. Develop a strategic communication plan tied to your district's mission, goals, and objectives.
4. Speak with one clear voice on behalf of your students and schools.
5. Establish a culture of effective, two-way communication and engagement with all stakeholders.
6. Demonstrate accountability through effective school governance standards supported by effective communication.
7. Make decision makers aware of accountability results so they continue a communication commitment for your schools.[8]

Questions

1. Some in the school district's executive cabinet have expressed skepticism about the links between communication and student achievement. Some are arguing that resources are better spent on other priorities than communication. List three key points you'd share to help them better appreciate the links between communication and student success.
2. Some in the community are questioning the superintendent's plan to spend money on communication research as a first step in devising a school communication plan. Explain why conducting such research would be a good

investment for the school system and its students. How might the research also help the district be accountable for future communication investments?
3. The superintendent wants to build a communications component into the evaluation of principals and has enlisted your help. What are three areas in which you might evaluate a principal's communications effectiveness?
4. Explain the importance of assessing communication efforts beyond just the dissemination of information.

Readings

Austin, Erica, and Bruce Pinkleton, *Strategic Communication Management: Planning and Managing Effective Communication Programs*, 3rd ed. Florence, KY: Routledge, 2014.

Bagin, Don, and Anthony Fulginiti, *Practical Public Relations*. Dubuque, IA: Kendall Hunt, 2006.

Cutlip, Scott M., Allen H. Center, and Glen M. Broom, *Effective Public Relations,* 11th ed. Upper Saddle River, NJ: Prentice Hall, 2012.

Institute for Public Relations Commission on Public Relations Measurement and Evaluation, *Guidelines for Setting Measurable Public Relations Objectives: An Update.* Gainesville, FL: Author, 2010.

International Association of Business Communicators, *Best Practices in Communication Planning and Implementation.* San Francisco, CA: Author, 2009.

Moore, Edward H., *The School PR Research Primer.* Rockville, MD: National School Public Relations Association, 2008.

National School Public Relations Association, *Rubrics of Practice and Suggested Measures.* Rockville, MD: Author, 2013.

National School Public Relations Association, *School Public Relations: Building Confidence in Education.* Rockville, MD: Author, 2007.

National School Public Relations Association, *Communication E-Kit for Superintendents.* Rockville, MD: Author, 2013.

Wilcox, Dennis L., and Glen T. Cameron, *Public Relations Strategies and Tactics,* 10th ed. Boston, MA: Pearson Education, 2011.

Endnotes

1. National School Public Relations Association, *Rubrics of Practice and Suggested Measures* (Rockville, MD: Author, 2013), pp. 6, 20, 29.
2. Lopez, Sonja A. "Experiences of Texas Public School Communication Directors in the 21st Century: A Phenomenological Study." Doctoral dissertation, Sam Houston State University, 2017, pp. 103–104.
3. Retrieved from the Internet, Nov. 27, 2017, https://www.nspra.org/superintendents-watch.
4. Retrieved from the Internet, Nov. 27, 2017, https://www.eschoolnews.com/resources-4-2/superintendents-center/tssa/nominate/.
5. Retrieved from the Internet, Nov. 27, 2017, https://www.nspra.org/files/docs/CharacteristicsOfEffectiveSuperintendents.pdf.
6. Edward H. Moore, *School PR Research Primer* (Rockville, MD: National School Public Relations Association, 2008), p. 9.
7. Ibid., pp. 31–52.
8. Taken from correspondence December 5, 2017, with Rich Bagin, Executive Director, National School Public Relations Association, Rockville, MD.

APPENDIX A

Organizations That Could Be Helpful

ASSOCIATION FOR WOMEN IN COMMUNICATIONS

1717 E Republic Rd. Suite A
Springfield, MO 65804
Phone: 417-886-8606
www.womcom.org

The Association for Women in Communications is a professional association whose mission champions the advancement of women across all communications disciplines by recognizing excellence, promoting leadership, and positioning its members at the forefront of the evolving communication era.

NATIONAL SCHOOL PUBLIC RELATIONS ASSOCIATION

15948 Derwood Rd.
Rockville, MD 20855
Phone: 301-519-0496
www.nspra.org

Since 1935 the National School Public Relations Association (NSPRA) has been providing school communication training and services to school leaders throughout the United States, Canada, and the U.S. State Department Overseas Schools worldwide.

NSPRA's mission is to advance education through responsible communication. NSPRA accomplishes that mission by providing diverse services to members and other school leaders.

NSPRA has a number of chapters working with school communication administrators locally. These include:

Alabama School Public Relations Association (ALSPRA) www.alspra.org
Arizona School Public Relations Association (ASPRA) www.azspra.org
California School Public Relations Association (CalSPRA) www.calspra.org

Chesapeake School Public Relations Association (CHESPRA) www.chespra.org
Colorado School Public Relations Association (COSPRA) www.cospra.org
Connecticut School Public Relations Association (ConnSPRA) www.connspra.org
Sunshine State School Public Relations Association (Fla.) (SUNSPRA) www.sunspra.org
Georgia School Public Relations Association (GSPRA) www.gspra.org
Illinois School Public Relations Association (INSPRA) www.inspra.org
Indiana School Public Relations Association (InSPRA) www.indiana-nspra.org
Iowa School Public Relations Association (ISPRA) https://iowaspra.wordpress.com
Kansas School Public Relations Association (KanSPRA) www.kanspra.org
Kentucky School Public Relations Association (KYSPRA) www.kyspra.org
Michigan School Public Relations Association (MSPRA) www.mspra.org
Minnesota School Public Relations Association (MinnSPRA) www.minnspra.org
Mississippi School Public Relations Association (MSPRA) http://mspra.schoolwires.net/MSPRA
Missouri School Public Relations Association (MOSPRA) www.mospra.org
New Jersey School Public Relations Association (NJSPRA) www.njspra.com
New York School Public Relations Association (NYSPRA) www.nyspra.org
North Carolina School Public Relations Association (NCSPRA) www.ncspra.org
Ohio School Public Relations Association (OHSPRA) www.ohspra.org
Oklahoma School Public Relations Association (OKSPRA) www.okspra.com

Oregon School Public Relations Association (OSPRA) http://oregonschoolpra.org
Pennsylvania School Public Relations Association (PenSPRA) www.penspra.org
South Carolina Chapter of NSPRA (SC/NSPRA) www.scnspra.org
Texas School Public Relations Association (TSPRA) www.tspra.org
Washington School Public Relations Association (WSPRA) www.wspra.com
Wisconsin School Public Relations Association (WSPRA) www.wspra.org

PUBLIC RELATIONS SOCIETY OF AMERICA

120 Wall Street, 21st Fl.
New York, NY 10005
Phone: 212-460-1400
www.prsa.org

The Public Relations Society of America (PRSA), headquartered in New York City, is the world's largest professional organization for public relations practitioners. The society's almost 20,000 members represent business and industry, counseling firms, government, associations, hospitals, schools, professional service firms, and nonprofit organizations.

Since it was chartered in 1948, PRSA has continued to provide a forum for addressing issues affecting the profession as well as the resources for promoting the highest professional standards.

AASA, THE SCHOOL SUPERINTENDENTS ASSOCIATION

1615 Duke Street
Alexandria, VA 22314
Phone: 703-528-0700
www.aasa.org

AASA, The School Superintendents Association (AASA), founded in 1865, is the professional organization for over 14,000 educational leaders across North America and in many other countries. AASA's mission is to support and develop effective school-system leaders who are dedicated to the highest-quality public education for all children. The organization is one of elementary and secondary education's longest-standing professional organizations.

CONSORTIUM FOR SCHOOL NETWORKING

1325 G St., NW, Suite 420
Washington, DC 20005
Phone: 202-470-2784
www.cosn.org

The Consortium for School Networking, founded in 1992, is an association serving school district technology leaders. It works to support school systems in using technology to create engaged learning environments.

NATIONAL ASSOCIATION OF SECONDARY SCHOOL PRINCIPALS

1904 Association Dr.
Reston, VA 20191-1537
Phone: 703-860-0200
www.nassp.org

The National Association of Secondary School Principals (NASSP) serves education leaders in middle-level schools and high schools, including administrators, teachers, students, and others interested in education and the welfare of today's youth.

Membership in NASSP includes a wide variety of people interested in secondary education. Although most members are principals and assistant principals in public, private, and parochial secondary schools, many are central office administrators.

THE COUNCIL OF CHIEF STATE SCHOOL OFFICERS

1 Massachusetts Avenue, NW, Suite 700
Washington, DC 20001
Phone: 202-336-7000
www.ccsso.org

The Council of Chief State School Officers (CCSSO) is a nonpartisan, non-profit organization of public officials who head departments of elementary and secondary education in the United States, the District of Columbia, the Department of Defense Education Activity, the Bureau of Indian Education, and the five U.S. extra-state jurisdictions.

INTERNATIONAL ASSOCIATION OF BUSINESS COMMUNICATORS

155 Montgomery Street, Suite 1210
San Francisco, CA 94104
Phone: 415-544-4700
www.iabc.com

The International Association of Business Communicators (IABC) provides products, services, activities, and networking opportunities to help people and organizations achieve excellence in public relations, employee communication, marketing communication, public affairs, and other forms of communication.

U.S. DEPARTMENT OF EDUCATION

400 Maryland Ave., SW
Washington, DC 20202-0498
Phone: 1-800-USA-LEARN
www.ed.gov

The U.S. Department of Education seeks to support student achievement by promoting practices that create educational excellence. As part of that mission, the agency collects data and disseminates research on key education issues. Its publications and online materials offer school communicators a wide variety of data and insights that can support public engagement and community-relations initiatives.

INDEX